APACHE WARS

APACHE WARS

An Illustrated Battle History

◆ ◆ ◆

E. Lisle Reedstrom

BARNES
&NOBLE
BOOKS
NEW YORK

Portions of Chapter 9 appeared in different form in the author's *Bugles, Banners and Warbonnets*, published by Bonanza Press, New York, 1986. Chapter 14 appeared in different form in a paper presented by the author before the United States Commission on Military History in Chicago in 1979.

This edition published by Barnes & Noble, Inc.,
by arrangement with Sterling Publishing Company, Inc.

1995 Barnes & Noble Books

ISBN 1-56619-959-X

Printed and bound in the United States of America

M 9 8 7 6 5 4 3 2 1

MUR

For my wife, Shirley

CONTENTS

PREFACE

While much has been written about the Plains Indians and their struggle against white civilization in the nineteenth century, in comparison relatively little has been published about the numerous and bloody campaigns waged against the Apache. Yet these hardy natives of the American Southwest resisted the white man's world longer than any western Indian tribe. From the Apache's earliest contact with the Spanish conquistadors, their relationship with the white man was marked by mistrust, on both sides. The Apache put forth a fierce resistance to the encroachment of white civilization and eventual domination by the whites, who waged long, weary, and seemingly endless campaigns against this cunning and very able warrior nation.

No western Indian had the reputation of the Apache. They were respected and feared by all who came in contact with them, and even other ferocious warrior tribes left them alone. Their very name, Apache, a Zuni word for enemy, was left unchanged, as the Spanish, the Mexicans, and finally the Americans, one after another, invaded their domain, learning that these guerrilla fighters were among the toughest people the world had ever seen.

An enemy such as the Apache posed a series of exceptional problems to the U.S. military establishment of the nineteenth century. To their credit, given the technology of the day, the officers and men who faced these problems head on did so with a resourcefulness and determination that has little equal in the annals of the frontier. The Army of the Southwest was relegated to the inglorious job of first being the peacemaker, and then afterwards the peacekeeper, police force, and punisher of those Indians who did not keep their part of an all-too-often one-sided bargain with their greedy white conquerors. As history has shown, the Army met its responsibility sometimes with fairness and impartiality, but other times its decisions were far less than just. This was an army that was considered largely unnecessary and was unpopular with the civilian population, not only in the East but often in the very frontiers that it guarded, yet it was expected to be all things to all people.

It is not the intention of the book to judge the soldiers who fought in the Apache Wars, but to look closely at the times and special circumstances in which they lived and campaigned, at the rules that governed their lives, and at the daily routines that they performed in the call of duty. By finding out what the soldier wore, what he ate, what arms and equipment he used, we can better understand the campaigns against the Apache in the late 1800s. This was an era of experimentation with weaponry, tactics, and equipment—a time when the hard-and-fast rules of Victorian ethics were pitted against the realities of relentless guerrilla warfare. It was also the twilight of pomp and ceremony and the dawning of common-sense uniforming and gear that was designed for a particular purpose in a given climate or terrain, rather than for show on a drill field.

To this end, the author has done an admirable job. As you read through these pages you'll gain a better feeling for the life of a trooper stationed in old Arizona, or some other desolate, sun-scorched Southwestern military camp. Ernest Lisle Reedstrom has poured through hundreds of volumes of military regulations, equipment memoranda, diaries, and other written records of the era. He has carefully scrutinized original firearms, military and civilian equipment, and related artifacts of the Apache Wars. He also has travelled to historic sites and museums, viewed collections, and in general tracked down everything of interest that related to the Apache Wars.

Reedstrom is no stranger to the West. As a young man he travelled west to work as a gold-and-tungsten miner, laborer, sign painter, and artist. Throughout his life he has remained true to his love of the Old West and its lore by writing articles and books, as well as producing some of today's most popular artwork on various Western subjects. For these efforts he has been awarded with such honors as the coveted Third Spur Award for Non-Fiction from the prestigious Western Writers of America for his book, *Bugles, Banners, and Warbonnets*. In addition, Reedstrom holds memberships in some of the nation's top historical organizations, such as the renowned Company of Military Historians, the Chicago Corral of the Westerners, Western Writers of America, Little Big Horn Association, and the National Association and Center for Outlaw and Lawman History.

So settle back and travel with Lisle Reedstrom as he takes you, in his own colorful way, back to a tumultuous time in United States history, when the white man and the red man were engaged in a dramatic struggle—one for dominance, the other for existence. This is how they looked and lived.

Phil Spangenberger, Black Powder editor for
Guns & Ammo magazine

1

APACHE OVERVIEW AND EARLY HISTORY

Before the move west by American settlers, the Apache Indians had begun emigrating south from the windswept plains of western Canada. The Southwest was originally populated by a group of cliff dwellers, the forerunners of today's Pueblo Indians. They were a peaceful people, moving from their cliff houses to the plains, where they did some farming and hunting. The Apache were followed by the larger tribe of the Navajo at some point in the fifteenth century. The Navajo were, at that time, a rather warlike nation of Indians and greatly outnumbered the impoverished Apache.

As with their eastern Canadian counterparts, the Algonquin, the Apache began to annex members of neighboring tribes. By around 1600, the numbers of Apache had begun to increase, and their approach to life had become decidedly more aggressive.

Sometimes they raided the tribal camps at night and stole captives or they made slaves of the captives. Tribes who were donors to the Apache were the Pima, the Papago, and the peaceful Pueblos. Then, through a complicated form of intermarriage and concubinage, the newcomers were made part of the Apache nation.

When their numbers grew large, small groups would split from the main body of the tribe and form a distinctive band of their own. The usual reason for a split had to do with the emergence of a strong, possibly warlike leader. The Mescalero, Lipon, and Jicarilla bands in the eastern part of the Apache territory began migrating south and west, entering the area that would become Texas. As they roamed, they raided the peaceful villages of local tribes, adopting still more people into their bands.

The Apache were primarily hunters, and the arid Southwest had little of the deer, antelope, and rabbits that were their favorite fare. So the growing bands continued to roam over Texas, New Mexico, Arizona, and Mexico. By the time of the Spanish explorations, the Apache had been in their new territory long enough to learn basket weaving, pottery making, and primitive agriculture.

However, the life-style of the Apache in their new home basically remained the same as it had been before. As fierce warriors, most Apache men felt it was beneath them to engage in any physical labor. Society dictated that their one and only responsibility was to their weapons—caring for them, whether bow and arrow or an occasional firearm, and using them when necessary.

Certain men were chosen by their superiors to take care of the more menial tasks, such as feeding the livestock and helping with heavy work. The Apache men, however, were very careful not to be seen doing anything that could, by any stretch of the imagination, be considered woman's work.

The women worked constantly. They cooked, cared for the children, found and carried firewood and water, built and maintained their homes, tanned hides, wove rugs, twined burden baskets, and made household implements and utensils. They also gathered wild plant foods when in season, made and attended to clothing, and took care of whatever farming was necessary.

Apache Country

When the men were relaxing in camp, they would sit around smoking and telling stories of their past war or hunting experiences. At the same time, they might busy themselves repairing or cleaning weapons and tools, or restringing medicine necklaces.

When conversation came to a close, the men headed home. Some Apaches lived in earth-covered lodges called hogans, like their close neighbors, the Navajo. The Lipon and Kiowa Apache used the buffalo-hide tipi of the plains. But most Apaches preferred the circular, dome-shaped brush dwellings called wickiups. These huts were carefully thought out and architecturally superior to other types of housing. The Chiricahua, Mescalero, Jicarilla, and western Apache all favored this structure for their home. If impending danger called for a hasty escape, they would set the wickiup on fire after retreating with their scanty belongings.

Traditionally, all Apache men dressed alike in long buckskin shirts, broad skin loincloths, and high moccasins, all made by the women. In the hot summer months, they went bare-chested. The loincloth was a long strip of buckskin hung over a belt in the front. The long end of the buckskin was drawn between the legs and tucked up under the belt in back, and fell as far as the knees or even the ankles.

The standard garment for the women was a two-piece outfit. This consisted of a midlength skirt and a top that extended past the hips. Later, during reservation days, colorful trade cloths were readily adopted with many curious designs. The women became quite famous for their truly voluminous multitiered ankle-length dresses of the brightest colors.

As with all North American Indian peoples, the Apaches possessed religious beliefs and practices that permeated and controlled their daily lives. Each of the Apache tribes had its "shamans," or medicine men, who would intercede on behalf of the others in the community thought to have less ability to communicate with the spirits.

The Apache believed that spirits could be unfavorably influenced by those using power for evil purposes. Witchcraft fears loomed large among the Apache for this reason. Extended illness, for example, was often attributed to witchcraft.

In their religious ideology, sickness and misfor-

Coyetena, an Apache bride. (Photo courtesy of Herb Peck, Jr.)

tune could also be the direct result of anger of a deity, or spirit. And failure to treat a personified natural force, such as lightning, respectfully could bring hardship to tribal members.

In addition, there were various animals that were considered to be hazardous to one's spiritual well-being. Owls, snakes, bears, and coyotes were dangerous and made people ill by their odor, touch, or sight. The owl and coyote were also favorite forms in which spirits of dead sorcerers and ghosts of relatives resided.

The Apache were intimately acquainted with

A Yuma-Apache and two early settlers. (Photo courtesy of Herb Peck, Jr.)

A Southwestern group, late 1860s. These Apaches were servants for a settler family, and the officer belonged to the 21st Infantry. Note the four-button fatigue blouses. (Photo courtesy of Bob McDonald.)

various aspects of tracking, and could thus determine many facts about those who made an imprint through the desert grass. By the appearance of the grass, they could tell how many days had elapsed since it had been trodden upon, whether the party consisted of whites or Indians, how many there had been, and if Indians, to what particular tribe they had belonged.

The difference between the crushing heel of a white man's shoe or boot, and the light imprint left by an Indian's moccasin, were too striking for any doubt. The different styles of moccasin used by the several divisions of the Apache tribes were well known among them. The time that had elapsed since the passage of the party was determined by the discoloration of the plants as well as by the amount of natural juice still left in the crushed grass. Numbers were arrived at by the multiplicity of tracks. When barley was discovered, the Apaches had reason to believe that the white man had been over the route. When maize was found, they were confident that the travellers had come from Mexico.

After 1540, when Coronado first visited the Southwest, the Apaches obtained horses from the Spaniards and began to use the animals not only to cover more territory in their search for food to feed their growing numbers, but to improve their chances in battle. By 1680, at the time of the Pueblo revolt, the Apache were noted for being hard and daring riders—stealing, raiding, and killing anyone unlucky enough to be in their path. Until 1850, settlers stayed as far away from the Apache strongholds as possible, and the Southwest was a place of terror.

Between 1850 and 1886, there was a desperate war between the Apache and the U.S. Government. Native weapons for waging war included

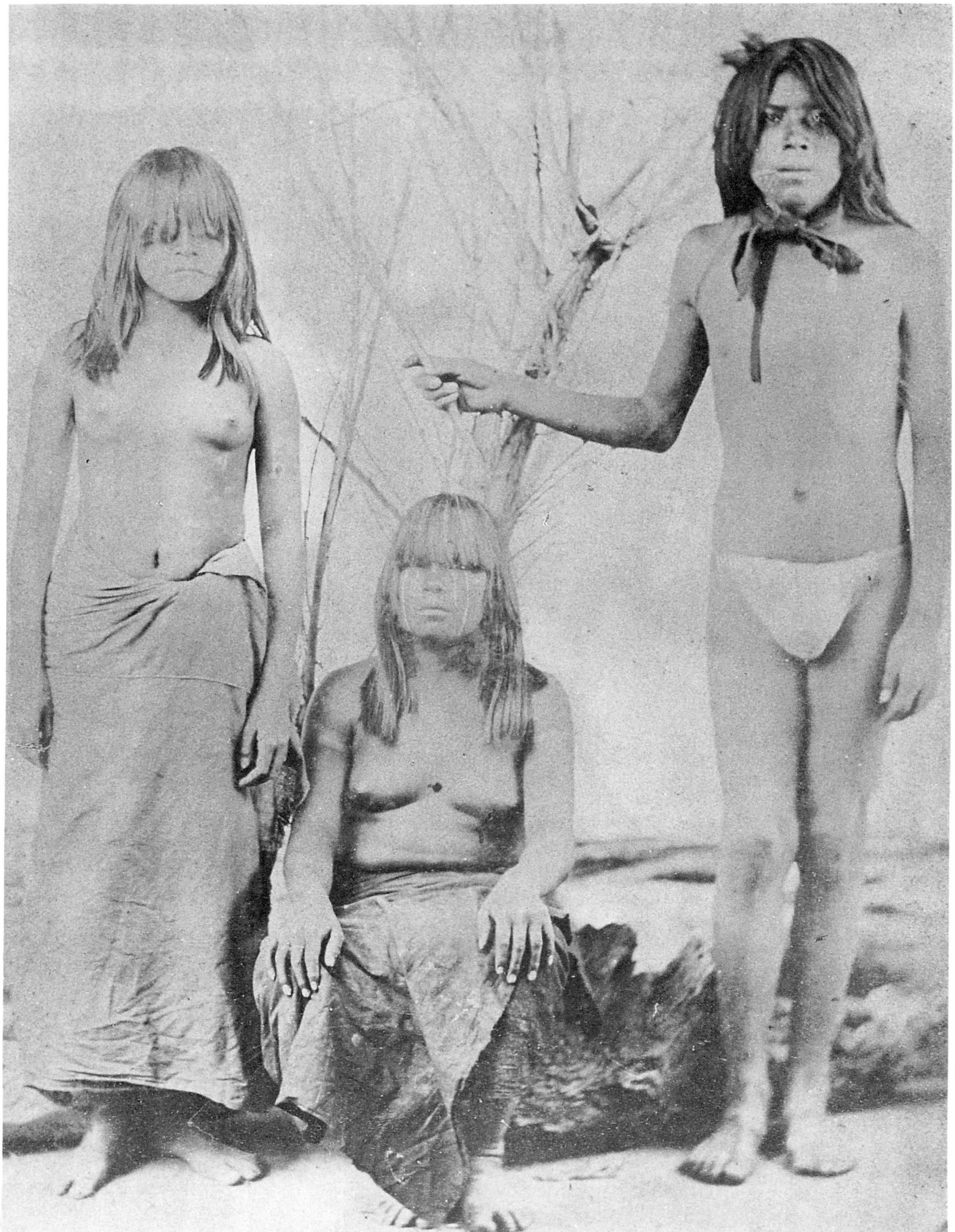

Typical early Apache everyday dress for young men and women.
(Photo courtesy of Herb Peck, Jr.)

bows and arrows, lances, clubs, and knives. To these, the Indians added a new arsenal of pistols and rifles, which they obtained by trading with or stealing from soldiers, trappers, and settlers. However, despite the growing availability of these gunpowder weapons, the bow and arrow remained the Indians' weapon of choice. The effect of one arrow shot by an Indian warrior was so mighty that it often went through the largest war horse, imbedding itself in the ground beyond. Apache warriors were known to shoot their arrows with such skill as to strike men with uncanny accuracy at a range of 150 yards. During the Apache Wars, it seemed as though the white man couldn't do anything to prevent the arrow from hitting its deadly mark.

So, the Apache were a force to contend with. Their stealth and sudden attacks allowed them to inflict great damage and then ride away like the wind, leaving the few survivors convinced that they had been visited by the Devil's forces. In addition, the Apache knew the mountains better than any newcomer could. As skilful pathfinders, they could catch up with large armies and pounce on them when least expected. And they proceeded to do just that, adding more weapons and horses to their supply as a result.

The ability of the Apaches to travel light and withstand temperature changes and lack of food and water made them even harder to track down. They could ride or run, clad in very little, living on cactus and scarcely any water for days, and survive in the freezing cold of the mountains or the parching heat of the desert. It was very hard to cut the supply lines of an army that seemed to travel on nothing and have little concern for their animals or human companions.

At the beginning of the Civil War, both the North and South attempted to win the Apaches as allies, but the Apaches made it very clear that they wanted no part of the white man's war. The Union Army was left with the primary job of quelling the Apaches after the Confederate Army withdrew into Texas. However, much of the Union Army had been withdrawn from the frontier posts to fight in the South, since their troops had been depleted by the drawn-out, hard-fought war. Some frontier garrisons had less than 40 percent of the troops that had been stationed there before the war, and many of these garrisons had been undermanned before the war. Now the Apaches withdrew to the mountains and started carrying out highly effective guerrilla raids on the posts and everyone else around.

As the Civil War continued, Indian outbreaks became more and more frequent and daring. The garrisons were further weakened as more men were transferred to the war theatre and Indian raids became increasingly damaging. Finally, the Federal Government had no choice but to divert men from the eastern battlefields to reinforce the western frontier. Confederate prisoners were urged to volunteer for frontier duty and wear Union blues. They had to swear loyalty to the United States to get released from the Union prison camps, and were called "galvanized Yankees" by the Regular Army recruits.

As the Civil War came to a close and the great rush to the West began, the Indians were fighting for their very existence. Broken treaties, thievery on the part of Indian agents, whiskey peddling, and gunrunning added fuel to the fires that already burned brightly in the Indian encampments, finally causing these encampments to erupt into war parties.

The Indian attacks were now so frequent and bloody that Union commanders were forced to withdraw troops from major battlefields to man the frontier. Launching one expedition after another, they searched the mountains and deserts for the bloodthirsty Apache in an effort to quell the violence.

2

GERONIMO

The Mexicans nicknamed him Geronimo—Spanish for Jerome—but his native name was Goyathlay, The One Who Yawns. In later life he became a medicine man and prophet of the Chiricahua Apache. Towards the end of the nineteenth century, the Chiricahua acquired notoriety through daring raids against the Mexicans and as a result of his refusal, with a few dozen younger renegades, to settle down on the Indian reservations.

He was born around 1829, at the headwaters of the Gila River in northern Mexico, near old Fort Tulerosa. Because his father, Taklishim, The Grey One, of the Chiricahua Apache, married a woman of the Bedonkohe Apache and joined her band, Geronimo could never be chief by hereditary right.

Geronimo's mother was called Juana. She was a strong woman, yet it was hard for her to have borne such a hot-blooded son with notions of his own. At the age of ten, Geronimo began to follow the hunters along the great trails of the antelope, elk, buffalo, and deer. It required more skill to hunt the deer than any other animal.

When he turned seventeen in 1851, Geronimo was admitted to the council of the warriors. Now he could wander wherever he wanted and do whatever he liked. When opportunity arose, he could now go on the warpath with his tribe and serve his people in battle.

Geronimo's roving eye stopped when he caught his first glimpse of Alope, the dutiful daughter of the warrior Noposo. Alope was a delicate, slender, shy girl; secretly they were lovers for a long time.

When the council granted Geronimo the privilege to see Alope's father concerning marriage, he found Noposo hard to bargain with since he asked for many ponies in exchange for his daughter. But in a few days, a determined Geronimo appeared before Noposo's lodge with a herd of ponies and took Alope for his wife. This was all that was necessary for the marriage to be recognized. From this marriage, three children were born.

It was the summer of 1858, and the Mexican towns as well as the neighboring Indian tribes were quiet and peaceful. On their way to Casa Grande, the entire band of Bedonkohe Apaches stopped at the small Mexican town of Kaskiyeh, and pitched camp outside the town for several days. Each day some of the Indians would go into town to trade, leaving their camp under the protection of a guard.

Then one afternoon upon returning from town, they found that Mexican troops had raided their camp, killing all the warriors, women, and children. Geronimo's aged mother, his young wife, and their three small children were among the dead. In addition, the ponies were gone, supplies destroyed, and the weapons confiscated. Their chief, Mangus Colorado, knew that they could not fight back successfully without arms, so he ordered them to start at once for their homes in Arizona. In their hasty retreat northward, they left the dead upon the field where they had fallen. Geronimo swore vengeance upon the Mexican troopers who had wrought such devastation upon his people.

In the summer of 1859, almost a year from the day of the massacre of Kaskiyeh, three Apache bands assembled on the Mexican border to go

Geronimo, in white man's clothing. (Photo courtesy of Herb Peck, Jr.)

Geronimo, wearing a woman's straw hat, 1880. (Photo courtesy of the Fort Sill Museum.)

Geronimo liked to present himself as a head chieftain, even though he wasn't one. (Photo courtesy of the Fort Sill Museum.)

Geronimo, in Mobile, Alabama, 1888. He's wearing a woman's top dress, probably given to him by townsfolk. (Photo courtesy of the Fort Sill Museum.)

upon the warpath against the Mexicans. Mangus Colorado had selected Geronimo to solicit the aid of the other two tribes.

The march began with the Apaches travelling in three divisions: the Bedonkohe led by Mangus Colorado, the Chokonen led by Cochise, and the Nednhi under Whoa. Geronimo acted as their guide into Mexico, following the river courses and mountain ranges, and keeping their movements concealed.

They set up camp near Arispe, and eight Mexican troopers rode out from the city to parlay with them. These troopers were captured and then killed and scalped. The next day a larger band of Mexican troops rode out by the Apache's camp, and instantly a general skirmish began, lasting most of the day.

Early the next day, the whole Mexican force came out with two companies of cavalry and two companies of infantry. Because he felt so deeply wronged by the Mexicans at Kaskiyeh—losing his entire family, unlike the others who had lost only one or two loved ones—Geronimo was given the honor of directing the battle. The battle lasted but a few hours, yet when Geronimo gazed over the bloody battlefield the enemy lay everywhere. Over the field the fierce Apache war whoop sounded. Geronimo and his warriors rejoiced; they had avenged the Kaskiyeh massacre.

It was at this battle that the Mexicans first called him Geronimo, the name he was called ever after by his Indian companions. For the white man, it was a name to be feared for the next twenty-seven years.

After the battle near Arispe, most of the Apaches seemed satisfied with the slaughter—except for Geronimo. He still had a desire for more vengeance, and finally succeeded in persuading

Geronimo is shown here posing reluctantly for a photographer, c. 1890. He is wearing his black-and-grey striped prison breeches, the five-buttoned blouse, and civilian boots. This photo was sold for one dollar. (Photo courtesy of University of South Alabama Photographic Archives.)

Geronimo, in white man's clothes, 1902. He acquired these photos from a promoter and sold them for fifty cents. (Photo courtesy of Fort Sill Museum.)

two other Apache warriors, Ahkochne and Kodene, to accompany him on another invasion of the Mexican countryside. But during a short battle, both of Geronimo's companions fell under heavy fire from the Mexicans, who seemed to have appeared everywhere. With the gathering darkness, Geronimo slipped away, retreating to Arizona, where the chase commenced.

Time and time again, Geronimo persuaded a few comrades to join him in raiding and butchering the Mexican troops, offering them plenty of dead Mexicans, captured loot, and Mexican women.

In the summer of 1860, he was able to take to the warpath again—this time with twenty-five loyal warriors. They lay in ambush along the slopes of the Sierra de Sahuaripa Mountains, waiting for a company of mounted Mexican troops to pass through a mountain defile. Geronimo thought that by properly surprising the Mexicans, he could defeat them. When the entire command of troops was visible, the signal was given to fire. The Mexican troopers dismounted without command, placing their horses on the outside of the company for breastwork, and staged a good fight against the Apache bushwhackers. Seeing that it was almost impossible to dislodge the Mexicans from their position without using up all of the Apache's ammunition, Geronimo led a charge. The warriors pressed in from all sides. The battle was fought hand to hand until all of the Mexicans were slain. When the echoing ring of the Apache war cry had finally died away, Geronimo was found lying unconscious where he had been struck over the head with the butt of a Mexican trooper's carbine.

Geronimo was able to march back to Arizona, but with a splitting headache. It wasn't until several months later that he finally recovered from the blow, although it left a scar that would always remind him of the incident.

In the spring of 1861, Geronimo and twelve warriors again went down to Mexico, where they attacked a large pack-mule train. The Mexicans rode away with their lives, leaving their property with the Apaches.

There were many engagements between the Mexicans and Geronimo, and the Apaches often escaped with minor casualties.

On one occasion, as the Apaches were heading northward through Sonora, Mexican troops overtook them while they were finishing breakfast. At the first volley from the troops, Geronimo was struck by a bullet at the lower corner of the left eye and fell unconscious. Thinking him dead, the Mexicans pursued the fleeing Indians. Geronimo lay there until the Mexican troops returned empty-handed. While still at some distance, they saw him stumbling to his feet and commenced firing at him. Desperately, Geronimo turned and ran in the opposite direction with bullets whistling from all sides. One inflicted a slight flesh wound on his left side as he ran, dodging from one bush to another, until he lost his pursuers in a steep canyon.

It had always been understood that should the Apaches have to break up into smaller bands in order to elude an enemy, they should meet at a rendezvous point in the Santa Rita Mountains in Arizona. From here they returned home minus their booty—and not even reporting a partial victory, Geronimo was blamed by his people and had no reply.

While Geronimo was resting from his wounds, many members of the tribe either packed up and left for a hunt up north or went to trade for blankets with the Navajo Indians. Early one morning, during this time, three companies of Mexican troops surrounded the settlement and opened fire. Of the remaining men, women, and children, many fell in the hail of Mexican bullets. The others, including Geronimo, fled to the hills, where the troopers could not follow. The encampment was burned to the ground, and the Indians' arms, provisions, and ponies were all confiscated. It was a long time before the Apaches were able to go on the warpath once more against their hated enemy, the Mexicans.

Many Apache women and children were carried away in various raids by Mexicans and compelled to work for them under strenuous circumstances. They were degraded and held as slaves. The Apache warriors who were captured by the Mexicans were kept in chains and held as hostages to be exchanged for Mexican captives held by the Apache. The captured Mexicans were not chained but kept in close confinement, seldom escaping. The Mexican men were compelled to cut wood and herd horses, but the Mexican women and children were generally treated as Apaches.

In the spring of 1862, Geronimo with eight men invaded Mexico once more to look for heavily laden pack-mule trains. One train with four drivers soon came along and spotted the Apaches ahead of them. In a matter of moments, they turned heel and rode for their lives, leaving a long train loaded with blankets, bolts of calico, tobacco, and loaf sugar. On their way home, the Apaches came upon another pack train, loaded with cheese, with only one driver. He, too, saw the Apaches and turned about, heading at a fast pace towards the mountains.

Several days later, Geronimo and his men arrived home. Mangus Colorado, their chief, assembled his people and gave a feast, where three pack mules were butchered and eaten. The spoils were divided, and the Indians danced all night.

It was Geronimo who suggested posting scouts to watch the trail should Mexican troops attempt to surprise them again. Several days later, the scouts came back to camp, reporting Mexican cavalry approaching. Mangus Colorado took com-

Geronimo (left) and Natchez (also spelled Naiche) at Fort Sill, Oklahoma, c. *1897–1908. (Photo courtesy of the Fort Sill Museum.)*

This photo shows Geronimo posing for a photographer who has had the old warrior dress in Plains Indian instead of Apache garb. He is staring at an old Colt percussion (a photographer's prop), probably wishing it was loaded. (Photo courtesy of the Fort Sill Museum.)

mand of one group of warriors and Geronimo another. They hoped to gain possession of the Mexicans' horses and weapons and to destroy the whole company. However, the entire Mexican command was saved by its own scouts who spotted the Apaches assembling for battle. After a short-pitched battle, in which ten troopers were killed, the Mexican cavalry was in full retreat. Thirty armed, whooping Apache warriors scrambled after their enemy and gave them no rest until the troopers were far inside Mexico. No other columns of Mexican troops pursued the Apaches for the remainder of that year.

In January of 1863, Mangus Colorado was killed by whites and his son, Mangus, was appointed the new Bedonkohe Apache chief.

That summer Geronimo selected three competent warriors and went on another raid into Mexico. Forty miles west of Casa Grande was a small village in the mountains, called Crassanas by the Indians. They camped near this town and decided to make an attack at high noon. Although hardly anyone seemed to be stirring, the Apaches cautiously stole into the streets with their spears and bows and arrows at the ready. Yet when they sounded their war whoop, Mexicans fled in every direction. No one made any attempt to put up any resistance.

When they saw that all the Mexicans had fled, they ransacked all the adobe huts and warehouses. They found horses and mules, and packed many provisions and supplies upon them. Once they were safely back in Arizona, they realized that the Mexicans hadn't bothered to follow them. This was Geronimo's greatest success. The booty was enormous; there were enough supplies to last the tribe for more than a year.

In the winter of 1864, there was another raid into Mexico by Geronimo and twenty warriors. They attacked several settlements and secured plenty of provisions. In Arizona, on their way home, they ran across a pack train at a place the Indians called Pontoco, a day's journey due west from Arispe. One pack-train driver was killed and two escaped. The train was loaded with wicker baskets full of bottles of mescal, a fiery liquor produced in Mexico from several species of agave. Soon after they pitched camp, the Indians began to get drunk.

The next day, about a day's march north from their previous camp, they captured some cattle from a wandering herd and drove them home. All that winter, the Apaches were peaceful, with plenty of meat to last until the end of spring.

In the late fall of 1865 when provisions were running low, Geronimo and four warriors went into Mexico again. Although the Apaches were accustomed to fighting on foot so that they could easily conceal themselves, this time they took ponies because they wanted cattle and knew that they wouldn't be able to handle the fast-paced animals on foot without losing half the herd. They went as far as the shores of the Gulf of California. Here, they saw what they believed to be a great lake extending beyond the limit of sight.

Nearby, they attacked several settlements and secured plenty of supplies. On returning with their booty, they also secured about sixty head of cattle northwest of Arispe. Afraid of being followed, they camped in a number of different valleys with the cattle. Upon reaching their village in Arizona, a feast was held and dancing followed. Everyone received gifts, and later the cattle were butchered and the meat dried and packed.

In the fall of that year, Geronimo headed a group of nine warriors, this time on foot, in a raid on Mexico. They attacked several settlements south of Casa Grande, collecting many needed horses.

On their return home, they followed a trail through the mountains near Arispe and made camp. Thinking they were not being followed, Geronimo turned the whole herd loose in a canyon surrounded by steep walls. They had set up camp at the mouth of this valley so that the animals could not escape.

Just as they were about to begin their supper, a scout ran back to report Mexican troops coming towards camp. When the Apaches started for the horses, other troops on the cliff above opened fire. Evidently, the scout had overlooked this maneuver while watching the rear trail. The Apaches scattered in every direction, losing everything they had captured.

Three days later they reassembled at their appointed rendezvous in the Sierra Madre Mountains in northern Sonora. The troops did not follow, and the Apaches returned to Arizona without their booty.

Geronimo was anxious to stage another raid into Mexican territory. Early in the summer of 1866, he took thirty mounted warriors and went south through Chihuahua as far as Santa Cruz, Sonora. He crossed over the Sierra Madre Mountains, following a river course at the south end of these mountains to the Sierra de Sahuripa Mountains, and then following that range northward. Along the way, Geronimo and his men collected all the mules, horses, and cattle they wanted, and drove them northward through Sonora into Arizona. The Mexicans saw them many times but did not bother to attack or chase them. When the Indians reached home, another feast and dancing commenced. During this expedition, the Apaches had killed about forty Mexicans.

The next year, 1867, the young chief, Mangus, chose eight mounted warriors, including Geronimo, and invaded Mexico once more. They rode south of Tombstone, Arizona, into Sonora. Here, they attacked some cowboys driving a herd of cattle. During this small skirmish, two of their number were killed; but they took possession of the herd, driving it northward. The second day out, a well-armed, well-mounted troop of Mexicans rode upon them. Mangus had had no scouts watching the trail. The Indians whipped their ponies and raced for the nearby mountains, leaving the herd behind. But the Mexicans gained on them rapidly. Reaching some timber, the Indians left their ponies to fight from cover. After a brief battle, the Mexicans gathered up the ponies and the cattle and rode across the plains towards Arispe, leaving the thieving Apaches empty-handed.

The warriors wanted to return to Mexico and raid again, but young Chief Mangus refused. So Geronimo took up the command, going on foot with only six warriors. They went directly to Arispe in Sonora and made camp in the Sierra de Sahuripa Mountains. They raided several settlements at night, capturing many mules and horses, as well as saddles and provisions. These raids were extremely profitable. The Apaches travelled at night with their own scouts at their heels, but the Mexican troops made no effort to follow them. Again, they feasted and danced and divided the spoils. Mangus, however, would not accept any gifts from the warriors.

A year later in 1868, the Mexican troops staged a surprise raid on a settlement not far from Geronimo's camp. They rounded up all the horses, ponies, mules, and whatever cattle remained. Evidently, the Apaches had been feeling secure—they had not stationed any scouts on the mountaintops. It is interesting to note that no raids were made into Mexico that year, as the Apaches were fairly well stocked with provisions.

Then it came to pass that two Mexican scouts were spotted near the Apache settlement and brutally butchered. But the Mexican troops had already located the settlement and had begun herding horses and mules before the Indians knew what was happening. Horseless, Geronimo took twenty warriors and trailed the troops to a cattle ranch in Sonora not far from Nacozari, where the stock was penned. They attacked the troopers there and killed two of them; then they drove the stock off along with other horses and mules.

Heading home, the Apache scouts reported that they were being trailed by nine Mexican troopers. Geronimo sent the stock ahead and, with three other warriors, stayed at the rear to intercept any advancing parties.

When the troopers were near the Arizona border, they pitched camp and bedded down for the night. The next morning when they awoke, they found their horses gone—and by that time, the Apaches were well into Arizona, heading home. It was more than four years until the Apaches crossed over into Mexico again for any raiding or were disturbed by the Mexican troops.

In about 1872, Mexican troops attacked a number of Apache settlements but were driven back and defeated. It was at this time that Geronimo and certain chieftains decided to make raids into Mexico again. They moved their entire camp—belongings, mules, and horses—into Mexico and settled in the mountains near Nacori. When they passed a Mexican farm or cattle ranch on their way, these farmers or ranchers would usually be killed, unless they totally surrendered to the Apaches, in which case they often would be taken prisoner.

Frequently the Apaches would change places of rendezvous and roamed in these mountains for more than a year, raiding Mexican settlements for supplies but having no engagements with Mexican troops. Finally they returned to their mountain hideouts in Arizona.

Then after about a year, they returned to Mexico and went into hiding in the Sierra Madre Mountains, establishing a stronghold near Nacori with many escape routes. Geronimo and Whoa, chief of the Nednhi Apaches, had just organized their warriors for a raid into Mexico when their scouts burst into camp, warning them that two companies of Mexican cavalry were coming to attack them.

Holding their ground, sixty warriors stood up and showed themselves. The troopers came to a halt, dismounted, and commenced firing. Somehow the Apaches encircled the two companies of Mexican cavalry and slaughtered all their horses. A war whoop was sounded and the Indians charged on foot. The attack came as a complete surprise to the Mexicans, who were lying behind

After his capture and while imprisoned, Geronimo posed for many photos such as this one. In order to make a few dollars, he consented to sign the photos, which sold for fifty cents. (Photo courtesy of Fort Sill Museum.)

Geronimo, after his capture. (Photo courtesy of Fort Sill Museum.)

their dead horses, trying to fire from this awkward position. The Indians jumped from boulders and overhanging cliffs, fighting hand to hand with the Mexicans. Soon, the Mexicans broke into a frenzied run for their lives, scattering in different directions. It wasn't long before they were all killed. The Apaches scalped the slain, carried away their own dead, and secured all the arms and ammunition that they needed. That night they moved the entire camp eastwards through the Sierra Madre Mountains into Chihuahua. They were not followed by any other troops and, after a year, returned to Arizona.

Just about every year, Geronimo and his warriors would stage raids into Mexico or live there in the mountains with their families. The Nednhi Apaches whose territory extended far into Mexico were their allies and would fight beside them. Their chief, Whoa, was like a brother to Geronimo, who spent much time in the Nednhi Indian territory.

In about 1880, Geronimo and his warriors were in camp in the mountains south of Casa Grande when a company of Mexican troops attacked them. There were about thirty Indians and twenty-four Mexican soldiers. The Mexicans surprised the Indians in camp, killing two in the first volley. The Indians scattered into the nearby timber, but Geronimo knew that if they staged a sudden surprise attack, it would surely scatter the troops and lessen the pressure. The Indians kept behind rocks and trees as they advanced, eventually killing all the Mexicans. This place was called Skolata by the Indians. After burying twelve warriors here, Geronimo secured what supplies the troopers had and headed northeast.

At Nokode, near Nacori, Mexican troops attacked the Indians again. There were about eighty warriors of the Bedonkohe and Nednhi Apaches against three companies of Mexican troops. Soon the Apaches scattered, firing as they fled, with the Mexicans in pursuit. The Apaches lost the troops in the Sierra Madre Mountains.

Four months later, the Indians and Mexicans met again at Casa Grande to parlay and make a peace treaty. The chiefs and all the men from town were there—shaking hands and promising to be brothers. Trading began and the Mexicans gave the Apaches mescal. When most of the Indians became drunk, two companies of Mexican troops from another town attacked them. Many Indians were captured and twenty were killed. The rest fled in every direction.

Geronimo blamed the chiefs at Case Grande for this surprise attack during a council of peace. He couldn't believe that the townspeople had nothing to do with the attack, and thought that the chiefs should have known that there would likely be spies among them in cahoots with the Government troops. The treachery and massacre at Casa Grande stayed with the Apaches for a long while, and they didn't reassemble until they returned to Arizona. Despite their distrust of the American military, they remained in Arizona for some time, living on the San Carlos Reservation.

In Geronimo's autobiography, *Geronimo, His Own Story*[1], he tells about his early days as a warrior, leading expeditions down into Mexico. Throughout the 1870s and 1880s, he says he used tricks, lies, and sometimes outright kidnapping to get his people to continue to fight the "white eyes" and the Mexican soldiers.

In April of 1876, Geronimo led a band of Chiricahua off the Fort Bowie Reservation in the first of his major transgressions against the new white expansion. For exactly one year, he and Victorio, leader of the Tcihende Mimbres Apache, remained at large, living across the border in Chihuahua. The "white eyes" were more determined to exterminate them than the Mexicans had ever been.

In April of 1877, pressed hard by U.S. troops, Geronimo came near Fort Thomas and surrendered to Apache Agent John P. Clum in a very tense scene. The presence of Clum's large squad of Apache police prevented the Indians from killing their presumptive captors. Victorio, having heard what had happened, arranged a conference with Clum and agreed to a transfer to San Carlos. Clum, distrusting Geronimo and his followers, had the Indians placed in chains before their departure. Victorio understood that resistance on his part would be useless. It would be better to go quietly to San Carlos and wait there for an opportunity to break out, which he felt certain would come.

Fortune was with Geronimo; Agent John Clum resigned his post, and with nobody to press charges of depredations against him, Geronimo was freed. After two or three flights into the mountains and cautious returns, Geronimo and Juh, a chief of the Nednhi Apache, on the night of September 30, 1881, fled once again into Mexico, after killing Albert Sterling, chief of the agency police, and whipping a detachment of the 6th Cavalry. This led to a struggle known as "The Geronimo Campaign" (see Chapter 7).

Geronimo's talent for camouflage was studied by the American army during World War II. It was then reproduced in uniforms with a number of colors—amber, green, and ochre—blending the soldier into the surrounding foliage to prevent him from being seen.

In *The Land of the Poco Tiempo*[2], Charles F. Lummis describes Geronimo's appearance:

> He was a compactly built, dark-faced man of one hundred and seventy pounds, and about five feet, eight inches in height. The man who once saw his face will never forget it. Crueller features were never cut. The nose was broad and heavy, the forehead low and wrinkled, the chin full and strong, the eyes like two bits of obsidian with a light behind them. The mouth was a most noticeable feature—a sharp, straight, thin-lipped gash of generous length and without one softening curve.

In his autobiography, *Geronimo, His Own Story*, the great patriot-warrior tells of the many wounds he received in battle against his enemies:

> During my many wars with the Mexicans I received eight wounds as follows: shot in the right leg above the knee, and still carry the bullet; shot through the left forearm; wounded in the right leg below the knee with a saber; wounded on top of the head with the butt of a musket; shot just below the outer corner of the left eye; shot in left side, shot in the back. I have killed many Mexicans; I do not know how many, for frequently I did not count them. Some of them were not worth counting.

Notes

[1]Published by Ballantine Books, 1971.
[2]Published by Charles Scribners and Sons, 1893.

3

GENERAL GEORGE CROOK AND THE 1872 CAMPAIGN

The Civil War was just a short interlude in General George Crook's military career; unlike other officers who staked their reputation on the War Between the States, Crook's star was already shining brightly before the blue and the grey left their blood on the hills "back East." Crook was, first and foremost, an Indian fighter, and to fight a man, one must know him. Crook knew the Indian, and developed a respect—even a fondness—for the mighty Indian chiefs who ruled from the Columbia River to the Rio Grande, and from the green fields of Illinois to the majestic Pacific shores. He understood and sympathized with "Mr. Lo," as the red man was frequently called by the frontier fighter. (When the whites were travelling west, the Indians soon found that they were being cheated, taken advantage of, and pushed off their hunting grounds. Back east, newspaper stories recounting their treatment would often begin by saying "Lo, the poor Indian . . ."—thus, the name.) Crook spoke often and plainly against the many injustices created by the white man in his treatment of the Indians.

Crook was asked to command the Department of Arizona, and time and again he refused. About this, Crook commented, "I was tired of Indian work." Besides, the climate of Arizona was fierce and Crook feared for his health. Crook was under great pressure to accept the post, and finally was given a letter from the adjutant general that assured him that the post would be temporary—if he accepted the post in May of 1871, a new assignment would be made in the fall.

Crook left San Diego by stagecoach, bound for Yuma, some 200 miles away, on the morning of June 3. The first 100 miles were over hilly country with some mountains. Then the coach crossed into the Colorado desert, and the heat—which he had heard about and dreaded—began to affect him. According to his autobiography[1], Crook said in his diary: "It was like being in an oven . . . during the day it must have reached 105° in the shade. Even at midnight, the heat was unbearable and rest or sleep was impossible."

He found the desert to be one vast expanse of shifting sand with a few mesquite bushes and a scattering of willow. The sand piled up into great dunes, twenty to thirty feet in height, without a blade of grass of any kind in sight. Although his stay in Yuma was short, he was briefed about the history of the adobe town.

Fort Yuma was established to protect the southern emigrant route to California and to control the bands of warlike Yuma Indians in the vicinity. Later it served as a supply depot for the various Army posts in Arizona. It was originally called Camp Independence; then its name was changed to Camp Yuma in March 1851, when the post was moved to its permanent site. It became Fort Yuma officially in 1852.

Not only did the little town have the roaming Apache to contend with, but it was a haven for every renegade outlaw from all points of the compass. By the 1870s, murderers, cattle rustlers, men on the dodge, and robbers had gravitated there; Yuma seemed to attract them all.

This photograph of General George Crook was taken at the end of the Civil War. (U.S. Signal Corps photo from the National Archives.)

After staying a few days in Yuma, Crook and his entourage went to Tucson. They rode in a horse-driven ambulance that bounced over every rock and pebble, and seemed to find the deepest potholes along the way. They were tossed about like so many beanbags, and the heat was as bad as it had been in the Colorado desert. Flies and dust added to the discomfort. Tucson was no relief. The temperature soared every day into the hundreds, reaching at least 103° in the shade daily, and sometimes pushing on to 116°.

Despite the heat, flies, dust, and other assorted ills, Crook set about organizing operations against the Indians. He remained in Tucson until September 11, making sure that the operations were ready. Tucson's governor and other prominent citizens urged Crook to enlist Mexicans for his campaign, pointing out that the Mexican mercenaries knew the country, the Indians' habits, and their modes of warfare—and with a little pinole and dried beef, they could travel all over the country without pack mules to carry their provisions. With ten days' rations on their backs, the mercenaries could march over the roughest country at a rate of thirty to fifty miles per day.

Satisfied with this recommendation, Crook hired fifty Mexicans for scouts. On July 11, 1871, he set out from Tucson bound for Fort Bowie at Apache Pass in the Chiricahua Mountains with five companies of cavalry and the fifty "destroying angels."

Three days later, the group reached Fort Bowie without seeing any Indians or signs of them. After resting and eating a meal, they moved out silently after dusk. Later that night they camped in an arroyo at the end of Sulphur Springs Valley, southeast of Dos Cabezas.

At daybreak the packers went out in search of water. To their astonishment, they found some livestock that had evidently been brought in during the night from Mexico. Surprised by the packers, the Apache had fled, leaving the stock behind.

Crook's company had been discovered by the Apaches. As they continued their march, watching very closely, they spotted a few more Indians, but no trouble occurred.

They marched to the foot of Graham's Mountain, where a scouting party climbed up and found a small party of Indians at the summit. The Indians fled posthaste across the north side of the mountain and over a steep precipice. Later, Crook spotted a dust cloud in the distance near Sulphur Springs Valley. Satisfied that the dust signified movement of a small Indian band, Crook sent Captain Moore to Cottonwood Springs, a spot located on a low range leading from the Dos Cabezas range to Graham Mountain. Crook stationed the remainder of his troops at various points along the valley, anticipating that the Indians would travel to the side of the valley where the troopers were well hidden.

The Indians, now aware of the Army troops in the general area, approached Cottonwood Springs cautiously late at night. For some reason Captain Moore led his men mistakenly onto the desert instead of moving directly to the spring, ostensibly to cut across the Indians' trail. But the tactic brought him in plain sight of the Indians, and his troops made their escape in the nick of time. Crook had lost the advantage. The Apache party would have been a prize, as it consisted of sixty warriors returning from a raid in Mexico.

Crook moved out, making good time, heading towards the San Carlos River. He and his troops camped on the stream where Camp Grant had once stood. After establishing a base camp, the group scouted the mountains on either side of the Aravaipa Canyon but found nothing. They continued to scout over the Gila River and up the San Carlos to the source of the western branch, but found no Indians. Nearing Fort Apache, Crook alerted his men, especially the Mexican scouts, to watch out for friendly Apaches hunting in the area.

The possibility of a skirmish between the friendly Apaches, whom Crook knew and trusted, and the Mexican scouts caused Crook to be uneasy. They continued their march until they struck Salt River, just below the junction of the White and Black forks. Crook then marched directly to Fort Apache, where he refitted his troopers and discharged the Mexican scouts, as his concern about the possibility of trouble outweighed their usefulness to him.

Crook had analyzed the situation. He needed scouts. But what could be more fitting, he thought, than enlisting the friendly Apache as scouts, to act in concert with his troops. Imagine! Indians chasing Indians. Letting the Mexicans go and using the friendly Apaches instead would be a much safer way of finding the hostiles without chancing a fight. The Mexicans were hot-headed, Crook had found, and they showed signs of refusing to obey commands by subofficers. The Mexicans hated all Apaches, and refused to distinguish between those who were friendly and those who were hostile.

After many long talks, Crook established a firm understanding with old "One-Eyed" McGill and Pedro, the principal Indians of the White Mountain Apache, or Coyoteros. (Coyoteros means wolfmen in Spanish, as their diet included coyote and prairie dogs.) They agreed to Crook's plan to subdivide the hostiles, and to take on the role of scouts.

Having organized his company of scouts, and having appointed Captain Guy V. Henry, 3rd Regiment of Cavalry, to command the first expedition, Crook prepared to move on to Camp Verde to organize similar expeditions.

At the end of August, Crook and his party left for Camp Verde without a guide, as they had been assured that the trail was visible and clearly marked. Before long, however, Crook discovered that his information was false. The trail lay along the summit of the heavily timbered Mogollon Mountains—an Apache stronghold penetrated by few white men—and all traces of it soon disappeared. The summit was broad in some areas, but in others it was cut by ridges and canyons. Travelling was very difficult. Not only was the trail hard to locate, but finding water was chancy. Most of the water they acquired was from heavy rains, secured by spreading canvas on the ground during a downpour and gathering up water from puddles with tin cups.

After floundering around for a time, Crook and his party struck a large, well-defined trail leading north. Following the trail for a short time, the party found a spring of soft water, which was immediately named General's Spring after Crook. Later, the trail itself became known as Crook's Trail.

Crook was usually the first man up in the morning, often at 2:00 or 3:00 A.M. Lieutenant John Gregory Bourke, who served as his aide and adjutant for years, makes these observations in his book, *On the Border with Crook*[2]: "In personal appearance General Crook was manly and strong, a little over six feet in height, straight as a lance, broad and square shouldered, full-chested, and with an elasticity and sinewyness of limb that betrayed the latent muscular power gained by years of constant exercise in the hills and mountains of the remotest West."

Crook was always the first saddled and ready for the trail. Dressed in his suit of canvas and seated on his strong, muscular mule, named Apache, with his rifle or shotgun carried across the pommel of his saddle, he was ready to lead the way.

This photo shows one of Tucson's many cantinas in the early 1870s, already near ruins. The adobe bricks kept the interior building cool during the summer months.

Crook preferred mules over horses because they withstood the heat better in the Southwestern desert, and they were more surefooted in the mountains. His movements were smooth and powerful, conditioned by years of exercise in the field. His keen blue-grey eyes could detect the slightest motion across the far horizon. Any sound instantly aroused his curiosity, and the faintest aroma awakened his suspicious mind.

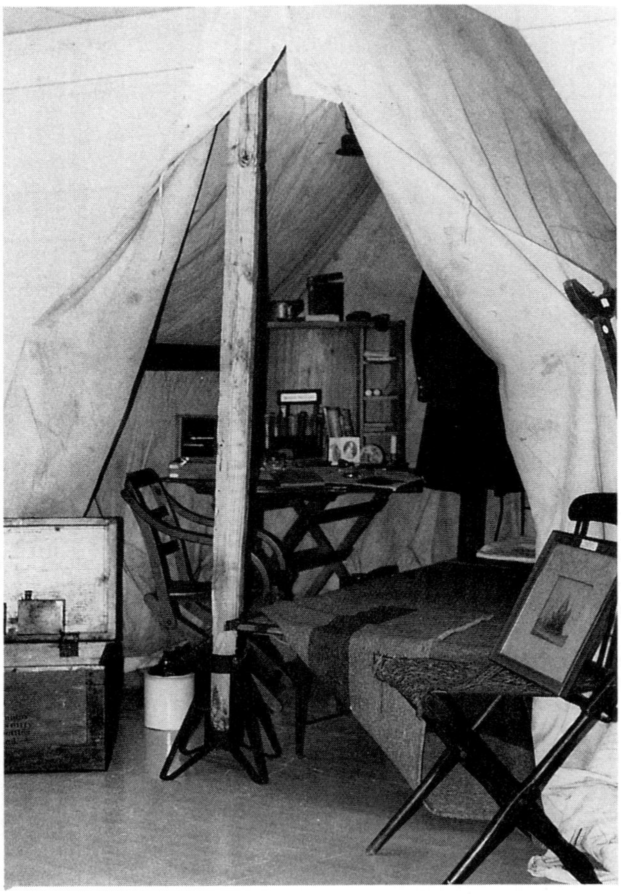

The inside of a typical officer's tent in the field, with all his personal gear, c. *1870s. Everything folded or could be broken down instantly.*

In *On the Border with Crook*, Bourke goes on to describe the general:

> His love for hunting and fishing, which received its greater impetus in those days of his service in Oregon and Northern California, increased rather than diminished as the years passed by. He became not only an exceptionally good shot, but acquired a familiarity with the habits of wild animals possessed but by a few naturalists. Little by little he was induced to read upon the subject, until the views of the most eminent ornithologists and naturalists were known to him, and from this followed in due sequence a development of his taste for taxidermy, which enabled him to pass many a lonesome hour in the congenial task of preserving and mounting his constantly increasing collection of birds and pelts.
>
> There were few, if any, of the birds or beasts of the Rocky Mountains and the country west of them to the waters of the Pacific, which had not at some time furnished tribute to General Crook's collection. In the pursuit of the wilder animals he cared nothing for fatigue, hunger or the perils of the cliffs, or those of being seized in the jaws of an angry bear or mountain lion.
>
> He used to take great, and in my opinion, reprehensible risks in his encounter with grizzlies and brown bears, many of whose pelts decorated his quarters. Many times I can recall in Arizona, Montana and Wyoming, where he had left the command, taking with him only one Indian guide as a companion, and had struck out to one flank or the other, following some sign until an hour or two later a slender signal of smoke warned the pack-train that he had a prize of bear-meat or venison waiting for the arrival of the animals which were to carry it back to camp.
>
> Such constant exercise toughened muscle and sinew to the rigidity of steel and the elasticity of rubber, while association with the natives enabled him constantly to learn their habits and ideas, and in time to become almost one of themselves.
>
> If night overtook him at a distance from camp, he would picket his animal to a bush convenient to the best grass, take out his heavy hunting-knife and cut down a pile of the smaller branches of the pine, cedar or sage-brush, as the case might be, and with them make a couch upon which, wrapped in his overcoat and saddle-blanket, he would sleep composedly till the rise of the morning star, when he would light his fire, broil a slice of venison, give his horse some water, saddle up and be off to look for the trail of his people.

After Crook's party found what was to be called General's Spring and moved towards the Verde River, they encountered some difficult riding through the rough canyons cutting across the Mogollon Plateau. They camped a few miles upriver from Fort Verde, some 40 miles east of Prescott. Fort Verde was the first white settlement in the area, and the troops there were trying hard to assure the safety of the primitive camp. With Crook's arrival, a courier began bringing in mail and dispatches.

From one such dispatch, the general was notified that Vincent Colyer was sent by the "Indian ring" to make peace with the Apache, by the Grace of God, and was travelling into the territory from New Mexico. (The "Indian ring" was a ring of Federal officials, contractors, and others, formed in Tucson, that had great influence in the national capital). Actually, in order to promote peace among the Indians and the white settlers, the Permanent Board of Peace Commissioners sent Colyer to Mexico and Arizona after Congress had appropriated $70,000 to place the Apaches of Arizona and New Mexico on reservations.

Although Crook had little faith in Colyer's enterprise, he figured that if he continued his operations against the Apache and failed, he would surely be charged with interference. So, he at once countermanded all of his orders to activate operations against the hostiles and directed his officers to assist Mr. Colyer in any way possible in order to carry out the plan for peace. Crook did not believe that Colyer's plan had any chance for success, and he anticipated that the Apaches would begin their raiding and depredations again. During this period of relative inactivity, Crook was able to resupply his troops, hire scouts and guides, and outfit the finest pack-mule train he could find in the territory. Everything was in readiness if Colyer's peace plan failed.

Colyer left Fort Apache, heading towards old Camp Grant on the San Pedro River. His lectures to (or at) the Indians about peace left a long trail of depredations following in his wake; the Indians were clearly showing their contempt.

But Colyer, unaware of the reactions to his pious preachings, was pleased by what he thought had been a successful tour with the Indians. Colyer expressed his appreciation of Crook, saying that the general agreed with his view of the situation. This made Crook a host of friends east of the Mississippi. Crook honestly told Colyer that he had little confidence in the peacemaking mission, but as Colyer had come to Arizona with the express authority of Crook's superiors, and as Crook had been directed to assist him, the general had conscientiously done so. If Colyer's peace policy should fail, it could not be laid at Crook's doorstep.

Not long after Colyer's triumphant return to the East with his news of peace among the Indians, word began to pour in telling of the outrages committed by the Apache. Life and property were unsafe again, and all business within the Arizona Territory had ground to a halt. By the time Colyer reached San Francisco, he heard of the outrages, and his confidence was very shaken. When he reached Washington, his friends shunned him. At this point, General Crook was given permission to continue his operations against the hostiles. However, not long afterwards, he was again ordered to cease his operations, as General O. O. Howard was being sent with even greater powers than those given to Mr. Colyer.

At their meeting in Yuma, General Howard came on strong. He intimated that he could use his powers to supersede Crook in command if he saw fit. Still, his respect for the veteran Indian fighter was great, and he didn't try to take advantage of Crook.

Along with General Howard came Reverend E. P. Smith, who was to become commissioner of Indian Affairs. He was bright, and tried to restrain many of Howard's excesses. He remained in the Arizona Territory only a short time before returning to Washington. Another member of Howard's entourage was an aide-de-camp, Captain Wilkinson, whose stock in trade was religion. He acted as a go-between for General Howard.

Howard took every opportunity to exercise his public speaking talents, and at the drop of a warbonnet would recite the tale of his religious conversion or the Battle of Gettysburg. (It was during General George B. McClellan's campaign on the peninsula during the Civil War that Howard commanded a brigade in the II Corps and lost his right arm at the Battle of Seven Pines.)

All the way from Fort McDowell to Prescott, Howard expressed his wish for a general council with the Indians. Word was sent to old Camp Grant calling for all of the Indians to gather for a council.

General Howard revealed to Crook that he thought of himself as Moses to the Negro for his Civil War exploits, and that he believed that he had been placed on Earth by the Almighty Himself for that reason. It then followed, surmised Howard, that God was sending him on another mission. General Crook was respectfully amused by these revelations.

It was the beginning of April, 1872. Camp Grant was situated on a little plateau, well above the San Pedro River, a stream about ten to fifteen feet wide and shaded by great cottonwood trees. Army personnel camped across the river from the fort. Crook watched as the Indians filed in, forming a large gathering. He thought he had never seen so many saucy, impudent cutthroats assembled in one place. Many carried the latest Army weapons, along with tribal lances embellished with "un-

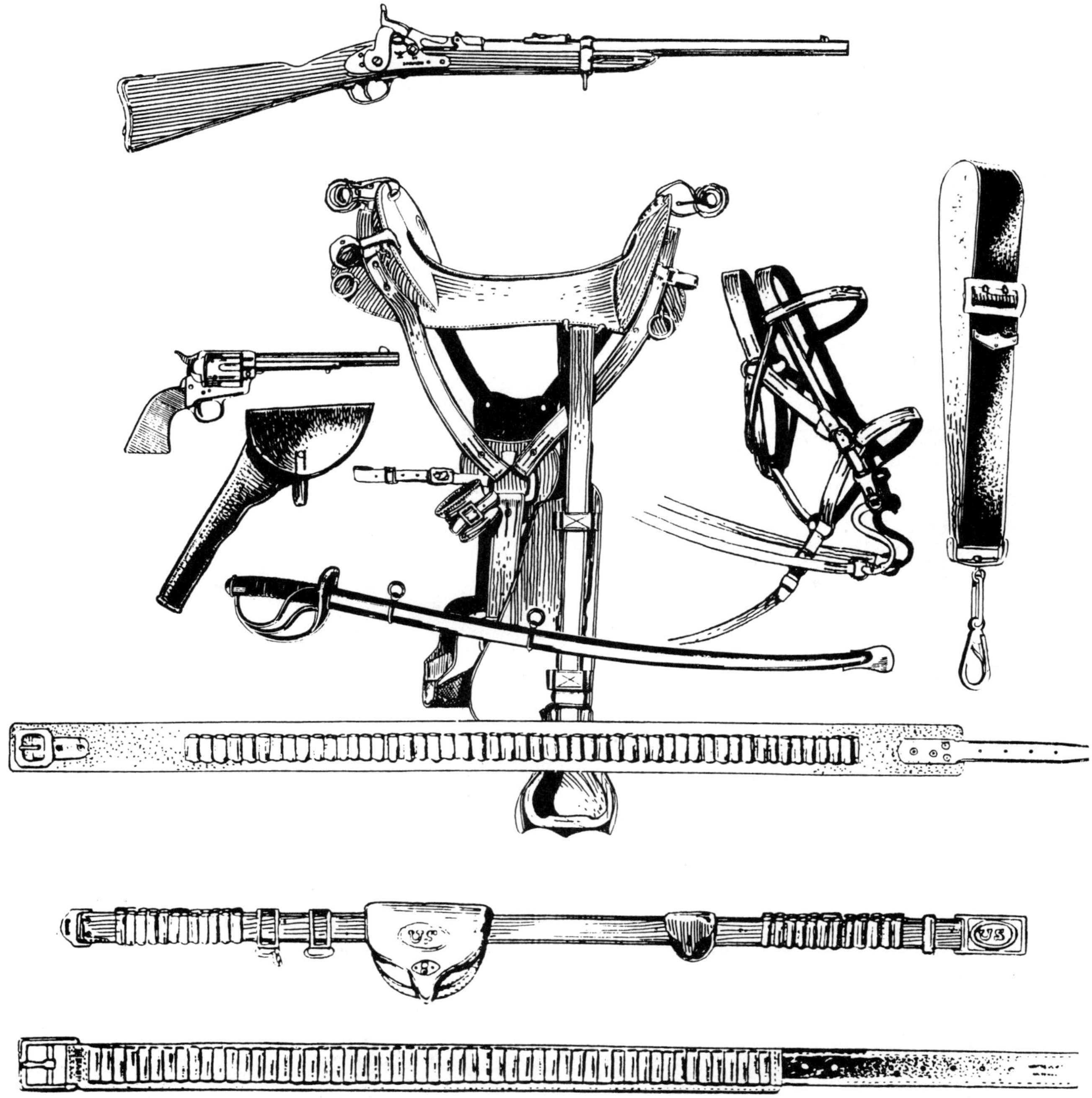

Field Cavalry Equipment, 1870s. Roughly, from top to bottom: Springfield .45-55-405, Trapdoor carbine, single shot, Model 1873; Model 1874 McClellan saddle (black leather); Colt, Model 1873, single action, .45-caliber (used from 1873 through 1891); holster from Civil War stockpiles; 1866 nonregulation leather belt made by Army saddlers; 1874 black leather belt with double-row sliding cartridge loops (Hazen); 1876 leather belt with light-brown canvas loops; 1875 bridle and halter with "S" bit; shoulder sling (Civil War vintage) for carbine; and U.S. regulation cavalry sabre.

speakable items." Several citizens from Tucson and elsewhere assembled to witness the council as well.

General Howard stood and made a friendly gesture with his one arm to open the council. Speaking through an interpreter, he informed the Indians that he had commanded 30,000 men during the War Between the States, and if they didn't obey his will and behave themselves, he would exterminate them all.

The head of the Indians, one Eskiminzan (or Skimmy), shouted, "Go to Hell!" contemptuously, and then disputed all of the points put to him by General Howard.

There was some basis for the Indians' contempt. A year before, in March of 1871, a party of citizens, provoked by the Indians' outrages against the whites, had marched on Camp Grant, killing Indian men, women, and children who were under the protection of the government there. These citizens had felt that the government was doing little or nothing to protect them from the Indians. This incident, known as the Camp Grant Massacre, was a rallying cry for the Indians against General Howard, causing his words and threats to fall upon deaf ears.

At Howard's council, another matter erupted. After the Camp Grant Massacre, several women and children had been carried off by the settlers to serve as slaves. Howard had induced the settlers to bring these children to the council, saying that if they had no living parents they would return to Tucson with the settler families. At the council, Skimmy demanded the return of all the children without question. After much argument, Howard decided it would be best to return the children to the Indians as a gesture of peace.

Many of the youngsters returned to the tribe with tears, because they were being separated from their mothers who were being kept as slaves.

Judge McCaffrey, the U. S. district attorney at Tucson, jumped up at the council and denounced General Howard as a liar and a brute. He said that Howard had deceived the settlers by telling them to bring in the Indian children under false pretenses. Howard defiantly denied the charges, although he was shouted down by McCaffrey and several others. Working himself into a towering

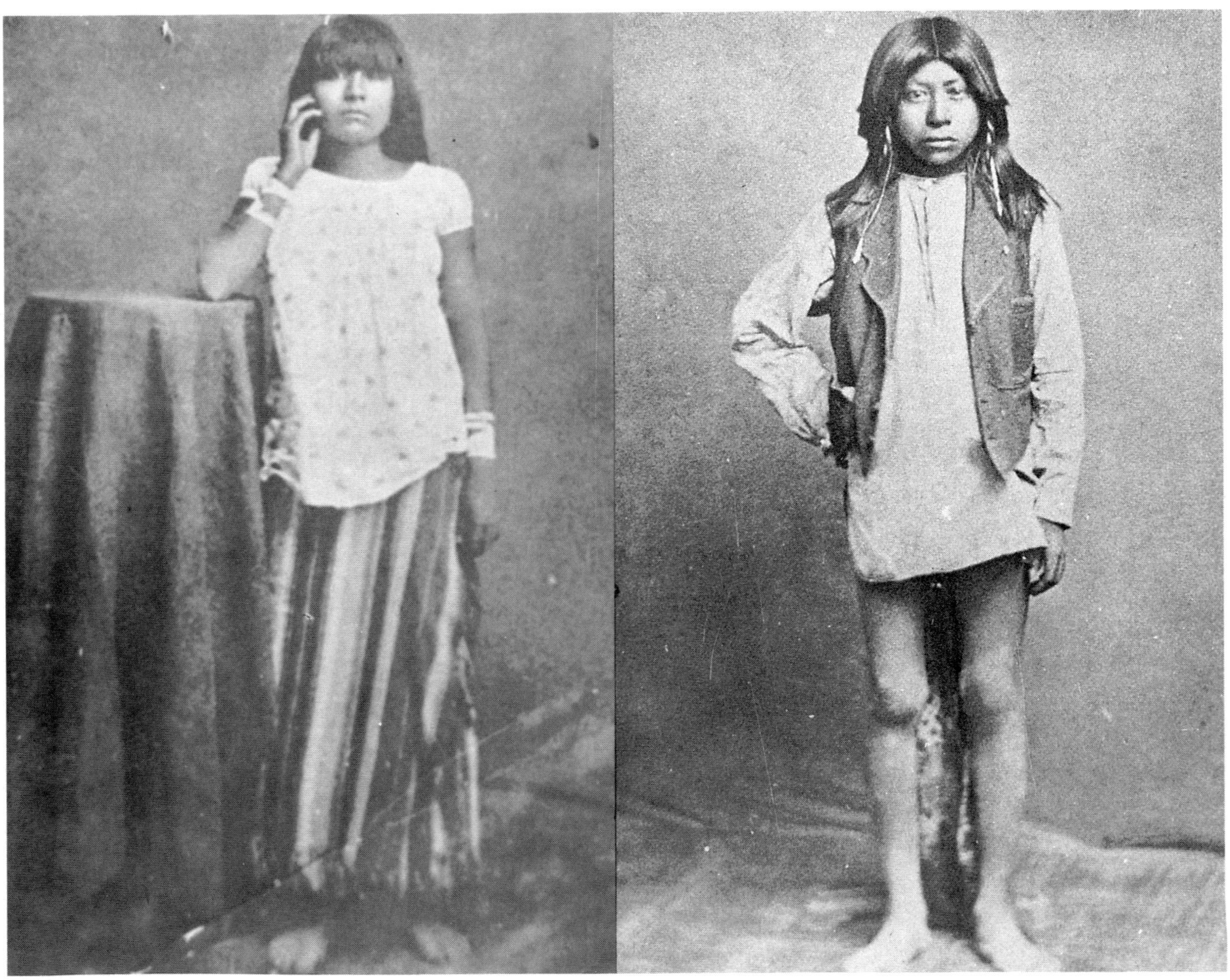

These two photos show two of the Apache children who were captured at the Camp Grant Massacre in 1871. Later, they were made slaves by their white captors.

rage, Howard threatened McCaffrey, telling him that he would have him removed from the position of attorney general. McCaffrey told him that fear of losing his position would not prevent him from speaking out against such outrages against decency and humanity.

When the council came to an end, Skimmy gave General Howard a stone, and said that the stone would melt before he would break his word. As Skimmy hadn't given his word on anything, it was a safe promise. General Crook, however, remembered the trail of such stones and was far from impressed. In addition, Crook was surprised at Skimmy's expressions of good will towards Howard, while ignoring himself. In his autobiography, Crook recounts the day:

> When General Howard and I returned to camp, he was very indignant that McCaffrey had spoken to him, which gave me an opportunity to make a few remarks myself. I said, "General Howard, these people have lost their friends, relatives and property to these Indians. They carry their lives constantly in fear, knowing not what moment is to be their last. Now, if instead of affording relief, you not only fail to give it to them but outrage their feelings besides, you must not expect your position to shield you from hearing plain words."

But General Howard gives a different slant. In his book, *My Life and Experiences Among Our Hostile Indians*,[3] he says that the children were sent in the care of a "good Catholic woman," and describes the close of the conference as follows: "Thereupon a wonderful scene followed. The Indians of different tribes double embraced each other, Apache and Pima, Papago and Mohave—and even the Mexicans participated in the joy that became universal. I said to myself, 'Surely the Lord is with us.' "

The Indians kept up a steady trail of rape and murder until September, when Crook was allowed to continue his operations against the hostiles. The fall of 1871 found Lieutenant Wheeler's exploring expedition from Nevada to Arizona terminated at Whipple Barracks, a mile northeast of Prescott. The stagecoach carrying several of Wheeler's party to California was passing from Wickenburg to Ehrenburg, and was attacked by Indians, who killed several people on board. Soon afterward, money in large amounts was brought to the agency on the Colorado River, along with other booty from the stagecoach, making it apparent that the Mohave had been involved with the attack. Crook's plan was to open the campaign by capturing the guilty parties.

On September 8, 1872, Crook's troops attempted to arrest the Indians at Date Creek. Shooting broke out, and several of the Indians were killed in the rifle fire. Discontented Apache Yumas attempted to kill the general as well, but Lieutenant Ross, Crook's aid-de-camp, deflected the rifle of the brave aiming at Crook. Several other members of the Army troop also narrowly escaped being shot. The Indians who were shot were primarily the Apaches who had led the attack on the stagecoach, making it clear that Indians could no longer murder white men under the cover of the reservation.

Shortly after the Date Creek incident, Colonel Mason of the 5th Cavalry, stationed at old Camp Hualpai, attacked some hostiles at Muchos Canyon near the Santa Maria Mountains. Several hostile braves were killed in the raid, and the entire band, while not totally destroyed, was completely demoralized.

On November 1, Crook sent Captain Brown of the 5th Cavalry to Fort Apache to assume charge of the Indians there. Brown was not to interfere with the duties of the Indian agent in any way, but he was charged with keeping the Indians in the fort under control, making a daily head count. When his work was completed there, Brown was to march to Fort Grant and repeat the same procedure there. He was then to meet with General Crook.

Before Crook left Fort Apache for Fort Grant, he organized his troops into commands of white troopers and Indian scouts, with a pack train for each so that they could act independently. Crook instructed no commanding officer to obey any outside orders—even from the president of the United States—until he approved them himself.

Upon arriving at Fort Grant, the first person Crook laid eyes on was Skimmy. Although he had ignored Crook not long ago, Skimmy praised him as a great general, a courageous man in battle, and considerate of the fallen.

Crook had collected all available troops in the southern part of the territory, organizing them into commands similar to those at Fort Apache. Camp Apache was commanded by Major George M. Randall of the 23rd Infantry with Chief of Scouts C. E. Cooley. Date Creek was commanded by Major George Price. Fort Whipple was superintended by Major Alexander McGregor. Troops at Fort Hualpai were Colonel Julius Mason's responsibility. Camp McDowell was commanded by James Burns, 5th Cavalry, and troops from Camp Verde were led by Colonel C. C. Carr.

General Crook's goal was to make the Apache Campaign short and decisive. On December 27, 1872, the Battle of the Caves won an important victory for the Army. Captain Brown's troops wiped out an entire band of Apaches, killing or capturing the whole party. From the Battle of the Caves to April of 1873, the various commands scored victory after victory—in many cases led by the Army Apache scouts.

On April 7, 1873, the last of the hostile Apaches surrendered to Crook's troops—with the exception of the Chiricahuas, led by Cochise, and the Tontos, led by Delshay (sometimes spelled "Delchay" or "Deltshay").

General Howard had personally taken the Chiricahuas under his wing, but they continued to battle the settlers. Their treatment of other humans—whites, Mexicans, and other Indians—was said to be so barbaric that their ragged and emaciated appearance failed to instill pity. The little band now had almost died out from starvation and exposure. They were constantly on the move, as most of their strongholds were now known.

Delshay (nicknamed The Liar and The Red Ant) said that last fall he had one hundred and twenty-five warriors, and now he had only twenty. Even the rocks had gotten soft, as his people couldn't put their feet down without leaving an impression that the soldiers could follow. Any movement aroused the Tonto camp into flight, as the possibility of attack from soldiers was always there. The lack of rest, food, and safety caused havoc with the little band. Deltshay had the worst reputation among all of the Indians of the Southwest for devilment and treachery. He was a direct competitor with Skimmy in making treaties with the solders using the melting stone routine. Too many times the stone "melted" before morning; meaning that, overnight many of the soldiers who trusted him had been overthrown and much of the livestock had been driven off.

Finally, the Chiricahuas and the Tontos were also subdued, and all of the Apaches were placed on the reservations under solemn promise to remain there and be peaceful.

General Crook then returned to Prescott, and for a month everything appeared calm and peaceful. Then a dispatch arrived by courier stating that the Tonto Indians had "fled to the mountains like a flock of birds." Crook sent the courier back with the message to signal the Indians with smoke and tell them to return at once. Surprisingly, they all returned like guilty little children with big ambitions.

Then Deltshay and forty followers left the reservation and did not return so peacefully. They trav-

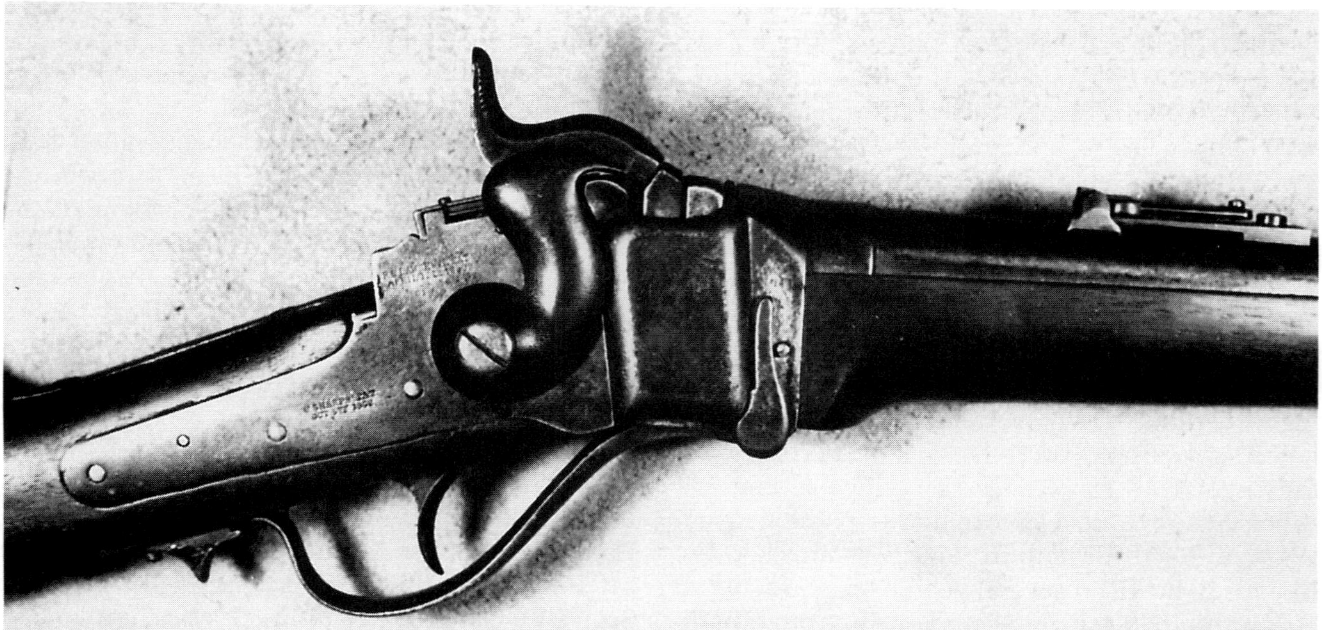

Sharps carbine, 1863 model, converted to a .50/70 cartridge. Many cavalrymen carried these weapons up to the early 1870s. (Photo courtesy of the Alan Feldstein collection.)

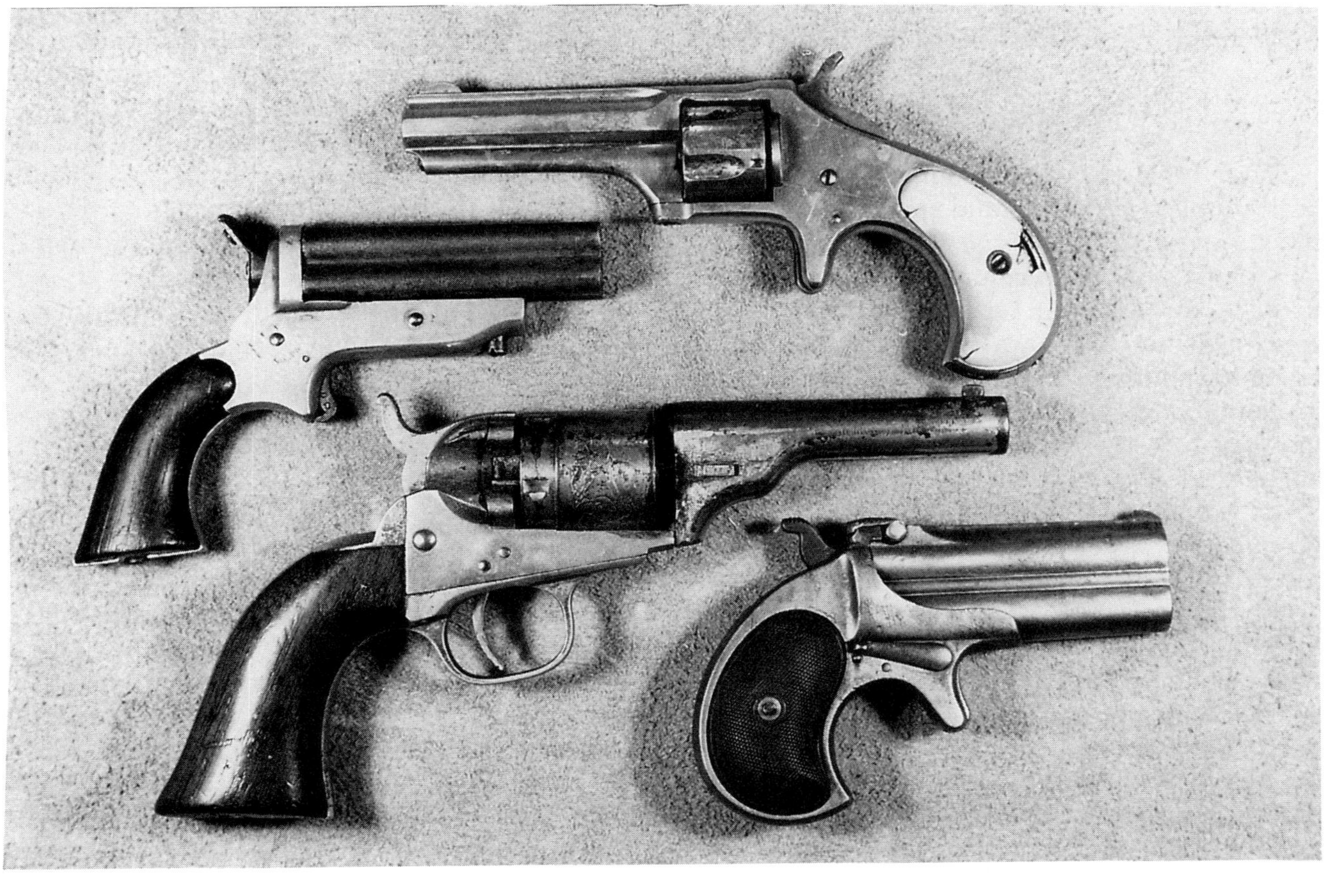

Officers and a few enlisted men would carry a boot gun or a second piece of artillery hidden somewhere on their person. Here are a few favored smaller pieces that could be easily hidden. From top to bottom: Remington .32 caliber, 1873; Sharps, four-barrel, .30 caliber rim fire, second model; Colt round barrel, no ejector, 38 rim fire, 1873; and Remington .41 caliber, over-and-under Derringer.

elled down the Verde River for some twenty miles, leaving no trail, and finally escaped into the mountains. Parties were at once dispatched to either force them back to the reservation or destroy them. They caught up with the Indians and some fighting occurred, but Deltshay was too wily to be killed.

Shortly after this incident, Indians at the San Carlos Agency escaped into the San Pedro Valley, murdering settlers' families, stealing livestock, and grabbing what they needed from the houses before torching them. The troops raced after them again, killing several in short, fierce skirmishes. The troops managed to separate a few, who returned to the reservation after their companions scattered.

Crook arrived at the reservation and initially refused to accept their surrender; but when they begged for mercy, he said he wouldn't harm them and finally allowed them to stay on the reservation. However, he plainly told them that he did not believe their promises, and that if they should go on the warpath again he would surely drive them back to the mountains and kill them. General Crook, now nicknamed The Grey Fox by the Indians, also told them that in exchange for letting them stay, they would have to bring him the head chiefs of certain tribes who were ringleaders of the rebellion. The contrite—or possibly very hungry—Indians responded by bringing in seven of the head chiefs Crook had demanded. Old Delshay even brought in two chieftains. Crook was satisfied that his order to bring in the head chiefs was honored by the Indians and that they were in earnest in their desire to remain on the reservation.

Still, small Indian parties would move about the hills, causing problems with the white settlements. Frequent expeditions were dispatched to these settlements, rounding up and sometimes destroying the war parties.

The last holdouts located themselves at the top of the Mogollon Mountains by the Little Colorado River. The area was rough country, cut with deep canyons, which even the Indians knew how to cross only in a few places. The hiding Indians were dislodged with great difficulty, and some of the smaller bands were totally destroyed in the attacks.

These Indians in the mountains had clearly been supplied with guns and ammunition, probably, surmised Crook, by the Moqui Indians. Captain John C. Bourke accompanied General Crook to the Moqui Village in October of 1874 to investigate the matter. Crook was content with his investigation, and the Moqui were so frightened by the incident that they ceased their part in the Apache terrorism.

The spring of 1874 found the Indians of the Verde Reservation transferred to the San Carlos Reservation, under General Howard. Along with the Apaches, they were made to work with broken grubbing hoes condemned by the quartermaster. Still, they managed with these inadequate tools to raise about 500,000 pounds of corn and some 30,000 pounds of beans.

The Army finally succeeded in relocating all of the Indians except Diablo's eastern band of White Mountain Apache. Diablo boasted that he would rather die than go down to San Carlos. Instead of chancing an outbreak of violence, the government permitted Diablo's band to remain in the mountains, provided that they would become self-sustaining.

General Howard's last act was taking old Eskiminzan with a few other selected chieftains to Washington, where he told authorities that old Skimmy was an Indian who knew guile.

As soon as most of the Indians had become settled on the various reservations, the Indian agents began their little games of plunder. For instance, the Hualpai Indians complained they were being cheated out of their annuities. The commanding officer of the post at Beale's Spring paid no attention to their complaints, which were becoming so noisy and obstreperous that the surrounding area feared an outbreak of real violence. After investigating the situation and making first-hand observations under cover, Captain Thomas Byrne became convinced that the Indians had cause for their agitation. Then he had the Indians bring their complaints directly to him and found, for example, families who were due ninety-five pounds of beef receiving fifteen. Captain Byrne took responsibility for the Indians' issues, and, as might be expected, acting Agent and Superintendent Dr. Bendall made charges against Byrne, accusing him of "high-handed acts on the part of the military." As superintendent of Indian Affairs for Arizona, Bendall ran essentially a one-man show, and was reticent to hand over authority to the military.

Captain Byrne asked for and received a Court of Inquiry into the matter. The court's investigation showed that Bendall's Indian agent was selling loads of beef and other Indian annuities to nearby mining communities, and pocketing the profits. He had furthermore rigged the government scales to show 300 pounds of beef weighing 1,300 pounds.

Surgeon E. Baily, president of the court, not only found Captain Byrne's actions to be proper, but also found that Byrne's close observation of the Indians' issues to be "both necessary and proper."[4]

General Crook was promoted to brigadier-general on October 29, 1873, as the result of his success in Arizona. In the spring of 1875, he was relieved of command of the Department of Arizona and ordered to take command of the Department of the Platte. On March 11, Crook departed for San Francisco, travelling by ambulance alongside the Mohave River up to Los Angeles, and from there by stage and railroad to San Francisco. The long-suffering Indian fighter and friend of the Indians was honored with a banquet in San Francisco.

Notes

[1]*General George Crook; His Autobiography*, M. F. Schmitt, Norman, University of Oklahoma Press, 1946.
[2]Published by Charles Scribners and Sons, 1891.
[3]Published in 1907.
[4]Department of Arizona; Special Orders No. 63 & 68, 1873.

4

ARIZONA CAMPS AND FORTS

Between 1865 and 1886, the government established a number of camps and forts within the Territory of Arizona to protect the small white population who lived in secluded, scattered areas. Many posts were of major importance, as they were carefully situated in strategic areas to keep the Mohave, Yuma, Navajo, and Apache Indians under surveillance. Other posts were garrisoned primarily for the safety and encouragement of stockmen, miners, and farmers who were settling permanent communities. To control principal roads and trails, as well as communications, into

This is a sketch of Fort Defiance, 1860. (Courtesy of the Arizona Historical Society Library/Tucson.)

Fort Apache. (Photo courtesy of the Arizona Historical Society Library/Tucson.)

Mexico or known Apache terrain, posts of lesser importance were also established. Many of these posts were used as temporary campsites, or as stepping-stones between major forts, and resting places for troopers engaged in running down renegades in the field. The military policy of the United States in the West was aimed at the control of the Indian, especially the Apache.

As early as 1832, military officers were perplexed by the many names given to the group of military buildings surrounding a parade ground, the center of which held the flagpole. Names such as post, camp, fort, presidio, barracks, or cantonment were often used, regardless of the size of the encampment.

In 1893–94, one Army officer stated the problem so aptly that his comments were made part of the Executive Documents for that year. (The quote that follows appeared in the *Army, Navy Journal*, December, 1893–94.)

> General Order 11 of 1832 directed that thereafter all cantonments should be called forts. With the lapse of time, however, a contrary practice grew up and although a partial reform was indicated by General Order 79 of 1878, certain anomalies still exist to the nomenclature of our military posts which might well be corrected, for the sake of uniformity and propriety. A very large number of military posts have been named from the locality where they are placed, some of which like . . . San Carlos . . . are not determined by any military appellation which is distinctive. A few posts bear the names of Indian tribes distinguished neither for friendliness nor other good qualities. We have named posts after Presidents and princes, general officers and lieutenants, Christian saints and heathen sinners, Spaniards, Frenchmen and Englishmen, who were in no way distinguished in, or connected with, the civil or military post which must of necessity comprise a variety of buildings and quarters for officers, as well as barracks for enlisted men. It is respectfully suggested that the order of 1878 be amended so as to reserve to the Secretary of War the naming of military posts, and to prescribe the prefix, 'Fort' for all permanent posts; that the title 'barracks' be dropped, and that all purely local names be eliminated from the nomenclature of military posts.

The buildings were variously described by the soldiers who lived in them as mud huts, adobes, wooden shacks with shingled roofs, or narrow claptraps thrown together over raw dirt and plastered or chinked with mud. These buildings were cramped and crowded—and hot during the summer months, and damp, drafty, and cold during the winter. During the heavy rains, the adobe roofs and buildings would become severely damaged. Many gave way completely, and the reliable "A" tents (three and one-half feet high) were pitched, accommodating two men to a tent. Animals, snakes, scorpions, and tarantula spiders always made a mad dash for these "A" tents whenever they were flushed out of their own underground homes. If the soldier was not fighting the renegade Apache, he was in battle with Mother Nature's small but deadly creatures. One problem after another caused every man to harbor thoughts of desertion.

The following is a list of the many posts that were situated in the Territory of Arizona, showing their date of construction and date of termination. This list includes the major posts and secondary campsites as well. Note the map on page 49 that shows where many were located.

Arizona Posts

Apache, Fort . . . . (1870–1924)
Arivaipa, Fort . . . . See Camp Grant
Barrett, Fort . . . . (1862)
Beale's Springs, Camp . . . . (1871–1874)
Bowie, Fort . . . . (1862–1894)
Breckinridge, Camp . . . . See Camp Grant
Buchanan, Fort . . . . (1856–1861)
Calhoun, Camp . . . . See Fort Yuma
Cameron, Camp . . . . (1866–1867)
Canby, Fort . . . . (1863–1864)
Clark, Camp . . . . See Fort Whipple
Colorado, Camp . . . . (1868–1871)
Colorado, Camp . . . . See Fort Mohave
Crawford, Camp . . . . (1886)
Crittenden, Fort . . . . (1867–1873)
Date Creek, Camp . . . . (1867–1874)
Defiance, Fort . . . . (1851–1861)
El Dorado, Camp . . . . (1867)
Goodwin, Camp . . . . (1864–1871)
Grant, Fort . . . . (1860–1905)
Huachuca, Fort . . . . (1877–)
Hualpai, Camp . . . . (1869–1873)
Ilges, Camp . . . . (1870s)
Independence, Camp . . . . See Fort Yuma
Infantry, Camp . . . . See Camp Picket Post
Infantry, Camp . . . . See Fort Verde
La Paz, Camp . . . . (1874–1875)
Lewis, Camp . . . . (1865?–1870?)
Lincoln, Camp . . . . (1864)
Lincoln, Camp . . . . See Fort Verde
Lowell, Fort . . . . (1860–1891)
McCleave, Camp . . . . (1864)
McDowell, Fort . . . . (1865–1890)
McKee, Camp . . . . See Camp Mason
McPherson, Camp . . . . . See Camp Date Creek
Mansfield, Camp . . . . (1863–?)

Quartermaster corral at Fort Apache, 1877. (Photo courtesy of the Arizona Historical Society Library/Tucson.)

Mason, Fort . . . . (1865–1866)
Mogollon, Camp . . . . See Fort Apache
Mojave, Fort . . . . (1859–1890)
Moore, Camp . . . . See Fort Buchanan
Nogales, Camp (near) . . . . (1887–1888)
O'Connell, Camp . . . . (1868)
Ord, Camp . . . . See Fort Apache
Pinal, Camp . . . . (1870–1871)
Picket Post, Camp . . . . (1871–?)
Pomeroy, Camp . . . . See Fort Whipple
Powers, Camp . . . . See Camp J. A. Rucker
Prescott Barracks . . . . See Fort Whipple
Price, Camp . . . . (1881–1883)
Rawlins, Camp . . . . (1870)
Reno, Camp . . . . (1867–1870)
Rigg, Camp . . . . (1864?–1870?)
Rucker, Camp J. A. . . . . (1878–1880)
San Carlos, Camp . . . . (1873–1900)
Skull Valley, Camp . . . . . See Camp Date Creek
Stanford, Camp . . . . See Camp Grant
Supply, Camp . . . . (1863)
Supply, Camp . . . . See Camp J. A. Rucker
Thomas, Fort . . . . (1876–1892)
Thomas, Camp . . . . See Fort Apache
Toll Gate, Camp . . . . See Camp Hualpai
Tonto, Camp . . . . (1864)
Tubac, Camp . . . . (1862–1865)
Tucson, Camp . . . . See Fort Lowell
Verde, Fort . . . . (1864–1890)
Verde, Camp . . . . See Fort McDowell
Wallen, Camp . . . . (1866–1869)
Whipple, Fort . . . . (1863–1913)
Willow Grove, Camp . . . . (1867–1869)
Yuma, Fort . . . . (1849–1885)

Much of the soldier's food was drab, with hardly any taste, and at times was scanty. A full month's menu may have included some beef or salt pork, rice, beans, dried fish, dried vegetables, and soft bread or hardtack (a Civil War vintage held over). "Rio" coffee, served all day, was strong enough to grow whiskers on your stomach lining.

It wasn't unusual for a few troopers to escape "extra duty," simply by planting and caring for a vegetable garden. They were regarded as The Kitchen Cook's Assistant (or Cookie, for short). No more than two enlisted men would carry out the task of watering and weeding each company plot.

Boredom often set in at these remote posts. Horseracing, hunting for fresh game, baseball, staging variety shows, sack races, card playing, and probably a host of other games were thought up by the officers to keep the men occupied. Underhanded, scheming individuals often brought their own tricks from civilian life to practise on their "bunkies" for a small profit.

Europeans were an easy touch. Because they couldn't speak or understand English very well, their Army pay slipped through their fingers freely. A few con men joined the Army just to fleece their bunkies of their money. Once they cleaned up, they deserted to the next territory.

A good example was the "Blacklegs," a sharper who knew all the tricks of the game in "pasteboards" (cards). He travelled the western railroads and took every sucker willing to enjoy a hand at cards. Nine times out of ten, he would inherit properties from the game table, but would sell them back rather cheap to keep the "saddle blanket" (dollar) moving across the table.

Field Day of a Soldier—an Account of Camp Life

The sky overhead was still dark, but the sentry on Post No. 3 was already walking his "company street" between two rows of enlisted men's tents. At each end were the officers' tents and a barricade of encircled wagons, with the horses picketed in the center. The wagons were being unloaded, sinks and fire pits dug, forage and grain set out, and wood chips, gathered by troopers along the route, stacked for the cook's fires.

Suddenly, the flap of the guard tent rose and fell, and the silhouette of an orderly trumpeter could be seen stepping forth. An instant later the notes of the first call for reveille rang out clearly, cutting the starlit air. In a moment muffled sounds were heard all over the camp, and the small tents on the company streets became faintly luminous, followed quickly by those on the officers' line. Dark figures darted to and fro, finally congregating in front of the tents for roll call.

Hacking coughs, many deep chested with accumulations of congested phlegm, were heard. And the men grumbled and cursed as the last stragglers, still dressing themselves, fell in the single line for roll call.

Here and there a lantern bobbed about in each street. The sergeant checked the company roll and

Forts in Arizona.

indicated who went on sick call, guard duty, or work detail. Ten minutes passed; then the trumpets blared out reveille and the work day had begun.

The teamsters had been feeding and grooming their mules long before roll call. The company cooks, quietly at work for some time, now served breakfast at the bugler's "mess call." Troopers dashed to the line carrying tin cups and plates; many eagerly pushed in line to get an early serving. Breakfast in the field was not an elaborate one—hot coffee, bacon, and hard bread. After being served, the soldier went where he pleased to eat his meal.

The longer the command remained in one place, the better the meals. Bean soup, beans, dried apples, biscuits, dried peaches, and fresh bread might be had. In a smaller command, every man

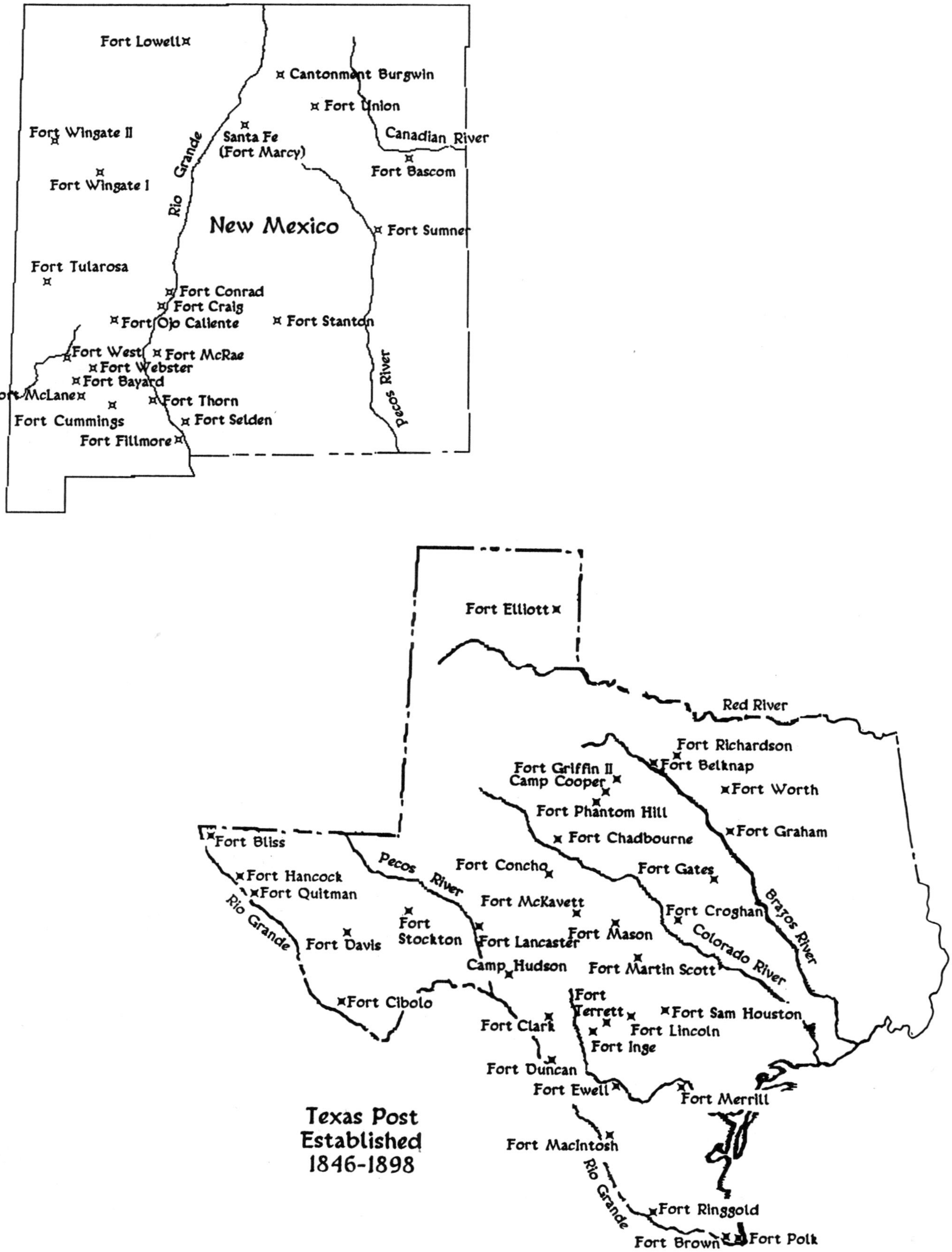

Forts in New Mexico and Texas.

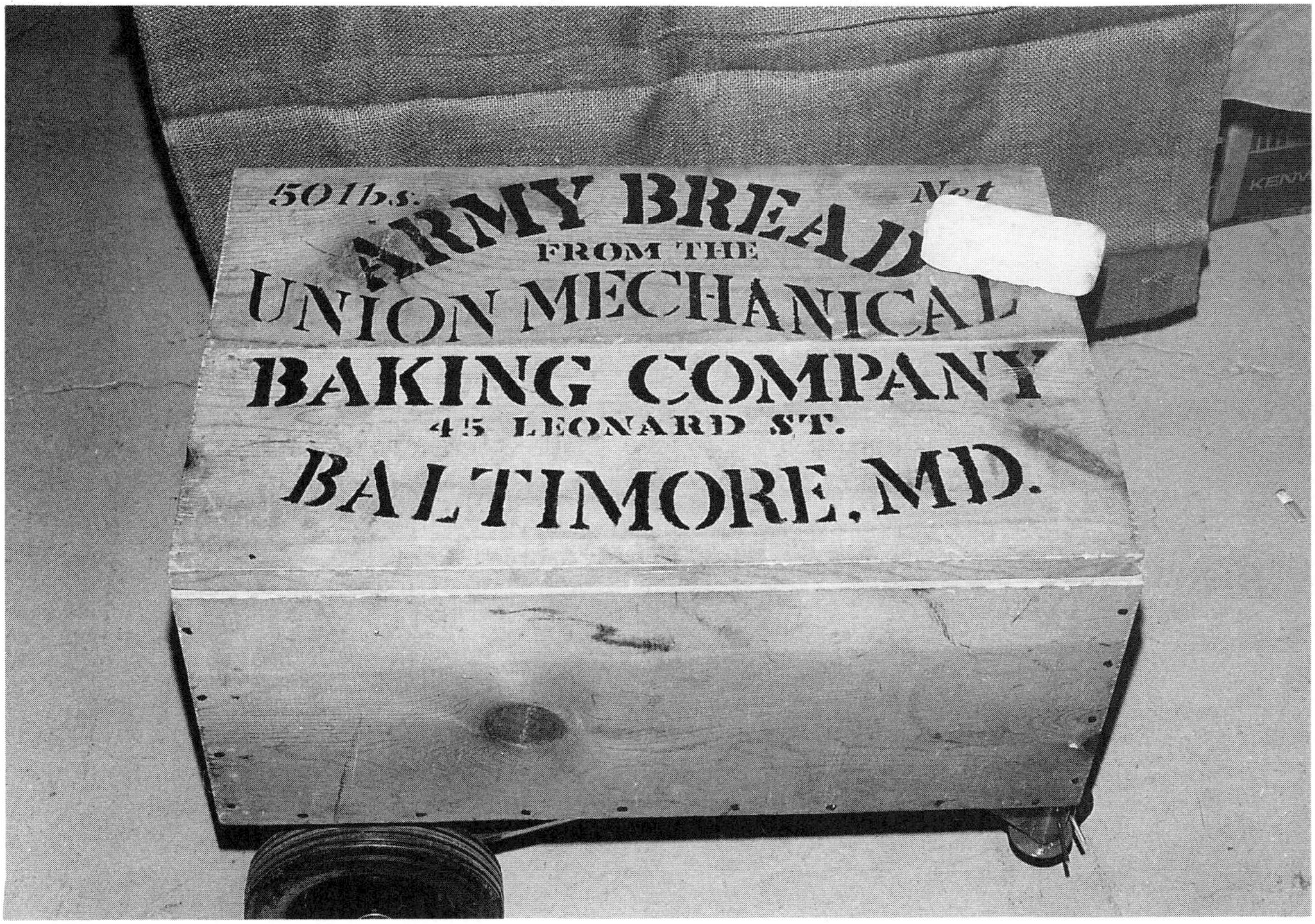

The old staple hardtack biscuit was still issued to western troopers, sometimes coming directly from the warehouses that stored Civil War goods. (One biscuit is shown on the upper right.) Almost all the boxes of hardtack were infested with maggots and weevils, riddling the crackers with tiny holes.

carried his own rations for the length of time he was in the field. Whatever he found, such as wild onions or berries, would be added to the standard menu of bacon, hard corn, coffee, beans, and hardtack. Volunteers were dispatched to find fresh meat or fowl. A double- or single-barrel shotgun was an issue item; there was one per command for these volunteers.

With mess call over, packing began. The wagons had already been driven up to a designated area, where they were now being loaded with everything except the enlisted men's tents, which had not yet been taken down. When the trumpets sounded the "general," the tents were simultaneously struck by the waiting camp guard, whether their occupants were ready to leave or not, and down came the tents. No notice was taken of indignant language or the rage of any soldier should he have to crawl out from beneath a dropped canvas tent. The rush to fold the tents and place them on the wagons before "assembly" sounded became a competitive game among several companies. The company that did it faster than the others qualified for lesser duties in the future.

Not much time was given for final preparations. Soon after the "general," the "assembly" was sounded. The battalion formed and the march began at the earliest indication of the sunrise.

Through the early morning mist, the commanding officer and staff rode ahead of the column, which appeared grey and indistinct, weird and ghostly, behind them. In hostile country the column moved with both advance and rear guards and flankers. The flankers rode well out on each side of the main body, watching eagerly for the slightest evidence of Indians.

Marching on the desert did not mean passing from one campground to another over a good road at a certain number of miles per hour. More than likely, a command had to depend upon its scouts to show the way and make the road as it went

Muster at Fort Huachuca, 1883. Company C, 1st U.S. Infantry; and troops I, H, and L, 6th U.S. Cavalry. (Photo courtesy of the Arizona Historical Society Library/Tucson.)

Fort Huachuca, c. 1880s. (Photo courtesy of the Arizona Historical Society Library/Tucson.)

This photo of Fort Huachuca shows the soldiers relaxing on the porches, probably on a Sunday afternoon, c. *1880s. (Photo courtesy of Fort Huachuca Museum.)*

Fort Huachuca, 1886. (Photo courtesy of the Arizona Historical Society Library/Tucson.)

Fort Defiance. (Photo courtesy of the Arizona Historical Society Library/Tucson.)

along. While on a trail or blazing one, no one knew what the day might bring. Canyon walls might be too narrow to allow passage of the wagons, and a work detail, already chosen, would have to hack at the hard rock walls with pick and shovel. Many obstacles, such as deep ravines and steep hills, caused delays and many precious hours were lost. It was on such journeys that the western soldier displayed his ingenuity and resourcefulness.

In the desert, sources of water were so infrequent that their appearance regulated all travel; thus, a day's march was commonly from source to source, and they could be anywhere from eight to twenty miles apart. When water did present itself, caution had to be taken. Scouts had to evaluate whether the water was fit to drink or possibly had been poisoned. These scouts were never wrong. If there were no dead insects lying about, the water was safe to drink. Then, empty canteens were filled, and the horses were allowed a little drink.

During the ten-minute halts that came in each hour, the men would romp around and amuse themselves, or lie on their backs and try to take a catnap. When the march was resumed, it took a few minutes for them to fall in and pick up their regular gait.

When they reached the evening camp, the men took care of their horses, removing bridles and saddles and checking their backs for galls or other skin irritations. The horses were walked to cool off for ten minutes and then allowed to roll with their blankets still on.

The soldiers would groom their horses by hand, using a curry comb and brush, or give them a hand massage, loosening muscles, but these were just for starters. Careful inspection of the horses' ears, eyes, nose, and hooves was very important, and officers saw to it that a lazy trooper took good care of his horse, if nothing else. Finally, before the troopers could retire, the mounts were all watered and fed.

The chunky, western-bred horses were considered the best for frontier service, where breed and speed were not as important as muscle and stamina. But when attacking Indian villages, it was the tough, swift, little Indian ponies that the troopers wanted as second mounts more than anything else. In turn, the Indians prized the huge army mounts for war and hunting. To clarify the differences between army horses and Indian ponies, it was the small Indian pony, grass-fed and light-footed, that could travel great distances. The army horse was much heavier and often became winded in a short time when chasing the ponies. Of course, the army horse was usually burdened with a rider, a saddle, and full equipment, including iron shoes.

Early morning Indian attacks on Army camps in the field were common. The braves would swing their robes in the air as they thundered down on the camp, attempting to stampede the corraled horses. While the soldiers rushed for their weapons, the bugler sounded "stable" or "water," alerting them to check for any runaway horses.

Fort Huachuca today. Many of the old buildings still stand. The post also has an interesting museum.

5

THE INDIAN WARS IN ARIZONA

These descriptions of the Arizona area during the Apache Wars have been taken from eyewitness accounts. The area was in the shape of a parallelogram that extended from Camp Verde east to the White Mountains, south to the San Carlos Mountains, west to Camp McDowell, and back up north to Camp Verde. It encompassed 15,000 square miles of rocky mountain peaks, canyons, sandy wastes, mountain streams, and dark pine forests. When the Army chased the Indians into this Apache stronghold, they faced a climb along a zigzag trail up the sharp, rocky ridges, followed by a steep descent. There were fields of grass useful for pasturing horses and pack animals, but they were limited, and surrounded by mountains that made them all but inaccessible. Overnight rest was usually followed by another interminable struggle up the mountain peaks.

In most wild mountain regions, the narrow edges of the streams, or the stream beds themselves, could be used to move pack animals up and down the mountains. However, the streams in the Arizona mountains were different, as they poured out in torrents through dark box canyons. The streams interrupted passage between the grassy areas, and movement between these areas was only accomplished by climbing the steep mountain faces.

The climate in the Arizona area offered all extremes. For the troopers who passed from the forests of the mesa to the barren river bottoms of the Salt and Gila rivers, the coolness of the pine forests and the burning sandy wastes must have

Beside a huge saguaro cactus (hundreds of years old), two Arizona cowboys study the valley to make certain that no renegade Apache camp is in sight before they herd their cattle through. Cowboys were easy prey for the hostile Apache.

In old Tucson (c. 1860s–1870s) Mexican homes, made of adobe brick and mesquite brush, were seen alongside newer buildings.

given rise to visions of Heaven and Hell. But travelling on the burning sands must have seemed easier than the journey into the cooler areas of wild, rocky mountains.

The rough terrain and difficulty in following a trail kept the Army in constant danger for many years. A record of some of the troops shows ninety-seven battles between 1871 and 1875, and describes the suffering and hardships that accompanied mountain scouting during that time.

Early in 1872, it became clear that the Camp Grant area was being used as a base for supplies by the Arivipa Apache. They would push their war parties in every direction, terrorizing all the settlements in the Arizona Territory, and then retreat into the towering mountains and burning sands.

Needless to say, the area provided many hiding and resting places for the Indians to recuperate after their brief hit-and-run forays against the Army.

The dread experienced by the settlers for these marauders is best appreciated when the character and mode of warfare of the mountain tribes are understood. You can get a fairly clear picture from these remarks by an old wagon master: "We have a horror of them that you feel for a ghost. We never see them, but when on the road we are always looking over our shoulders in anticipation. When they strike, all we see is the flash of the rifle resting with secure aim over a pile of stones, behind which, like a snake, the red murderer lies at full length." This quote originally appeared in *Life Among the Apaches*, by John C. Cremony (*Arizona Silhouettes*, 1951).

All the Apaches were footmen, mountain climbers. They would steal horses and use them, but when they were driven into the mountains the horses often became a part of their rations. Graceful, well formed, light and active as a cat, with legs that seemed to be made of steel wire, the Apache on the rocky hillside was nearly unapproachable. To fight him, with any chance of success, he had to be attacked with skill and great caution before sunrise in his bivouac far up among the rocks. Many a surprise attack was made by night marches through natural fortresses absolutely unassailable in the daytime, and where, if the Indians had discovered the ascending columns, even in the night, they could have repulsed them with great slaughter.

As a first step in the campaign, the commanding general ordered all warriors receiving rations to be counted every day, at a place to be selected within five miles of the post. So that the officer detailed for this duty could identify and keep a record of the young men, a metal tag stamped with a number was issued to each brave of fighting age. Many of the Indians received this order with sullen dissatisfaction because, if carried out, it would checkmate their rovings. Seated on their heels in increasing concentric circles in front of the general, they crouched and glared—and with their brilliant

This is a close-up of a typical mid-1880s cavalry trooper, posing for the folks back home. (Photo courtesy of Herb Peck, Jr.)

beadlike eyes, they reminded the soldiers of snakes, coiled and ready to strike. It was clear that when the opportunity arose, the Indians would resist this effort to thwart them by the most deadly means possible.

The next day the cavalry officer detailed for this task rode out four miles from the post, accompanied by one orderly, to meet the young braves and make the first count.

The officer selected was a lieutenant who had seen considerable service and fighting, but he subsequently confessed that he would have been glad to exchange this duty for a detail to lead a hopeless charge over a breastwork. However, he had been told by the general that it was undesirable to send a force to meet with the warriors, since some of them might become alarmed, and in their ignorance make trouble, and that the object was to give the Indians a fair chance.

So, out he rode, with his heart in his throat, aware that unless he kept his wits about him, some young brave would stab him in the back, and thus distinguishing himself, take to the warpath. The place selected was at the foot of a hill on which was situated the largest Indian village of the reservation. Upon his arrival, the lieutenant was met by the whole band rushing down the hillside with yells and shouts. As they came closer, he had the horror of perceiving that they were nearly all drunk. They had been "celebrating" the disagreeable order of the day before with a "tiswin" spree. (Tiswin is a fermented liquor made from sprouted corn.)

The lieutenant received the charge by dismounting and standing, with a nonchalance that was far from natural, at the foot of a large cottonwood tree. The orderly remained mounted, holding the horses a few yards in the rear. It was soon apparent that several of the chiefs had stayed sober, and were doing their utmost to prevent trouble. As a result of their exertions, the wild crowd was halted about twenty yards from the tree and the Indians attempted to seat themselves in their usual half-circle formations. The lieutenant then approached, with book and pencil in hand, and although aware of the possibility of assassination, resolutely passed along the front of each half-circle, checking off the numbers on the tags.

Many of the Indians, with impudent drunken leers, shook their tags in his face, and one fellow refused to show his. Passing the mutineer for the time being, the lieutenant concluded the checking

Indian scouts. (Photo courtesy of the Arizona Historical Society Library/Tucson.)

process. He was now confronted by a formidable problem: Either he must capture the drunken young Indian, or submit to the indignity of seeing the orders entrusted to him for execution treated with contempt, of which the Indians were sure to take advantage. At this point, the lieutenant called up the orderly with the horses, and then turned to one of the most reliable chiefs standing nearby, and made signs to him to bring up the young man and force him to show his tag. The young fellow came forward when bidden by the chief, but stood immovable, staring at the government representative with drunken insolence. Giving the orderly, who was still mounted, a few words of direction, the lieutenant mounted his own horse as if to ride off. Then at the lieutenant's signal, the orderly, a fine old soldier, suddenly drew his revolver and covered the young rascal, while making an imperious sign to him to jump up behind the lieutenant. The old chief took in the situation instantly, and seizing the fellow under the arms, almost threw him up on the rump of the horse behind the lieutenant—and so, covered by the steady pistol of the orderly, they rode off. The Indians were quick to appreciate the defeat of the braggart, and followed the little procession of prisoner and captors with yells, screams, and jeering laughter. The prisoner was safely landed in the post guardhouse, a witness to the nerve and courage of a resolute officer who would not be intimidated by the fury and insolence of the Apache.

Such captures were not always made so successfully. A few months later, two soldiers were just about to arrest a young Indian who was seated on the ground wrapped in a blanket. As they approached him, the Indian quickly threw off the blanket; then, by a right and left stroke with a knife, he killed one soldier and severely wounded the other.

No further trouble occurred at the daily verification of the Indians, and a correct estimate of their number resulted from this counting process. The young men who preferred war to steady rations quietly slipped away, with the exception of two desperados, Chontz and Cochenay. Aspiring to be war chiefs, they committed a cold-blooded murder within the limits of the military post, and then fled to the mountains, followed by their immediate relatives. This party was promptly pursued by an officer and ten cavalrymen summoned from the drill ground.

The soldiers, reenforced by three Apache scouts from the band of Casadore (who had always remained friendly), took up the trail from the scene of the murder, where lay the body of an inoffensive young Mexican, brained from behind by the cowardly assassins. Following the trail, they soon came to a place where there was a mark drawn in the dust across the path and a red flag stuck up on a stick, plainly indicating war.

The trail then led over country that was the roughest imaginable. Down deep into the bowels of the earth it seemed to go before reaching the stream at the bottom of the first box canyon, and then up, up it went along the slanting, slippery crevices worn in the face of the opposite rocks. Going forward all day on foot, leading their stumbling horses over the broken rocks, the soldiers and scouts pushed on. They halted only after dark, when the trail could no longer be followed, spending the chilly winter night on the bare rocks without food and with only their saddle blankets for cover. For days the party kept up this search, but, unfortunately, without success. This pursuit, however, was to be a prelude to a tragedy in which Chontz and Cochenay, who were natural leaders and desperados, were principal characters.

Some time later, after the agency had been moved to the San Carlos Reservation, these desperados, taking advantage of a stormy night and a sudden rise in the Gila River, which separated the camp of the cavalry from the Indians, boldly entered the Apache village.

It so happened that many of the young men that night, feeling confident that the soldiers wouldn't interfere on account of the swollen stream between them, were drinking "tiswin," and fast ripening into a mood fit for mischief. This habit of the Apaches' deliberately intoxicating themselves by using a liquor made by the squaws from fermented corn was a very difficult thing to deal with. Parties of soldiers under determined young officers were frequently sent into their camp to break up the drunken sprees—and while these dangerous duties were always successful, there was no way to prevent the Indians from stealing or buying corn and making "tiswin" again.

When Chontz and Cochenay with their followers entered the Indian camp, they harangued the bands, and said that all young men not cowards would follow their lead. Taunts, reproaches, and appeals at such a time produced an explosion. A rush was made for a wagon train loaded with supplies for the troops that was on the Indian side of the river directly opposite the cavalry camp. The teamsters were instantly killed and the wagons plundered, and then with wild yells the whole tribe started for the mountains.

There was work to do indeed. Hurrying from Fort Apache, the nearest post, two cavalry troops made the seventy miles in one march, bringing with them a company of the gallant and faithful White Mountain Apache, enlisted as scouts.

Taking up the trail, these troops followed in the wake of the devastating Apaches. The trail led straight for the settlements on the San Pedro River, and was found returning up the valley of that stream and heading for the mountains north of the Gila.

There was no need to follow the trail to the ruined homes of the white settlers down along the San Pedro. At the point where it was encountered, the troopers saw torn dresses, children's clothing, and broken household utensils scattered along the path, and knew that the "red devils" had swept through the peaceful colony like a whirlwind, leaving nothing but wreckage. And so it proved, as those who later visited the scene reported finding dead women, the lifeless bodies of helpless little children, and men who had been scalped and mangled—an all too familiar sight after the raid of an Indian war party.

After much suffering in the mountains and three days of absolute fasting, the advance troops finally reported that they had located the entire Indian band on the top of the Pinal Mountains, in a position unassailable by direct attack. The commanding officer of the San Carlos, a man of nerve, and one familiar with all the vicissitudes of Apache character, had by this time secured the services of a renegade from the hostiles, who promised to lead the troops into the natural fortress under cover of darkness.

The expedition started at once. It included the soldiers from Fort Apache and the cavalry troops summoned from the nearest posts. They marched only at night, concealing themselves during the hours of daylight, and by dawn on the third morning, reached a point fifteen miles as the crow flies from the Pinal Mountains.

As the sun rose, the outlines of the Indian stronghold became plainly visible. Then curling pillars of smoke could be seen, which apparently the Indians made no effort to conceal. This unusual sight of campfire smoke was disheartening evidence of the Apaches' confidence in their impregnable position along the rocky ridge. It was clear that the defiant Apaches felt secure.

Fort Apache. (Photo courtesy of the Arizona Historical Society Library/Tucson.)

Although they were only fifteen miles away as the crow flies, the renegade insisted that it would be necessary to make a detour to the north in order to avoid the dangerous chasms that intervened, and that twenty-five miles of the roughest country in Arizona must be crossed to reach the crest of the mountain.

Early in the afternoon, the party set out. Only the very best of the men were taken. All marched on foot. The sick and exhausted left behind took charge of the horses and pack mules, and were told to keep everything well hidden from any outlying enemy scouts.

Single file, in one long column, the troops pushed out, led by their White Mountain allies. Stripped to their breechcloths, lithe and graceful, the Indian scouts, like a pack of greyhounds, surrounded and guarded the renegade guide. Officers and men alike carried two days' rations on their backs, but had divested themselves of all superfluous weight. Saving their breath by silence, they strove manfully to keep up with their fleet-footed guides.

A terrible task was before them. The country was one mass of broken rocks, and canyons with precipitous sides crossed the trail at frequent intervals. All night long they stumbled, struggled, and scrambled forward. How they succeeded in crossing the gloomy, pitch-black canyons no one in the party were ever able to say. Keeping within touch of each other, and guided by faith, they groped their way to the bottoms of the dark chasms—and, in the same order, panting for breath, toiled up the opposite sides. Treachery on the part of the Apache scouts would have turned any one of the dark holes into a slaughter pit.

The briefest halts for rest were made, for should daylight come before the crest was reached, discovery, repulse, and death to many would follow. Before the glimmer of the dawn appeared, it was apparent that they were climbing up the side of the last and highest ridge. With increased caution, the men pulled themselves upwards from rock to rock. From the steep face of the ridge, sharp rocky spurs projected at intervals in the direction from which the troops advanced.

The attack was made in three parties, each ascending by one of these natural scaling ladders. So well timed was the operation that when, just at the first streak of dawn, the White Mountain scouts opened fire and charged the startled hostiles, the troops had gained the top of their rocky spurs, and the fortified camp—which, had it been warned of the attack, could have repulsed a brigade—was carried in three places.

The capture of this natural fortress, which Chontz and Cochenay had tried to prove to the bands was impregnable, broke up the unity of the tribe, shook their confidence in their leaders, and increased their fear of the troops. The Indians who weren't killed or captured dispersed in small parties into the surrounding mountains. The soldiers in like manner separated, and in small squads scouted the mountains in every direction, giving the hostiles no chance to attack the settlements.

Before long, runners came in to the San Carlos Reservation from the scattered tribe, asking for peace and permission to return. The commanding general told every such messenger that the Indians could return as long as they would surrender one or all of four named outlaws: Chontz, Cochenay, Pedro (one of the most active leaders in the murders on the river of that name), and Sondazzy (the "tool" of Chontz in the killing, a short time before, of a cavalry officer at the agency). He also told them that if they could not surrender the outlaws named alive, they themselves should mete out the punishment of death, and that upon proof that a just fate had overtaken the criminals, any or all of the other Indians could come back and live in peace.

So, it finally turned out that the Indians themselves punished the outlaws, furnishing satisfactory proof that justice had been done, and before summer the Arivipa tribe was reestablished at the San Carlos Agency.

6

THE 1884 REPORT OF BRIGADIER-GENERAL CROOK

The following appeared in the Report of the Secretary of War, *Messages and Documents*, 1884.

SIR: I have the honor to report that during the year just past the condition of military affairs in the Department of Arizona has been eminently satisfactory. The last of the Chiricahua Apaches is now on the reservation, and for the first time in the history of that fierce people, every member of the Apache tribe is at peace.

Efforts were made early in the spring to put the Chiricahuas at work for their own living. They are allowed to select farming lands in the vicinity of Fort Apache, such seeds and farming implements as could be obtained were issued to them, and under the instruction of Capt. Emmett Crawford, Third Cavalry, assisted by Lieut. Britton Davis, of the same regiment, ground was broken and farming begun. The results have been such as to warrant the most hopeful anticipations. The two chiefs—Geronimo and Chato, who last year were our worst enemies—have this year made the greatest progress and possess the best-tilled farms. The other Apache bands continue to do excellently well, and with the exception of a few, who did not receive seed in time, or whose farming lands were injured by freshets, have produced large crops of vegetables and cereals, the surplus of which will be purchased for cash for the use of the military posts upon the reservation.

I regard this as one of the most important features of any policy which has for its object the advancement of the savage beyond a state of vagabondage. He must be made to work, and he will do that with full heart only when he sees that he can always find a ready cash market for the fruits of his labor.

Farming in Arizona demands much preliminary knowledge and entails much preliminary expense. Irrigation is indispensable, and long and deep ditches must be excavated. When besides this we have an inadequate provision of seeds and farming implements, many of the Indians being compelled to plant with sticks hardened in the fire, and to reap with ordinary case knives, some idea may be formed of the difficulties overcome but; in spite of these difficulties the following crops have been raised this season:

Three million eight hundred and fifty thousand pounds of corn, 550,000 pounds of barley, 54,000 pounds of beans, 20,000 pounds of potatoes, 50,000 pounds of wheat, 200,000 pumpkins, 50,000 watermelons, 40,000 muskmelons, besides small quantities of onions, cabbage, and peppers.

The bans living in the vicinity of Fort Apache lost one-third of their crops by late spring rains and early frosts; while those living closer to the San Carlos Agency were even more unfortunate by reason of freshets in the Gila River.

Upon my reassignment to the command of the department, just two years ago, the Chiricahuas and many of the White Mountain Apaches were on the warpath, and the others were mainly loafers and beggars, hanging about the agency for an occasional dole of rations.

Farming labor, indeed labor of any kind, was regarded as drudgery to be done, if done at all, by squaws, but no stronger proof can be adduced of the anxiety of the Apaches to improve their condition than the fact that more than half of the work of this year has been performed by men and boys.

It is not perhaps necessary to repeat the views held by me in previous reports upon all that relates to Indian management. Years of practical experience with the savage under all possible circumstances have merely confirmed the theories formed and followed in my earlier service. The Indian will never cease to be a nuisance and a terror until he be enfranchised, but it is not just to endow him with the ballot until he be competent to hold land in severalty and be taught how to utilize it for his own support.

The facts above cited in the case of the Apaches speak for themselves. They demonstrate that with but little honest encouragement, this Indian will drop from the list of worthless idlers and relieve the Government from the responsibility of caring for him.

I therefore earnestly recommend that no further delay be allowed in forwarding to all the Indians on the White Mountain Reservation a full equipment of plows, tools, and wagons, and a supply of such seeds suitable to this country as they may not possess. They would then be placed in a position to make their own living and lay by something for the future.

There should also be erected one or two mills for grinding wheat by water power. Their cost would be but trivial, while the advantage would be great and immediate.

The request continually made by the Apache for the establishment of additional trading stores should not be disregarded. The prices they have to pay to the present traders for the commonest articles are extortionate and much greater than those demanded by the store keepers in the little towns outside; hence arises a very natural desire to go to those places where they can get the most for their money. But in the gratification of this desire they have sometimes to go great distances and thus incur the risk of unfriendly collision with the settlers. The remedy for this is the one the Apaches themselves suggest; the introduction of competition which will beat down prices.

There have been no troubles with the Apaches during the past year, excepting the case of the young chief Ke-e-te-na, last spring. This chief asserts that he is a Mexican Indian, that his home has always been in the Sierra Madre, and that neither he nor his band has ever been on a reservation. The restraints of his new surroundings proved irksome to him, and he manifested a disposition to oppose the discipline imposed upon the other Apaches. He made a speech at a dance, in which he referred to past victories gained over the whites, and expressed a hope for a renewal of such glories. On other occasions this chief had clearly shown an unruly temper and an aversion to the new order of things. When it became evident that this influence was exerted in antagonism to peace and good order, there was no alternative left but to make an example of him. He was arrested by a detachment of native soldiers, of his own tribe, tried by an Apache jury, found guilty, and sent to Alcatraz Island, California, for imprisonment.

This system of trial by Indian juries has been introduced with happy results, and offenses committed within the tribe are tried and punished with certainty, promptness, and justice.

Captain Crawford, Lieutenant Gatewood, and Lieutenant Davis, the officers having military charge of the Apaches, deserve the warmest praise for the intelligent and conscientious manner in which they have performed their arduous and thankless duties, handled the most difficult questions, introduced good order among the Apaches, and placed them so far on the road to civilization and self-maintenance. Careful attention is invited to their reports, hereto appended, marked A.

The starvation which last winter threatened the Hualapai in the northwest part of the Territory has been provided against by the issue of supplies, under the special appropriation made for the purpose. Capt. F. E. Pierce, First Infantry, has labored hard with these people and has managed their affairs judiciously and economically.

They number between seven and eight hundred, and although a small tribe, are distinguished for individual courage, as well as for the fearfully rough country—that in the vicinity of the Grand Canyon of the Colorado—to which they retreat when pressed. When on the warpath they occupied the constant attention of a full regiment of cavalry.

In my opinion a suitable reservation should be provided for them as soon as possible. To issue rations and not place the Hualapai at work is no great favor. Life may be prolonged, but the debauchery of men and women is increased, not averted.

The reports of the chiefs of staff bureau, on duty at these headquarters, are attached, marked respectively, B, C, D, E, F, and G. I concur in their recommendations, especially the following:

Major McGonnigle, chief quartermaster, complains of the meager appropriations made for the support of this department, which rendered it impossible to keep public animals in condition for effective service. It seems to be a false and short-sighted economy to half feed horses and mules in a department containing so many Indians lately on the warpath. Had circumstances compelled our troops to begin an active campaign last spring, most of the cavalry would have been on foot.

Lieut. T. A. Bingham, engineer officer, renews the request so often made, that he be furnished with a small amount of money for the purchase of paper and other materials needed in making maps and for other necessary purposes.

The sum asked for is so small—$375—and the advantages to accrue from a correct mapping of Arizona so great, that I trust no further application on this head shall be necessary.

Maj. A. K. Arnold, who during the greater part of the year performed the duties of inspector general, recommends certain changes in the components of the ration which should receive careful consideration. I believe that ours is the only army in the world which endeavors to give a soldier the same food in Arizona as that which he would receive in Alaska.

This question of food is in Arizona of grave importance. Military posts are from a variety of causes often prevented from maintaining vegetable gardens and the soldier must consequently look more and more to his superiors for good, wholesome rations; a failure to supply these will often breed discontent, the logical sequence to which is always inefficient service or desertion.

A very marked proficiency in rifle practice has been gained by the officers and enlisted men serving in Arizona. Much credit for this gratifying progress is due to Lieut. G. H. Morgan, Third Cavalry, the officer in charge.

I regret extremely being obliged to again call attention to the inferior character of horses supplied to the cavalry. Very many of them are vicious and intractable, totally unsuited to the requirements of service. Soldiers have been killed by them or maimed and disabled for life.

In my last annual report I recommended that animals needed for Arizona be bought in Missouri or adjoining States, where good, sound saddle horses are raised for market. I was led to understand that such purchases were in the future to be made, but, for reasons not known to me, the old system is adhered to and the same objectionable class of animals has again been sent here for issue to the Third and Fourth Cavalry. The first installment arrived at Ash Fork last week, and a few days after at Whipple Barracks. Of the total number, forty, invoiced here, one "bucked" itself to death, one died of an obscure disease, one gave out on the road, and sixteen others have been condemned by a board of survey convened for their examination by the regimental commander Third Cavalry.

It is a useless waste of money to buy such horses, not to mention the injustice to the soldier to compel him to ride them. It has been reported to me by regimental commanders that men have deserted rather than incur the risks of riding and managing them.

Finally, I would beg leave to urge that the proper department be requested to push the matter of the return by the Mexican authorities of the Apache women and children held captive by them. Their restitution cannot fail to develop a happy state of feeling among the Chiricahuas and other bands. It is scarcely necessary to enter into argument upon this point. It must be evident to any comprehension that so long as those members of their tribe are in the hands of the Mexicans the Apache will have cause of irritation and complaint, and that temptation will constantly be held out to impetuous young men to raid into Mexico to resume war and make reprisals. The Chiricahuas have shown their good faith by delivering up thirteen women and children captured and held by them as hostages. Mexican interests are as deeply involved as our own in the permanent settlement of border troubles, for which reason I am anxious to see removed the last source of provocation for their renewal.

Very respectfully, your obedient servant,

George Crook,
Brigadier-General, commanding.

APPENDIX A

To the Assistant Adjutant-General, Whipple Barracks, Ariz.:

SIR: In reply to your letter of 21st of August, 1884, I have the honor to make the following report: The police control of the reservation having been placed under my charge by General Order No. 13, series 1883, Headquarters Department of Arizona, I, since that time, have exercised it in accordance with instructions at various times received by me from my superiors, and with results that I trust are as satisfactory to them as they are gratifying to me. I respectfully submit a statement of the incidents of importance that have occurred since my last report, and certain recommendations suggested by my observations of the condition and habits of the Indians.

In fulfillment of promises given General Crook in the Sierra Madre, various parties of Chiricahuas, some large, some small, have during the past year made their way, some under guard from the Mexican line, others by mountain trails, to the reservation. The last party of these hostiles reached here in April, 1884, and for the first time since the establishment of the reservation all the tribes of the Apache nation in their entirety were upon it.

The Chiricahuas were then allowed to choose any part of the reservation upon which to live, and having selected a camp on Turkey Creek in the northern part of it they, five hundred and twenty men, women, and children, were moved to that place in May, in which vicinity they are at present under the charge of Lieut. Britton Davis, Third Cavalry.

Although it was late in the season, they set to work to raise such crops as could at that time be planted. Those that had distinguished themselves most in their desultory warfare in times past set them the example, for today Geronimo and Chato have the best farms belonging to the tribe. These Indians have under cultivation about 75 acres of land, and have raised an estimated 45,000 pounds of corn, a considerable amount of barley, besides many melons, pumpkins, and other vegetables. With the above products of their industry applied to their support I have been able to order a reduction in certain portions of the rations heretofore issued to them.

Since their return these Indians have been extremely tractable, with one exception, that of Ke-e-te-na, chief of the Chiricahua and Warm Springs Indians, who, on the night of the 21st of June, undertook at a dance to recall to his tribe their success in the fights in which he had led them, and at the same time hinted of future engagements in which they might hope to be equally fortunate. For such expressions Ke-e-te-na was, by the order of Lieutenant Davis, promptly arrested by Indian scouts of his own tribe, and sent here under guard, where he was tried by an Indian jury, and sentenced by me to three years' confinement (in irons) at Alcatraz Island, to which place he has been sent.

The present contentment and quietness of the Chiricahua Indians is due greatly to the intelligence, patience, and firmness of Lieut. Britton Davis, Third Cavalry, immediately under whose care they have been since they camped on Turkey Creek.

The Apache-Yuma Indians have their camp on the south bank of the Gila River and opposite the agency. I would recommend that they be moved some distance up the river, for the following reasons, namely, the amount of possible farming land where they are is too small for the number of workingmen in the tribe. Its lay is such as to make it extremely difficult, if not impossible, to water it by means of an irrigating ditch, and the proximity of the camp to the agency and this post permits the men and women of the tribe to loaf around these places, satisfying their natural curiosity and habituating themselves to lives of idleness. I think these people will work as well as any on the reservation, if a large, easily watered farm is selected for them, which can be done within ten miles of this place.

A large and properly arranged guardhouse is much needed on the reservation; the cells of the one at present used are too small, poorly ventilated, and very insecure. There are no separate accommodations for women that circumstances make it absolutely necessary to confine. At a very slight cost an adobe guardhouse could be built with two systems of cells, and two yards, so arranged as to prevent communication between male and female prisoners. With such a place of confinement at my disposal, prostitution, so prevalent among the Yumas, Mojaves, and Tontos, could be made a misdemeanor, and the interests of morality very much subserved. There are often cases in which the proper immediate punishment of a woman would prevent serious subsequent trouble.

It may be said that the only articles raised for sale by the Indians are barley and corn. No matter what amounts of these have been brought here they have been received and paid for. Last year about one-tenth of the grain fed to public animals at this post was delivered by them; this year two-thirds of the amount required for the same purpose has already been purchased of them. Judging from the increased ratio of the supply of such grain, it can easily be seen that the amount produced will soon be in excess of our requirements; other markets are distant, limited, and unprofitable. When we consider that the number of the Indians raising large crops is small in comparison with the number that incited by their success will, in future, engage more extensively in farming, the necessity of directing the attention of the Indians to the raising of other crops than corn that they can consume is apparent. These Indians at present buy large quantities of flour at $7 a hundred, an exorbitant price. Wheat can be raised by them with as little skill, labor, and attention as barley, and should grist mills be erected for grinding this wheat (and I strongly recommend that they be built, which can be done without expense to the Government, one on the Gila River, and another near Fort Apache), they will soon provide themselves with their principal article of food. The original cost of such mills will willingly be stood by parties who want permission to build on the reservation, where they can obtain the exclusive privilege of grinding the grain for the Indians. Water power for running the mills can be easily obtained in the neighborhood of their suggested sites. Rules for their management and toll to be paid, should be fixed by the authorities on the reservations.

One of the greatest obstacles to the advancement of the Indians in the want of farming implements, seed, and wagons. Two and a half cents a pound is but a poor price for barley planted and harvested with a case knife. Most of the ground is prepared for crops with shovels. The work required to do this is too much for the remuneration obtained. Two hundred plows, 2-horse, with necessary single and double trees, 200 harrows, 400 single sets of plow-harness, 600 heavy hoes, 600 long-hand shovels, 200 picks, and 30 small fans for cleaning grain, if immediately bought and judiciously distributed, would probably be all the implements that ever need be given to the 4,000 Indians camped around this place. There is also need of about 100 wagons. With this assistance, surely not much in comparison with the results to be attained, I am confident that in one year all the Indians on the reservation will be self-supporting.

I made a similar statement in my report last year; since then, time and time again, have the Indians assured me that, could they be given the implements necessary for planting and harvesting their grain, there would be no need of feeding them longer.

I would suggest that the Indians be permitted, subject the certain regulations, to work for whites living in the vicinity of the reservation. By this means numbers of them will be instructed in farming and other pursuits, that may in future be of use and followed by them.

During the past year confidence in the military and their ability to control the turbulent element on the reservation, has led to a general desire on the part of the Indians to take up farming lands even at a great distance from the agency. Today every Indian goes without fear to the remotest limits of the reservation, and as a consequence there has been a great increase of the land under cultivation. When praised on account of the number of sacks of barley raised, the Indians almost invariably reply. "We will do better next year."

The work on the farms is not now by any means

performed entirely by the women; in fact, I believe the greater part of it is done by the men. I take pleasure in reporting that the manufacture of "tiswin," the most fruitful source of trouble on the reservation, is broken up; those that still insist upon making it rarely escape discovery; upon conviction they are surely punished.

There were but three murders committed on the reservation during the past year, and at present there are but 13 prisoners in the calaboose.

Appended is an estimate of the amount of land cultivated and crops raised by all the Indians on the reservation.

Very respectfully, your obedient servant,
Emmett Crawford,
Captain Third Cavalry, Commanding.

The estimate of the amount of land under cultivation and crops raised by Apache Indians on the White Mountain Indian Reservation, during the year 1884, 4,000 acres of land, upon which have been raised the following crops:

Corn	pounds	3,850,000
Barley	do	550,000
Beans	do	540,000
Potatoes	do	20,000
Wheat	do	50,000
Pumpkins		200,000
Watermelons		50,000
Muskmelons		40,000

Besides small quantities of onions, cabbage, and peppers.

The White Mountain Apache, to whom two-thirds of the above may be accredited, lost about one-third of their crops by reason of late spring rains and early frost.

The Yuma Indians had all their barley destroyed by an overflow of the Gila River along which they are camped.

7

THE GERONIMO CAMPAIGN

It was late in May of 1885 that Geronimo and about 150 members of the Chiricahua and Warm Springs Apache broke out of their reservation at Fort Apache and headed for the Mexican Sierra Madre. Geronimo is spoken of as the leader of the renegades or hostiles, as they were called by the beleaguered Army, but in fact he was the medicine man of the tribe, not the chief. That role was cast to Nachez, a son of Cochise and a man of great ability and leadership. Geronimo had leadership, too; but, according to Lieutenant W. E. Shipp, a member of the forces charged with keeping the Indians contained, he had a "diabolical appearance with a character to correspond," which appealed to the "bad side of the Indian nature," causing the Indians to "listen to him in preference to better men." Geronimo took the role of war chief, a sort of second in command. It was only the band led by Geronimo that headed for the Sierra Madre; other bands, led by Hosanna as war chief, Chatto (who served as first sergeant of scouts for Captain Crawford's command), and Martinez, stayed off the

Arizona Territory's famed photographer C.S. Fly shot this picture while on campaign with the cavalry against Geronimo in 1885. It is a view of Lieutenant Marion Maus's Apache scouts, armed with .45/70 "Long Tom" Springfield Trapdoor rifles. (Photo courtesy of the Phil Spangenberger collection.)

Natchez (left) and Geronimo at Fort Bowie, 1886. (Photo courtesy of the Arizona Historical Society Library/Tucson.)

warpath, and in many cases were called on by the Army to help track down their brothers.

Therein was the rub. General Crook, the commander of the Western Army forces charged with maintaining the peace, chose to use Apache scouts to help fight the Indians. While there were certain advantages to his plan—the Indians understood the strike-and-run tactics of Geronimo's band, and certainly knew the craggy heights of the Sierra Madre as no white man did—there were disadvantages as well, such as the matter of trust.

The rugged terrain of the Sierra Madre served the hostiles well. Until a recent treaty with Mexico made it possible for the U.S. Army to cross into that area, the mountains had been a safe haven for the Apache; thus, the Indians knew every nook and cranny, while the Army was still exploring new terrain. The use of Indian scouts, despite the soldiers' nagging feelings of distrust, was virtually essential.

So, when the news of Geronimo's breakout came, Crook organized two expeditions heading into the interior, trying to beat the hostiles at their own game. Crook was located at Fort Bayard. From there, Lieutenant Britton Davis left quickly in pursuit of Geronimo, with Chief Chatto as first sergeant of scouts. Captain Emmet Crawford formed a company at Deming, New Mexico, with Quartermaster Chief Packer H. W. Daly as his wagon master and confidant. Crook had pledged to provide enough troops to guard every watering hole, as well as a small number of scouts to ride the area between the water lines, to add a bit more security to the fighting troops. The combination of the guarding of the water holes and the troops pursuing the renegades was expected to provide protection for the settlers living within 100 miles of Guadaloupe Pass should the hostiles decide to reenter Arizona and New Mexico. Guadaloupe Pass was located directly between Fort Apache and the Sierra Madre Mountains, and would be a likely spot for the Indians to stir trouble.

Crawford was joined by Chief of Scouts Al Seiber, Captain Kendall, and Lieutenants Elliot and Hannah, with a troop of the 6th Cavalry. The command joined Lieutenant Davis and his pursuit party at Skeleton Canyon, arriving June 8. From there, the combined troop moved south and west

Apache head chief Natchez. (Photo courtesy of Herb Peck, Jr.)

Famous frontiersman and Chief of Scouts Al Seiber had this photo made sometime in the late 1880s or early 1890s. He is posing with his saddled horse, holstered revolver, and 1886 Winchester rifle. (Photo courtesy of the Phil Spangenberger collection.)

to the Opata Mountains, and then to the village of Opata. Then the trail of Geronimo became apparent, as the news filtered in that the renegades had rounded up some cattle and slaughtered the animals for food. The Indian scouts determined that Geronimo's band had made camp in the foothills of the Sierra Madre, not far from Opata. That night, June 22, Lieutenants Davis and Elliott, Chief of Scouts Seiber, and about fifty scouts were sent to locate the hostile camp, attack it, and try to obtain a surrender.

On June 23, a runner brought back the information that one of Geronimo's followers had been killed, one or more of them were wounded, and about fifteen had been taken prisoner, without any loss to the Army.

That afternoon, Lieutenant Davis returned to camp with the fifteen prisoners, and Nana was among them. Nana had been war chief to Victorio, chief of the Warm Springs Apache. He was one of twenty-five survivors of the massacre at the Tres Castios Mountains in 1881, when General Terassas overcame the Warm Springs Apache after three years of continuous raids on the settlers of New Mexico.

The next day, Lieutenant Hannah started for Fort Bowie with the prisoners, guarded by some troopers, and guided by an Indian scout named Dutchy. According to the account of Quartermaster Chief Packer H. W. Daly, Dutchy obtained some potent mescal in the village of Opata, and proceeded to raise hell all the way to Fort Bowie, where he was clapped into irons in the guardhouse. Then Lieutenant Hannah started back on the trail of the renegades.

In a *Cavalry Journal* article, Daly describes the route to the renegades:

> Our scouting was along the southern flank of the Sierra Madre Mountains, which were cut up by seemingly impassible ravines and hills covered with pine, fir, oak, mountain mahogany, scrubby cork trees, giant cacti, and of thorny undergrowth. The small tributaries of the Jarras River rushed madly down between boulders of immense size, making fording them a perilous undertaking.[1]

The trip into the mountains led the troop to Lang's Ranch, where Lieutenant James Pettit was in command of the supply camp. There, troops under Captain Budd and Lieutenant Huse joined Pettit's troops and headed for Crawford's camp.

At that point, the command was divided, and a portion headed for Fort Bowie. The remainder moved northwest, into the Sierra Madres. After five days of climbing into the hiding places of the Apache, word came that five of the renegades had been surprised by Lieutenant M.W. Day's scouts and killed. In addition, several Indian women and children had been captured. Caught by surprise, Geronimo's followers had jumped into ravines to escape, and had been separated into smaller groups, with part heading down the divide on the northwest side and the larger group moving down the face of the great divide towards the east. Crawford decided to follow the main party, but elected to send the pack train back to Lang's Ranch. Feed for the pack animals had become scarce, and the condition of the animals wouldn't support a long, tough climb.

Crawford's group moved towards the crest of the high Sierras, making camp where the Indians had abandoned camp two days before. Remains of ponies slaughtered to feed the small band of Indians told the story of the poor condition of the renegades. Crawford, feeling that the Army might now have the upper hand, sent out an advance scouting party under Lieutenant Davis and Chief of Scouts Seiber, while the rest of the party, clinging to the steep peak, endured a fierce mountain storm. A few days later, the advance party reported that the trail had been scattered; so Crawford decided to send a larger force, with a small pack train for support. His instructions were to "stick to the trail at all costs" and force a surrender if possible. Five days later, after the group had endured storms that, according to Daly's account of the campaign, "soaked every blanket and piece of canvas" in the camp, Captain Crawford sent Lieutenant Elliot with twenty-five scouts and support troops to overtake Davis and report back. Crawford and the remaining troops followed, passing the crest of the Sierra Madre at noon the next day. A day later, they reached the headwaters of the Casa Grande. The Sierra Madre had been crossed by mounted troops with pack animals, a feat considered impossible by the Mexicans who lived on the two sides of the divide.

Five days after starting out, Crawford's troops reached the town of Casa Grande and learned that Lieutenant Elliot and his scouts and packers had been captured and were imprisoned by the Mexican forces, acting on their own. Davis and his party had crossed the Casa Grande a mile from town, and were pursuing the hostiles. Crawford effected the release of Lieutenant Elliot and his

Bakeitzogie, The Yellow Coyote, otherwise known as Dutchy—a Chiricahua scout. He was accused of numerous murders of white people. (Photo courtesy of Herb Peck, Jr.)

Geronimo (right) and three of his warriors in the Sierra Madres, c. March 25–27, 1886, before surrender. (Photo courtesy of the Fort Sill Museum.)

men by visiting the mayor, and the combined force rode out to Casa Grande and then on towards the boundary.

Part of the troop was ordered to the southern flank of the Chiricahua Mountains. While camping outside Fort Bowie, Daly, who was with that group, reported the arrival of a scout called Navajo Bill with messages from General Crook to Captain Carpenter, stating that Geronimo and his group of renegades were making their way down the Stein Peak Range. Carpenter was to cut across the valley below and intercept them.

Early the next morning, Daly and Navajo Bill set out on the back trail to Fort Bowie. Near the mouth of the ravine, signs of the hostiles were seen, followed by the discovery of a burro with its rider shot and killed. The renegades had captured ponies at a shack near the mouth of the ravine and shot the owner. As the pair followed the trail, it became obvious to them that the Indians would camp at the top of the divide so that they could watch for troop movements on both sides. Retracing their steps, Daly and Navajo Bill then crossed a range and headed towards Fort Bowie, full tilt, to report their findings.

After about a five-mile ride, they were intercepted by several riders galloping for dear life, shouting, "Indians, Indians!" The riders had been chased away from their homes, and feared that their neighbors might have been butchered by the renegades. After moving their livestock out of harm's way, Daly and Navajo Bill rode posthaste to Fort Bowie.

Captain Cyrus Roberts, Crook's adjutant general, met the pair, and took them immediately to General Crook to report their findings. After some discussion, Captain Thompson and his 4th Cavalry troops were sent to follow Captain Crawford and render assistance.

By the end of the summer, the hostiles had moved towards New Mexico. Lieutenant Davis and Al Seiber both resigned their commissions after angry words with General Crook, and left the campaign for civilian life.

As winter came upon the mountains, Captain Crawford began to enlist new scouts for another campaign, and on November 29, left Fort Bowie with a hundred Indian scouts under the command of Lieutenants M. P. Maus and William Shipp. Tom Horn and William Harrison were designated chief of scouts for the commands, and two pack trains completed the troops. The company headed across the Dragoon Mountains, on through Mexico's Cumpas Valley range, and then towards Nacori. They arrived in Nacori near the close of 1885.

In early 1886, there was evidence that some of the Indian scouts might not be telling all they knew about the whereabouts of the hostile band under Geronimo. The various groups of Indians had their own scores to settle, just as did the white men, and there had been incidents before where the scouts may have been using their position in the Army to settle their own intertribal disputes. The day after a meeting between Crawford and the scouts (Noche and his medicine man), the scouts reported that they had located the renegades' camp, and that they were sun-drying beef and not particularly alert to troop movements.

Crawford decided to travel very light in order to surprise the renegades, and set out at twilight on January 3, 1886. The officers and scouts wore moccasins, and the group was equipped to include a rope corral to provide as much security as possible. Six days later, some of the scouts returned to the base camp with word that Crawford was hot on the trail of the renegades, and that a supply train would be needed. One of the scouts would accompany the supply train and provide a shortcut. Early on the morning of January 11, the supply train, headed by H. W. Daly, picked up Crawford's trail.

Before noon, a message came from Lieutenant Maus that Captain Crawford had been severely wounded by a shot from Mexican troops. The supply train at first started towards Crawford's camp, but then got word that the troops were bringing the wounded captain to the supply train. A camp was made at the foot of the mountain, and

This photo was taken at Fort Apache, Arizona, c. 1885–1886. These are undoubtedly White Mountain Apache scouts, who served so faithfully against Geronimo. (Photo courtesy of the Phil Spangenberger collection.)

Dress parade at Camp Bowie. Note the company of Apache scouts to the far right. (Photo courtesy of Herb Peck, Jr.)

Geronimo, Natchez, twenty-three warriors, and two youths, heavily armed—plus four women, Sierra Madres, March 1886. (Photo courtesy of the Fort Sill Museum.)

the captain was brought to a hastily constructed shelter. Two days later, Lieutenant Maus decided to return to the line, and a travois was rigged to carry the unconscious captain, who died during the journey. During the march to bring the captain to Nacori, where he was buried in the town cemetery without ceremony, the renegades moved off towards the mountains.

By forming a rope corral, Crawford had been careful to keep the scouts from leaving camp and warning Geronimo and his followers. The Indians had depended on their friends among the scouts to inform them of an impending battle so that they could move their camps or find a way to surrender if they so desired.

The night before Crawford was shot, there had been a visit from a squaw who had confirmed that the camp about to be attacked was the camp of Geronimo, and who had said that she had been sent to request a parley between Crawford and the war chief. But before the parley could take place, Crawford was shot.

The shooting had taken place early on the morning of January 11, when the camp was awakened by rifle shots and shouts of "Nacoya, mucho Nacoya" (Mexicans, lots of Mexicans). The Apache scouts, who hated the Mexicans, opened fire and added to the bedlam. According to Daly's account, Crawford, in an attempt to stop the carnage, took Dutchy, the scout who was periodically in trouble and under suspicion, to the top of a large boulder, where he attempted to identify himself and Dutchy. According to the account, a Mexican took careful, deliberate aim, and shot Crawford. Dutchy claimed to have killed the Mexican. Whether Dutchy did indeed attempt to protect the captain is not known, but he did go through Crawford's pockets, removing all the money he could find—or so the story goes.

During the days that followed, Geronimo and his company visited the Army camp, finally arranging a meeting with General Crook across the boundary in Mexico. Geronimo asked for five or six weeks in order to gather his people, and promised to signal his approach with smoke signs.

On January 22, 1886, the troop left for the rendezvous between General Crook and Geronimo. The promised smoke signals were seen in mid-March, and were investigated by Lieutenant Maus and his scouts.

Then, at about 10 o'clock the next morning, Geronimo, Nachez, and Chihuahua, with their companies, rode through the carefully prepared camp and disappeared from view. They could be heard across the stream, selecting the site for their camp and setting it up. The next day, some of the Chiricahuas were chatting with the scouts and packers when Geronimo appeared out of nowhere, asking when General Crook—The Gray Fox, as the Apaches called him—would arrive.

It turned out that Crook didn't come for nearly ten days. In the meantime, the Apaches found the establishment of one Charles Tribolett, who had set up a shack filled with mescal, vile whiskey, and stale tobacco. Tribolett sold his wares to anyone who had the money, and the Chiricahuas whiled away their time in a drunken frenzy.

On his arrival, Crook visited Tribolett's camp for a good meal. After Crook had eaten, Keyetana, a Warm Springs Apache belonging to Victorio's band, entered the packer's camp with Nana, and shook hands with the general. According to Daly's account of the event, Geronimo and Nachez followed with many of the Indians, and General Crook decided to hold the council there. Tribolett entered the camp as well, to listen to the outcome, but was sent away by Lieutenant Maus, against the advice of Daly and others. Captains Bourke and Roberts, also of General Crook's staff, attended the council.

Crook selected the ground for the council and made his seat at the base of a little knoll, with Captain Bourke; interpreters Montoya, Antonio Besias, and Jose Maria; Lieutenant Maus; and Noche, an Apache scout, on his right. Captain Roberts, Lieutenant Faison, and Lieutenant Shipp were on the general's left. Geronimo centered himself in the Apache delegation, with Nachez, chief of the Chiricahuas, on his right and Nana on his left. Hosanna and other Apache chiefs stood behind Geronimo, while the Quartermaster packers and Mayor Strauss of Tucson stood behind General Crook.

Crook asked Geronimo, through the interpreters, why he had left Camp Apache. He cautioned the war chief to be thorough in his discourse, as his answers would all be taken down in writing, for posterity.

Geronimo conferred with Nachez for some time, and then began his oration. And what an oration it was! Geronimo explained that the Apaches had gathered at Camp Apache two years ago, based upon promises made to them by the general, whom he called Father, and that the Indians had been glad to be there. He went on to say that "The Long-Nosed Captain" (Lieutenant Gatewood) had been promised to them as a friend and mediator, and that the Indians had been happy with The Long-Nosed Captain. But the general had taken away their friend, complained Geronimo, and sent another, who favored Chatto's village and gave his own people the leftovers. The harangue went on for a long time, with Geronimo complaining about the unfairness, the favoritism. Finally, soaked with sweat and worked up to a fever pitch, the mescal-soaked war chief shouted, "I want no more of this!"

Crook answered, through Captain Bourke:

> I have heard what you said, and why is it that more than forty men were afraid of two or three; why did you, after leaving the reservation, kill innocent men, women and children and steal their horses? The white people hold me responsible for all of the innocent people that you have killed. You are no child to listen to every foolish story told you by the old women in your camp, and you know better than to believe them. You say that you were told that you were to be arrested at Apache, which was all nonsense, as there were no orders or thought of them. Yet you spread this story among your people to make them dissatisfied. You promised me in the Sierra Madres that the peace made then would last forever, but you have lied to me about it. When a man lies to me once, I want something better than his word before I will believe him again. Everything that you did on the reservation is known to me, and it is useless for you to talk nonsense to me. You sent some of your people to Lieutenant Davis' camp, and then spread the report that they had been killed by him, and by that means persuaded them to go on the warpath, sneaking through the country like a pack of coyotes, killing innocent people. You must make up your minds to surrender unconditionally to me or to stay on the warpath. If you decide to stay out, I will keep after you until the last one is killed, if it takes fifty years.[2]

Crook instructed Geronimo to think this over during the night, and to reach a decision by the morning. During the council, the Army officers were unarmed, as were the Indians, but Indian firearms were stacked less than fifteen yards away in readiness.

During the next day, the interpreters scurried back and forth between the Indian and the Army camps, reporting on any signs of progress. Finally, as the mescal wore off, some of the Indians realized that they were in desperate straits, and decided to make the best deal that they could.

At about noon on March 27, Chihuahua appeared as chief orator in a meeting with the Army, and surrendered unconditionally to General Crook. Geronimo and Nachez, now jealous of the attention given to Chihuahua during the discussion, tried to force Crook to permit them to return to Fort Apache. But Chihuahua had unconditionally surrendered, and it became clear that Crook would insist that the Chiricahuas be sent to the Atlantic coast for a period of time before being allowed to return to their native habitat. So the conference fell apart, with dissatisfaction on the part of several groups of the Apache. The mescal may have been flowing again, and the Apaches spent a noisy night yelling, hooting, and finally shooting over the tents of the Army officers. The mood was decidedly ugly.

There was news the next day that Nachez had shot his squaw in the leg during the melee, and that the groups were at great loggerheads. Finally, Geronimo and all of his band mounted up and rode away from the camp, screaming and swilling mescal. Chihuahua and his band stayed in the camp, giving every indication that they intended to keep their bargain. Later that day, General Crook started his journey towards Fort Bowie, leaving the troops to escort that portion of the Apache back to the fort, while the rest of the renegades spread fear and terror among the settlers.

After General Crook had left for Fort Bowie, Geronimo and his band took every opportunity to obtain whiskey and mescal from Tribolett, and their tempers became still more inflamed. It was rumored that Geronimo and Nachez were more than a little angered by Crook's demeanor towards them, and especially by the favoritism he seemed to show towards Chihuahua. According to H. W. Daly's account, "There is no doubt that Geronimo made up his mind that night to play a trick on General Crook that he would never forget, and to prove that Chihuahua was not the whole push."[3]

Shortly after Crook left, Lieutenant Maus broke camp and led Chihuahua's band towards Fort Bowie, followed by Daly's pack train and some scouts. Daly recounts the trip:

> When about four miles from the Cañon de los Embudos, one of the Chiricahuas came running up to me and said, "John Daisy Mantan (Mule Captain), Geronimo is very drunk, come and see him." I halted the train and followed the Chiricahua to where Geronimo lay on the ground in a drunken stupor. I shook him and tried to rouse him, and finally he rolled over and recognized me. He spoke to me in a mixture of Apache, Spanish and English, and said, "Natan, mescal heap no good; mucho sick; give me agua." I gave him a drink of water and finally got him up and on his pony, and then he wanted a drink of whiskey or mescal, which I, of course refused to give him. I, however, promised him that I would give him a drink and a good supper when we got to camp, and told him he would feel all right then. His eyes were bloodshot and bulging, and generally he was a pitiable spectacle.[4]

After spotting Geronimo, the Chiricahuas refused to continue farther that day, and unsaddled their ponies, forcing Lieutenant Maus to make camp many miles before he had intended. This was before noon on the first day of March, and, before lunch was ready, it became clear to the men that the Indians were up to something. Geronimo and Nachez sat at the table with Lieutenant Maus and a few others, and Geronimo got his drink of mescal, reports Daly, but it was a tense situation and the men thought that trouble was clearly brewing.

The morning of March 30 dawned, and the procession began again, with the Chiricahuas and Lieutenant Maus leading, followed by the pack train and scouts. But before the sun had reached overhead, the column halted and the Indians unsaddled their ponies and made camp. To Daly and others, this was a clear indication that the Chiricahuas didn't intend to get any closer to Fort Bowie than this. Geronimo and Chihuahua selected their campsites, and the Army camped across the trace from them, a little distance away but with a clear view of the hostiles. Although several of the soldiers believed that Geronimo would leave the camp before morning, Lieutenant Maus apparently thought that the Apaches intended to stand by their word.

After dark, the soldiers and quartermasters were sitting around their campfire when a shot rang out over their heads. Later, two Indians entered the Army camp and apparently told the troops to retire. After the troops had, in fact, retired, stirrings could be heard in the Indian camp that drew suspicions that an escape was underway.

Indeed it was. While Chihuahua and eighty of his band remained at the site across the trace from the Army, Geronimo and all of his band plus some of Chihuahua's headed for the Sierra Madre. A scout, Kyetena, rode off to try to pick up Geronimo's trail, but Chihuahua expressed the opinion that Geronimo would never return except by force. Lieutenant Maus then decided to send the Chiricahua that remained and Chihuahua on to

Fort Bowie, and to mount a search party to follow and try to recapture Geronimo.

Maus and his party were able to follow Geronimo's trail to the Bavispe River, about fifteen miles from the ill-fated base camp. There, the hostile band split. Apparently, the women and children were sent into the Sierra Madre, and the men went on up the river to form a raiding party so that they could replenish their supplies. At this point, Maus decided against trying to follow Geronimo any farther, and headed back to Fort Bowie.

On their return to Fort Bowie, some Army scouts spotted signals made by two Chiricahuas, who had ridden away from camp in a drunken stupor but couldn't keep up with the furious, driven Geronimo. These Indians joined the Army troop, saying that if Geronimo and his braves had not gotten hold of the mescal, none of them would have left camp, and all of them would have returned to Camp Bowie.

But Daly and others have reported that the way Geronimo and Nachez were humiliated by Crook set the stage for the outbreak and the trouble that followed. Many of the men felt that General Crook failed to comprehend the significance of Geronimo's complaints of uneven treatment by the Army officers. The War Department had been pressing Crook on other affairs, and he misjudged the proper handling of Geronimo. In any case, Crook, who appeared to take the escape very hard, was recalled to other duties. The task of restraining Geronimo and his followers fell to General Nelson A. Miles, who assumed command of the Department of Arizona on April 12, 1886.

Miles continued the practice of using Indian scouts, troop trains, and few Army personnel. However, he added another dimension to the fight against the hostiles, with the introduction of heliograph lines between mountain peaks, permitting information about Indian movements to be forwarded rapidly. (For more about the heliograph, turn to Chapters 16 and 17.) More army troops were added to the force as well, and on May 2, Captain Lawton arrived at Fort Bowie to command an expedition to force the surrender of Geronimo. Accompanying Lawton was Assistant Surgeon Leonard Wood. Lawton's troops contained thirty-five men of Troop B, 4th Cavalry; twenty-five men of Troop D, 8th Cavalry; Lieutenants Terret and Johnson; and twenty Indian scouts under Lieutenant Finley, with Tom Horn as chief of scouts.

Assistant Surgeon Wood and two pack trains of fifty mules and fourteen packers each started from

General Nelson A. Miles, when he took over operations in Arizona.

Arizona towards the Sierra Madre. During the troop movements towards the Mexican mountain stronghold of Geronimo and his band, the wily Apache made a fast trip of his own. In early April, Geronimo and his braves rode into the Fort Apache area, where he found that troops were on the move, and bearing down on his trail. He again divided his band into two groups. The squaws and children were first secreted in the lofty Sierra Madre; then he and his raiders moved to the Patagonia Mountains and nearby areas, farther west and thickly populated, compared to the Sierra Madres. His reason for doing this was probably to wear out the Federal troops who would try to follow them, but at the same time leave the squaws and children in relative safety.

The Apache braves were accustomed to travelling fast on horseback, keeping several horses tied and running along beside them. When a mount carrying a brave tired, the animal was cut loose as the Indian jumped to a fresher horse and continued to gallop at top speed. Thus, the Indians could travel 100 miles in a day, while the heavily laden Government horses grew short-winded and picked up stones in their hooves. Since the Government horses couldn't keep up the Indian pace, the only chance the Army had to catch the braves

Captured Apaches would play cards while awaiting their trip to Florida.

was to surprise the tribe and attack them before they knew that the Government men were in the area.

After Geronimo left Fort Apache, he passed south through the San Catalina, Colorado, Whetstone, Mustang, Patagonia, and Penito ranges. While crossing the Penitos, Captain Lebo's 10th Cavalry men surprised the Indians and did battle. Then, on April 15, the Indians were surprised by an attack from Troop D, 4th Cavalry, under Captain Hatfield. The troopers scattered the Indians, who lost their camp gear and ponies. Then the Apaches followed Hatfield's forces, attacking them, recapturing their ponies, and killing one of the troopers.

After this attack, the Chiricahuas separated again, with one group moving east and north towards Fort Apache and the other moving northwest towards San Carlos. Captain Lawton divided

Once the Apache Wars were settled and the hostile Indians were sent to Florida, desert-basin cities such as Phoenix and Tucson began to flourish and attract Eastern visitors, c. *late 1880s.*

Apache prisoners of war (Geronimo's group) in transit to Texas, September 1886. (Photo courtesy of the Fort Sill Museum.)

After the Apache Wars, white settlers could picnic in the Arizona deserts without fear of being butchered, c. *late 1880s.*

Chiricahuas at Mount Vernon Barracks, Alabama, c. 1890. From left to right: Chihuahua, [unidentified], Loco, Nana, and Geronimo. (Photo courtesy of the Alabama Department of Archives and History.)

Geronimo, in captivity, 1905. (Photo courtesy of Fort Sill Museum.)

his command so that the two parties could follow both groups of hostiles. The troopers joined again at Calavasas at about the first of June after following the Indians but not engaging them.

However, the Tucson Rangers, under the command of Dr. Samaniego, attacked the Indians as they approached the San Catalina Mountains. The Indians released a Mexican child during the attack, and then fled towards the Catalina Mountains, where they were surprised by Lieutenant R.D. Walsh of the 4th Cavalry. Walsh's troops captured the ponies and camp gear of the Indians once again, and then followed the Indians into the Azul Mountains, where the tribe turned southwest towards the squaw camp. At this point, the Army called off the Geronimo campaign for a time, and temporarily turned to other business.

But by the first week of July, Geronimo and his followers were causing too much trouble to be ignored. So, Captain Lawton and a detachment of scouts and some infantry headed towards Tonababa, from where they had heard reports of depredations.

The diaries of H. G. Daly include comments on this period: "As I was still suffering from sciatic rheumatism, Captain Lawton informed me that he was going to send me back to Oposura. He said that in case I met General Miles, I was to tell him that he (Captain Lawton) did not want any more infantrymen, and told me to say to him that he might as well try to hunt Indians with a brass band."[5]

In the meantime, Geronimo passed along the Cumpas range, killing some miners, and then contacted some officials in Mexico to effect a surrender. At this point, Lieutenant Gatewood, a friend of the Apache and trusted by Geronimo, was on his way to the Mexican area to try to locate Geronimo and convince him to lay down his guns.

Two friendly Chiricahuas accompanied Gatewood, and made contact with Geronimo using smoke signals. Geronimo met with Gatewood, and told him that he would always be safe and welcome at his (Geronimo's) campfires. When Lawton joined Gatewood, Geronimo immediately requested supplies for his people. Lawton replied that his pack train was nearby; then Geronimo demonstrated his tracking ability by relaying the news that Lawton's pack train was lost, and probably two or three days away.

Geronimo then agreed to move inside the lines to Skeleton Canyon to confer in person with General Miles. This was after much concern on the part of Geronimo, who believed that the Army was out to surround and destroy him. Miles arrived on September 3. After conferring with Geronimo and Nachez, General Miles rode the Army ambulance with the two of them to Fort Bowie. Captain Lawton rode with the remaining Chiricahuas, arriving at Bowie on September 8, at which time the Indians boarded railroad cars bound for Florida.

Notes

[1]"The Geronimo Campaign," *Journal of the United States Cavalry Association*, October, 1908.

[2]Ibid.

[3]Ibid.

[4]Ibid.

[5]Ibid.

8

APACHE SCOUTS

General George Crook was the first to enlist Apaches as scouts; the way he put it was, "The best way to pursue Indians was with other Indians." Crook studied the Indians' techniques of rapid movement and decided also to use mules rather than wagons to carry supplies, cut the amount of provisions, and train his troops in the mechanics of long and rapid campaigns.

Scouts were easy to secure, for various tribes had age-old animosities. When one band began

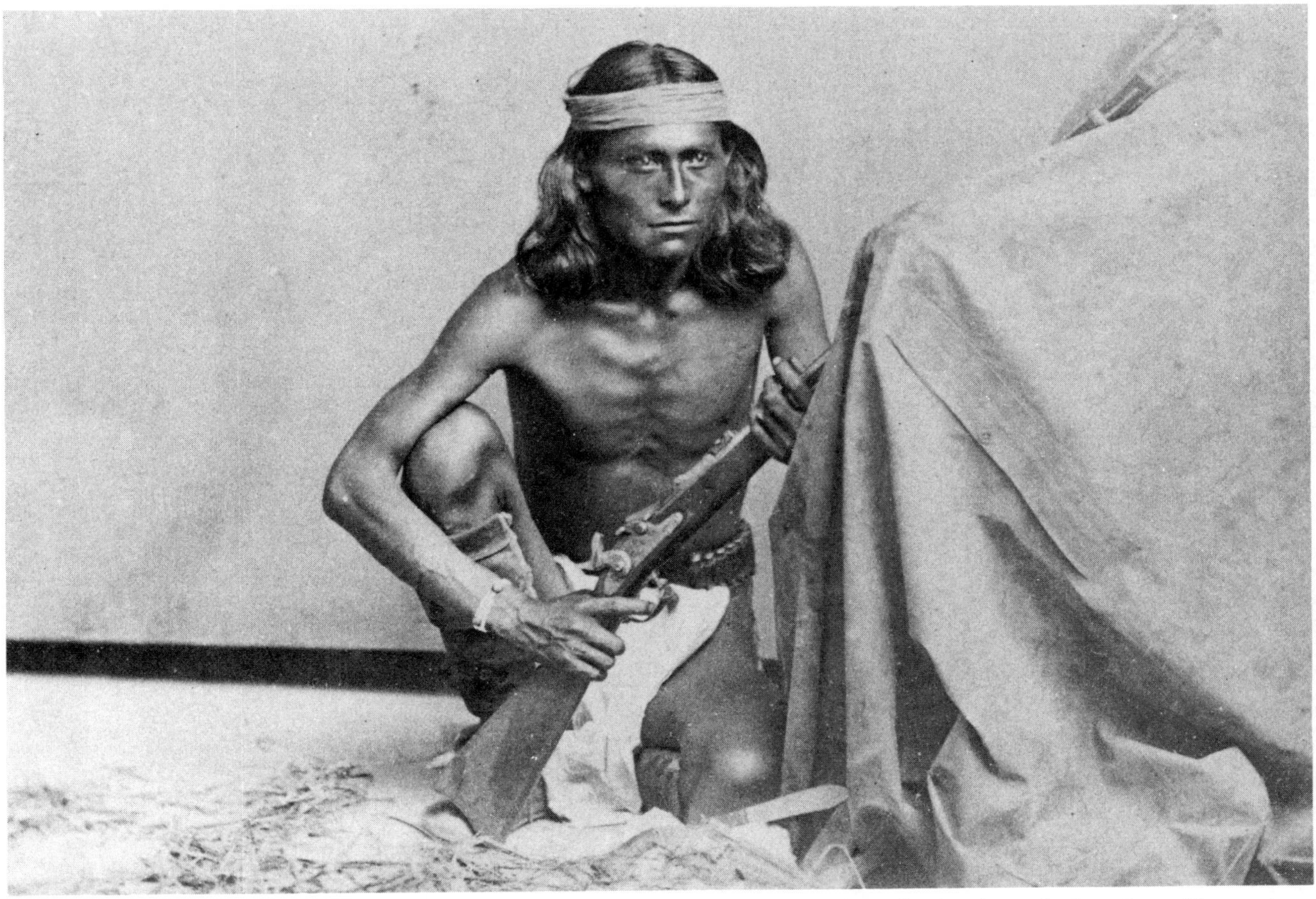

Nantagira, an early Apache scout. Even though scouts were outfitted with a military uniform, they usually stripped to the skin when a battle commenced. This scout carries the .50/70 Springfield Trapdoor rifle. Reflecting the sun's glare, these rifles caught the enemy's attention, so Ordnance had them blued. (Photo courtesy of Herb Peck, Jr.)

An Apache scout, wearing the red turban that distinguished scouts from hostiles. This came about at the end of the 1870s.

Warm Springs Apache scouts, in and out of uniform, all holding the seven-shot Spencer Carbine. Having no cartridge belts, they were issued only a handful of cartridges. These scouts were merely to trail the hostiles, not fight them.

raiding another, Crook would go among the enemies and enlist them. They were eager to join just to settle old scores. The enlistments into the Army were usually for a six-month term. Should their enlistment term be less than six months, the Indians would be obliged to furnish their own horses and other equipment.

The scout generally wore, from the waist up, a four-button blue tunic—fresh from the quartermaster's stockpiles of surplus uniforms left over from the Civil War—and a Hardie hat. From the waist down, he wore a Mills looped cartridge belt, a loincloth, and moccasin-type boots made of loose leather. It was not until August 1890, that a full and complete uniform was furnished to the Indian scouts, along with a prescribed guidon with white crossed arrows and company letters against a scarlet background. When battle seemed apparent, however, the Apache scouts would strip down to their loincloth and kick off their moccasins to get a firmer footing on the rocks.

By November 1872, companies were mustered and ready when Crook took to the field. Riding ahead of the command on their little ponies, cradling a Springfield carbine or rifle in their arms, and carrying a long butcher knife tucked into their cartridge belts, these Indians looked more menacing than the gaudily painted warriors of other tribes.

No Apache would, unless it couldn't be avoided, go on a scout without a bag of his precious powder, called hoddentin, somewhere on his person—but generally attached to his ammunition belt. Hoddentin is the yellow pollen of the tule, a variety of the cattail rush.

Whenever an Indian was wounded, hurt, or taken sick, the medicine man of the party would walk in front of the horse or mule ridden by the ailing Indian and scatter at intervals little pinches of hoddentin, that his path might be made easier. Whenever an Apache went on the warpath, or to hunt or plant, he always threw a pinch of hoddentin to the sun, saying, "With the favor of the sun (or permission of the sun), I am going out to fight (or hunt or plant, as the case might be) and I want the sun to help me." When worn out after a lengthy scout, Apaches put a pinch of hoddentin on their tongues as a restorative. It was also eaten by the sick as a remedy.

Before starting out after enemies, the scouts took a pinch of hoddentin and threw it to the sun, and then put a pinch on their tongues and another on the crown of the head. When they came back, they held a dance. The next morning, before the raid, they threw pinches of hoddentin to the rising sun and then to the east, west, south, and north, and to the four winds, ensuring their safe return.

In 1883, when General Crook's expedition reached the Chiricahua stronghold in the heart of the Mexican Sierra Madre, a couple of unusual items were found in Geronimo's rancheria, to which, it was learned, the Indians attached the

San Carlos Apache police, c. 1876. Most of their trousers and shirts were given to them by Arizona settlers. Any boots were issue items. At low center is Agent John Philip Clum, wearing an African sun (cork) helmet similar to that of General Crook, who tried to have them issued to officers in the southern campaign. (Photo courtesy of Herb Peck, Jr.)

Juan (pronounced Whain), chief of scouts. (Photo courtesy of Herb Peck, Jr.)

This photo, taken at the San Carlos Reservation in 1883, shows four Tonto-Apache scouts. Also, standing behind the man with the child on his lap is "Squaw Mack," a white man who lived with the Indians. The identities of the man and child are not known. (Photo courtesy of the Herb Peck collection.)

greatest importance. One was a very small piece of hard wood, cedar or pine, about two-and-a-half to three inches long and a half a finger in thickness, and the other was a small section of the cane indigenous to the Southwest and of about the same dimensions. The first was a scratch stick, and the second a drinking reed.

According to a rule among the Apache, the first four times one of their young men went out on the warpath, he had to refrain from scratching his head with his fingers or letting water touch his lips. How to keep this vow and at the same time avoid unnecessary discomfort and suffering involved the use of these rather insignificant-looking pieces of equipment. Instead of scratching his head with his fingers, the Apache used this scratch stick. And rather than letting water touch his lips, he sucked it into his throat through this tiny tube. A long leather cord attached both the stick and reed to the warrior's belt and to each other. Whether these items had to be prepared by the medicine men or by the young warrior himself in a special ceremony is not known.

Reference has also been made to the Indians engaging in a ceremonial plastering of mud on their heads. When General Crook was returning from his expedition into the Sierra Madre in 1883, the scouts, upon reaching the San Bernardino River, made free use of the sweat bath. With much singing, this was part of the ceremonial purification that all warriors had to undergo as soon as possible after being engaged in battle. Although most Apache bands did not apply mud to their heads, the Apache-Yuma did.

So that the scouts would not be mistaken for hostile Indians, Crook came up with the idea of having them wear a red turban around their heads. The Apache scouts gave no quarter to wounded enemies, and when they advanced on them, it was to silently cut their throats or send a bullet through their brains when the Army wasn't around. There literally were no survivors.

Officers outside the Indian territory questioned why these scouts were so efficient. The answer came from experienced troopers who said that they knew the country like the veins on the backs of their hands and were extremely self-reliant. Also, their tribal systems inured them to hardship. Their advantage in horsemanship, marksmanship, and tracking needed no comment.

Scouts and police were generally full-bloods from such bands as the White Mountain, Membreno, Chiricahua, Yuma, Mescalero, Mojave, and Tonto. People of mixed ancestry, such as Mickey Free (who was Mexican and Irish, and became a valued interpreter for Chief of Scouts Al Sieber), participated, but were not always trusted. While other Southwestern tribes were employed in the beginning of Crook's campaigns, it was the Apache that took preeminence.

So long as there was a plentiful supply of good ponies available, the Indian scouts were very valuable to the little Army in the West. The scouts were truly splendid horsemen, and when led by vigorous, energetic officers whom they trusted, they could keep the country in front of a column of soldiers thoroughly scoured of trouble, preventing loss of life and promoting rapid troop movements.

Still, there is an isolated incident that needs to be mentioned concerning the Apache scouts that General Crook so trusted. A dispatch of August 13, 1885, from Silver City, New Mexico (originally published in the *Army, Navy Journal* on August 22, 1885), stated:

> On August 8, Lieutenant Davis, with his company of Apache scouts, accompanied by two troops of

Apache scouts at Fort Apache, c. 1890. *(Photo courtesy of the Arizona Historical Society Library/Tucson.)*

An Apache policeman at one of the reservations, c. *1890s. (Photo courtesy of Herb Peck, Jr.)*

the Fourth Cavalry, were operating in the State of Sonora, Mexico. It seemed certain that the renegades would be overtaken, when suddenly Chatto, the chief in command of the scouts ordered a halt and called on the officers for a council. Lieutenant Davis promptly issued orders to move forward, when Chatto and five or six other Indians drew off to one side and moved toward the hills to the north of the trail, which was leading almost due west. Upon being commanded to halt, Chatto and his men started upon a run, when the command to fire was given. One of the companies of troops with a 200 yard range opened fire upon the fleeing scouts with splendid effect, killing Chatto and two of his men, wounding another, and bringing the others to a sudden halt. The scouts who had remained in line seemed to be stupefied by the suddenness of the affair, but after it had been ascertained that Chatto was killed they all assumed an air of sullen anger, which boded ill for the future. At the time the courier left, the command was again moving forward, but the feeling was general among the troops that the scouts would require close watching. Chatto was the Indian who led the murderers of the McComas family in their march of 1883. He had also been regarded as one of the worst of the Warm Springs band of Apaches, and was with Victorio in all his raids from 1879 to 1882. He was a sub-chief, ranking with Bonito and Natchez, and had considerable influence not only with his own band but among the Chiricahuas. Not a little surprise was expressed on the frontier when it was learned that General Crook had placed so turbulent a spirit in command of his Indian scouts.

However, the following article that appeared in the *Saturday Globe* newspaper (Utica, New York) on October 25, 1902, pays tribute to the Apache scouts:

THEY KNOW THE DESERTS
SOUTHWEST SCOUTS AT HOME AMID TRACKLESS WASTES

Trailers That Are Keener Than Bloodhounds—The Scouts Who Led Lawton's Men in Their Pursuit of Geronimo

In northern Mexico, New Mexico and Arizona there are men who far surpass the bloodhound, when it comes to trailing. Men who served during the campaign against Geronimo and the hostile Apaches, many of them expert trailers, were from day to day overwhelmed with astonishment at the almost superhuman instinct of the Mexican and Indian scouts, who in that memorable pursuit followed the fleeing Apaches over sand deserts harder than asphalt and floors of solid rock upon whose bare surfaces the soldiers could see no trace of the horsemen who had passed that way.

In a recent interview with an officer of Troop B of the Fourth Cavalry, a military organization that acquitted itself creditably during that campaign, a reporter learned much of interest concerning the human sleuth hounds who were employed in the southwest during those days.

"I served all through the latter part of the Geronimo campaign under Gen. Lawton, who was then a colonel," said the trooper. "We were out six months and during that entire period not one of us had a change of clothing. The campaigning was through one of the most mountainous countries in the world. Sometimes we would climb up the side of an almost perpendicular slope and at other times the descent was so steep that we were obliged to let our horses down over ledges of rocks by lariats tied to their tails.

"Accompanying our command were about 100 friendly Indians, enlisted and used as scouts. Talk of trailing! Why, I never until then dreamed that it was possible for human beings to do what these men did every day of the campaign. Frequently we would descend mountains, along the slope of which old scouts of my company were able to barely make out the trail of the Apaches, until we reached a valley about half or three-quarters of a mile in width, the surface of which was as hard as adamant. Here we could see nothing, but the scouts ahead on coming to such places never hesitated one minute, but struck boldly across, following the trail up the mountain side again.

"As we crossed these valleys and mounted once more up the side of the high ridges we would again catch traces of the Apaches in the softer and looser soil of the mountain side and many a time we have wondered at how our Indian trailers were able to follow the track on ahead of us over the valleys, where the surface was as hard as asphalt and crossed by fresh trails of hundreds of cattle that had passed up or down the depression after the Indians.

"The most remarkable case of trailing that ever came under my notice, however, occurred in 1887, when the San Carlos Apaches broke out of their reservation and went on the warpath south into Mexico. This occurred shortly after the Geronimo campaign, at a time when the War Department had discharged all the Indian scouts attached to the southwestern posts, thinking that the trouble was all over and that there would be no longer any use for them. Consequently when we received a hurry order at Fort Huachuca to go in pursuit of the San Carlos Apaches we were obliged to leave without taking any of these human bloodhounds with us.

San Carlos Apache scouts, Arizona Territory c. *1886–1895. They are wearing early prairie belts (1885 models), and the red headbands that they used to distinguish themselves from hostile Indians.*

"We soon began to feel the need of them, however, and although two-thirds of the men in the command were accomplished scouts, they could not begin to do the work with the skill and certainty of the Indian scouts trained to the task from infancy.

"Along about the eighth day out we crossed a range of mountains into one of the most peculiar depressions I ever saw. It was surrounded on all sides by high mountains, but the singular feature was that the bottom rose up like an inverted bowl. This curious formation was solid rock that in some past period of time had been lifted up and tilted in such manner as to leave no hollows in which sand or soil could gather. Up to this time we had made slow progress tracking the Indians, but when we reached this spot we gave up the task in disgust, as there was no earthly means, so far as we could see, of tracking them across such an expanse of naked stone.

"We sat down to think the matter over, when Col. Lawton, in stirring about, ran across an old Mexican riding along on his burro. The colonel asked him if he would be our scout and whether he felt himself capable of taking up and following the trail of the Indians. The old fellow gave a grunt of assent, two minutes later had found the trail and, to our unspeakable astonishment, was leading us almost on a run across the barren spot and up the mountain. In three hours' time he brought us in sight of the Indians encamped in a hollow. We charged down upon them, but failed to make a capture, as they saw us in time to escape.

"This old Mexican served as our trailer for the rest of this brief campaign until we finally overtook and captured our recalcitrant Indians. In all that period he never once missed the trail, notwithstanding the fact that we frequently passed over places where no signs of tracks were apparent to us. This, to my mind, was the most astonishing piece of tracking that I ever witnessed or heard of and I believe that the clever Mexican above all others was justly right to the title of human bloodhound."

General Nelson A. Miles arrived at Fort Bowie on April 11, 1886, and that afternoon conferred with departing General Crook about the Apache problem. He reviewed the troops and made a speech to the Apache scouts, including all the Chiricahua and Warm Springs Apaches, whom he ordered home to Fort Apache for discharge.

Miles intended to use Indians in small groups of threes or fours, primarily as trackers. All the fighting was to be done with regular soldiers. Next, he set in motion the most elaborate military preparation ever to be undertaken in Arizona. At great expense to the government, he constructed and manned a complex network of heliograph stations, covering southeastern Arizona and part of northern Sonora. Under Miles's command were five thousand troopers with which to fight only thirty-eight hostiles.

On the reservation the scouts were ordered to be issued only four to five rounds of ammunition because, it was stated, cartridges served as currency to the Indian and were worth 25 cents each.

Sadly enough, when the dust settled and the renegades were gathered up and shipped to Florida, it wasn't long before the Apache scouts, who generally had served so loyally, went to the same jail that the hostiles occupied, as prisoners of war.

9

THE FRONTIER ARMY

Recruitment

Recruiting an army for frontier duty depended mostly on voluntary enlistment. The term for service was five years, although there was a short term of three years that came later. In all the principal cities around the country, the recruiting office was usually located on a side street near one of the main thoroughfares. It was designated by an American flag not too ostentatiously displayed, along with several posters with slogans such as "Call to Arms" or "Patriots, Come Forward!"

In front of the doorway, and only in favorable weather, stood a neat, dapper, well-dressed man in uniform, with polished brass buttons, stripes running down his trousers, and chevrons sewn closely to his sleeves. This was the recruiting sergeant. And although he wasn't supposed to practise any of the wiles employed by the English recruiting sergeant for securing troops, he undoubtedly painted a rose-colored picture of service to the inquiring young men seeking adventure and military glory.

To qualify for service, you had to be age eighteen to thirty-five, able bodied, of good character, and with no ill habits or severe past records. The first inquiry into the candidate's qualifications was in regard to his physical fitness for the service, and so he was critically examined by an army surgeon.

The cavalry requirements in 1874 favored the lean, wiry type. With saddle, weapons, ammunition, and accouterments, the horse would be carrying a little over 240 pounds, so this limited selection to men between 5′5″ and 5′10″ and not over 140 to 150 pounds. However, horsemanship was not part of the requirements, as the cavalryman's early duties had little to do with riding a horse.

If all counts were satisfactory, the candidate was received as a recruit, dressed in the fatigue uniform of a soldier, and dispatched to the rendezvous at Jefferson Barracks in St. Louis if he enlisted in the cavalry, or Columbus Barracks in Ohio or Fort Monroe in Virginia if he chose the infantry or artillery. At the rendezvous he was taught his duties and was drilled to a fair state of soldierly perfection. Then he was assigned to his regiment and conducted to his new home on the frontier.

* * *

Actually, Army recruits during the time of the Apache Wars were often of poorer quality than Americans like to admit for their fighting men. The Department of the Army seems to have sacrificed the mental and moral fitness of its men to the fitness of their physique. Now, deserters were not being considered for reenlistment, and the "stupid and vicious" were not wanted in the force, because to include them frequently meant disaster in battle. Also, public opinion was demanding a higher character of its fighting men.

Recruiting stations were only given to the best officers of the service. Regimental commanders usually had long and distinguished service before being given their post, and tried to select good men for recruiting officers, seeing that term as one of some relaxation and as reward for good and faithful service.

This drawing from the National Archives shows the uniforms worn by cavalry and artillery officers in 1888.

The Enlisted Man

Once on the frontier, the enlisted man would either be building bridges, laying roads, cutting ice, or sawing wood—or spending endless hours in dreary guard duty. When he finally found himself seated in a saddle, he would be escorting a slow-moving immigrant train or an ox-drawn "bull wagon."

Army pay for recruits in the cavalry, infantry, and artillery regiments was as follows: for the first and second year of enlistment, $13 per month; for the third year, $14; for the fourth year, $15; and for the fifth year, $16. Thereafter, while the soldier was in continuous service, his pay increased to $18 per month for the next five years, with an additional $1.00 per month for each subsequent period of five years' continuous service.

The pay for a corporal ranged in the same ratio, from $15 to $20 per month, according to his length of service, and that for a duty sergeant from $18 to $23 per month. First sergeants were paid from $25 to $30 per month, according to their length of service.

The total allowance of clothing for a private in

This National Archives drawing shows the full-dress uniforms worn by enlisted men in the cavalry and infantry in 1888.

These are the soldiers of the 3rd Cavalry, stationed at Fort Davis, Texas, in the late 1880s. They are wearing the 1850 wide carbine slings and the 1880 Mills cartridge belt (the 1885 version had the leather billet and bar buckle). The belt plates are the old 1851 eagle pattern. Their holsters were either the 1885 model or the 1874 model with the wide flap cut off. In terms of clothing, they are wearing the 1883 drab campaign hat, 1884 fatigue blouses, 1883-pattern blue flannel shirt with double pockets, and the 1884-pattern boots. Their weapons are Smith & Wesson, Schofield model, .45 caliber. (Photo courtesy of Fort Davis Historic Site, Fort Davis, Texas.)

the army for his first three years was the following: one overcoat, two uniform dress coats, three woolen blouses, three canvas fatigue blouses, seven pairs of uniform trousers, seven pairs of kersey trousers, three pairs of canvas fatigue trousers, three pairs of overalls, seven dark-blue woolen shirts, nine undershirts, nine pairs of drawers, thirty-six linen collars, twelve pairs of cotton socks and twelve pairs of woolen socks, nine pairs of shoes for the infantry and two pairs of boots and five pairs of shoes for the cavalry, four fatigue caps, three campaign hats, two helmets, two woolen blankets, twenty-four pairs of white gloves, and three pairs of suspenders. In addition to the above, the cavalrymen were furnished two pairs of leather gauntlets and two stable frocks.

Cavalrymen scheduled for a lengthy campaign had to be ready as early as the season of the year permitted. First call for reveille sounded at the crack of dawn, after which the men turned out promptly, struck their tents, and packed their saddles. Fifteen minutes later, reveille was sounded again and the men fell in for roll call. After roll call, the first sergeants marched their men to the stables, where they watered, groomed, and fed the horses. Then the men were dismissed for a breakfast of hardtack, bacon, and coffee. Half an hour before departing time, "boots and saddles" was sounded, followed fifteen minutes later by "to horse," when the roll was called again. First sergeants reported the results of the roll call to troop commanders, who in turn reported them to the adjutant. Troop commanders then ordered "prepare to mount," and moved out when the "advance" sounded.

After thirty minutes of marching, the troops were halted, and the men dismounted to check packs and tighten girths. Such short halts were usually made at the end of each hour, and, if the march was lengthy and the terrain rough, a halt of an hour was made around midday. The horses were generally watered once during the day's march.

If there weren't any obstacles on the trail or road, a trot was ordered. There was no reason for using up all the horses' strength on a gait that was any faster. When they reached their campsite, the troopers unbridled, tied up the horses, and wiped the saddles and bridles. If water was available, they would sponge off the horses. After this, the men refreshed themselves during a short interval before "stable call" was sounded. At this point, saddles were removed, and the horses were watered, groomed, and fed. The troopers also inspected the backs of their mounts, and applied hot poultices to any infected areas to prevent inflammation.

Retreat sounded at sundown, and the men were allowed to go to bed if they wished. The signal to "extinguish lights" was sounded at 8:30 P.M., after which no loud talking or noises were permitted.

Black Army Units

By an act of Congress on July 28, 1866, provisions were made for black men to serve in the regular peacetime Army. To the six regiments of cavalry then in service, four more regiments were added, two of which were composed of black men with white officers (the 9th and 10th Cavalry Regiments). Also, two regiments composed of black men with white officers were added to the Infantry Regiments (the 24th and 25th Infantry Regiments). By this legislation, Congress had opened a new chapter in American military history and afforded the former slave an opportunity to play a major role in settling the West.

Of the special provisions stipulated by Congress, chaplains who were normally assigned to a particular post now were assigned directly to a black regiment. There, they had both spiritual and educational duties, for they also were to instruct the soldiers in the fundamentals of reading, writing, and arithmetic.

Although the Army had no experienced black officers at the time, Congress still specified that all officers of the new regiments were to be white, and required them to take a special examination before a board of officers appointed by the secretary of war. At least two years of active service in the Civil War were required of all officers, with two thirds of those holding the rank of captain or above drawn from the volunteer regiments and one third from the Regular Army list. Officers of lower rank were drawn from volunteer services.

Most white officers simply refused to serve with black units. It mattered little to them that the promotion cycle was greatly improved for those serving with black units on the frontier. There were a few good officers, however, who freely joined the black units, remaining for a substantial period of

This photo shows a black soldier wearing a buffalo coat. The Indians would call the black troopers "buffalo soldiers" since they often wore these coats.

Tenth Cavalry black soldier, by Frederic Remington. (Drawing courtesy of the National Archives, Washington, D.C.)

time. But there were others who, after a short tour with these units, were willing to swap their post for whatever was available with a few dollars thrown in to cover expenses.

Many young black men enlisted for the five years of service because the Army afforded an opportunity for social and economic betterment that was all but closed to them in civilian life. Thirteen dollars a month seemed meager pay, but it was more than a black man could expect as a civilian, and there was also the allotment for food, clothing, and shelter. His betterment and advancement seemed to be well assured.

The 9th and 10th Cavalry Regiments were authorized to help dispatch the hostile Indians to their appointed reservations. When, in 1877, Victorio and his band of Ojo Caliente Apaches jumped the reservation to begin their trail of depredations, the task of containing and returning them fell for the most part on the 9th and 10th Regiments.

These black troopers spent more than half their time marching and countermarching in Indian campaigns, leaving the frontier Army so thinly spread over such a vast area that its task was almost impossible to perform. With no experience at "reading" the indications the Indians left behind when taking flight from their pursuers, the black troopers seemed to be frustrated at every turn. Yet these men—in many instances, assisted by the 24th and 25th Infantry—continued to scout the mountains and plains as best they could.

As the 1870s progressed, the black troops suffered even more. During these hard campaigns, their condemned horses and mules had practically collapsed; so many troopers went barefoot, with their soles bleeding from the sharp rocks and sand burrs. With their clothing in tatters, some wore only underwear. They also were beset by dysentery and other maladies. Besides all this, the Army Quartermaster Department invariably sent them inferior equipment. The outdated weapons and ammunition made the black soldiers' job even more difficult.

The Army food was disastrous. As in the 1850s, it included a meat ration of three-tenths bacon and seven-tenths fresh beef. The bread was made at night in the post bakery, and nearly every kind of flying insect was found in it. "That's an extra ration, Bunky!" the sergeant would shout after hearing complaints. Beans were always included in the menu, thickened with cornstarch to help swell a hungry belly. There were occasional scurvy epidemics, so the post surgeon suggested that they plant a garden. The officers eagerly accepted this idea, and sent for onions, cabbages, and a variety of melon seeds. Perhaps because, as civilians, the quality of their food hadn't been much better, blacks were less critical than whites in their regular meals and they usually ate their entire ration.

Desertions were not as frequent with black soldiers as they were with white, but a few blacks did slip away from their posts, taking everything they could with them on horseback or over their shoulders. They usually headed across the Mexican border, where they joined other blacks who were already bonded with Indian and Mexican outlaws and were committing depredations equal to the Apaches'.

Report on Black Troops for the Year 1886–1887

The black troops in service during this year consisted of two regiments of infantry, two regiments of

"A Pull at the Canteen," by Frederic Remington (courtesy of U.S. Government Printing Office).

cavalry, four ordnance sergeants, three quartermaster sergeants, and 126 unassigned recruits, making an aggregate mean strength of 2,142 men. Included in this number were only two commissioned officers, both regimental chaplains.

The following table[1] shows the regions in which black troops were employed, as well as a comparison between them and the white troops serving in the same regions, as to mean strength, and rates of admission to sick report, constant noneffectiveness, death, and discharge for disability. The mean strength shown by the returns of the adjutant general has been used in calculating the death and discharge rates for the whole Army, but not for the several regions.

In the regions of the "Atlantic Coast" and "Central Timbered Plains and Hills," the mean strength of the black troops was so small that any compari-

An Apache scout communicating by sign language with a black trooper. (Drawing by Frederic Remington, courtesy of U.S. Government Printing Office.)

	REGION OF:													
	Atlantic Coast		Northern Lakes		Central Timbered Plains and Hills		Prairies		Great Plains		Cordilleras		Whole Army	
	W.	B.	W.	B.	W.	B.	W.	B.	W.	B.	W.	B.	W.	B.
Mean strength	2,194	31	989	203	1,028	86	3,593	265	5,559	899	5,410	658	21,430	2,142
Ratio per 1,000 of mean strength of:														
Admissions	1,390	2,194	825	562	2,180	2,651	1,247	1,374	1,316	1,709	1,043	1,369	1,239	1,490
Constant Non-effectiveness	41	77	26	19	73	106	38	39	42	43	34	44	39	43
Deaths	10.9	.0	9.1	4.9	12.6	.0	11.4	7.5	8.1	7.8	8.9	10.6	9.0	7.2
Discharges	25.1	32.3	12.1	34.5	30.2	34.9	23.9	45.3	31.5	23.4	27.0	19.8	24.9	24.6

son based upon it would be of little value; in the other regions, however, the force was larger, and the ratios given are thus more reliable.

In the region of the "Northern Lakes," the rates of admission to sick report, constant noneffectiveness, and deaths were decidedly in favor of the black troops, but their rate of discharges for disability was nearly three times as large as that of the white troops. In the region of the "Prairies," all the rates of the black troops were higher than those of the white, except the death rate, which was considerably lower. In the region of the "Great Plains," the black troops gave lower death and discharge rates than the whites, but higher admission and noneffective rates. In the region of the "Cordilleras," all the rates of the black troops were higher than those of the white, except the discharge rate, which was very much lower. For the whole Army, the admission and constant noneffective rates given by the black troops were considerably higher than the same rates for the white troops, but their death rate was lower. Discharges for disability occurred in about the same proportion for both groups.

The following table[2] shows the principal causes of disability, as well as their rates of occurrence, of which a notable disparity is shown to have existed between the white and black troops.

A black soldier of the 24th Infantry, Company B. (Photo courtesy of Herb Peck, Jr.)

Principal Causes of Disability, and Differences in the Rates Between White and Black Troops

In favor of the white troops			In favor of the black troops		
Diseases	Admission rate per 1,000 of mean strength for: White	Black	Diseases	Admission rate per 1,000 of mean strength for: Black	White
Influenza	.37	3.73	Enteric fever	.93	4.25
Measles	1.40	4.20	Malarial fever, cont'd.	.00	2.05
Rheumatic fever	3.17	9.34	Remittent fever	11.67	19.04
Articular rheumatism (subacute & chronic)	32.20	96.17	Typho-malarial fever	.00	1.87
			Cholera morbus	1.40	7.00
Epilepsy	2.38	6.07	Erysipelas	.00	2.38
Headache	24.03	49.49	Venereal epididymitis and orchitis	1.87	6.49
Neuralgia	36.21	58.82			
Snow blindness	.05	2.33	Alcoholism and results	4.67	50.21
Asthma	1.68	8.87	Insanity	.47	1.49
Catarrh and colds	75.69	133.05	Gastritis	.47	2.15
Pleurisy and results	2.66	6.07	Synovitis	.93	2.15
Tonsilitis	40.04	75.16			
Colic	18.62	28.48			
Constipation	19.93	48.09			
Orchitis, nonvenereal	3.17	9.34			

Desertions

By 1885 the issue of desertions was paramount, and was being considered by the inspector general. A number of posts required a great deal of daily labor from their servicemen, and this undoubtedly contributed to their high desertion rates. In addition, the experience of the Civil War, with its expectations of a "quick win" and the resulting high rate of desertions that occurred when it wasn't forthcoming, had set the stage for problems on the frontier, where a quick win was not very likely. Desertions were on the decrease, but were still a problem requiring attention. Some officers thought that the $30 reward for apprehension of a deserter should be increased sharply—possibly to $100 or more—as the sympathy of the people was often with the deserter. Some thought that a more equitable way of settling clothing accounts might prevent some desertions. All charges for overdrawn clothing would be postponed until the second semiannual settlement following enlistment.

From October 1884 to July 1885, desertions were approximately 30 percent, compared to 40 percent for a similar period in 1883. Still, the rate was extremely high, and made protecting the frontier very difficult. At garrisons where desertions were frequent, rigid orders were issued for examinations into their manner of being governed. Officers were held accountable for desertions, so guarding the soldiers became more stringent.

The company commander was guardian of both his mens' rights and their instruction and discipline. The percentage of desertions was found to be correlated to the commander's stewardship: If he was faultfinding without ever commending his men, if he was wanting in soldierly sympathy and frequently lost his temper, if he showed little interest in the welfare of his men, the percentage of desertions increased and the commander might be asked to resign, or might be severely punished. Some officers favored branding the deserter, or a more permanent solution. Generally, it seemed that most of the officers had the best interests of their men at heart, and tried to help them all they could.

As early as December 1868, soldiers who deserted were tried before a General Court Martial. If found guilty, they were dishonorably discharged from the service, forfeiting all pay and allowances. The deserter's head was shaved and his left hip was branded with the letter "D," which prevented his reenlistment at some other post.

With the desertion rate still high in 1885, it was thought that the adoption of a more rigid system was necessary. Now, recruiting officers were held accountable for the enlistment of "stupid and vicious" men, evidence attesting to their character and habits was required before men could be accepted for service, the reward for apprehending deserters was increased to $100, and a persistent effort was made to catch the deserters.

A new law made aiding or abetting desertion a Federal crime, as did harboring or protecting deserters by any citizen. Such crimes were punishable by fine and imprisonment. The law stated that it was the duty of a United States marshal to apprehend and prosecute those who in any way aided or abetted the deserter. Men were required to take an oath before enlistment, in which they stated their habits, any other names they used, previous vocations, whether they had criminal records, and other information. As the majority of desertions occurred during the first year of service, regulations now required that recruits be held at depots until they were thoroughly instructed in their duties, and accustomed to their daily performance, and until they understood the personal restraint that was needed in the service.

A new edition of the Army Regulations was called for. Over 450 paragraphs had been changed or struck out, sixteen percent of the total regulations. So that the new manual would reflect the real needs of the Army, some 274 general orders were studied carefully. These orders had been issued between 1881 and 1885, and formed the backbone of the new Army Regulations.

Notes

[1]From the Report of the Quartermaster General to the Secretary of War, Beginning of the Second Session of the Forty-Eighth Congress (Vol. 7), 1884.
[2]Ibid.

10

TALES OF HEROISM

Following an Indian Trail

Early in the spring of 1868, a few months before the great Indian uprising that was to be known as the Apache Wars, two troops of the 8th Cavalry left Camp Verde, Arizona, on a mission to quell the Indians who were becoming increasingly difficult. The troops were headed for the Tonto Basin, a march that took five days. Many of the raw recruits were more afraid of finding the Indians than of getting saddlesore, so they continued riding in the warm spring air with a minimum of the usual Army complaints. Still, many were quaking in their boots, and seven stole out of camp at night, making tracks away.

The Tonto Basin was a valley with steep, high sides, and getting down to it from the 4,000-feet-high sheer cliffs took all of the sixth day. But by evening, all of the troopers were assembled in the basin, having pitched camp by a little stream, and were awaiting the sure-to-come welcoming party from the Apache. Early in the evening the welcome came—a rain of arrows and bullets that actually caused little damage but a lot of consternation. Forty troopers chased the Indians, but they got away fairly easily in their familiar surroundings.

The next morning, a couple of the troopers took off for a two-day scouting trip, leaving the remainder of the cavalry and supply trains in the basin. Four cavalrymen were charged with the difficult job of getting the train back up the basin walls. An old, grizzled trooper named Cap Shere was to be their guide. Shere didn't like the prospect of climbing over the rocky cliffs, and without a word, saddled his mule and got ready to leave the camp.

Two of the troopers, Privates Aston and Cubberly, accosted the old fellow and demanded to know where he was headed. Rubbing his whiskers quizzically, Shere replied, "I aim to hunt up a trail. Must be some way out of this valley, I reckon." This sounded good to Aston and Cubberly, who then rushed for permission to accompany the old-timer.

After hiking for about a mile towards the foot of the hills, the three saw signs of an Indian party. Carefully, they continued on the trail until they spotted about nineteen Apaches ahead of them. Keeping a distance from the braves, they moved on, filled with trepidation. Shere questioned his young companions about their resolve, and both Aston and Cubberly assured him that he was in charge, and that they would follow him.

Shere led the pair up a small hill, and found that the Indians had left the trail and disappeared from view. He noted that if they turned back, the Indians would surely attack—and if they went ahead, the Indians would "lay for them" as well. But the appeal of finding a useable trail out of Tonto Basin was so great that the trio slogged along for another six miles to the top of a rise—and from there, a trail was plainly visible.

Their elation at finding the trail was somewhat tempered by their knowledge that the Indians would be certain to ambush them as they retraced their steps back to Tonto Basin. However, the importance of their find gave them courage to move along.

After retracing their steps the six miles to their first stopping place, Shere turned to Aston and

Cubberly and told them to turn their horses loose and drive them down to him so that he could lead them to the bottom of the hill. Shere started down, with their horses, and reached the bottom without an arrow appearing. However, when Aston and Cubberly had carefully picked their way through the scrub pine for about 150 yards, the Apaches came forth, all war whoops and missiles. Still, the pair continued their descent, furiously firing their carbines. The Apaches returned the rain of fire, but without hitting either trooper, and the men crossed the canyon to safety.

Their horses had been hit, although not fatally, and Shere had lost a lock of hair, which had been shot from his forehead as clean as a razor slice.

Both Aston and Cubberly were awarded a Medal of Honor for their valor in finding the trail and thus allowing the pack train to follow the Indians.

Backed into a Canyon

During the summer of 1872, the Apaches had their way with the land, the cattle, and just about everything else in the area near the military post of Camp Crittenden in southern Arizona. Camp Crittenden afforded little protection against the Indians, as it was garrisoned by a small troop, F Troop of the 5th Cavalry, and over half the troop was debilitated by a particularly virulent fever.

Still, the F Troop tried its best to maintain some kind of order with the Apaches. So, on the morning of July 13, 1872, when a Mexican rancher came to the post with news of a band of Apaches herding large numbers of cattle in the vicinity, Lieutenant Hall, with a detail of seven troopers and First Sergeant Henry Newman, struck out to chase the Indians and retrieve the cattle.

One of the troopers, Private John Nihill, wrote this in his diary: "The trail was found within 600 yards of the post, and, as it had been raining the day before, the ground was soft and there was little difficulty in following it while on open country. It headed towards the Whitestone Mountains, which were distant about fifteen miles, southeast of the post. We traveled as rapidly as the nature of the ground would permit, hoping to overhaul them before they reached the mountains."

As the troopers neared the mountains, they spotted some abandoned cattle, which indicated that the Indians would probably box themselves into a canyon, where it would be impossible to get at them.

Entering a deep canyon, the troopers dismounted to continue the chase, when, sure enough, they were attacked from about 800 feet above, where Indians were hiding on the sides of the canyon.

It was almost impossible to shoot back. Some of the troopers were wounded by Indian fire, but Private Nihill had followed the trail to the other side of the canyon, and was able to provide some cover for them. Then Lieutenant Hall decided to retreat, and gave the men orders to move out. Hall and First Sergeant Newman would hold the rear, assisted by Private Glynn. Glynn drove off eight of the Apaches himself, killing or wounding five of them. Nihill was watching for a shot and hadn't noticed that the other troopers were retreating faster than he was. Quickly dismounting, he moved as quietly as possible to join the other men, when an Indian fired a shot at him. However, the Indian's gun misfired, and Nihill was able to kill the Indian before he could fire another shot. Three other Indians attempted to cut Nihill off, but he was able to escape by turning his horse loose and retreating on foot while the Indians concentrated on the horse.

Sergeant Newman and Privates Nihill and Glynn were all awarded Medals of Honor for bravery in the action.

The Chase of Chief Victorio

In 1879, a band of warriors led by Chief Victorio swept across much of New Mexico, leaving a wave of cold, hard fear among the settlers. The hostiles' hit-and-run attacks occurred late at night or in the first blush of morning, causing confusion and chaos. Their first attack was against the E Troop of the 9th Cavalry; despite the loss of fifty horses, human loss was relatively small, with eight men killed.

The settlers decided to organize and help the soldiers fight the Indians. However, the citizens' force was defeated at Hillsboro. Ten men were killed and dozens were wounded and scalped, and all of the livestock was taken away by the Indians as booty.

Captain Dawson was sent to chase Victorio, but his troopers were attacked and returned to the fort in shambles. Although later reinforced by Captain Beyer's troopers, the combined force had to withdraw after an embarrassing loss.

Then a group of 200 soldiers commanded by Major Morrow was ordered to chase Victorio north and stage an attack near Ojo Caliente. This troop fared better, recapturing about sixty horses and mules, some belonging to the E Troop. Morrow learned the position of Victorio's braves and surprised them at night. Victorio's camp was captured and destroyed, although the Indians faded into the darkness and disappeared. Morrow's command, reduced in fighting strength to about 100 men, continued the chase through rivers and into canyons.

The last confrontation between Victorio and Morrow was on a dark, moonlit night. The troops circled the Indian stronghold and charged. The Indians put up a brief, fierce fight before the few survivors fled into the darkness.

The soldiers moved on towards Fort Bayard, New Mexico, confident that they would not be attacked again. They reached the post on November 3, 1879, after a two-month chase of the wily Victorio and his small but fierce band.

Disobedience Saves the Lieutenant

During the early days of the Indian uprising, a military post was lacking in Arizona, so the Army sent a young surveyor, Lieutenant King, to survey the territory for such an installation. The post was to be near Sunset Pass, where the Apaches were becoming more and more difficult to control. King was also considered to be an Indian fighter, and several troopers accompanied him into Arizona to spread the word among the Indians that they were not to be trifled with.

King was riding well ahead of his troopers when he was ambushed by a group of Apaches, who hit him in the face with an arrow and in the arm with a rifle ball. King immediately slumped to the ground, half-conscious.

His troopers quickly arrived at the scene, with Sergeant Bernard Taylor galloping to the aid of the lieutenant, snatching him from the ground, and tossing him over his shoulder. Running and dodging arrows and rifle fire, Taylor carried his com-

This photo shows a company of soldiers in their new white summer helmets and fatigue caps, c. 1880s. One soldier wears a bowler (back row, left) and another wears a straw "skimmer" (sitting, right).

mander for half a mile to safety, disobeying King's repeated orders to, "put me down and save yourself."

For behaving with great valor (though disobeying an order), Taylor was awarded the Medal of Honor.

The Saving of Tularosa

Old Fort Tularosa was too near the Mescalero Agency on the Fort Stanton Reservation for safety from the Indians, and the Army troops stationed in the area were too sparse. So, when a hostile band of Indians from the reservation went on the warpath in the cold of early January 1880, the town of Tularosa, just outside the undermanned fort, was hardly protected.

All of the cavalry in the district were called to block off the area and secure the towns that the Indians hadn't already sacked and pillaged. While one regiment led by Colonel Grierson pushed the Indians north, another led by Colonel Hatch pushed them south. The plan, developed by Generals Pope and Ord, was to trap the renegades between them both and capture the hostiles. The plan worked well, and 250 of the approximately 300 Indians in the band, led by old Chief Victorio, were killed.

The remaining fifty, encumbered by captured livestock, were boxed into Dog Canyon by a portion of Hatch's forces, commanded by Major Morrow. Three of the warriors were killed in the skirmish, and twenty-five head of cattle and horses were reclaimed by the Army for the settlers.

But Victorio and enough of the braves had escaped to continue to cause trouble. Almost five months after the initial engagement, Sergeant George Jordan of K Troop, 9th Cavalry, was ordered back to old Fort Tularosa to again hold down the town outside the fort. Jordan and his men arrived, tired and thirsty, only to find that the hostiles were heading for town.

The soldiers were now on the move again. However, problems through the mountains near the fort slowed their progress, upsetting their wagon train and allowing the Indians to come nearer.

When they had almost reached the town, the Indians attacked, but the soldiers managed to muster themselves enough to surprise them. The Indians tried again and again to gain control of the town, but were not able to push back the tenacious troopers. The Indians tried firing into cattle herds nearby to cause a stampede, but this, too, failed. After a short but frustrating battle, the Indians withdrew.

Shortly afterward, Major Morrow, accompanied by four troops of the 9th Cavalry, again engaged Victorio and his shrinking band of hostiles, killing fifty five of the remaining Indians. Then on June 5, 1880, Morrow met the Indians head on in Cooks Canyon, killing ten and wounding three more of Victorio's henchmen, including the son of the chief, who again had managed to escape into the mountains of old Mexico.

This picture, obviously posed in a photographer's studio, shows an Apache brave wearing the Army 1883-issue campaign shirt of blue wool flannel and a civilian modified, woven, webbed cartridge belt, along with the typical white trousers or Army-issue underwear, and muslin or cotton breechcloth. He also wears the traditional high-topped buckskin Apache boots with the heavy rawhide soles and the silver-dollar-kicker toe piece. This toe piece was the turned-up portion of the toe area of the sole, and protected the wearer as he travelled through the cactus country of Arizona and New Mexico. (Photo courtesy of the Phil Spangenberger collection.)

Black Soldiers Honored for Courage

Chief Nana was one of the most notorious of the White Mountain Apache, and by 1881, his murderous band was one of the most feared in the territory. He was especially active in the midsummer of 1881, when, during his forays out of the San Andreas Mountains in New Mexico, he and his band were dealing death and destruction to the unfortunate settlers who lived in the area. After one particularly devastating ride by Nana, Colonel Hatch was sent into the mountains with eight troops of the 9th Cavalry to punish the Indians and recapture some of the plunder.

A detachment of nineteen men under Captain Parker struck Nana's band, although there were easily three times as many Apaches as troopers. The troopers forced the Indians to withdraw, but this was after one soldier was killed, one was taken captive, and three were wounded.

A few days later, on August 16, Troop I, under First Lieutenant Valois, was recuperating from a difficult campaign against the Indians when a local Mexican man came running into camp, shrieking that the Indians had murdered his wife and children and were coming up the canyon to ravage the town. Lieutenant Burnett led the first detachment out of camp to investigate the situation, and chase the Indians back into the mountains or fight them if he could. But the Indians were already retreating towards the Cuchilla Negra Mountains, encumbered by great amounts of booty.

A number of Mexicans, armed and on horseback, joined Burnett at the devastated ranch, bringing Burnett's forces to about fifty. It appeared that there were about 100 Indians. Burnett split his forces, sending the soldiers under his first sergeant, Moses Williams, to the right and a group of the Mexicans to the left, while he and a few soldiers remained in the middle. The Indians fired heavily as they rode away, and soon Burnett's men had to dismount and continue on foot. The Indians also dismounted, firing from behind every bush and knoll. Both adversaries fought hard for several hours, until they finally reached the foothills of the Cuchilla Negra Mountains, where the Indians made a stand. The troopers were not able to outflank the Indians on the right, so Lieutenant Burnett decided to try to attack them on the left, with about fifteen soldiers, to keep the Indians from reaching the mountains, where the troopers would surely lose them.

Things were not going well with the detachment. The Indians kept moving nearer, and the situation was very grave, when Trumpeter John Rogers volunteered to carry a message to Valois. Trying to crawl away without being noticed, Rogers became frustrated with his slow progress and ran to his horse and mounted it, riding off through a storm of bullets.

Rogers, riding his wounded horse, found Lieutenant Valois and delivered his message, sending Valois to take a large hill to the right of the fighting. Attempting to take the objective, Valois and his troopers met with stiff resistance from the Indians, who had anticipated this move. As several of Valois's men had been wounded—including Valois himself—Lieutenant Burnett ordered a charge on the Indians to allow Valois to move his wounded to the rear. Then the line fell back, to try to figure a way out of this increasingly desperate situation.

Lieutenant Valois was starting the move back towards relative safety when one of his men panicked, crying out to Valois not to leave the men who were unable to move. Valois didn't hear the call, but Burnett did, and asked for volunteers to help these wounded men.

First Sergeant Williams and Private Walley answered the call for volunteers, and started the rescue operation, while the rest of the troop attempted to crawl quietly backwards. Williams and Walley, both of whom mounted their horses in record time, rode forward to the wounded men, while apparently being ignored by the Indians.

The Indians, however, did not ignore Burnett, whom they recognized as an officer among the black troopers. After three of the rescued men were moving in the direction of safety, another one of them was seen wandering around, confused, heading for the Indians. Burnett quickly mounted and rode towards the dazed trooper, staying between him and the Indians. The trooper finally joined the rest of the soldiers, and Burnett was able to retire from the center of attention. In the melee that had ensued, the Indians, who had a clear shot at Burnett, missed their fire and wounded his horse instead.

In the meantime, Valois's troopers and the Mexican citizens had taken up a new position, fighting the Indians and keeping them at bay and recapturing the horses. By nightfall, however, their ammunition had run short, so they returned to the camp to rearm. At daybreak, they again hit the trail, chasing Nana and his men. Finally, after another brief encounter, Nana and his warriors were chased into old Mexico.

Medals of Honor were awarded to Lieutenant Burnett and his two black troopers, Williams and Walley, for their courage in the face of fire.

Heroes and Treachery at Cibicu Creek

Until the summer of 1881, the White Mountain Apaches had been living fairly peacefully for several years alongside the whites on their reservation near Fort Apache. So, it seemed strange that this band, considered among the most intelligent and sophisticated of the bands in the Arizona Territory, would suddenly change its course and start a battle.

The band probably would have continued its peaceful coexistence with the whites had it not been for the shenanigans of a medicine man by the name of Nockay det Klinne. According to reports, Klinne was well on his way towards amassing real wealth, which was mostly extorted from his own people. In order to keep his hand in the wampum belt, however, he knew he had to come up with some bold new plan. So, he promised his people that he would raise the dead; then he qualified this by saying that all of the dead had already risen but their feet were being held down until the whites were driven out of Indian country. Whether by design or accident, Klinne's story so inflamed the White Mountain Apaches against the whites that they eventually went to battle.

Although part of the White Mountain Reservation, Fort Apache was some distance from the middle. Colonel E. A. Carr (6th Cavalry) was serving a temporary stint at the fort in 1881. As the Indians began to show their anger, Carr talked with Klinne and several of the chiefs, and explained to them that efforts to run the whites out of the territory would only hurt the Indians. Not satisfied that Klinne would stop his wild claims, Carr ordered Klinne to report to Agent Tiffany at San Carlos. Although Tiffany sent his police escort after Klinne, the wily medicine man retired to his camp on the Cibicu Creek, about forty miles from Fort Apache, and stuck to the terrain like a burr. Agent Tiffany then asked Colonel Carr to arrest Klinne.

This turn of events caused Carr to telegraph the department commander, asking for back-up troops. He hoped that a show of force would convince the Indians that an outbreak would be futile, and would thereby possibly prevent an uprising. But the troops were not sent, so Carr attempted to keep the peace by speaking directly with the Indians, who were growing more insolent by the hour. Eventually, more troops were dispatched; but, because they came so late, they were not very effective. Then Agent Tiffany made a formal demand ordering the military force to bring in the medicine man, dead or alive.

During this delay in Klinne's arrest proceedings, Klinne had held dances, and the Indians' frenzy rose higher and higher—probably supported by large quantities of "tiswin," a corn liquor known to be a "frightful intoxicant."

When Agent Tiffany telegraphed the order for Carr to arrest Klinne, the Indians immediately cut the telegraph line and occupied the only useable road to the fort, thereby severing the garrison from outside help. And, more alarmingly, stories began to circulate, linking the Indian scouts on the garrison with some of the disobedience.

Carr sent a runner to the camp, who told Klinne that he would not be harmed if he reported to Agent Tiffany as requested. Klinne's answer was evasive, and he was apparently planning more and larger festivities closer to the garrison. However, attempts to catch the tricky medicine man at the dances failed. And at about this time, Carr removed the ammunition from the scouts.

On August 29, Carr took stock of his little organization, and moved his command of seventy-nine troopers and twenty-three Indian scouts towards Cibicu Creek. A small infantry company stayed back at the garrison. While in camp in a gorge of Carizo Creek, Carr had a plain talk with the Indian scouts, in which he explained the objective of the expedition. Then, as he thought that the scouts had been unfailingly loyal up to that time, he restored their ammunition.

Sergeant Mose moved on ahead to inform the Indians in camp that there would be no hostilities if Klinne reported to the post as requested. With no answer from Klinne, the next morning the troops moved up the trail to the top of the canyon and crossed to the valley of the Cibicu. The scouts took the high trail, leading along the creek, while Carr and his men moved along the higher open ground. Suddenly, Sanchez, a chief of the White Mountain Apache, rode up to the soldiers, and shook hands with the officers at the head of the column. After counting the men quite deliberately, Sanchez then galloped back to his camp.

Somewhat perplexed by Sanchez's behavior, the command nevertheless marched forward into the camp. There, Klinne surrendered without incident. Carr's interpreter stated that Klinne and his family were going to be taken to the agent and that they would not be harmed. However, he went on to explain, if Klinne attempted to escape, or anyone tried to rescue him, the medicine man would be shot immediately.

On the return, the men were separated by an accidental missing of the creek crossing, so that the prisoners and scouts were on one side of the creek and the soldiers were on the other. As the soldiers were making their camp, they spotted Indians riding to the camp on the opposite bank. At this point, Carr sent Lieutenant Hentig to warn the Indians to leave right away, and Lieutenant Carter to bring the scouts and prisoners over to the main camp. The scouts left the tribesmen, and crossed the creek, but hesitated to make camp, claiming that the ant hills were too large. The scouts instead arranged themselves across the front of the campground.

Hentig, who was well-known to all of the Indians, called out, "Ukashe!" (Get away!) to the 100 or so Indians who now invaded the main camp. Then a young brave gave a war cry, and a volley of shots rang out in the canyon. Hentig and his orderly were wounded in the first volley, and had to be rescued by Carter and carried to the rear. The dismounted soldiers, caught by surprise, grabbed their arms and proceeded to attack the Indians and the scouts. Carr calmly walked to the area where the scouts had stood and ordered Sergeant McDonald, in charge of the guard, to "kill the medicine man." McDonald was only able to wound Klinne before being shot himself by the scouts. All during this time, Klinne was boisterously telling the Indians to fight and trying to reach the scouts. Klinne said that he would come to life immediately, should he be killed in the scuffle.

Lieutenant Carter's orderly moved towards the guard with a saddle kit, and at Carr's command, drew his revolver, thrust the gun into Klinne's mouth, and fired. Klinne's squaw was permitted to run from the camp, and was heard uttering a death chant as she scurried.

Having been driven from the creek, the scouts and the Indians in the band now took up new positions in the hills, where they continued to fight. As the night fell, the Army buried its dead in a single grave inside Carr's tent, while the fighting went on. The column then prepared to return to Fort Apache.

Before leaving the battlefield, Carr sent Lieutenant Carter to see if Klinne had died of his wounds. Surprisingly, the medicine man was still alive—a situation that Carr could not permit to continue. He then sent a guide named Burns to complete the job, using a knife to keep any more shots from being fired. Burns, afraid that he might botch the job, crushed the forehead of the medicine man with an axe, a "signature" immediately adopted by the Apache.

On September 1, the Indians who had preceded Carr's command back to the garrison killed a number of citizens on their way and looted the area as well. The word went out that Carr's command had been massacred, and the general concern for the safety of the territory was high. When the Carr party unexpectedly arrived on the second, a call for rejoicing rang out through the territory.

The Expedition of 1882

The spring of 1882 saw the 6th Cavalry and troops of the 3rd still chasing the Apaches, who were then apparently hiding in the crags and crannies of old Mexico, so the Army was thus able to celebrate the Fourth of July with true American vigor. But on July 9th, the Army received a telegram, stating that a band of hostiles had made a run on San Carlos, killing the chief of scouts, a number of Indian policemen, friendly Indians, and all of the white settlers and townspeople they could find. They had ridden towards Tonto Basin, and the 6th Cavalry and other available troops were ordered to march, posthaste, to Cibicu Creek, and from there intercept the renegades when they crossed the Black River.

Two companies of the 3rd Cavalry headed out

Troop C, 3rd Cavalry, stationed at Fort Davis, Texas. The officer in the foreground with the white horse wears a straw hat, which could be drawn from any supply depot in any Southwestern state. (Photo courtesy of Fort Davis Historic Site, Fort Davis, Texas.)

after the Indians, starting from Fort Thomas, and a third group, a troop from the 6th Cavalry plus some Indian scouts, rode out from Fort McDowell, under Captain Chaffee.

Troops E and I of the 3rd Cavalry, and E and K of the 6th, combined under Major Evans, also rode out towards Tonto Basin. A week later, on July 16, they found signs from the Indians, warning the troops to beware. That night, Captain Chaffee, who was camped only an hour away from the main camp, rode in to consult with Major Evans. The two commanders agreed that it would be likely that they would contact the Indians the next day.

So, at the crack of dawn, Chaffee and his command broke camp, and started the ascent of Tonto Basin. At about eleven Chaffee sent word to Major Evans that the Indians had been spotted and were apparently spoiling for a fight. It was later revealed that the Indians had seen only Chaffee's group, otherwise they would have picked a better spot for a battle. The spot was a branch of the Canyon Diablo, a great gash in the earth separating the trails from the Apache and the Navajo Reservations. A party of soldiers advanced as noiselessly as possible, while the I Troop skittered along the bank, firing at the Indians to attract their attention. At the same time, two other troops moved around the main body of the Indians, attempting to reach the other side of the canyon and then to box them in.

Early in the afternoon, the Indians opened fire, still believing that they greatly outnumbered the troops and feeling sure of an easy victory. Four troops moved towards the other side of the canyon to the right and rear of the Indians. Troop I then ran the Indians' pony herd apart, killing the herders and capturing the ponies. The Indians were now aware that they had bitten off much more than they could chew, and began to fight for a way out. The I Troop started out after the Indians through the forest, but found the going tough—several men were wounded and a few were killed.

When the melee was over, the Army had recaptured seventy horses as well as camp plunder, and the Indians were so weakened that they were forced to head back to the protection of the Sierra Madre in Mexico, at least for the time being.

The Number of Depredations Committed by Each Tribe and the Amount Involved During the Period from 1812 to 1889[1]

Tribe	No.	Amount	Tribe	No.	Amount
Comanche	1,031	$ 3,116,169	Ponca	25	$ 38,621
Apache	759	3,548,466	Pottawatomie	23	7,887
Cheyenne	638	2,309,777	Oregon	19	124,229
Sioux	637	2,703,498	Sac and Fox	19	269,645
Navajo	464	1,687,780	Yakama	18	75,998
Kiowa	310	1,411,111	Wichita	17	6,821
Chippewa	184	155,062	Crow	16	30,120
Pawnee	169	214,520	Puyallup	12	14,145
Osage	160	227,115	Omaha	11	4,067
Nez Perces	157	357,390	Creek	10	59,472
Ute	135	489,166	Modoc	10	29,334
Rogue River	134	431,226	Cayuse	10	38,242
Bannock	119	280,883	Shoshone	9	54,265
California Indians	96	708,659	Caddo	9	18,120
Arapaho	68	295,078	Walla Walla	8	64,093
Nisqually	66	118,109	Coquille	7	12,027
Winnebago	58	73,251	Skaquamish	7	3,676
Keechie	52	55,365	Pima and Maricopa	6	9,752
Klikatat	50	138,678	Flatheads	6	11,505
Washington Territory Indians	48	84,527	Menominee	6	580
Blackfeet	40	216,561	Hualapais	5	42,769
Kansas or Kaw	36	65,261	Otoe	5	3,564
Piutes	35	335,140	Eluha	3	398
Snake	34	149,343	Iowa	3	252
Cherokee	29	84,220	Prairie Indians	3	13,325
Southern Refugee Indians	29	5,909	Lipan	3	6,760
Kickapoo	27	53,146	Pend d'Oreille	3	1,740
Cow Creek	25	30,151			
				273	941,407
	5,590	19,345,651		5,590	19,345,651
				5,863	20,287,058
Miscellaneous and unknown tribes				102	312,945
Committed by white persons, including United States soldiers, emigrants and rebels				88	322,936
Total				6,053	$20,922,939

[1]Report of the Secretary of War, *Messages and Documents: 1890–1891*, p. 725.

Except for the Comanche, the Apache committed more depredations than any other tribe.

11

ARMY MEDICAL TREATMENT

The Hospital Corps

The Hospital Corps was a body of soldiers permanently attached to the Medical Department, and all the duties passed down to the Medical Department were discharged by it. It consisted of non-commissioned officers (hospital stewards) and privates, a small proportion of the latter being graded as acting hospital stewards.

This corps was recruited by the voluntary transfer of men from other branches of the service who had served at least one year, and had thus become trained in military discipline, or by direct enlistment of soldiers whose terms of service in other organizations had expired. In times of peace, not more than ten civilians could be enlisted in the Hospital Corps, but each of them had to be attached to a company of the line for at least one year, to become thoroughly instructed in the duties of a soldier.

The qualifications of a private in the Hospital Corps, in addition to the physical soundness required of all soldiers, were the ability to read and write, natural intelligence, temperate habits, and good general character. No married men were accepted, and if a private married, he could not be reenlisted.

The acting hospital stewards were detailed by the secretary of war from the privates, after having served at least one year in the corps, and passing an examination in pharmacy, arithmetic, dictation, the regulations of the Medical Department of the army, the principles of cooking, minor surgery, and nursing. They could lose their position for misconduct, on the recommendation of a medical officer or by sentence of a court-martial.

Hospital stewards were non-commissioned officers of the highest grade, ranking as sergeants of the non-commissioned staff. Following examination, they were selected from among the acting hospital stewards after at least one year's service in that grade. They were examined in the same subjects as the acting stewards, but more thoroughly, and their capacity to control men also was taken into account. They had to be men of good habits and of unimpeachable integrity. They could not be reduced to the ranks. Their pay was $45 a month.

At every post in the Army there were at least one steward and three privates, and at the very large posts there could be as many as three or four stewards or acting stewards and twelve or fifteen privates. They were subject to the same conditions of subordination and discipline as the other enlisted men, and differed from them only in the nature of their duties. They were equipped as infantry, except when serving in the field with cavalry or light artillery, when they were mounted, but they carried no offensive weapons. Instead, they were armed with a large knife, and about a fourth of them carried a medicine case.

They were instructed in their special duties both theoretically and practically, every man being required to learn all forms of work necessary in a hospital. This instruction was given by the medical officers, by the stewards, and by the privates longest on duty. Once well-instructed, they were assigned to the duties for which they were best suited.

Besides their indoors duties, they were drilled in the use of litters and ambulances, which involved the careful and expeditious transportation of a

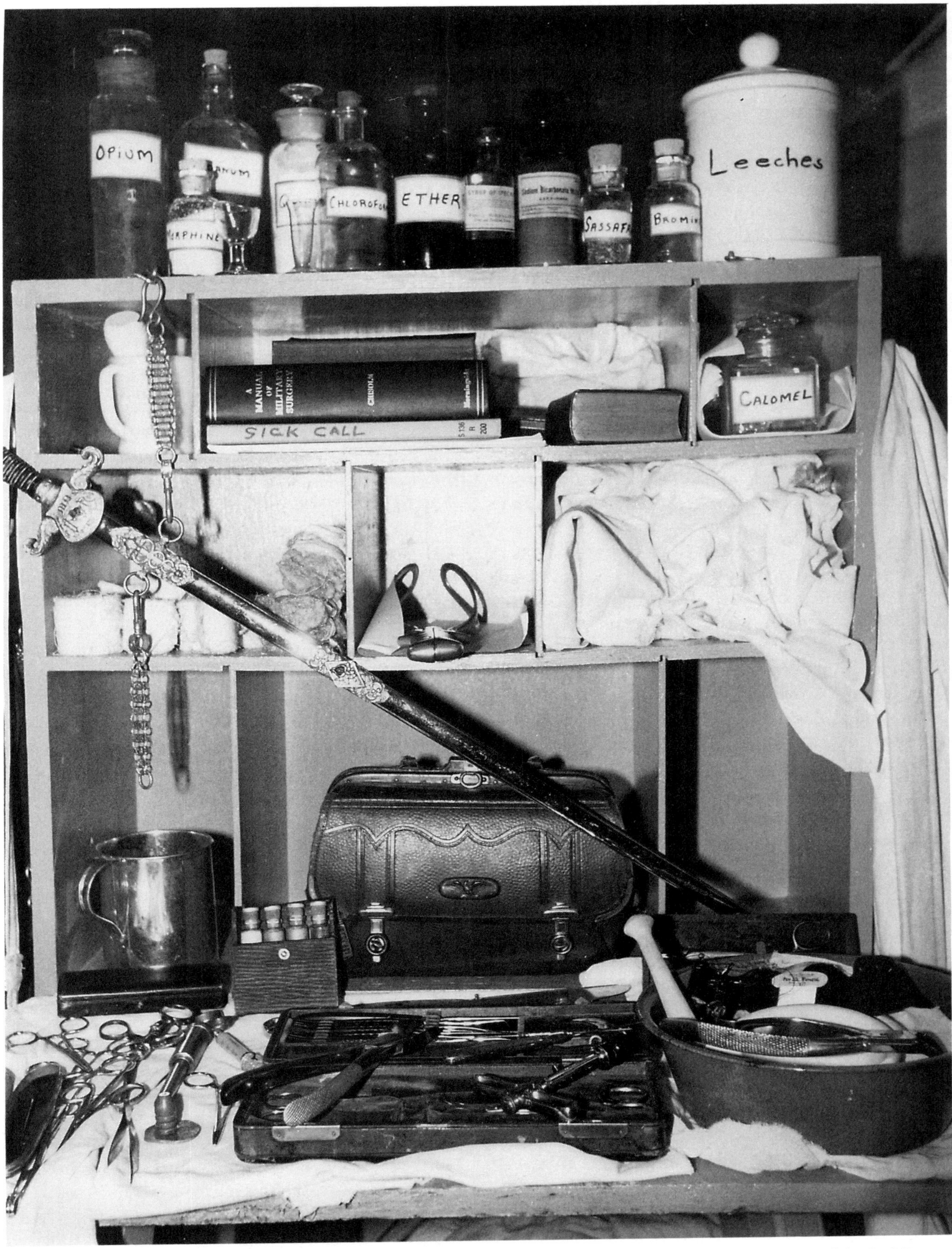

Doctor's field desk, c. *1860–1870. Contains instruments, drugs, reference books, and a Bible. The sword is from the Mexican American War,* c. *1840–1860. (Photo courtesy of the Carl Rumps collection.)*

wounded man from the place of casualty to the bed of the hospital. These drills in and out of doors were carried out with the precision and attention to detail that mark other military exercises.

A day in a military hospital for the enlisted men of the Hospital Corps was much as follows: Most of the men rose at reveille; the cook, his assistant, and the mess-room attendant rose earlier. In the wards the men employed as nurses saw that the patients allowed to do so washed and dressed themselves, opened their bedding for airing, and later made their own beds if they were strong enough. They washed those patients who were unable to get up, and made sure they were comfortable. Next, they carefully swept the floors; opened windows and ventilators as the weather allowed; dusted all chairs, tables, windows, and other objects; cleaned the spitoons and any vessels belonging to the bedridden; and prepared the wards for the medical officer's morning visit. While breakfast was being prepared, the nurses saw that the patients who went to the table were neatly dressed. They brought in the breakfasts of those who could not go to the table, and gave them such assistance as was necessary. All day the nurses were involved in keeping the wards tidy, administering the medicines or arranging the dressings that were ordered, and keeping everything in the wards and the adjoining washroom and water closet scrupulously clean. In the rougher and more ordinary part of this work, they were assisted by the more convalescent patients. The nurses were in military charge of the wards, and were responsible for the good conduct of the patients, who were bound to obey them. In case of disobedience, the nurses at once reported to the steward, who exercised his authority, or, if the steward was unavailable, reported the case without delay to the medical officer. The right of appeal to the medical officer always existed.

The nurse saw that there was no disorder at any time during the day and no noise at night, the lights being extinguished at a fixed hour, except when necessary for the care of the sick. The nurse carefully observed the sick, and at any sudden change for the worse, he promptly notified the steward. When patients required special watching or care, other patients were drafted for temporary duty.

The privates not directly employed as cooks or nurses began their duties at reveille. They kept the administrative parts of the hospital, the grounds, and the outbuildings in order; took care of the cows and the garden; and generally discharged the several duties to which they were assigned. As they usually were intelligent men of good habits, all this work was done regularly and uniformly with little urging. Nevertheless, the stewards exercised a general supervision, and were held responsible for any lapses in neatness or discipline.

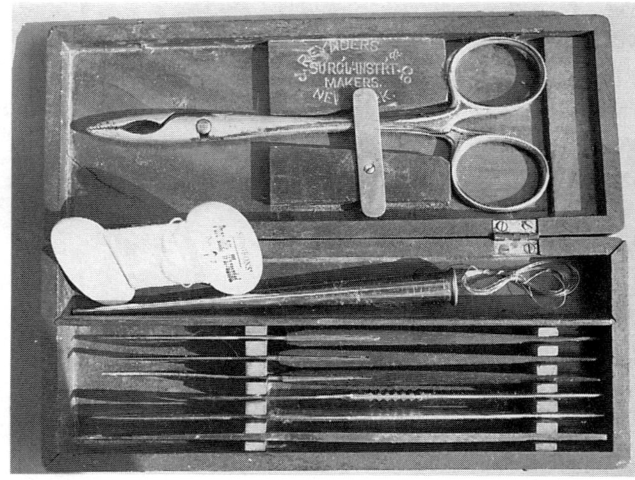

Small pocket amputation kit, containing scalpels and suture material, c. 1868–1870. (Photo courtesy of the Carl Rumps collection.)

At about nine o'clock every morning, a medical officer inspected the sleeping rooms of the hospital corps, just as a company officer inspected the company barracks. He visited the wards and examined the patients at least twice daily, and at least once a week carefully inspected the whole hospital and every man in it. To be ready for these inspections required constant and intelligent work by the men of the corps.

The stewards were directly occupied with dispensing, with acting as dressers for the graver cases, with drawing and distributing the rations and supervising the cooking, with attending to the large amount of detailed clerical work, and with constantly overseeing the more seriously sick or injured patients following the medical officer's instructions.

Arrow Wounds

Many experienced military surgeons who had seen their share of Indian arrow wounds between 1866 and 1889 remarked upon the rapidity with which the American Indians discharged their arrows during a skirmish with the troops. They also stated that it was exceptional to see a single wound, because if one arrow found its mark, it would be immediately followed by two or three others.

Early methods of removing arrows from wounds involved the use of the famous "duck-bill forceps." With every conceivable modification, this instrument continued being used from the Dark Ages up through the American Indian wars. In extracting arrows, it was recommended that the entrance wound be dilated, the barb of the arrowhead crushed by the strong pliers, or protected between the grooves of a split reed, and thus withdrawn without further laceration of the soft parts.

Most arrows were twenty-four to twenty-nine inches in length. The feathers were chiefly taken from the eagle or wild turkey. The war arrowhead is easily distinguishable from the hunting arrowpoint. If the arrow could be pulled back and out of the wounded man, it was a hunting arrow. War arrowheads were barbed, and either had to be cut out or pushed on through the body. The war arrowpoint was attached to the shaft at a horizontal plane against the vertical notch of the other end of the shaft because the ribs of a human being are horizontal. The arrowhead of the hunting arrow was vertical, in line with the notch cut in the other end of the shaft for the string, as animals' ribs are vertical. By placing the end feathers at certain angles that controlled the arrow in flight, hardly any rotary turn occurred, and by the time the arrow hit its mark the tip found its position smartly between the ribs of man or animal. Eight out of ten were successful hits. It must have taken hundreds of years for the Indian to calculate this system.

Time was of the essence in removing an arrow from the wound. Body heat would begin to soften the arrow glue and sinew that held the arrowhead to the shaft. If the shaft remained in the body for

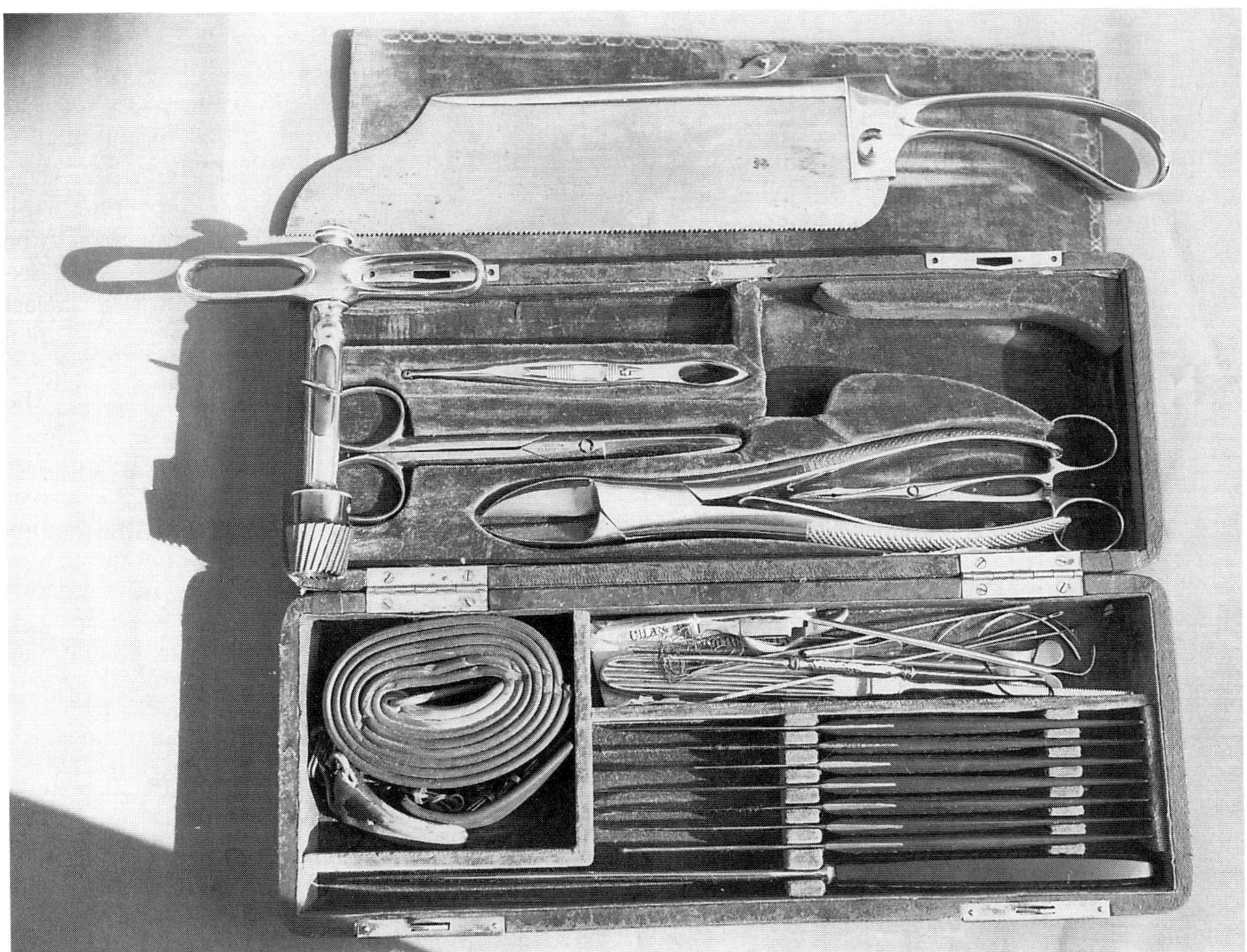

Amputation kit, c. 1860–1870. Top: amputation saw. Left: skull drill. (Photo courtesy of the Carl Rumps collection.)

more than half an hour, it would be certain that on extracting it, the arrowhead would be left in the wound.

The more arrow wounds that occurred, the more the surgeons experimented, either in the field or on the operating table. New techniques were devised, along with several ingenious instruments for removing barbed arrowheads when they were buried in soft tissue or large cavities, or when impacted in bone. When removing the point by means of a snare (Fig. A), the arrow shaft was used as a guide for the wire, and the great danger of detaching the head from the shaft was avoided.

Fig. A. Wire loop for extracting arrowheads embedded in soft parts.

Where arrowheads were lodged in bone and could not be detached by slight traction aided by a gentle rocking motion of the shaft, the surgeon was advised to procure a piece of well-annealed iron wire, two-and-a-half feet in length, to pass the ends through the holes in a long suture-wire twister, and to secure them to its handle (Fig. B),

Fig. B. Twelve-inch wire twister recommended by surgeons.

leaving a loop at the distal extremity (Fig. C). The loop passed over the feathered end of the shaft was to be thrust down to the other extremity and made to snare the arrowhead, and, the wire being tightened, the foreign body and instrument were to be withdrawn together.

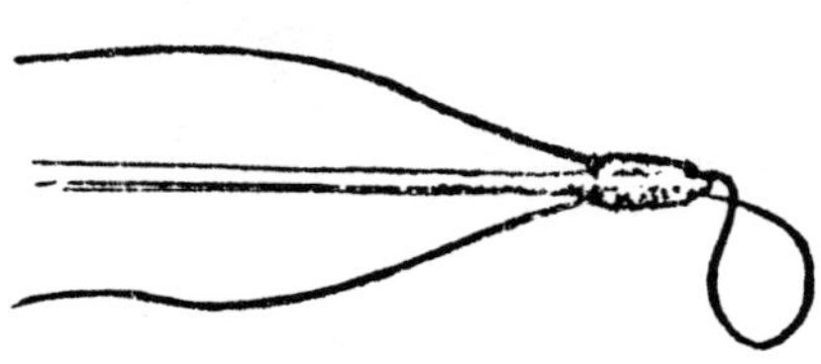

Fig. C. Wire loop twisted once on itself for snaring impacted arrowheads.

More than seven out of every ten with an arrow wound would die due to shock, blood poisoning, a severed artery, or infection caused by one of the many arrowpoints painted with snake venom or the decayed livers of animals. All took their toll. The great fatality percentage of arrow wounds to the vulnerable abdomen was well known—and so well known to the Indians that they always aimed directly at the umbilicus. Thus, the Mexicans, who were more knowledgeable about fighting Indians, often protected their abdomens with many folds of a blanket.

Since many Apache braves picked up the new Army metallic weapons in battle, the need for bow and arrows was thought to have decreased. However, even as late as 1885, hostile Apaches were found in possession of both modern arms and bow and arrows, which were used as a second weapon or standby.

The following are just a few serious cases of arrow wounds taken from a "Report of Surgical Cases Treated in the Army of the United States from 1865 to 1871." The complications were carefully noted in each case and recorded by the surgeon of the post. The cases come from many different areas on the Western frontier.

CCCCLII.—Report of Death from Multiple Wounds, most of which were from Arrows. By W. H. Smith, M.D., Acting Assistant Surgeon.

Private Robert Nix, Co. G, 11th Infantry, was wounded near Camp Lincoln, Arizona Territory, in October, 1868. He received a gunshot flesh-wound in the upper portion of left arm; a slight cut from an arrow in the left ear; two flesh-wounds from arrows, from one of which the haemorrhage was profuse; two arrow wounds in the right knee, the synovial membrane having been penetrated, but no bones broken; one gunshot wound in the right elbow, but not through the joint; and another through the metacarpal bone of the third finger of the right hand. During the eight hours following, while being conveyed to camp, he became very weak from loss of blood, and riding part of the time on a horse with a comrade, and the remainder in a Government team. He suddenly died the next morning. Decided symptoms of fatty degeneration, with dilatation and hypertrophy of the heart, had been previously observed.

CCCCLIII.—Note of a Case of Multiple Arrow Wounds. By R. B. Hitz, M.D., Acting Assistant Surgeon.

Private Constand Queswelle, Co. E, 13th Infantry, aged 26 years, received May 24, 1868, while on herding duty about half a mile from Camp Reeve, Montana Territory, seven arrow wounds. One arrow entered the cavity, through the eighth dorsal vertebra, and one through the ninth; three passed through the forearm, one between the fifth and sixth ribs on the right side, and one through the palmer surface of the right hand. Death was apparently instantaneous.

CCCCLIV.—Report of a Case of Death from Arrow Wounds. By G. L. Porter, Assistant Surgeon, U.S.A.

Nate Crabtree, a citizen, aged 38 years, while looking for his cattle, April 24, 1868, was shot by Indians, receiving nine arrow wounds; one in the post gluteal region, one in the left lung, one in the abdomen, one penetrating the humerus, one in the hand, one in the testicle, one in the back of the left of the dorsal vertebra, one in the bladder, and a glance shot five inches long below the ninth rib. He was admitted to the post hospital at Camp Cooke, Montana Territory. Some of the arrows had been removed by his friends, and five, including the one in the gluteal region, which had penetrated ten and a half inches, were taken out at the post. The man died a few hours after admission to hospital.

CCCCLVI.—Report of a Case in which the Patient received Five Arrow Wounds, and was Scalped. By S. M. Horton, Assistant Surgeon, U.S.A.

Private Patrick D. Smith, of Co. 11, 18th Infantry, was attacked about six miles from Fort Philip Kearney, Dakota Territory, on the evening of September 26, 1866, by three Indians, who inflicted five arrow wounds, and removed part of his scalp. On the next morning he was seen by two physicians. Two of the arrows still remained in his body—one in the right side below the region of the kidney; the other had pierced the cartilage at the junction of the first rib with the sternum, inflicting a wound three inches in depth. The arrows were extracted, the wound dressed, and the patient supported until 10 o'clock the next morning, September 28th, when he expired. At the autopsy it was found that the wound in his chest had been the cause of death. The arrow had cut the edge of the right lung, and had inflicted a slight wound, one-eighth of an inch in length, in the descending vena cava. The right lung and surrounding tissues were considerably infiltrated with blood, and a large amount of coagulum was found in the cavity of the thorax.

CCCCLVII.—Account of a Case of Fatal Wounds from Arrows. By C. S. DeGraw, Assistant Surgeon, U.S.A.

Private James Spillman, Troop B, 7th Cavalry, aged 22 years, was wounded on the morning of June 12, 1867, about a mile from Fort Dodge, Kansas, by a party of Kiowa Indians, who made a dash upon the herd of horses he was guarding, and inflicted three arrow wounds: the first in the right shoulder; the second in the right side, the arrow glancing from a rib, and making a wound similar to a stitch about three inches in length; and the third through the right lumbar region, penetrating the abdominal cavity to a depth of about eight inches or more. The arrow causing the wound in the side was removed by cutting the arrow in two, and then drawing out the parts. The arrow in the lumbar region was removed with great difficulty. The wound being enlarged, two fingers were inserted on either side of the shaft until the base of the iron head was reached, the fingers thus inserted serving as a guide and as a protection to the parts, when, traction being made, the arrow was withdrawn. This latter wound proved mortal, the man dying the next day about 3 o'clock, P.M. His true name was Wise, of Washington. No post-mortem; the two arrows removed were contributed to the Army Medical Museum, and are numbered 5651 in the Surgical Section.

CCCLX.—Memorandum Relative to the Skull of a Mexican Killed by an Arrow. By W. M. Notson, Assistant Surgeon, U.S.A.

An unknown Mexican was killed by an arrow wound in an Indian fight, which occurred seventy-five miles northwest of Fort Concho, Texas, on February 22, 1868. The arrow perforated the frontal. When I opened the skull, I found an incision extending clear across the opposite hemisphere, touching the dura mater just above the tentorium. The dura mater was stained, but I could find no mark on the skull. When I made the post mortem I found the arrowhead in the brain. When the Mexican was hit he seized the arrow shaft with both hands and pulled it out, then dropped and of course remained unconscious until he died, in about six hours. The specimen was forwarded to the Army Medical Museum . . . The arrowhead has been removed from the cavity of the skull and fastened at the point of entrance. Apart from the lesion, the skull is a highly interesting specimen.

CCCCLXI.—Memorandum of an Arrow Wound of the Face. By P. Middleton, Assistant Surgeon, U.S.A.

Private William Drum, Co. G, 14th Infantry, aged 20 years, was wounded in a fight with Apache Indians on November 11, 1867. One arrow entered over the malar bone of the left side of the face, passed along the lower border of the orbit to within half an inch of the nose. Another arrow entered through the tendon of the latissiumus dorsi muscle on the right side, and passed directly backward toward the spine under the deep muscles, penetrating two and a half inches. He was admitted to the post hospital at Fort Whipple, Arizona Territory, on the following day. On November 19th, I cut down upon the arrowhead in the side, and removed it. The parts healed by the first intention, and on December 3, 1867, the patient was returned to duty.

CCCCLXIII.—Report of an Arrow Wound of the Neck. By B. Semig, Acting Assistant Surgeon.

Private Thomas Dutton, Co. K, 32d Infantry, aged 23 years, was wounded in an attack by Apache Indians upon a wagon train in the lower Senorita Valley, Arizona Territory, on May 8, 1869, by an arrow which caused a flesh wound of the posterior portion of the neck. He was admitted on the next day to the post hospital at Camp Crittenden, Arizona Territory. He recovered, and was returned to duty May 17, 1869.

CCCCLXV.—Note of an Arrow Wound of the Chest. By F. Damour, M.D., Acting Assistant Surgeon.

Private George Duggan, Troop K, 8th Cavalry, was wounded near Camp Willow Grove, Arizona Territory, November 8, 1867, by an arrow, which penetrated the posterior side of the right chest. He died December 17, 1867. At the autopsy, the arrow was found to have penetrated the chest a little above the diaphragm, with which the head of the arrow was lying in contact. There was also an abscess containing much purulent matter.

Arrow Wound of the Abdomen—Three instances of penetrating wounds of the abdomen by arrows have been recorded among the cases of multiple wounds in an earlier portion of this section. Special reports were made of six other cases of this class. Of the nine cases seven were fatal, and in the two cases of recovery, there is room for doubt whether the arrowhead penetrated the peritonaeal sac.

CCCCLXXI.—Report of an Arrow Wound of the Abdomen. By H. S. Kilbourne, M.D., Acting Assistant Surgeon.

Private Samuel Brown, Troop F, 10th Cavalry, was wounded near Canadian River, Texas, December 2, 1868, by an arrow, which entered the abdomen in the left hypochondriae region, making a punctured wound three-quarters of an inch in length, through which about eighteen inches of the small intestine protruded. The intestine was cut in four places. The wounds in the intestine were closed by suture, and the protruding portion of the gut returned through the wound, which was enlarged for that purpose. When found, the man had lain out all night, and was in a state of collapse. He was carried along in an ambulance, but died on the second day, not having rallied from the shock of the injury.

CCCCLXXV.—Report of an Arrow Wound of the Back and Kidney. By Calvin DeWitt, Assistant Surgeon, U.S.A.

Private Conrad Tragesor, Troop I, 8th Cavalry, was wounded in an engagement with Apache Indians, at Sunflower Valley, Arizona Territory, March 9, 1870, by an arrow which entered the left side, about four inches from the spine, and above the crest of the ileum, from below upward. The kidney evidently was injured, as the patient passed bloody urine in small quantities, and frequently. His face was pale, anxious, and expressive of great pain; pulse weak. He was conveyed in an ambulance to Camp McDowell, Arizona Territory, a distance of thirty miles, over a rough, stony, and hilly road. He died the next day. At the autopsy, it was found that the arrow had transfixed the kidney, entering it on the external border, at the juncture of middle and lower thirds emerging from the posterior surface near the internal border, a few lines below the pelvis. A large irregular piece, about one inch long, and half an inch thick, was torn from the posterior border of the kidney at the place of entrance, evidently by the traction made in extracting the arrow, leaving the head behind. The kidney was otherwise normal; the abdomen was filled with blood.

CCCCLXXXIV.—Memorandum Relative to an Arrow Wound of the Testis. By A. H. Smith, Assistant Surgeon, U.S.A.

While serving at Fort Bliss, Texas, in 1866, I had occasion to attend a Mexican herdsman, who had received a wound in the testis from an arrow shot by an Apache Indian. The hoop-iron arrowhead had lodged in the testicle, and the external wound had nearly healed over at the time I saw him, about three months after the reception of the wound. It was not difficult, however, to detect the position of the foreign body and to extract it. Upon its removal the wound cicatrized finely. The specimen was transmitted to the Army Medical Museum.

12

CHANGING WEAPONRY SYSTEMS

Immediately after the Civil War, the U.S. Army continued to use the basic infantry and cavalry arms that had been employed during the conflict.

The 1861–1864 Springfield .58-caliber muzzle-loading musket was the infantry shoulder arm. It used a .58-caliber, hollow-based, picket-type bullet, contained in a paper cartridge with sixty grains of 2Fg black powder. The cartridge was loaded by exposing the powder after the paper was torn with the teeth, and then ramming the whole cartridge down the forty-inch barrel with the ramrod contained in the stock. A musket-sized

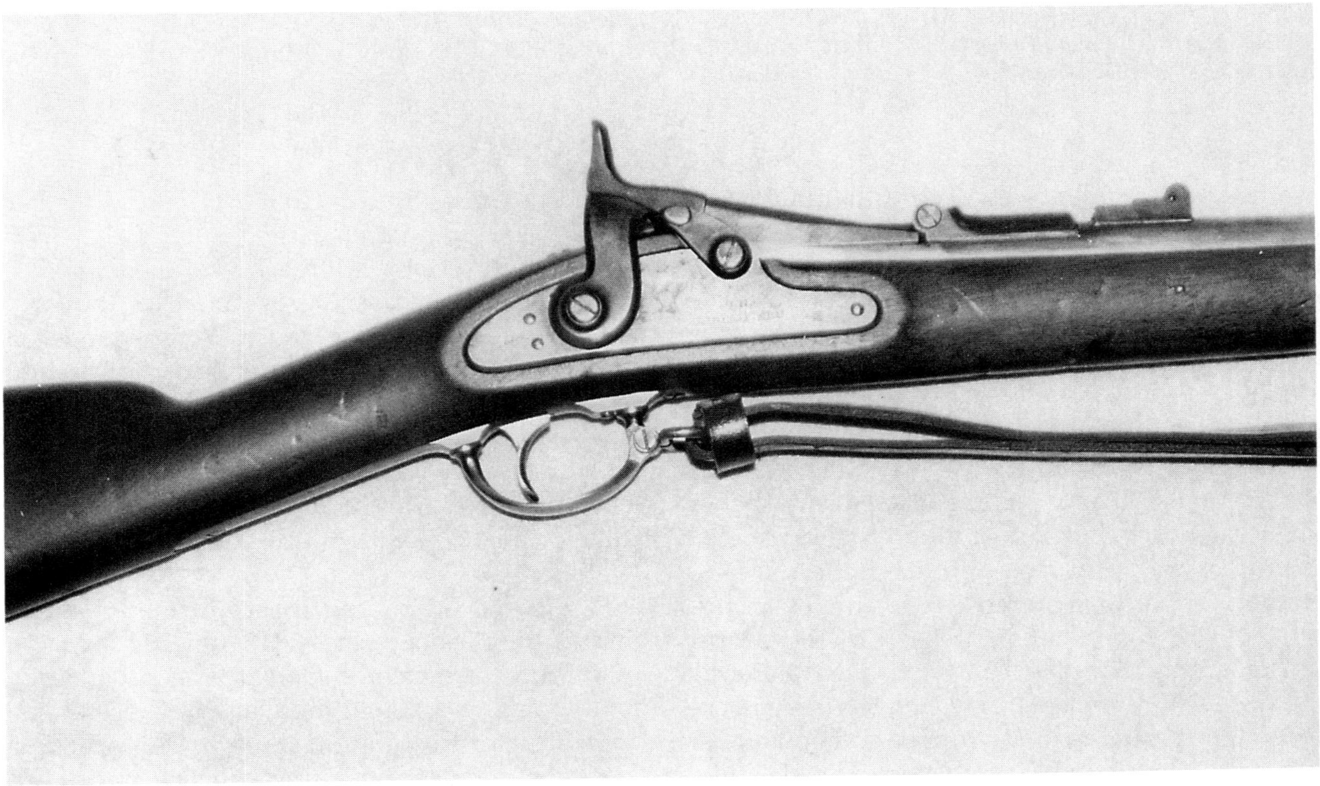

This is an 1866 Springfield Trapdoor rifle, .50/70 caliber—the second Allin conversion from the 1864 .58 caliber Springfield musket, made by sleeving the barrel to .50 caliber and applying the breech-loading mechanism to cut off the rear end of the barrel. It has the original forty-inch Civil War barrel length and three barrel bands. (Photo courtesy of Alan Feldstein.)

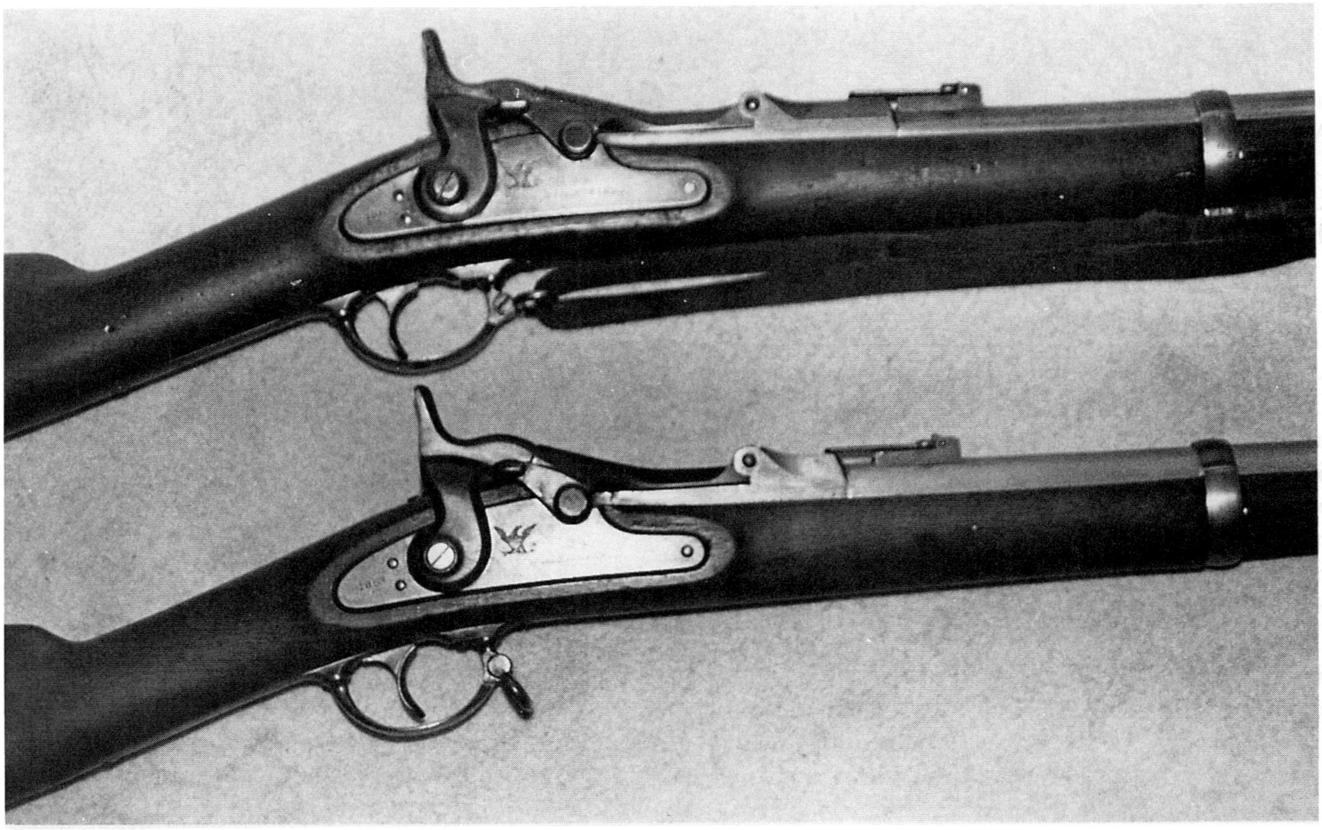

Top: the 1868 Trapdoor Springfield rifle, .50/70 caliber, erroneously called the "third Allin conversion" by collectors. Note the length of the front of the receiver, and its relation to the rear-sight clamping lower barrel band. Bottom: the 1870 Trapdoor Springfield rifle, .50/70 caliber, erroneously called the "fourth Allin conversion" by collectors. Note the shorter receiver, solid barrel band, and rear sight. Both rifles finished in "National Armory Bright," and issued interchangeably. The 1870 model is the immediate predecessor of the 1873 .45/70 Springfield. (Photo courtesy of Alan Feldstein.)

percussion cap was then placed on the nipple beneath the hammer. When the hammer was brought to full cock, the musket was ready to fire. This was a slow process, indeed, when one considers that the breech-loading shoulder arms were almost exclusively used by the Civil War U.S. cavalry.

Two breech-loading cavalry carbines were manufactured and issued in larger quantities than other weapons during the Civil War. These were the .52-caliber Sharps carbine that used a paper or linen cartridge similar to the .58-caliber musket cartridge, and also used an outside primed percussion cap, or the Lawrence repeating pellet priming device, found to be unreliable by the troops.

The second cavalry carbine issued in large quantities was the legendary Spencer seven-shot repeating carbine, with its copper, self-contained, rim-fired cartridge that was loaded through a tube in the butt-stock of the weapon. The Spencer carbine was way ahead of its time; it was faster firing and more rugged in service than any other weapon. These two cavalry arms continued to be issued during the post–Civil War period for use against hostile Indian tribes.

The huge success of breech-loading arms during the Civil War posed a dilemma for the Ordnance Department. The general temperament of Congress after the war (as after every war fought by the United States) was of a mind to reduce the war budget below necessary limits for the needs of the time. So the Ordnance Department started to look for ways to convert large quantities of the .58-caliber muzzle-loading muskets into breech loaders.

Erskine S. Allin, the master armorer at the Springfield Armory since 1847, devised a way of modifying the muzzle loaders to breech loaders by milling out a section at the rear of the barrel and applying a forward-hinging breech block over this. The cartridge used was a .58-caliber rim-fire cartridge, not unlike the Spencer cartridge.

A board of Ordnance officers, probably biased in their decision by a need for economy, chose this design over others, and in late 1865, ordered 5,000 Model 1861 Springfield muskets to be remanufactured by the Allin process. The muskets were completed in 1866, and issued to the troops for field trials. This weapon is listed in the Springfield Armory records as the Model 1865 Breech-Loading Rifle. To present-day collectors, it is known as the First Allin Conversion and also as the first Springfield "Trapdoor" rifle.

Whatever the name, the design had severe problems. Allin was called back to the drawing board in 1866 to modify the design. His second effort, known as the Model of 1866 or the Second Allin Conversion, met with success in the hands of the troops. This modification used the Model 1864 Springfield musket, which was reduced to .50 caliber by sleeving the barrel with a .50-caliber rifled tube. The cartridge was a .50-caliber, inside-primed, center-fire cartridge, with a 450-grain lead bullet backed by 70 grains of 2Fg black powder, and known as a .50/70 or .50 U.S. cartridge. Both the 1865 and 1866 models maintained the original forty-inch barrel length. The 1866 Springfield was the factor in the successful defense by the Army at the Wagon Box and Hayfield battles against Red Cloud's Sioux in 1867.

From a distance, the Model 1866 looked like the Model 1864, from which it was derived, and which was previously used by the troops. The Indians knew that their best tactics against infantry armed with muzzle loaders was to draw the soldiers' fire and then leap up and close in while the troops reloaded the slow-to-load muzzle loaders. During the Wagon Box fight, the Cheyenne were surprised by a second withering volley from the 1866 breech loaders when they used their customary tactics. The Cheyenne mounted assault after assault, moving in close to take advantage of reloading time, and were met with rapid volley after rapid volley. After sustaining severe losses, they finally retreated, dejected, from the field of battle.

The success of the breech loader was assured. However, the Model of 1866 was unwieldy for waging war against hostile Indians, because of its excessively long barrel. Again, Allin modified his design. The new Model 1868 used the lock of the

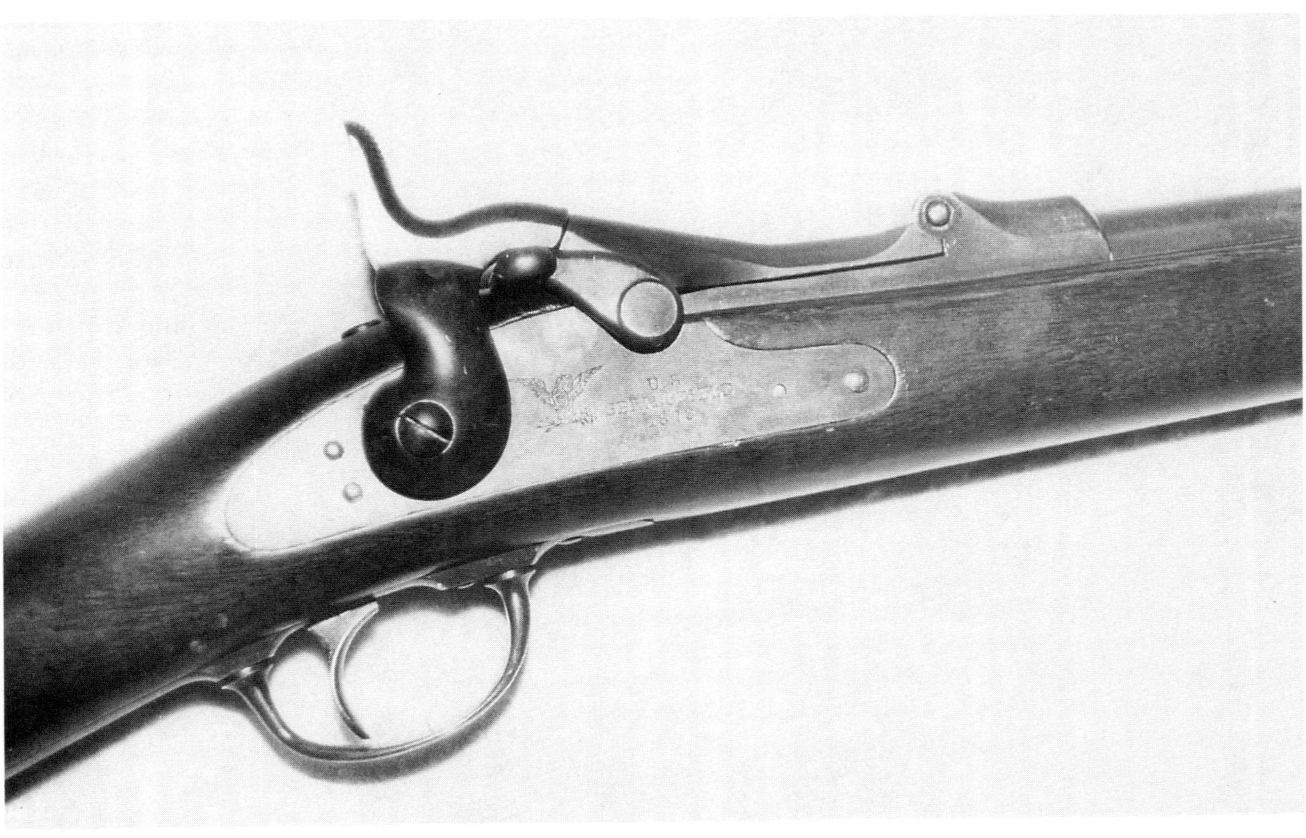

Early 1873 Springfield Trapdoor carbine, .45/55-405 caliber with closed breechblock. (Photo courtesy of Alan Feldstein.)

Civil War musket with a new hammer. The barrel was reduced to 32⅝ inches and threaded to a new, stronger receiver, and the .50/70 cartridge was retained. The 1870 Springfield was almost identical; only the receiver was slightly shorter. There were other minor differences apparent only to the trained eye. Both models were issued interchangeably. There were carbine versions of both models of the 1868 and 1870 rifles that were manufactured by the Springfield Armory, but only four Model 1868 carbines and 361 Model 1870 carbines were manufactured. These were considered experimental and were unlikely to have been used in battling the hostile Indians.

The percussion Sharps carbine was altered during the late 1860s and early 1870s to use the .50/70 cartridge that had been used in the Model 1866 Springfield rifle. Some of these carbines used the original .52-caliber barrel, while others had their barrels lined with .50-caliber, three-groove liners. These Sharps carbines, along with the .52-caliber Spencer Civil War carbines altered to .50 caliber, and the .50-caliber '65 and '67 Spencers were the main cavalry shoulder arms used until the Model 1873 Springfield "Trapdoor" carbine was issued in 1874.

On September 3, 1872, a board of Army officers, under Brigadier-General A. H. Terry, met to test and adopt a new shoulder arm for the infantry and cavalry. This new shoulder arm needed longer range and improved impact power over the .50/70 caliber weapons then in use. The board selected a slightly modified 1870 Trapdoor rifle with bore reduced to .45 caliber, out of the more than 100 rifles of both American and European design submitted. No one testing the designs alluded to the Army's experience with repeating arms.

On May 28, 1873, the Springfield Armory began to retool in order to manufacture the new rifle and a half-stock carbine version with a short 22-inch barrel. By December 31, 1873, the armory had finished 1,940 of the new carbines and two rifles. It is unlikely that any of these arms reached the troops before the first quarter of 1874.

The real innovation was the .45-caliber cartridge employed by the new rifle. It was copper and cen-

Top: box of .45/55 carbine ammunition for the Springfield Trapdoor, Model 1873. Bottom: box of cartridges for the .45 caliber Colt, 7½ inch barrel. (Photo courtesy of the Emmet O. Hussar collection.)

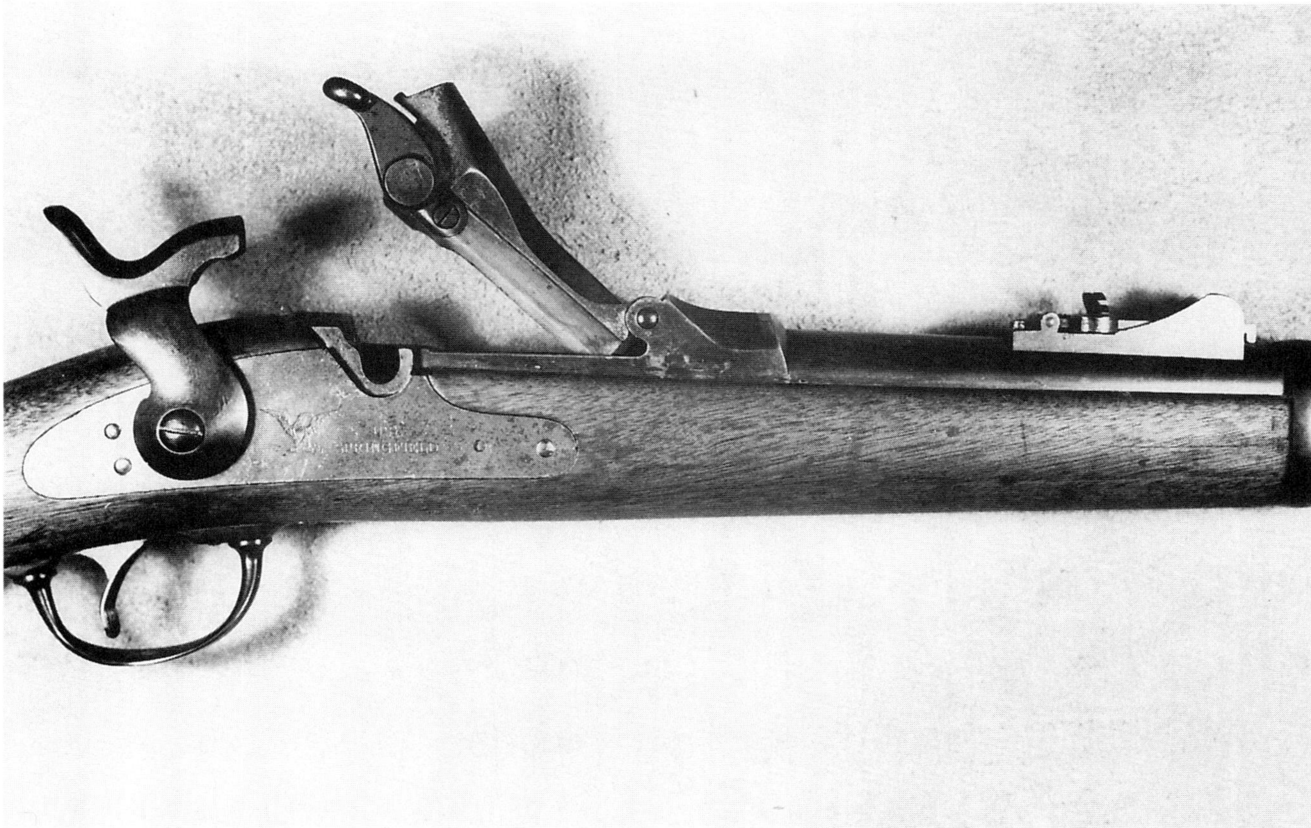

The 1873 Trapdoor Springfield carbine, .45/70 caliber, with modifications of 1879. Note the rear sight. The late grooved trigger was applied after 1883. (Photo courtesy of Alan Feldstein.)

ter fired, and an inside-primed cartridge case employed a 405-grain lead bullet backed by 70 grains of 2Fg black powder. The cartridge was all that could be expected from a ballistic standpoint, but the cartridge case material caused some problems. During the nineteen years that the cartridge was used, it underwent constant modification. The copper case was tin plated to prevent corrosion and then changed to brass. Priming was changed from inside center fire to outside center fire to make it reloadable if corrosion was prevented by removing the priming mixture and black powder immediately after firing.

The desire for improved shocking power led to increasing the bullet weight to 500 grains; then it was taken back to 405 grains to reduce the punishing recoil. The carbine round had carried 55 grains of 2Fg black powder; the recoil generated by 70 grains, when used in the light carbine, could be enjoyed only by a masochist. A common practical joke was to plant an infantry cartridge among the carbine cartridges used by fellow troopers during target practice. The expression on the face of the victim due to the pain felt upon discharge of the infantry cartridge usually brought amusement to the jokester. The official designation of the cavalry cartridge was .45/55/405.

The 1873 rifle and carbine both underwent many modifications and improvements during their service life. Complaints about the carbine's performance during the Custer debacle triggered the addition of a trap in the butt plate to hold a three-piece cleaning rod and a headless shell extractor to clear cartridges that had their heads torn off by the strong action of the extractor. (Development of the brass cartridge solved this problem later.) The weak wrist of the stock was strengthened by shortening it, thereby thickening it at its weakest point. The carbine with these two modifications was designated the Model of 1877, although stamping on the breechblock continued to read Model of 1873. The stock wrist modification was also applied to the infantry rifle. Other modifications continued to the officially designated Model 1877 carbine and 1873 rifle until 1886, when both arms were redesignated Model 1884, and the breechblock stampings

Captured Apache warriors posing before the camera, displaying their ancient bows and arrows, as well as a .50/70 Springfield Infantry rifle and a spear.

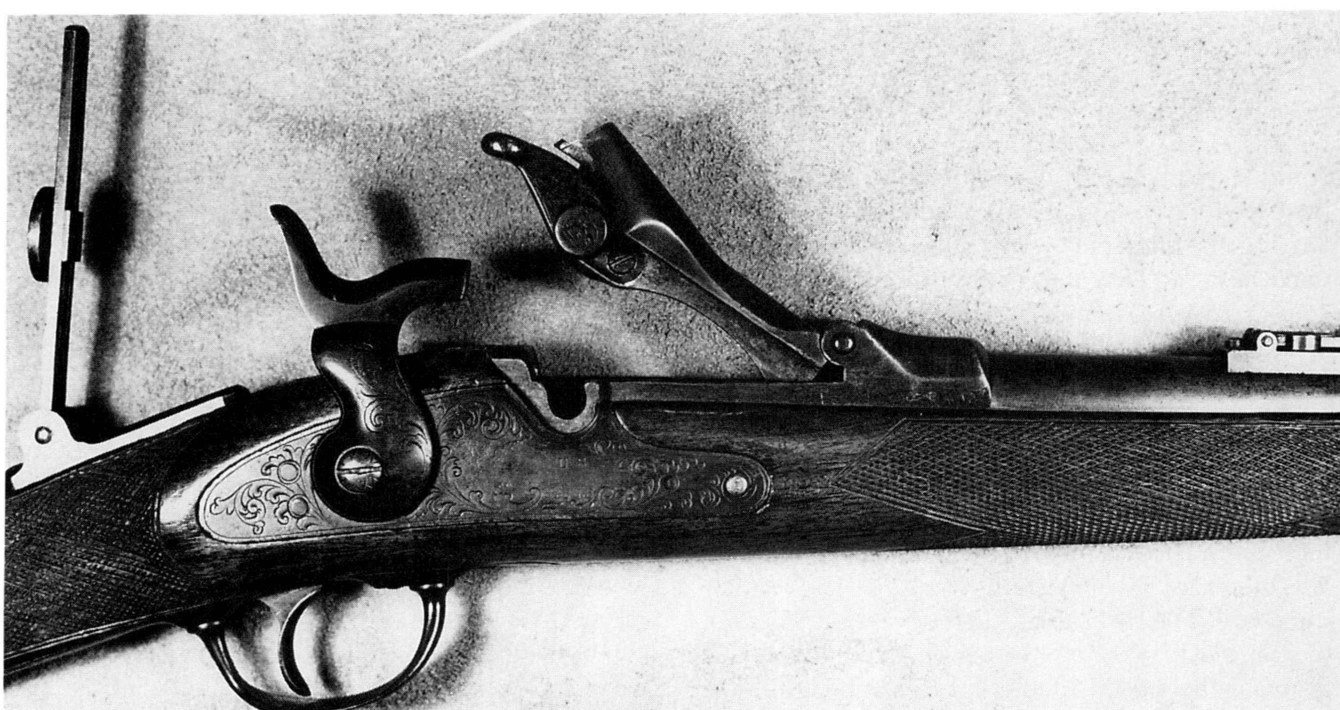

This is an officer's model Springfield, .45/70 caliber, with the checkering on the stock and the scroll engraving on the lockplate and hammer. The open breechblock shows the high arch of early models. The tang peep sight is probably an early replacement by the original owner for longer range. (Photo courtesy of Alan Feldstein.)

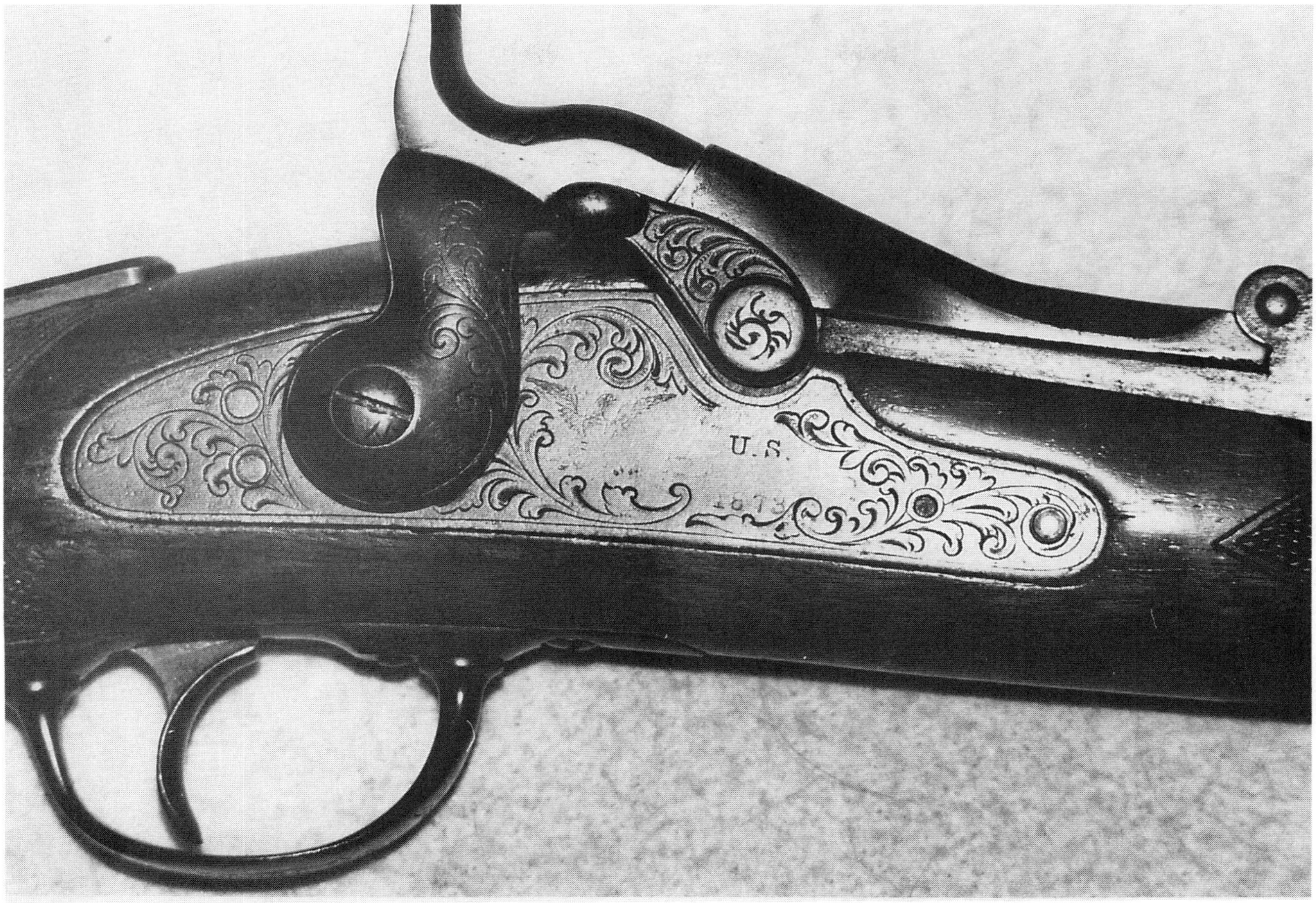

An 1875 officer's model .45/70 rifle, manufactured very early in the production of 477 total. This rifle is half-stocked, with an engraved German silver stock tip. It has a single-set trigger, tang peep sight in addition to service sight on the barrel, checkered stock at wrist and front end, and profuse scroll engraving on the metal. It also has a folding globe front sight and a brass-tipped hickory cleaning rod in the stock. Later models had a detachable checkered wood pistol grip as well. (Photo courtesy of Alan Feldstein.)

were changed. After this, the official designation of the carbine and rifle was Model of 1884 to the end of the Trapdoor production, in spite of unofficial collectors' designations such as Model of 1879 or 1890, until the advent of the 1888 Ramrod Bayonet Model. The carbine remained the Model of 1884.

All of the U.S. Army weapons of the Civil War and post-war era were occasionally acquired by the Indians during the period of Apache warfare through theft, capture, and barter. The Indians also acquired civilian weapons by murdering their owners, stealing, barter, and trade. The muzzle loaders, plains rifles, Henry and Winchester repeaters, and Sharps hunting rifles all appeared in Indian hands, which extended the period of warfare. It's interesting to note that the Indians, already used to the percussion rifles, didn't know how to load the cartridge weapons. They thought the cartridge was the ball, and tried ramming it home at the muzzle. Needless to say, the method didn't work. A photo of Geronimo's band, taken during a truce on March 27, 1886, shows one warrior clutching a Model 1873 Winchester rifle, and other warriors with Trapdoor carbines. In another photo, Geronimo is shown with a Trapdoor rifle with a shortened stock and barrel. Yet another photo of Captain Crawford's Apache scouts shows all of them armed with the Model 1873 Springfield Trapdoor rifles. However, the bow and arrow were always within reach of the Apache warrior, right up to their final days of battle. This century-old weapon needed no alterations, and was just as deadly and effective.

Cartridge-loading rifles called for cartridges—lots of them—and something had to be devised to carry them in. Two early cartridge boxes were distributed to the infantrymen for use with the

Top: the 1884 Springfield Trapdoor rifle, .45/70 caliber. Bottom: the 1889 Springfield Trapdoor rifle, .45/70 caliber. This rifle uses the ramrod bayonet. Note the detachable metal pistol grip used on late rifles and carbines and variations between trigger guards. Both rifles employ late-model Buffington rear sight, adjustable for windage and elevation. (Photo courtesy of Alan Feldstein.)

Trapdoor Springfields. First, the pattern 1872 Hagner Type 1, made of leather and holding twenty-four cartridges, with a tool in a side compartment. Then the Hagner Type 2, which was smaller but still held twenty-four cartridges. Both boxes were supported with a brace yoke attached to the belt. The two boxes provided forty-eight rounds of ammunition. When a soldier was on garrison duty or drilling, he wore a single box, supported by the waist belt and placed either in front or back. Inside the box, cartridges were held by shellacked loops of cloth, sewn in three rows of eight loops each.

Civil War carbine socket. Almost any of the carbines carried by the cavalry would fit this socket, which was used up until 1886. (Photo courtesy of the Alan Feldstein collection.)

But the Army continued to be plagued by the knowledge of the soldier lugging around lots of cartridges with the necessity of keeping them properly cleaned so that they would not stick in the gun barrel and blow him to kingdom come. Many methods of transporting the little agents of death and destruction were designed, tried, and dropped. Most of these designs were made in the arsenals. One, the Dwyer pouch, was shaped like a half-moon and carried forty cartridges in its wool lining. It, and several modifications, were well accepted by a number of troops and then later discarded.

Before the adoption of General Anson Mills's

looped webbed belt in 1878, the waist of every soldier was badly cluttered! Each trooper carried sliding ammunition boxes on black belts, along with pistol and holster, sabre straps, and a rectangular buckle. Foot soldiers carried their cartridge boxes sliding on the waist belt, as well as a bayonet and scabbard, and later a Model 1880 hunting knife. With all of this paraphernalia hung about the waist, it was hard for a soldier to bend, reach for the instrument of destruction or protection he wanted, and generally make headway marching.

The cartridge boxes had other disadvantages besides the problem of space. When the soldier was riding at a run or full gallop, the cartridges flopped around and often spilled out onto the ground, leaving the hapless fighting man at the mercy of his mount's speed or his enemy's rifle sights.

The last of the mountain men showed up at a number of the frontier posts sporting a looped cartridge belt of their own design as early as 1866. The all-weather properties of this arrangement were questioned by some, but the design was swiftly picked up by the soldiers, who had them duplicated by the company saddlers. The soldiers called them "fair weather Christian belts." Cartridges were slipped into a number of loops on a leather belt, the loops being in single or double rows.

Enamored of the new belts, the soldiers began to throw away their cartridge boxes. But the belt design had its problems, as some soldiers soon discovered. Tannic acid used in curing the leather reacted with the bullet lubricant, and the combination formed a tacky green verdigris on the brass or copper casings of the shell. The coating would stick to every particle that touched it, so that dirt, dust, sand, woolen fibres from the uniforms, and anything else that got in the way, would adhere. The big sticky cartridges stuck in the belt loops, the gun barrels, and the craw of the soldier who

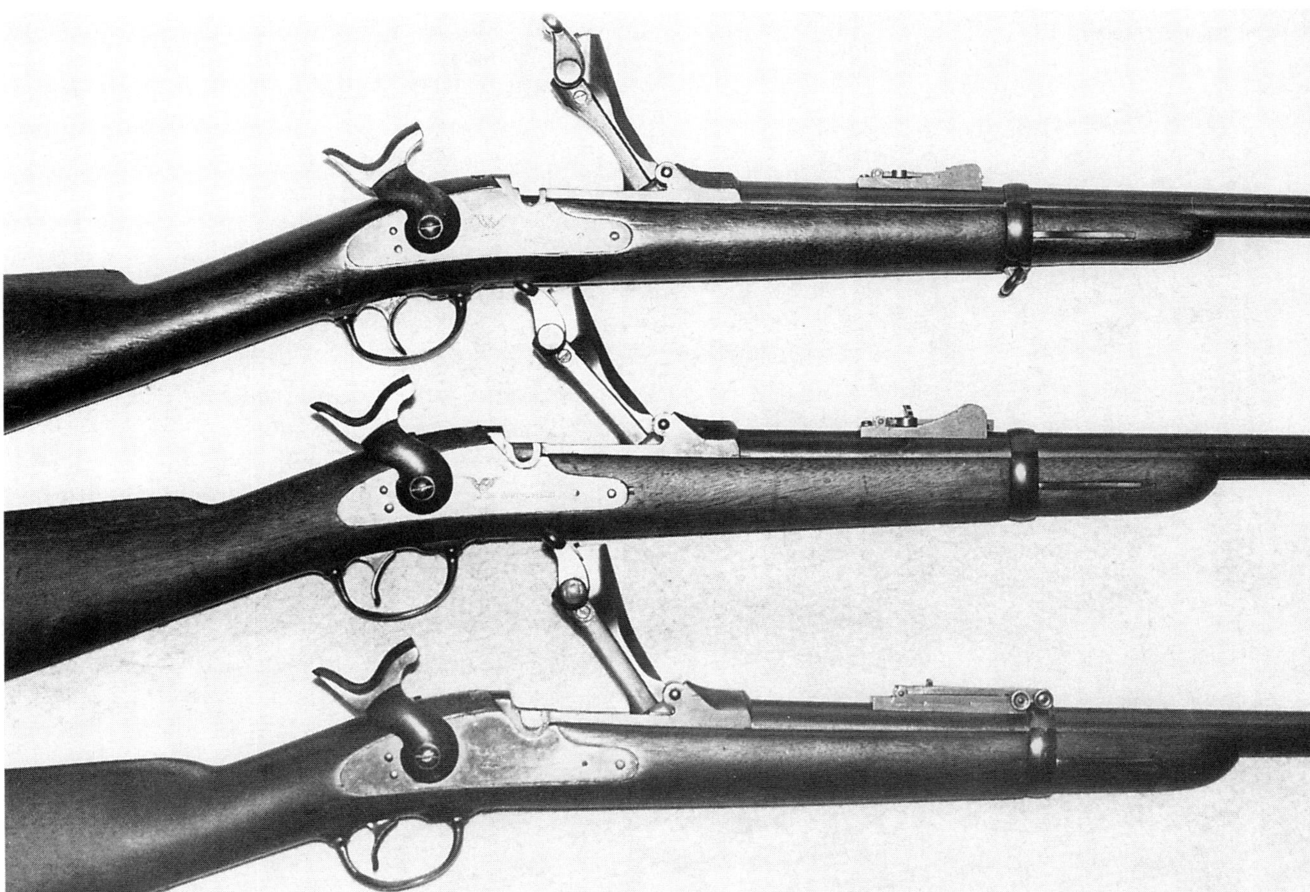

Three variations of the .45/70 Trapdoor carbine. Top: early 1873 model, with high arch under breechblock, long-wrist stock, early 1873 sight, and stacking swivel on barrel band. Middle: 1879 modified model, filled in under breechblock, with short-wrist stock and 1878 buck-horn rear sight. Bottom: 1884 carbine with all 1879 modifications and Buffington rear sight; also, the top of the barrel band is notched to accept the overhang of the rear sight. (Photo courtesy of Alan Feldstein.)

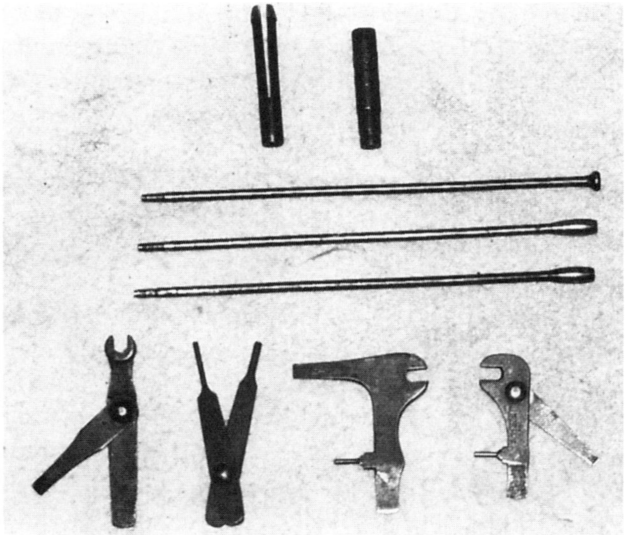

All these tools were manufactured for the Springfield. Top, left to right: Model 1877 headless shell extractor, and Model 1882 shell extractor. Middle three pieces: cleaning rod after 1877 for Springfield Trapdoor carbine. Bottom: disassembly tools, from left to right: mainspring clamp (1870 model) for Springfield Trapdoor, band-spring punch and tumbler punch (1866), combination tool (1874), improved combination tool (1879). (Photo courtesy of the Alan Feldstein collection.)

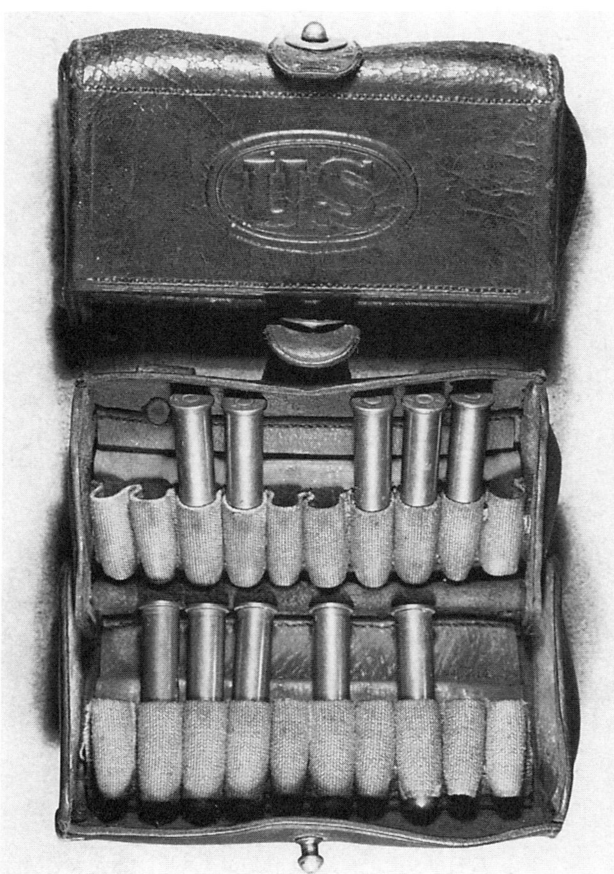

McKeever cartridge box, Model 1876. It held twenty rounds of .45/70 cartridges. A later model had a swell on the side for a gun tool.

had abandoned his regulation cartridge box for the new design. Company commanders were not overjoyed with the action, either.

But the looped belt would have its day. The leather was removed and cotton canvas took its place. After experiments with different sizes of belts to accommodate the full-flap holster, scabbards for the hunting knife, and additional equipment, the Model 1876 cartridge belt, made from canvas and leather and called the Prairie Belt, was adopted.

Although the looped belt was much more functional, the black polished waist belt (Model 1874) and the McKeever cartridge box were used for garrison and parade functions, and were retained as issued items. A further derivation of General Anson Mills's looped belt appeared in 1881. These web belts carried fifty of the .45-70 cartridges, easily accessible to the soldier. By the mid 1880s, these belts were all the rage among the U.S. soldiers who wore the blue, tan, or grey belts into the Spanish American War and later the Philippine Insurrection. All of these webbed belts, including the unofficial variants developed in the field, saw duty, and were also adopted by European armies all over the world.

The Anson Mills woven cartridge belt seemed to be a popular dress item for Apache warriors. They wore it constantly about their waist, whether it was loaded with cartridges or not. When the belt's single loops were completely loaded with .45/70 cartridges, the belt weighed around five pounds, and riding and tracking the hostiles all day with this cumbersome belt around their middles caused many scouts, as well as white and black troopers, to complain of back problems and sore muscles.

The Infantry Board recommended retention of the McKeever cartridge box (Pattern 1874) as it was neat in appearance, and in the opinion of the Board was better adapted to garrison service than the canvas belt. Experience had shown that it was necessary for soldiers, in order to present a clean, soldierly appearance at parades and inspections, to have two sets of accoutrements—one for service in the field and one for service in garrison.

The Colt Revolver

Gradually, hand guns came to share the spotlight with the rifle or musket. Among them was the Colt

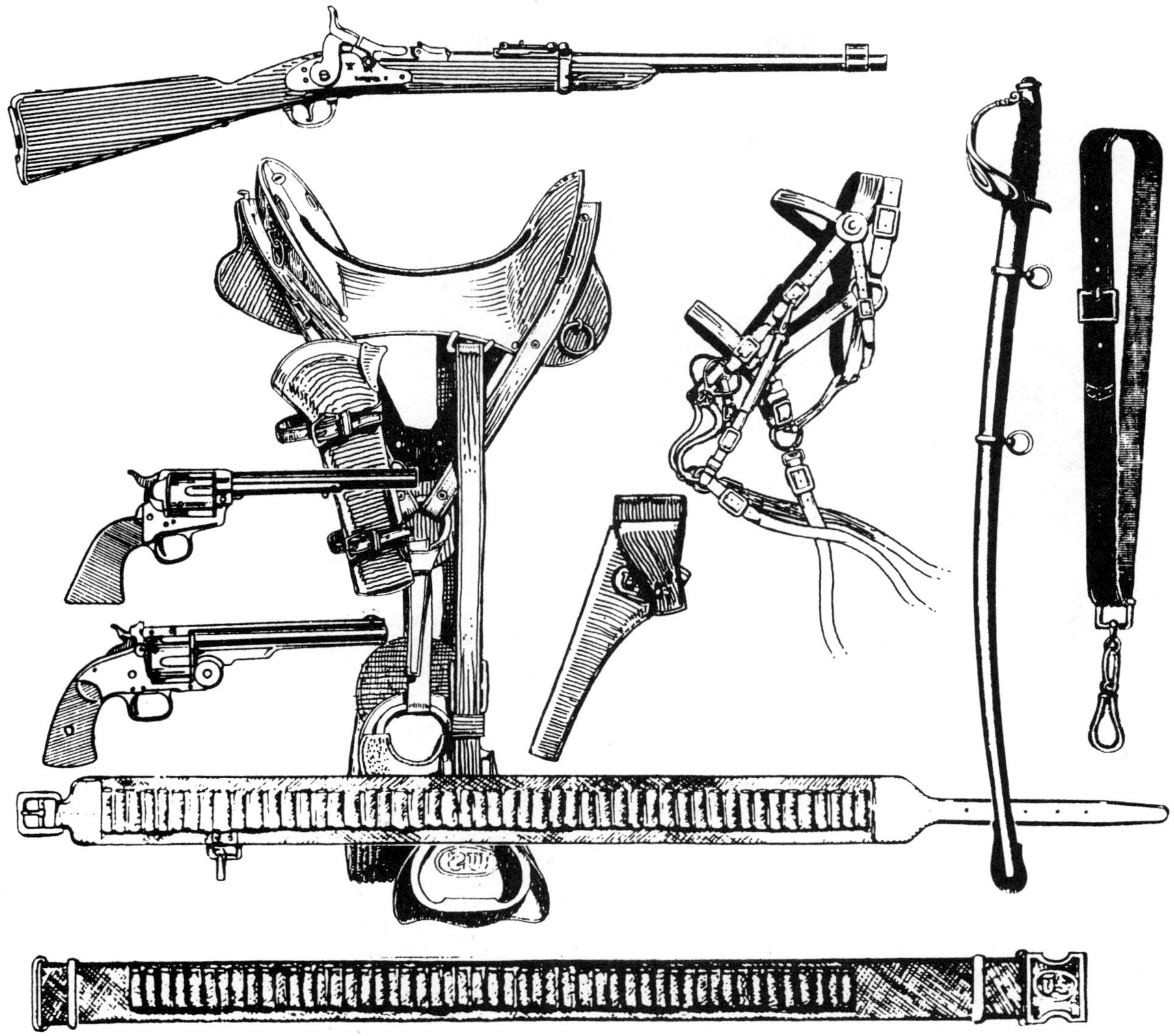

Cavalry field armament equipment, 1885. Roughly, from top to bottom: Springfield carbine, Trapdoor Model 1884; Model 1885 McClellan saddle (black leather); 1885 bridle and halter with a shoemaker bit; U.S. regulation sabre for cavalry; 1872 carbine sling, worn in place of the Civil War sling; single-action, .45 caliber, six-shot Colt, Model 1873; single-action, .45 caliber, six-shot Smith & Wesson, Army Model 1875 (top break open); Model 1885 pistol holster for either the Colt or Schofield (Smith & Wesson); 1885 leather belt with grey webbed loops; and 1887 Mills grey, blue, and tan webbed belt.

revolver, a 7½-inch barrel, six-shot, six-chambered weapon designed for use with a .45 caliber metallic center-fire cartridge. The cartridge carried a 235-grain lead bullet backed by forty grains of black powder. The U.S. Government supplied the troops with cartridges to fit this model, made at Government arsenals, but loaded them with thirty grains of FFg black powder instead of forty. The Colt revolver sported a black leather holster, half-flop, with a loop to attach the sidearm to a regulation leather belt. Later, in 1878, the holster was fitted with a larger belt loop to accommodate the thimble cartridge belt. The Colt was a well-balanced, accurate weapon.

Many of the great shots of the West could put six bullets into a telegraph pole with this revolver while galloping past it. The better shots could hit a man at seventy or seventy-five paces, off-hand shooting.

Snap shooting was a popular pastime with this single-action Colt during the middle 1880s. Snap shooting involved standing solidly, bringing the pistol up into the air in one swift motion, and then cocking the pistol. In the same motion, the shooter would lower his arm and extend it full length, pistol at the ready, pointing directly at the target. He then let the hammer slip. Nine times out of ten a good marksman would score. And the effect of

The single-action, .45 caliber, six-shot U.S. Army–issue Colt, with 7½ inch barrel, was the officer's sidearm and the cavalry trooper's defensive weapon at close range, besides their .45/55 carbine. Problems evolved with this weapon: The cylinder lock bolt wore down quickly, and the ejector-housing screw worked loose after each firing. However, this weapon was much preferred over the Smith & Wesson.

these motions was like throwing the bullet out of the barrel.

Shortly after the Army's adoption of the new service revolver, the Colt .45 began to acquire some unusual names. To the soldier, it was a "thumbbuster" or an "Army .45." To the lawman, it was a "peacemaker" and "equalizer." Civilians tagged it a "hogleg" or a "plowhandle." Regardless of its name, the Colt .45 was accepted gladly by those who had use for its block-busting effects.

The trooper was repeatedly reminded that proper care of his Colt metallic cartridge pistol was important; with constant care, it would last the soldier almost indefinitely. The trooper used the pistol in every type of climate, although it was certain to rust and foul when subjected to rain and snow. Generally, the men in the garrisons took to oiling their weapons and keeping them in top shape. But it was a different story for the men in temporary encampments in the more remote areas. There, many resented the time spent cleaning the pistol and felt it was up to the manufacturer to produce a pistol that could cope with all conditions.

The greatest fault with any rifle or pistol can be traced to the owner. Most gunsmithing problems originated with the individual who tinkered with the mechanism or otherwise mistreated the weapon. Black powder and corrosive primers act as fouling agents and can bind up an intricate mechanism. The Colt was a strong weapon, and at times continued to function faithfully despite abuse. However, to guard against any abuse or malfunctioning, sergeants and officers held frequent pistol inspections.

The soldiers occasionally tightened the screws in the Colt, as this was only necessary after lengthy firings with 40-grain black powder load. The main objection to the pistol was its ejector, which often blew off after the weapon had been fired for some time and which was slow in ejecting spent cartridges.

Other problems appeared, albeit infrequently. Sometimes the ejector tube housing would loosen when the small holding screw loosened after the weapon had been fired repeatedly. A trooper kept a small screwdriver handy, or used the tip of his knife to tighten the screw. But taking time out during an Indian raid to tighten a screw could be disconcerting, to say the least. Sometimes, bolts or bolt springs would break, a problem that could not be dealt with by a soldier. Occasionally the bolt locking the cylinder in place would break and the gun had to be repaired by a regimental arms artificer. At times the cylinder did not align with the barrel when the hammer was ready to fire, and the pistol could burst. Even a slight misalignment problem could cause lead slivers to fly forward of the cylinder.

This new Colt pistol was designed for the .45 caliber metallic cartridge ball made at the Frankfort Arsenal as early as 1873. By 1874, the cartridge had evolved from the 1.26-inch case to the shorter 1.1 inch Smith and Wesson Schofield-model that fit both revolvers. This shorter cartridge was first manufactured in August of 1874. It had a copper casing, referred to as the Bloomfield Gilding Metal, and was inside primed. The primer was often called a cup anvil primer. It had a straight, rimmed case with a reinforced head.

Company returns indicated that the average service life of a cavalry percussion pistol was from four to five years. This was calculated for times of active service in war with ordinary repairs. The cartridge pistol also had the same service life.

The soldiers liked the new metallic cartridges, and had little difficulty with them; however, improvements were certainly needed. The paper and linen cartridges proved to be a real hazard to the troopers.

Entrenching Tools

As the Indians gained mounts and became more expert marksmen, the soldiers felt an increasingly stronger need for a means of digging a shelter. One of the first tools to be developed for this purpose was the Rice-Chillingsworth Trowel Bayonet, which appeared around 1873. The invention of Edmund Rice and Felix Chillingsworth, it was issued with the first production of the Model 1873 Trapdoor Rifle. The unit could be used solely as a digging instrument or as a sidearm, making it somewhat versatile.

But the soldiers often used it affixed to the gun barrel—with disastrous results. With a little heft behind the gun, the soldier could cause serious damage to the muzzle of the rifle. And by digging with the bayonet affixed to the rifle, the barrel could also be bent or the muzzle become plugged with dirt. The soldier who fired his weapon after plugging the muzzle was in for a nasty surprise: The barrel frequently exploded, often leading to

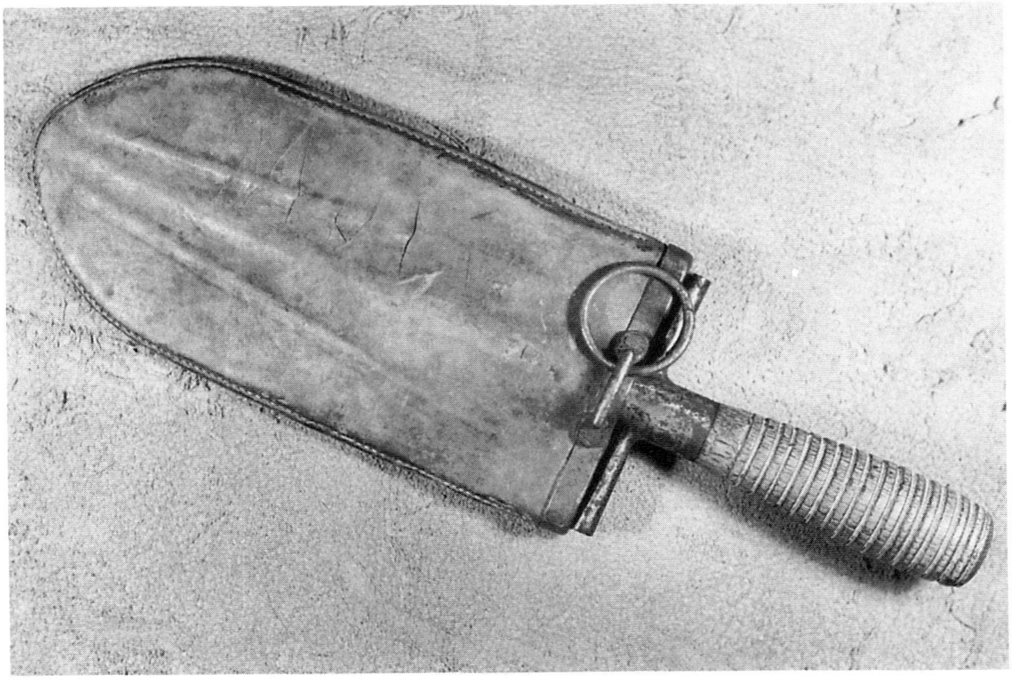

This is the early Model 1873 Hagner entrenching tool, a shovel-shaped trowel and carrying scabbard, which was issued before the Rice-Chillingsworth model.

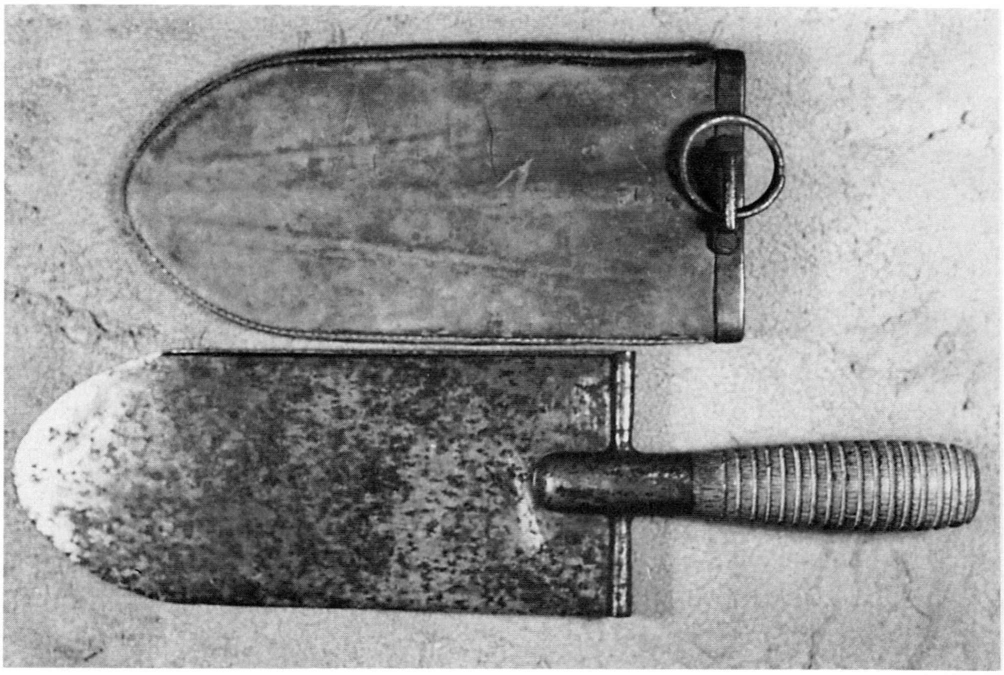

Hagner entrenching tool, opened.

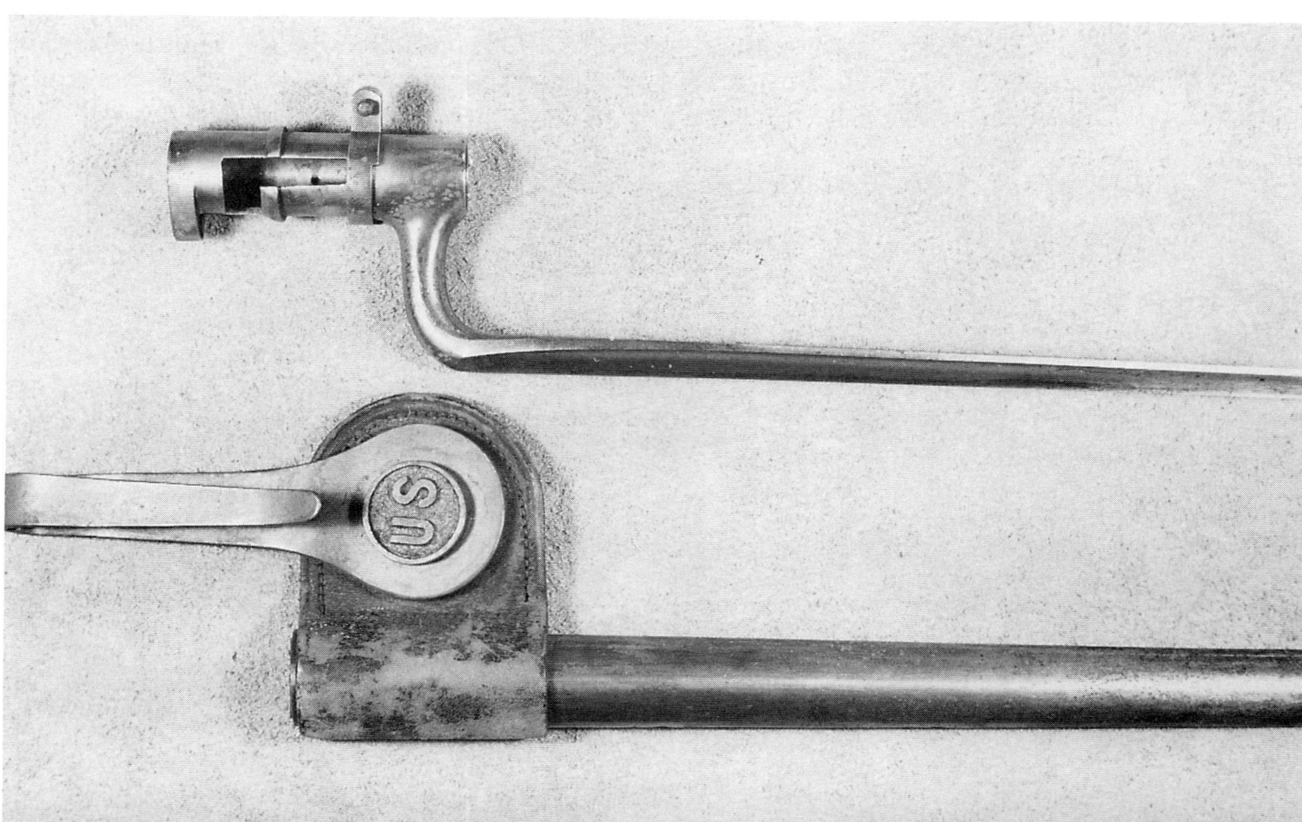

Top: the 1873 socket bayonet remanufactured from the Model 1855 Civil War bayonet. Bottom: the bayonet scabbard later issued for use with Mills webbed cartridge belt. (Photo courtesy of Alan Feldstein.)

The entrenching knife bayonet, or the trowel bayonet, commonly called the Rice-Chillingsworth, appeared sometime in 1873, and was the first of these tools to be used on the muzzle of the 1873 Springfield Trapdoor rifle. Affixed to the muzzle, it was to be used as a shovel for digging trenches, but had disastrous effects. As a separate piece, however, it was used as a hand trowel and dug a viable trench.

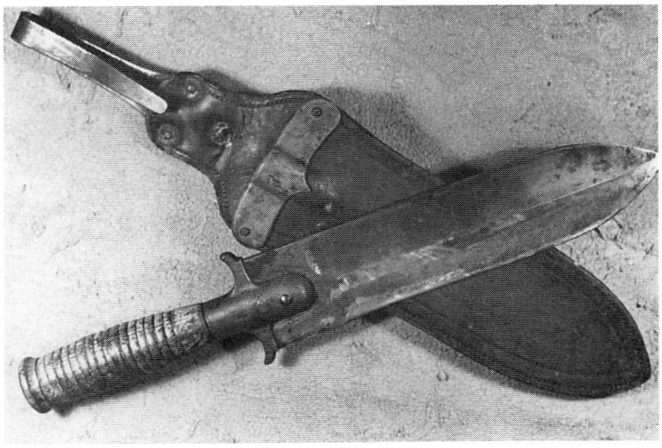

On February 20, 1881, one thousand of these hunting knives and scabbards (Model 1880) were issued to field units. It was just what the troopers needed.

serious wounds. By 1879, the various trowel-bayonet models were discontinued by the Army as they were considered too dangerous to be included in the enlisted men's gear.

That left the Model 1873 Hagner Entrenching Tool, a shovel-shaped trowel and carrying-ring scabbard that had been issued long before the Rice-Chillingsworth models. This unit was held by hand and carved out a suitable trench for protecting troops under attack. Some troops favored the entrenching tool, particularly those who had some warning before an Indian attack. This unit was included in the enlisted men's gear after the discontinuance of the Rice-Chillingsworth models and until the adoption of the 1880 hunting knife.

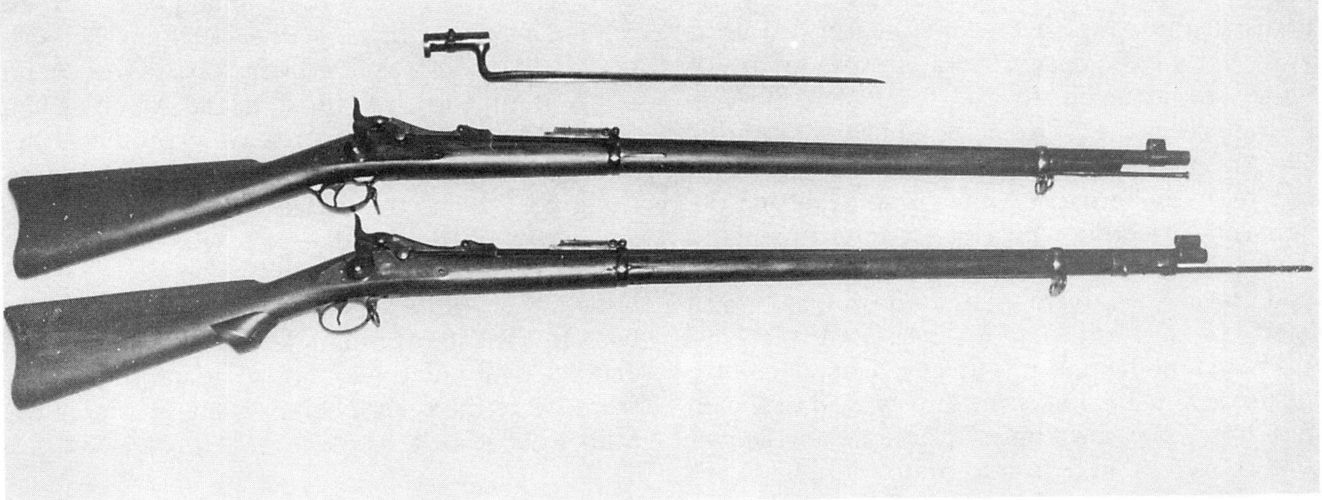

Top: the 1884 Springfield rifle with socket bayonet and milled front sight cover. Bottom: the 1889 Springfield rifle, with ramrod bayonet partially extended, snap-on front sight cover, and detachable metal pistol grip. (Photo courtesy of Alan Feldstein.)

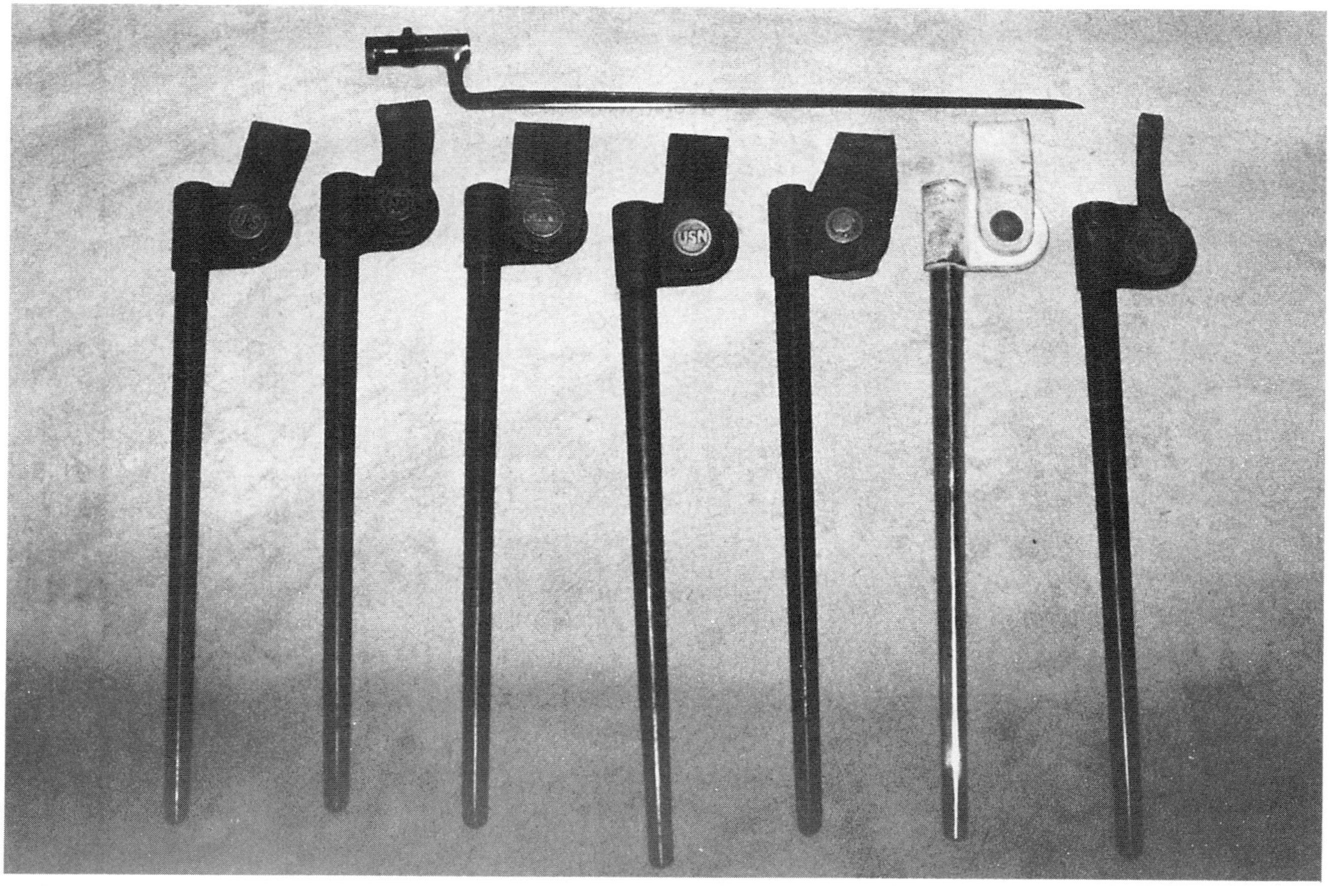

Top: the 1873 socket bayonet. From left to right, various scabbards for it: 1873 U.S. Army, 1873 New Jersey, 1873 Massachusetts, U.S. Navy, Hoffman's limited traverse, nickled dress with white buff leather frog, and 1884 for use with the Mills webbed belt. (Photo courtesy of Alan Feldstein.)

In a letter written by an experienced artillery officer to the chief of ordnance, a suggestion was made to include a serviceable butcher knife and sheath as part of the appendages of the belt, in addition to the trowel bayonet. This letter, written on November 17, 1877, expressed a consensus of many of the troops serving in Indian country. But it wasn't until August 18, 1879, nearly two years later, that a basic design for a hunting knife was authorized and sent to the National Armory in Springfield by the Office of the Chief of Ordnance. The Armory responded with three sample knives and two scabbard designs. These scabbard designs, one of leather with a loop for attachment to a waist belt or cartridge holder, and a similar one made from steel, were submitted on October 21, 1879. The decision to adopt the leather scabbard was based on the findings that even small dents in the metal housing made the knives hard to sheath in a hurry. So the knives, clad in their leather jackets, were issued, first to troops supplied with the 1880 Springfield Triangular Ramrod Bayonet Rifle.

The arsenal at Watervliet received the design to produce the knives and leather scabbards on September 24, 1880. On February 28, 1881, a thousand of the units were completed and issued to field companies.

There were several models of the leather scabbard. The first, designed by Captain A. L. Varney, offered a swivel-hinged leather belt loop. The second early model was fitted with a brass throat and hook, stamped R.I.A. (Rock Island Arsenal). Ten thousand of these scabbards were produced between 1883 and 1885. The hook was a modification designed to accommodate the Anson Mills webbed, looped cartridge belt, which was growing in popularity. Two other models were also issued, one with a leather loop to attach the scabbard to the infantryman's leather waist belt, and another with enlarged loops to attach the leather scabbard to the prairie belt or a later model of the Mills webbed belt.

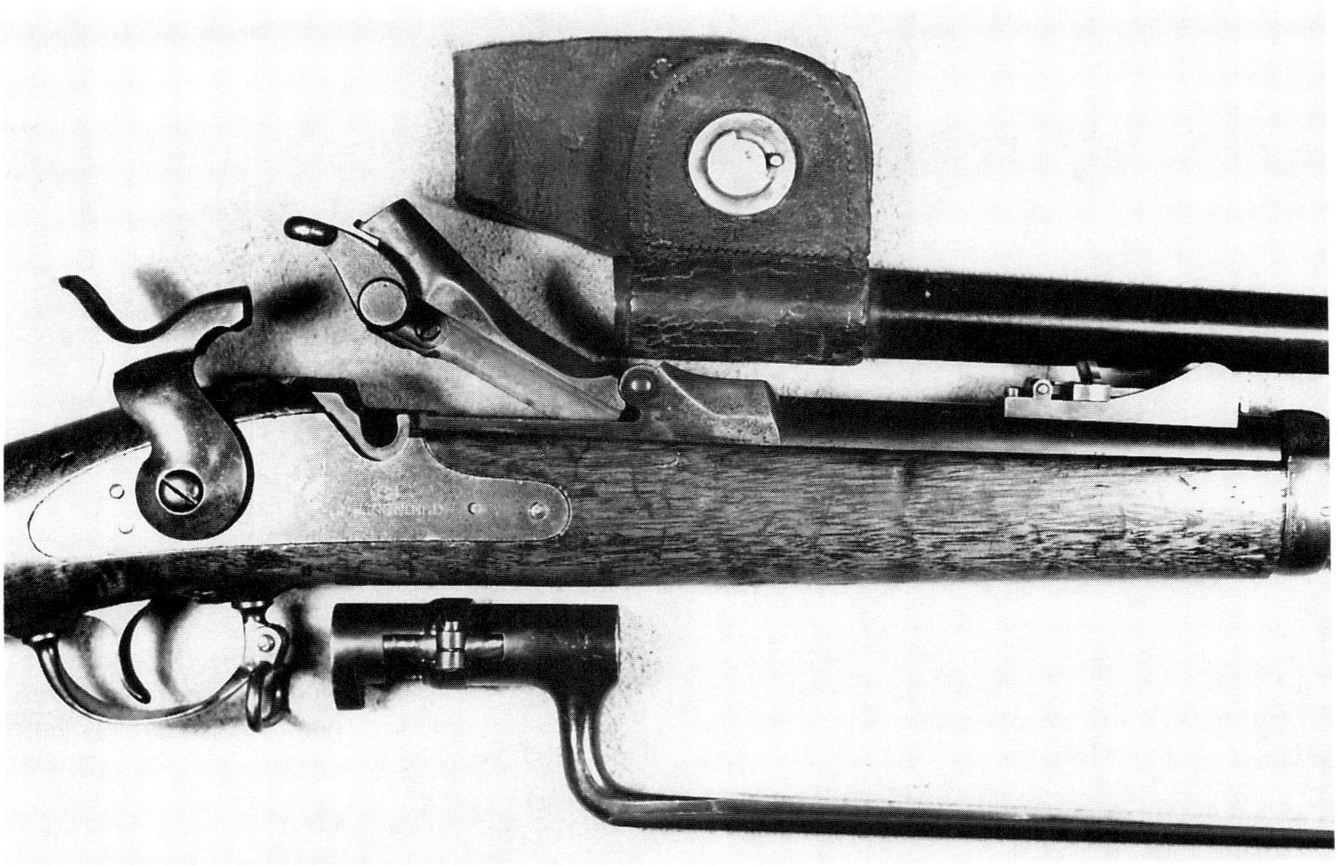

The 1879 Trapdoor rifle with blued socket bayonet and Hoffman's limited traverse bayonet scabbard. (Photo courtesy of Alan Feldstein.)

13

THE ORDNANCE DEPARTMENT

The Ordnance Department was formally established by an act of Congress in 1812. But as early as 1794, three or four arsenals were provided for, and between 1791 and 1812, more than $8,000,000 had been appropriated for ordnance purposes.

When established in 1812, the Ordnance Department consisted of a commissary-general of ordnance, having the rank, pay, and emoluments of a colonel of infantry, and thirteen other officers, eight of whom had the rank of second lieutenants of infantry. The duties of the department, as prescribed by this act, were to procure by purchase or manufacture the armaments for sea-coast defenses, and the arms, equipment, and all other ordnance stores for the army, the militia, the Marine Corps, and for all the executive departments, to protect public money and property. In addition, the colleges authorized by law to receive arms for instruction were supplied by the Ordnance Department.

In 1813 the number of assistants of ordnance was increased to sixteen, and their pay raised to that of a first lieutenant of infantry. By an act of Congress in 1815, the duties of the department were reiterated, and the senior officer of ordnance, no longer called the commissary-general of ordnance, was given general control of the public armories. Six years later the Ordnance Department merged with the Artillery Department, and ordnance duties were performed by artillery officers selected by the president.

In 1832 the Ordnance Department was reestablished, and in 1838 the number of officers increased.

The present organization of the Ordnance Department is as follows: a chief of ordnance, with the rank of brigadier-general; three colonels; four lieutenant-colonels; ten majors; twenty captains; and sixteen first lieutenants.

All vacancies in the grade of first lieutenant were filled by transfers from the line of the army. Promotions to the other grades were regular, with the exception of the chief, who was appointed by selection.

The Ordnance Office was at the War Department in Washington, and was supervised and controlled by the chief of ordnance, with several assistants. The arsenals of construction were the National Armory and the Frankford, Watervliet, Rock Island, Watertown, and Benicia arsenals. The arsenals of storage were the Allegheny, Augusta, Fort Monroe, Indianapolis, Kennebec, New York, and San Antonio. Besides these, there were a number of powder and ordnance depots located at points in the country most convenient for the purposes of supply.

From 1875 to 1882, an officer was designated as constructor of ordnance, and to him was entrusted, under direction of the chief of ordnance, the designing and construction of all guns and carriages. In 1882 this office was abolished, and its duties were assumed by the chief of ordnance. While utilizing the services of officers stationed elsewhere, the chief had a staff of officers in Washington mainly employed on construction work, and officers employed as resident inspectors at private foundries and establishments engaged in work for the government, such as the West Point and South Boston foundries and the Midvale and Cambria steelworks. These inspectors were the medium of communication between the chief of ordnance and the establishment to which they were attached. It was their duty to supervise every detail of the work, and make the various inspections provided for in the contract and in the ordnance instructions.

Intimately associated with the Ordnance office since 1875, the Ordnance Board consisted of three members, with stations at the New York Arsenal, Governors Island. The members of the board, associated with two other officers, constituted the board for testing rifle cannon. The proceedings of this board, limited to experiments with rifled cannon, were forwarded through the chief of ordnance to the secretary of war.

Another board, designated the Board on Ordnance and Defense, was established, relieving the two previously mentioned boards of much work. Being a mixed board, it was independent of the Ordnance Department, except in the matter of expenditures for ordnance purposes.

The ordnance proving ground was under the command of the president of the Ordnance Board, with an officer as assistant in charge. It was here that all new constructions in the way of guns and carriages were mounted and proved. All experiments with powders, high explosives, projectiles, fuses, sabots, primers, and so on, were made here as well. The proving ground was provided with the most modern ballistic instruments of the time, with devices for the analysis of gunpowder, and with a testing machine for metals. There was a machine shop at the station where all repairs were made, as were occasional original constructions of considerable importance. Prior to the completion of the testing machines at Watertown Arsenal, all the metal employed in gun construction was tested here, and the specimens were cut out and turned.

It was at the proving ground that the various inventions presented by civilians from any part of the country were tested. The inventor, through his congressman, approached the secretary of war with his war balloon, his contrivance for firing dynamite shell, his improved projectile, sabot, or fuse. The invention was referred to the chief of ordnance, who in turn referred it to the Ordnance Board, which carefully examined the plans and specifications. Unless the device was palpably absurd, the inventor was then given the opportunity of having it tested.

The National Armory was established at Springfield, Massachusetts, in 1794. Except for occasional experimental work, the only products of the armory were rifles, carbines, and side arms. Pistols and Gatling guns for issue were obtained by purchase, but they were inspected by officers and employees of the armory. In 1888, 41,310 rifles and carbines were manufactured, but it was stated that the armory could turn out 1,000 rifles per day. During the Civil War, from 1861 to 1865, there were 805,537 rifled muskets made at this armory.

As a result of the National Armory, the government educated many skilled workmen who were often later employed in the various private establishments in the country, and a great number of the labor-saving and accurate machines were developed that were universally used in the fabrication of small arms.

Frankford Arsenal, in Philadelphia, was established in 1816. Its productions were limited to the manufacturing of ammunition for the rifle, carbine, pistol, and Gatling gun; and of fuses, primers, and military pyrotechnics. The powder used was obtained from private manufacturers, after inspection by ordnance officers.

In 1887, the principal productions of the Watervliet Arsenal were leatherwork, harnesses, and other equipment and acouterments. That same year it was selected by the Gun Foundry Board as the most eligible arsenal for the concentration of the government plant, and it became one of the most important ordnance establishments. Machinery was transferred from Watertown and from the South Boston ironworks. With the facilities already existing, in September, 1888, it had the capacity for about fifty field guns and one eight-inch and one ten-inch gun per year. As funds became available, the plant was increased, enabling the government to make limited quantities of twelve-inch calibre guns as well.

The Rock Island Arsenal was established as an arsenal of storage and repair, but from its inception it was hoped that it might be developed into an arsenal of construction commensurate with the requirements of the Mississippi Valley and the West. In 1865, General Rodman assumed command, and commenced the preparation of plans for the construction of an establishment that would be both an arsenal and an armory. Eight immense finishing shops, one forging shop and foundry, and one forging shop and mill were constructed and provided with the most up-to-date appliances. A large part of the stores for issue to

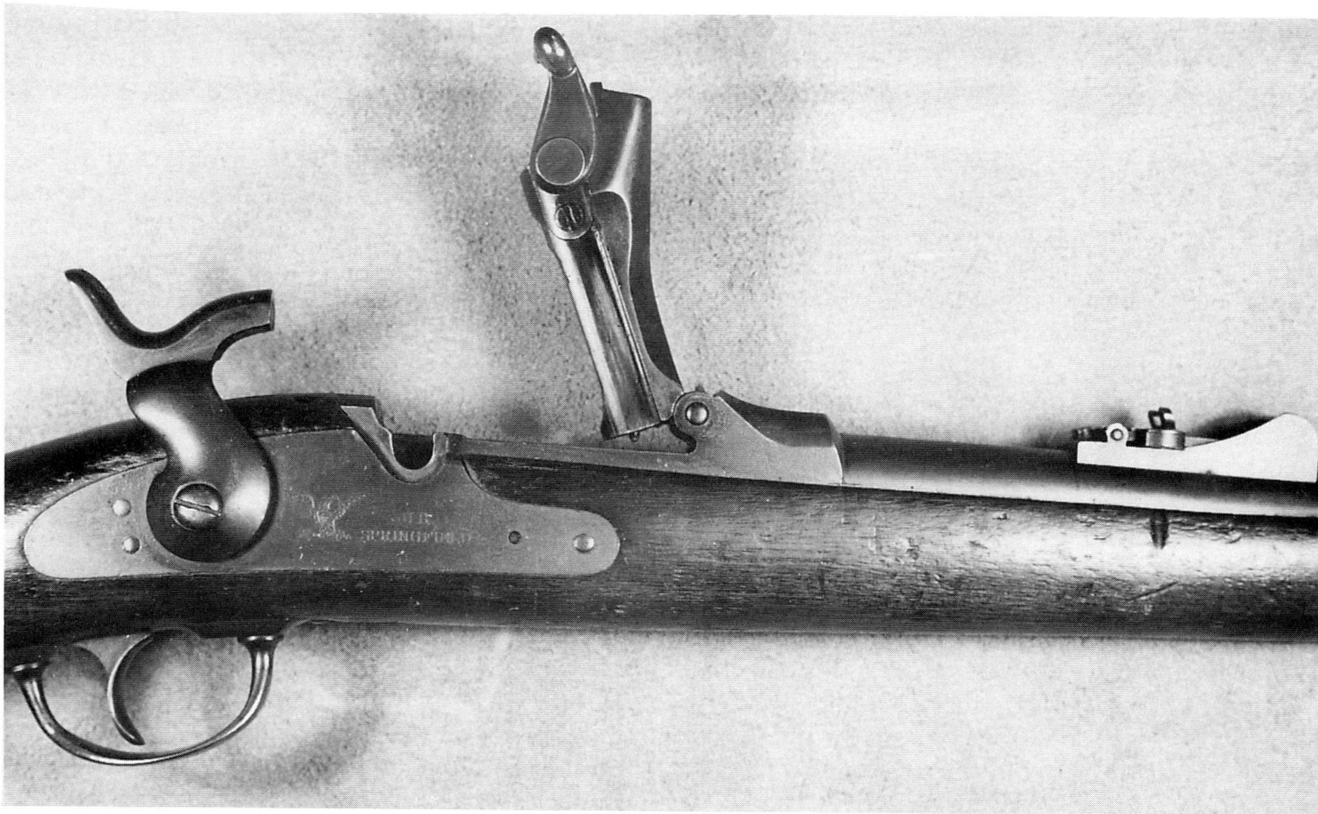

The 1873 Trapdoor carbine, with the earlier smooth trigger used before 1883. (Photo courtesy of Alan Feldstein.)

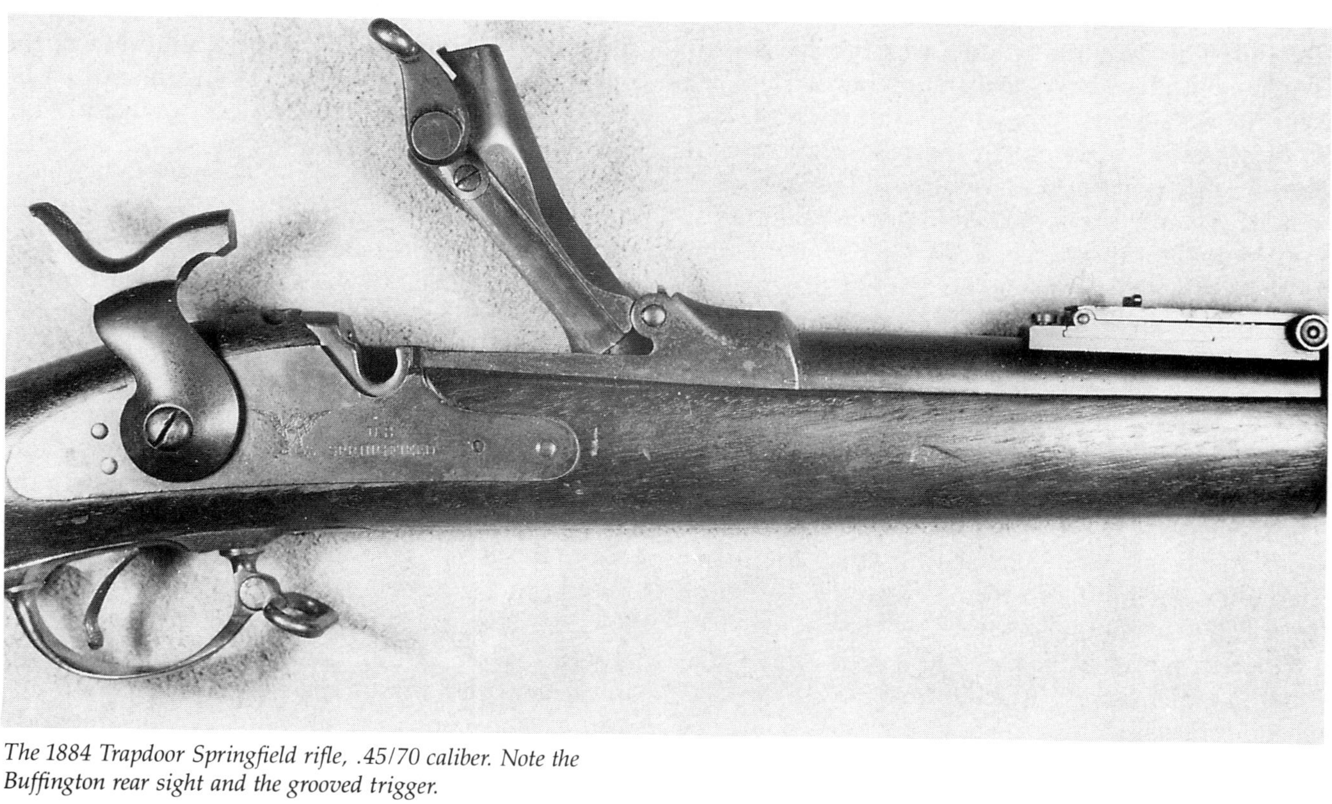

The 1884 Trapdoor Springfield rifle, .45/70 caliber. Note the Buffington rear sight and the grooved trigger.

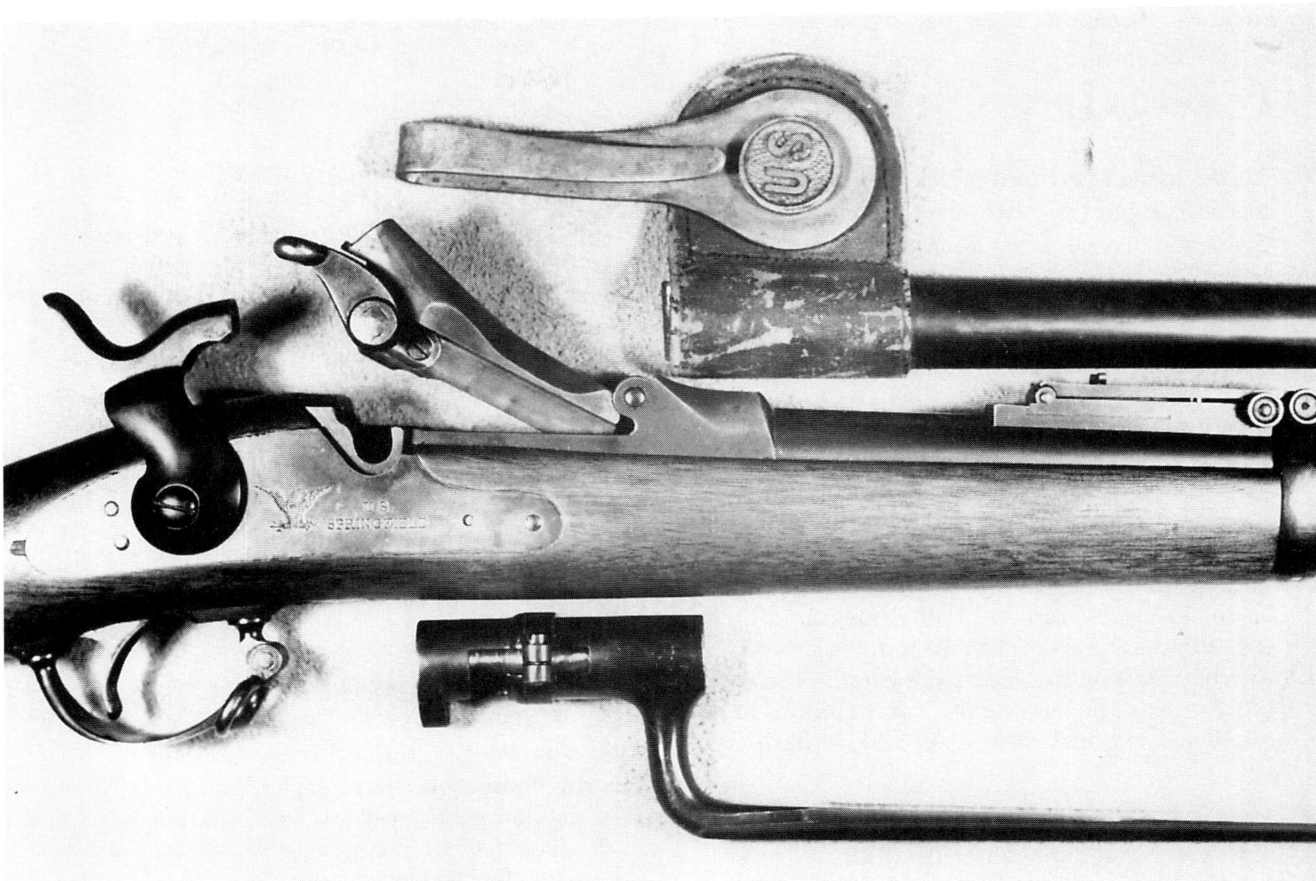

The 1884 Trapdoor rifle, with blued socket bayonet and late scabbard. (Photo courtesy of Alan Feldstein.)

the Army were made at this arsenal. These included equipment for horses, cavalry acouterments, infantry equipment, targets and supplies for target ranges, arm racks, and other similar appliances.

The Watertown Arsenal, near Boston, Massachusetts, was established in 1816. The principal work undertaken there was the manufacture of field guns and projectiles, the alteration of sea-coast gun carriages, and the manufacture of various experimental siege and sea-coast guns.

The United States Testing Machine, the finest and most elaborate machine in the world at that time for testing the strength of materials, was located at this arsenal. It was in almost continual use on work connected with civil pursuits as well as on work for the government.

Benicia Arsenal was important in that it was the only manufacturing arsenal on the Pacific coast. It was dependent upon other establishments for most ordnance supplies.

The way officers were appointed to the Ordnance Department resulted in its being filled by some of the brightest and most talented officers in the service. Among the young officers were those who, by earnest application, mastered and became eminently proficient in the courses taught at the Military Academy or the colleges of the country, and who, having carried their habits of study and application into the Army, were tested and then admitted into this important corps. Many people thought that by using this method of appointment, the Ordnance Department recruited much of the best material in the Army.

Cavalry Guidons

There have been many questions about the guidons from 1861 through 1885, so let's settle the controversy once and for all with this inclusion from Colonel W. A. Graham's report, "Custer's Battle Flags," written especially for the Westerners' *Brand Book*, Los Angeles Corral, 1950.

REVISED REGULATIONS FOR THE ARMY OF THE UNITED STATES 1861

1441 The flag of the guidon is swallow-tailed, three feet five inches from the lance to the end of the swallow-tail; fifteen inches to the fork of the swallow-tail, and two feet three inches on the lance. To be half red and half white, dividing at the fork, the red above. On the red, the letters U.S. in white; and on the white, the letter of the company in red. The lance of the X X X guidons to be nine feet long, including spear and ferrule.

* * *

G.O. NO. 4 HEADQUARTERS OF THE ARMY,
Adjutant General's Office,
Washington, January 18, 1862.

1. Under instructions from the Secretary of War, dated January 7, 1862, guidons and camp colors for the Army will be made like the United States flag, with stars and stripes.

* * *

Changes and Additions to Army Regulations up to June 25, 1862.

8. Guidons and camp colors for the Army will be made like the United States flag, with stars and stripes.

* * *

REGULATIONS OF THE ARMY OF THE UNITED STATES
Date: February 17, 1881
Guidons for Cavalry

2792 To be made of silk, with stars and stripes like the National flag; made swallow-tailed. Stars to be gilt, one and one-eighth inches in diameter from point to point.

The guidon to measure from the lance three feet five inches to the end, and fifteen inches to the fork of swallow-tail, and two feet three inches on the lance.

The fork of the swallow-tail to be equidistant from the top and bottom of the guidon.

The letter of the company to be embroidered in yellow silk, or painted on one of the white bars of the flag.

* * *

G.O. HEADQUARTERS OF THE ARMY,
ADJUTANT GENERAL'S OFFICE
Washington, February 4, 1885

By direction of the Secretary of War, par. 2792 of the regulations is amended to read as follows:

2792 The flag of the guidon is swallow-tailed, three feet five inches fly from the lance to the end of the swallow-tail, and two feet three inches on the lance. To be cut swallow-tailed fifteen inches to the fork. To be made of silk, and to consist of two horizontal stripes, each one-half the width of flag, the upper red and the lower white; the red to have on both sides in the center the number of the regiment in white silk, and the white to have the letter of the troop in red silk, the letter and number to be block-shaped, four and three-fourths inches high, and held in place by a border of needle work embroidery three-sixteenths of an inch wide, of same color.

14

A BRIEF HISTORY OF U.S. CAVALRY TACTICAL MANUALS

The American troops were drilled using the English Tactics during the early part of the War of the Revolution. In 1779, Congress adopted Baron de Steuben's abridgement of the Prussian Tactics. This was used by the United States Army until the beginning of the War of 1812, and by the Militia until 1820. In 1812, a very imperfect abridgement of the French Tactics of 1791, by General Alexander Smith, was published under the sanction of the War Department.

In 1813, Lieutenant Colonel William Duane, an ex-editor, produced a handbook of instruction for the squad and company, which was used to some extent in the Army. In this particular year, Congress requested the president to prepare for its approval "a military system of discipline for the Infantry of the Army and Militia of the United States."

This resolution was not acted upon owing to the occupation of the officers with field service, and during the War of 1812 tactical instruction was in a state of chaos, with every officer concerned in this matter being a law unto himself. De Lacroix had published in Boston a bad translation by Macdonald of the French Tactics, and with this and a copy of the original French, General Scott, at the camp in Buffalo in 1814, personally instructed two brigades of Brown's division. This was the first introduction here of the French system in its entirety.

With some modifications, it was adopted by the War Department and is known as The System of 1815. Its use by the Militia was made compulsory in 1820. The System of 1825 was adapted from the French by a board consisting of Scott, Brady, Fonwick, Thayer, and Worth. It was originally taken by the French from the Prussian system of Frederick the Great, and was used throughout the Revolutionary and Napoleonic wars in France. Under authority of Congress, General Scott in 1834, prepared the adaptation of the Prussian system known by his name. The improvement in firearms finally compelled a change from the formal movements of Scott, and Hardee's translation of the French system for their *chasseurs a pied* (hunters on foot) was adopted as far as the school of the battalion.

Because of its peculiar double-quick stop, it was familiarly known as the Shanghai Drill. Casey's revision of Hardee's system was authorized during the Civil War, and continued in use until it was superseded August 1, 1867, by Upton's Tactics, which gave place to a newer system, that of Drill Regulations of 1891.

The majority of the Union Cavalry fought the Civil War in double-rank deployment, under the 1841 Cavalry Tactics, or "Poinsett Tactics." The double-rank system was derived from Scott's 1834 Tactics, wherein a regiment of eight troops, each made up of four officers and seventy-six men, was organized into four squadrons of two troops each. Squadrons formed up, mounted in two ranks, two

Photos of U.S. Cavalry soldiers in the field are scarce. This one shows a troop, c. 1885–1887, in the Southwest. While some images are blurred because of movement of the horses, the picture still offers a rare glimpse into the everyday campaign life of the frontier soldier.

feet from head to croup. The Cavalry Tactics, adopted February 10, 1841, by order of Secretary of War J. R. Poinsett, modified the organization somewhat, the main change being that a regiment now consisted of five squadrons or ten companies. The Poinsett Tactics was used by the Eastern armies all through the Civil War, and by the Western cavalry up until 1864. French influence dominated both Scott's 1834 Tactics and Poinsett's Tactics, in that both new drill regulations were in the main translations from French sources.

It was not until 1854, during the Crimean War, that the War Department selected young professional officers to observe and study first-hand the various foreign military systems in order to incorporate their best features and revise the Army's tactical manuals. Captain George B. McClellan was among those chosen, and one result of his report was the introduction of the Russian system of carrying a pistol on the waist belt.

The Poinsett Tactics, used by the cavalry during the Civil War, was designated "The system of Cavalry Tactics, adapted to the organization of Dragoon regiments." When it was adopted in 1841, the cavalry consisted of the First and Second Regiments of Dragoons only, but it prescribed in detail the training of dragoons, chasseurs, hussars and lances. The following is a brief review of its contents.

Both dragoon regiments were armed with sabres, muzzle-loading pistols, and a Hall's muzzle-loading carbine. Double rank was prescribed. The hussar saddle was recommended by the Scott Board of 1824, and the soldier was taught to sit down in the saddle at a trot. The recruit was given a period of two months' instruction on foot before being advanced to the next phase: instruction on horseback. The School of the Trooper included 120 lessons, two each drill day. After sixty further lessons in the School of the Platoon, the soldier proceeded to the School of the Squadron.

During field duty, the horse was equipped with curb and snaffle bits, a blanket folded into twelve or sixteen thicknesses, and the hussar saddle with a buckled girth, breast strap, and crupper. Slung from the soldier's waist was a heavy sabre. Strapped on the left side of the pommel was the holster housing a percussion pistol. The carbine was at times attached to a shoulder carbine sling, with its muzzle nosed into a small leather boot attached to the off side of the saddle just behind the trooper's thigh.

There were no marching regulations prescribed in the 1841 manual, even though it consisted of three volumes: Part 1, Dismounted; Part 2, Mounted; and Part 3, Evolutions of a Regiment. The third volume contained the manual of the Colt's revolver. In 1864, a one-volume edition was printed by order of the War Department.

In 1864, the cavalry in the West began to use the Cooke Tactics system, which had been officially adopted on November 1, 1861, by order of Secretary of War Simon Cameron. It was published as "The System of Tactics and Regulations for the Cavalry of the United States, by Col. Phillip St. George Cooke, 2nd Cavalry." Cooke's tactics were based on the single-rank formation; however, this formation was not adopted until 1874.

The War Department did not receive Cooke's Tactics until January, 1860, and it was not approved until almost two years later, after the war between the states had been going on for several months. Until that point, the cavalry continued their battles in double rank, under the Poinsett Tactics.

Cooke, an 1827 graduate of West Point, served with the infantry until 1833, when he was transferred to the First Dragoons. Twenty-seven years of fighting, marching, and camp life qualified him to write the tactics for the cavalrymen.

The rules and regulations for cavalry service in the field, as described in Cooke's manual, were very complete. One chapter in particular, "Special Service of Cavalry in the West," is worthy of study. The basic principles governing cavalry marching and campsites were formulated on two constituents: Indians and grazing. The following is an excerpt from this chapter.

> It is very certain that bodies of cavalry, performing the same amount of marches and duties—one, under a commander ignorant, or injudicious and careless in this respect, will have broken down horses, whilst the other may maintain them in good condition.
>
> A commander in the west is subject commonly to the great difficulty and risk of necessarily grazing his animals at night, whilst they must be protected from an enemy. The camp should be formed early; sometimes it is protected in rear by a wide river, and the squadrons disposed on three sides of a parallelogram; sufficient space is included for night grazing.
>
> To encamp regularly, the squadrons are formed in line with squadron intervals; they are dismounted; without forming ranks, the troopers unsaddle and unbridle; they deposit the saddles in line in front of all the horses, and place upon

> them their sabers; the horse blankets are retained surcingled to the horses; if to be picketed, under charge of an officer they are let out as far as is safe in order to preserve the nearer grass for the night.

The author proceeds with a set of march regulations that have been rated as the best ever published in any cavalry manual:

> The march should generally be in columns of fours, the squadrons 4 with 40 or 50 paces interval, in order that a check in one squadron should not extend its disturbing influence by causing the next to stop; it also tends to the avoidance of dust. From 40 minutes to an hour after the march, a halt of five minutes should be made, the squadrons to be dismounted, informally in column, at the command "dismount" from their Captains. If there be grass, the squadrons should oblique from the road before dismounting. The horses should be encouraged to feed at the shortest halts; at those for ten minutes or more, as when watering, the commander should give the command "unbit."
>
> Every hour, a halt from two to five minutes should be made.
>
> Troopers are prohibited to leave the ranks for any purpose on the march, unless on foot, leaving the horse led.
>
> About noon, or about the middle of the march, when circumstances allow a choice of time, the "watering call" should be sounded; the troopers should generally dismount and unbit. The watering is superintended by the officers. Often the horse would fail to be watered from the impatience or want of perseverance of the trooper. This halt is from 20 to 45 minutes. Videttes or sentinels from the advance guard are posted.
>
> After one of the halts the troopers should lead, about 45 minutes; or twice for 30 minutes.
>
> There are several advantages in trotting a part of the march; by it the horses are sooner relieved of the saddle burden, and have longer time for feed and rest. Horse and man are relieved from the constant motion and fatigue of the same muscles and parts. It avoids a bad carriage of the person of the troopers, sometimes injurious to the horse; it awakes and relieves him. It is found, from experience, to lessen the liability to sore backs.
>
> Long marches or expeditions should be commenced very moderately. The horses, if untrained, must be gradually inured to their labors; in other words, the march must be a training. Fifteen miles a day at first; afterwards they will be equal to twenty-five.

On July 17, 1873, Secretary of War William W. Belknap approved a revised set of tactics for artillery and cavalry known as "Upton's Tactics." The author, Lieutenant-Colonel Emory Upton, 1st Artillery, was the instructor of tactics at the U.S. Military Academy. He was graduated from West Point in 1856, and was assigned to the 4th Artillery. He commanded the 121st New York Infantry from October 1862 until May 1864, when he was promoted to brigadier-general of volunteers. His distinguished Civil War record included brevet promotions to major general.

When Upton's manual was approved, the cavalry was organized into ten regiments of three battalions each, with twelve companies to a battalion. Each company had one captain, one first lieutenant, one second lieutenant, and seventy-seven enlisted men. The McClellan saddle, single (curb) bit bridle, and six-fold blanket were now regulation. The mounted trooper carried a light cavalry sabre suspended from the waist belt. A pistol was carried on the right side, butt forward, in a large flapped holster (Civil War vintage). And a single-shot, breech-loading .45 caliber carbine hung from a carbine sling, and was tucked into a leather socket affixed to the saddle behind the trooper's thigh. Dismounted, companies now formed in double rank, and mounted in single rank.

The march and camp instructions covered in Upton's tactical manual are much the same as in Cooke's Tactics:

> Commanding officers must bear in mind that the efficiency of cavalry depends almost entirely upon the "condition of the horses," which alone makes them able to get over long distances in short spaces of time. The horses must, therefore, be nursed with great care, in order that they may endure the utmost fatigue when emergencies demand it.
>
> Reveille, ordinarily, should not be sounded on the march before daylight, as horses rest better from midnight until dawn than at other times.
>
> The average march for cavalry is from fifteen to twenty miles per day. The walk is the habitual gait; when the ground is good, the trot may be used occasionally for short distances.
>
> Long marches or expeditions should be begun moderately, particularly with horses new to the service. Ten or fifteen miles a day is enough for the first marches, which may be increased to twenty-five miles when necessary, after the horses are inured to their work.
>
> In campaign, the usual precautions against surprise are taken, and an advanced guard and flankers are thrown out.
>
> The march is usually in columns of fours; when

practicable, it may be in double columns of fours; in small commands it is often in columns of twos.

In small commands, not in campaign, distances of forty to fifty yards may be taken between the companies, so that checks will not extend from one to another and cause unnecessary halts. A halt of from five to ten minutes is made at the end of every hour, for the purpose of adjusting equipment, tightening girths, etc. The companies are dismounted in column at the command of their captains; if there be grass, each captain first obliques his company a short distance from the road to let the horses feed, as horses must always be encouraged to graze as much as possible on the march. When troops march for the greater part of the day, a halt of from twenty to forty-five minutes is usually made about noon. In campaign, videttes are posted during the halts.

On long marches, officers and men, except the sick, are required to dismount and lead from twenty to forty minutes every second or third hour; to save their backs, horses will be led over steep ground, and particularly down hill.

In passing obstacles, each company commander halts at a sufficient distance beyond the obstacle, and requires his men to close up at a walk. When necessary, the column is halted by the commanding officer for the companies to close up.

When water call is sounded, the Captains cause their companies to dismount, and usually to unbit. The watering is superintended by the officers, who see that all the animals are watered without confusion. No horse of a cavalry command on the march should be watered unless all are watered.

In each company, the chiefs of platoon, and particularly those in rear, are held responsible that the troopers do not lounge in their saddles, so as to chafe their horses' backs. Any man who fails to sit up squarely on his horse, must be made to dismount and lead.

No enlisted man will be permitted to leave the ranks for any purpose, except on foot, leading his horse.

The chapter on camping goes into detail as to sanitation, and gives specific instructions governing precautionary measures to be taken while in "hostile Indian country."

Thus far the best tactical manual for the cavalry, Upton's Tactics was used until October 1891, when Secretary of War Redfield Proctor authorized the Cavalry Drill Regulations, to be prepared by a Board of Officers from all three branches of the service. In this publication, the word "regulations" was used, instead of "tactics."

On the frontier, Upton's Tactics was received by officers with mixed comments. Letters to the editor of the *Army and Navy Journal* reflected this, as did the Journal's own views:

> Brigade movements mounted are not prescribed to be made by general commands, but by dispatched orders and bugle calls. So far as all these movements, and those of divisions and corps, are concerned, the changes are in the right direction, and the Cavalry Tactics are amply sufficient to meet all the necessities occurring in maneuvering either large or small bodies of horse, in the simplest and most rapid manner. . . . As the tactics stand now, it would save the Government a good many dollars, and our so-called "cavalry" much needless trouble, to have every sabre used by an enlisted man turned into the arsenals.

Sabre exercises, with all their useless flourishes and cuts at the empty air, were retained in Upton's Tactics because of tradition. Although these exercises were practised in the cavalry, sabres were only meant to be used in "pomp and ceremony." In some regiments, however, by disregarding the instructions put forth in the Tactics, the men were made into fair swordsmen, and would charge with the sabre. When the tactics were followed, firing carbines was the cavalry's only recourse.

Astonishing as it may seem, during the first three years of the Civil War, reports of 105 sabre wounds were recorded. But as the war was coming to an end, the use of the sabre was diminishing, and was mostly used to club the enemy when close up.

Charging Indians with sabres may seem preposterous, but it did happen. According to an entry in the *Army Navy Journal* in 1867, an Oregon paper reported one instance of soldiers using sabres to fight Indians. The account tells about a band of Snake Indians running off a pack train near Camp Watson, and about their pursuit by Brevet Lieutenant-Colonel John P. Baker's First U.S. Cavalry command. When about twenty miles from the post, the troops came up against the Indians and charged on their camp. The Indians stood their ground; but during a preceding snowstorm, their rifles had become damp, so they failed to fire. The soldiers, observing the state of affairs, drew their sabres and cut the hostiles down, killing fourteen men and capturing five women and all the stolen mules, together with ten horses. In the battle, a great amount of Indian supplies were destroyed, and it was considered one of the most complete victories gained over the Snake Indians.

This photo of a cavalry trooper, posing for the folks back home, is from the mid to late 1880s. Although he wears his sabre, it was generally not taken on campaigns. (Photo courtesy of Herb Peck, Jr.)

English and German soldiers often were seen fencing, and most of them developed a certain interest in it. However, confidence in this weapon was entirely lacking in the U.S. Cavalry, mainly because American troopers rarely used it, and when they did it was usually to cut at the air in exercise. Since the troopers knew little about how to guard against cuts or point in actual battle, the inclusion of the sabre exercises in the tactics manuals seemed irrelevant to many of them.

Generally, Army officers voiced little complaint concerning the wisdom or judgment expressed in the cavalry's tactical manuals. These manuals were written by veteran cavalrymen in the "day of the horse," when travelling anywhere was done by or on the horse. They expounded a system with organization and theory, and generally exhibited practical common sense. Despite changes in equipment, training, and tactical use of the mounted trooper, the principles involving mounted men and wagons travelling successfully over land changed but little. The greatest value of the cavalry was in its mobility, which enabled it to arrive in time for effective action. Four elements of a successful campaign, as advocated in the manuals, had to do with equipment, horse rations, footing, and timing. The fifth tactical principle, added by seasoned troopers, had to do with surprise in battle. Details on the subject of training young horses, gaits, seating, and equitation aids were also included in the manuals, as many recruits knew nothing about equitation and horse management, and cared less until their lives depended on it.

15

THE PACK TRAIN

Primitive man had always sought a mode of transportation other than the personal burden, naturally utilizing the most docile and tractable of the animal kingdom available, such as the elephant, camel, llama, ox, horse, mule, burro, reindeer, and even dog.

Pack saddles of various designs had been adapted to the conformation of each animal employed. With certain care, throughout the years, the "crosstree," or "sawbuck," and the "aparejo" have been used by civilized man, but which antedated the other remains a question.

The crosstree may be said to be universal, as it has been in use in European and Asiatic countries for centuries. It is believed that the Romans carried it into Gaul (France) and Britain in their conquest of these countries under Julius Caesar. And the French and British carried it into Canada and the United States in their settlement of these territories.

In the mountainous portions of Switzerland and the British Isles, you can still see people carrying marketable supplies in wicker baskets fitted over the forks of the saddle and strapped to the donkey by the "cincha" and tightening strap. It was not unusual for baskets to be unequally loaded, and often the loads were balanced by the addition of a billet of wood or a few stones thrown in. Generally, overloaded pack animals would drop and commence rolling about, trying to eliminate the burden.

On the discovery of gold in California, the miners saw how the pack mule could be adapted for carrying supplies into mining camps not accessible by wagons. The mule and aparejo were in constant demand, and the employment of pack trains became a source of profit to many people.

The "bell horse" travelled ahead of the pack train. This was a horse with an ordinary sheep bell attached by a strap to its neck. The tinkle of the little bell could be heard from one hill to another. Should any animal fall behind or wander off by itself unnoticed by the packer, it would rejoin the pack train guided by the familiar sound of the bell.

After the close of the Civil War, General George Crook employed the services of civilian aparejo pack trains in operations against the hostile Paiutes, Shoshones, and Bannocks in Nevada, Oregon, and Idaho. Crook's utilization of the pack trains was so satisfactory that the U.S. Government purchased three of them, and Crook may well be called the "father" of the pack service in the U.S. Army.

On the assignment of General Crook to the Department of Arizona, these trains were transferred with him and others were organized for the campaigns against the hostile Apaches. Known as the Tonto Basin War, the campaigns lasted from 1871 to 1875. The trains were under the supervision of Thomas Moore, as chief packer, and Dave Mears, as assistant chief packer. The names of Hank and Yank, Jim O'Neil, Harry Haws, Chileno John, Frank Monack, Sam Bowman, the two Crooks ("Long" and "Short" Jim), Bill Knight, Nat Noble, Charley Hopkins, Bill Duklin, Manuel Lopez, and Lem Pyatt, all packmasters, are inseparably connected with those campaigns against the Apaches.

In 1875, a number of these government trains were transferred to the Department of the Platte, taking station at Camp Carlin, in Cheyenne, Wyo-

General George Crook, in his younger days.

ming, under Major J. V. Furey, depot quartermaster. There, they were joined by other trains for the expedition of 1876, known as the Sioux Campaign. Likewise, these trains were under the supervision of Thomas Moore, as chief packer, and Dave Mears, as assistant chief packer. The names of packmasters Dick Closter (better known as "Uncle Dick"), Johnny Patrick, Ed Delaney, John Jaycox, Frank Houston, Pat Nolan, Tom McCaulif, Tom Mason, and Dave Young are all inseparably connected with the Sioux Campaigns.

General Crook's success in being able to cut loose from his wagon transportation, rendering his command thoroughly mobile by the aid of pack trains, led to their further employment by other army officers. Generals Mackenzie, Howard, Terry, Custer, and Miles used them in the subjugation of the hostile tribes—notably the warlike Sioux, Cheyennes, Nez Perces, and Arapahoes in the Northwest; the fleet and vindictive Kiowas and Comanches through the Middle West; and last but not least, the wily, slippery, and bloodthirsty Apache tribes overrunning Arizona, New Mexico, and Texas. Through all the arduous field service necessitated by campaigns against these various tribes, the pack mule has borne its part, and was thoroughly identified with the U.S. Army as an essential means of transportation.

It's worth mentioning a case in which pack animals were employed on a continuous basis—the Geronimo Campaign, which lasted from May 1885 to September 1886 (see Chapter 7). Several pack trains followed the troops, taking part in the various operations. These trains were always on the move, travelling through the territories of New Mexico and Arizona, as well as the states of Sonora and Chihuahua in old Mexico. They crossed the Sierra Madre Mountains at their highest and most precipitous part, from Opata in Sonora to Casas Grandes in Chihuahua. Through such hazardous country any other form of transportation would have been utterly impossible.

The mules carried loads averaging 250 pounds. An average day's march was thirty miles, except when climbing mountains, when about fifteen miles per day was the rule. The mules subsisted entirely on the grasses that grew in the country, and when the campaign was over, were returned to their posts in good condition.

Marches and Loads of the Pack Mule

The following is an excerpt from the *Manual of Pack Transportation; Quartermaster Corps*, by H. W. Daly, published by the Washington Government Printing Office in 1917.

> Under ordinary conditions, the pack mule carrying a load of 250 pounds will travel from 20 to 25 miles per day, and maintain a rate of speed of 4½ to 5 miles per hour.
>
> With occasional days of rest he may be expected to perform this amount of work steadily; and this, too, without the aid of grain or hay.
>
> It must be remembered, however, that except on extraordinary occasions pack mules should never be tied to a picket line, but should be herded as much as possible. In bivouac they should be taken to graze at night as well as day, packers being detailed as herd guard.
>
> The 'bell' horse being hobbled or picketed in the vicinity, there is no danger of the mules stampeding, as they will not leave the 'bell.'
>
> If allowed to graze, mules will always keep in average condition, and on nutritious grasses will stand a twelve months' campaign and keep fat.
>
> *Mountainous country.*—In rough and moun-

From left to right: Apache scout Dutchy; Crook mounted on his mule, named "Apache" (Crook is wearing his prized African cork helmet); and Apache scout Alchesay. Circa 1880s. *(Photo courtesy of the National Archives.)*

tainous country, the pack mule will carry the same load (250 pounds), and travel from 10 to 15 miles per day. He should not, however, be forced when traveling up or down a mountain, unless the occasion is very urgent. Uphill work is hard on man and beast.

Forced marches.—In forced marches the pack animals should not be loaded in excess of 200 pounds.

If traveling with cavalry, the pack mule may not be able to spurt off at a 10-mile gait, but he will be pushing the horse before 30 miles are covered, and he has the horse at his mercy in a march of 75 to 100 miles in twenty-four hours.

The following instances, out of a great many, may be briefly mentioned:

In the campaign of 1881, under Colonel Buell, Fifteenth Infantry, against Chiefs Victorio and Nana, of the Warm Spring tribe of Apaches, a company of Indian scouts and one pack train made a march of 85 miles in twelve hours, loaded 200 pounds to the pack animal.

Later, in pursuing Indians of the same tribe, a company of Indian scouts and one pack train marched from old Fort Cummings to Fort Seldon, on the Rio Grande, about 60 miles, from sunrise to sunset; then went by rail to Fort Craig, New Mexico, loaded 250 pounds to the mule; marched across the valley, some 30 miles, to the San Mateo Range; struck the trail of Chief Nana and party; and, without making an all-night camp, followed the hostiles into old Mexico, south of the Hatchet Mountains.

This was a running fight the entire way. A distance of about 300 miles was covered in about four days.

During the 'Loco' outbreak from San Carlos Agency, Ariz., in 1882, one company of scouts and one pack train, loaded 200 pounds to the mule, made a forced march of 280 miles in three days.

Evolution of the Diamond Hitch

The following is another excerpt from the *Manual of Pack Transportation; Quartermaster Corps*, 1917.

This form of hitch has its origin in the crosstree hitch. The early trappers of the Hudson Bay Company introduced the crosstree hitch among the Indians of the Northwest, and later the Americans gave to this hitch the name of the "squaw" hitch; along the Pacific coast, in sections where sheep raising has become an industry, it is known as the "sheepherder's" hitch, and by miners and prospectors as the "prospector's" hitch.

In the use of the aparejo, in forming the crosstree hitch in bringing the loop of the running rope under the boot of the aparejo instead of around

Army packers found it easy to overload the mules. Often the pack outfit had to struggle to keep up with the command. (Photo courtesy of the Signal Corps, National Archives.)

Forming the diamond hitch. (Drawing from an Army technical manual, courtesy of the Government Printing Office.)

the "side" pack on each side, evolved the "double" hitch, and in not bringing a loop of the running rope under and forward of the standing rope—that is, forming the loop in rear of the standing rope—led to the formation of the "Oregon" diamond hitch, so named in being first practiced in that Territory before it became a State.

The practice of first throwing the lash rope cincha under the animal's belly to the off packer, in forming the regular diamond, in contrast to the crosstree and Oregon hitches, in which the lash rope is first thrown over the load and under the animal's belly by the near packer, may be said to date with the advent of the Americans after the discovery of gold in California, 1848–49. This I have heard disputed by some of the old-time packers of the early fifties, who stated the regular diamond was practiced by the Mexicans of California. However this may be, it may be stated the regular diamond hitch is used in the States bordering on the Rio Grande. In the Santa Rosa mines, State of Coahuila (Mexico), I have seen the diamond in use in 1878. In Mexico it has been the custom of using the crosstree and stirrup hitches, with the employment of the donkey, and aparejo made of matting; in the case of the stirrup hitch a cincha two feet long, having a ring at each end, is employed; in forming the hitch the cincha is held under the animal's belly, using the ring on each end instead of forming the stirrup.

The double diamond hitch was used in the days of freighting by civilian pack trains from The Dalles to the mining camps in the interior when barrels of flour, vinegar, pork, etc., had to be transported. This hitch had become a lost art in government service, due to a lack of necessity for its use, and is known to very few packers of the present day, the double hitch being erroneously called the "double diamond."

The pole hitch has been erroneously called the "squaw" hitch; the fact that the Indians have never used the aparejo confirms this statement. It cannot be used with the crosstree or riding saddle, as no portion of the rope in the formation of the hitch encircles the body of the animal.

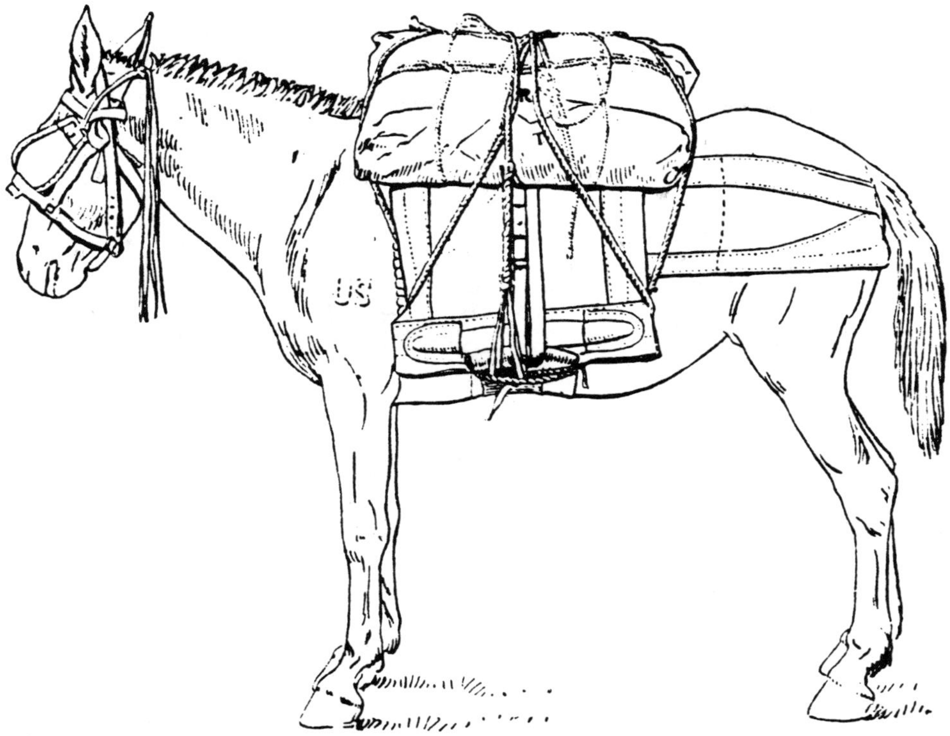

The double diamond. (Drawing from an Army technical manual, courtesy of the Government Printing Office.)

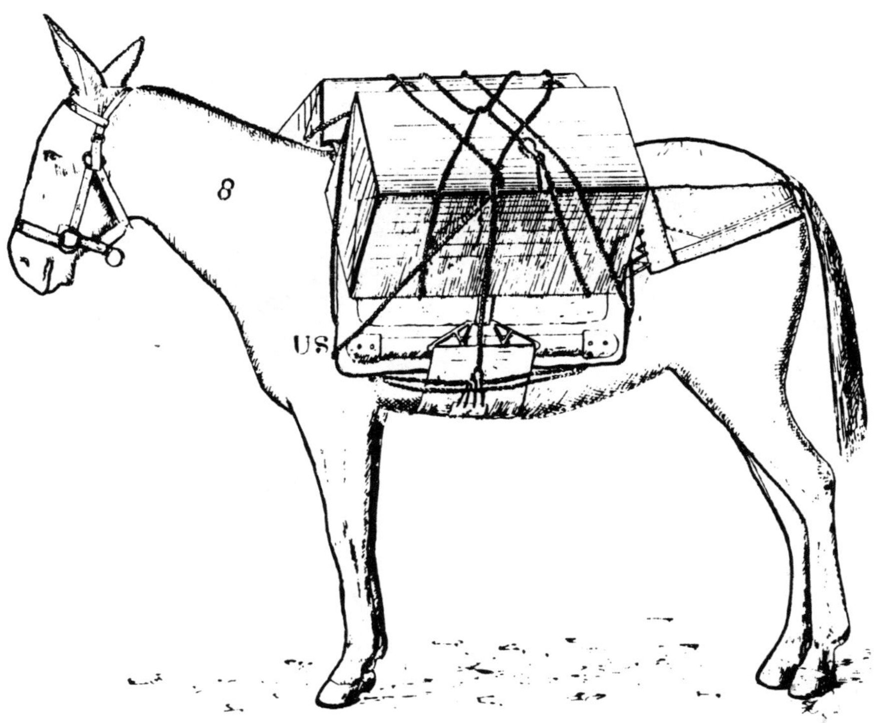

This drawing, from an Army technical manual, shows a mule loaded down with mess boxes. (Courtesy of the Government Printing Office.)

Almost every packer has his own variation of the famous diamond hitch. This is the basic pattern

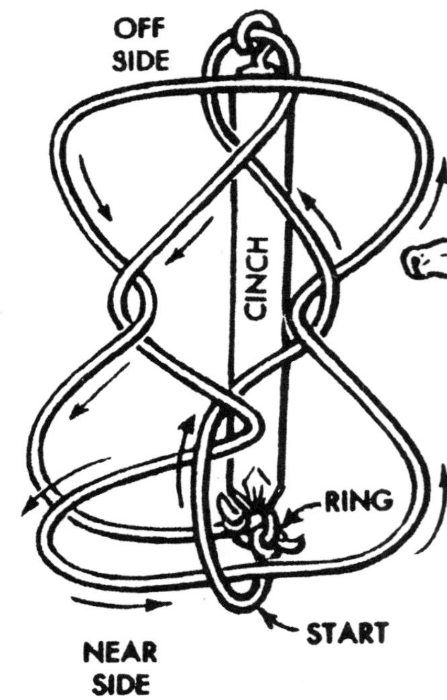

DIAMOND HITCH

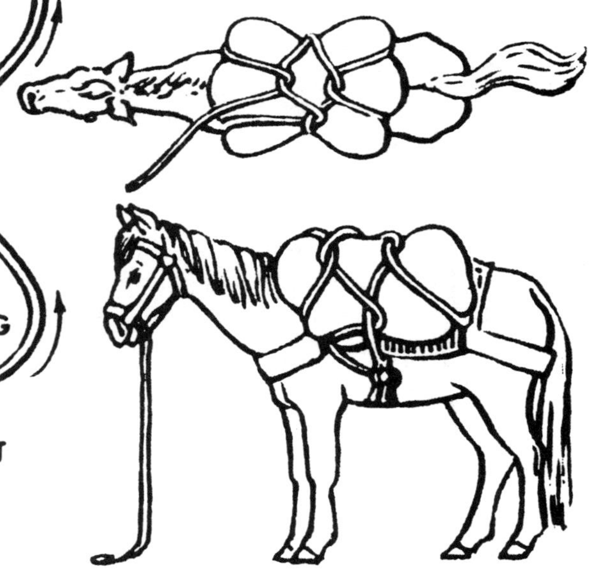

Two types of sawbuck pack saddles, the center rig and the double rig, that are standard for pack horses

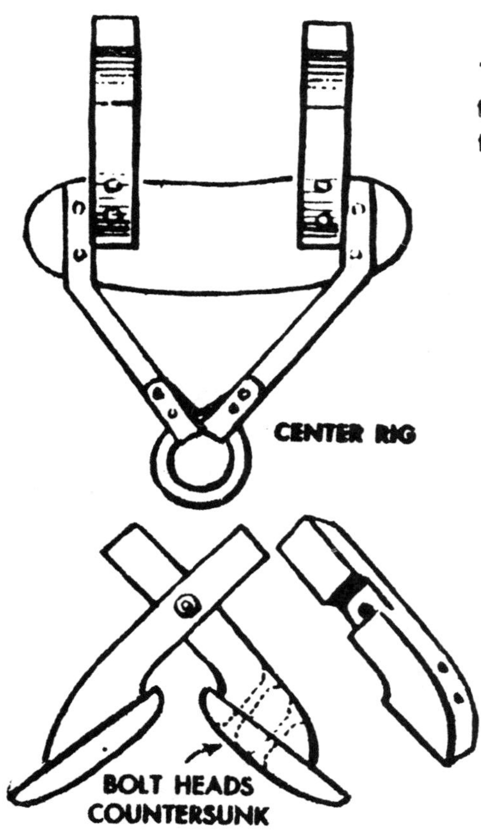

SAWBUCK PACK SADDLE

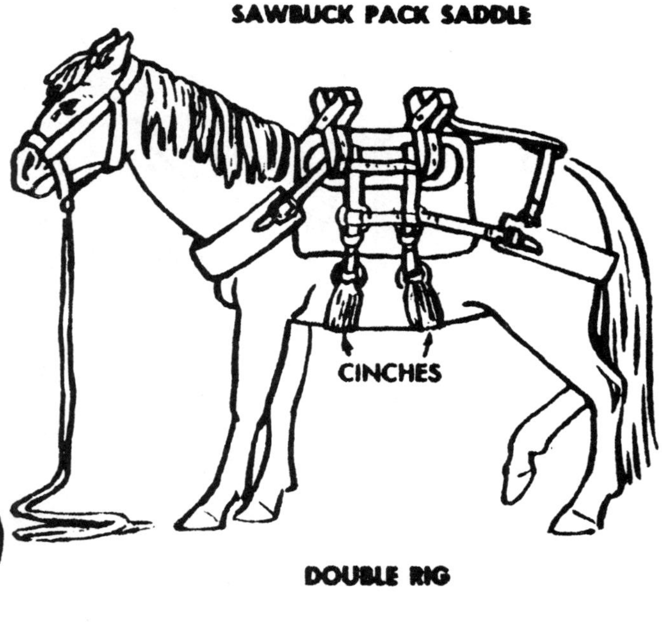

DOUBLE RIG

These drawings are from the book, Wildwood Wisdom *by Ellsworth Jaeger, copyright 1945 by the Macmillan Company, and are used with their permission.*

Frederic Remington sketched this packer hitching up a cinch in Arizona, c. 1886. Mules wore blinders while being packed. The average load was 200 to 250 pounds, according to the animal's weight. (Drawing courtesy of the Government Printing Office.)

Glossary

This Glossary also appeared in the *Manual of Pack Transportation; Quartermaster Corps*, 1917.

Aparejo (ap-pa-ray-ho): A pack saddle.

Bag, war: A clothes sack.

Bell: Ordinarily a sheep bell, attached by a strap to the neck of the lead horse or mule.

Bell horse: A horse with a bell strapped about its neck and used to lead a pack train of mules; sometimes alluded to as the "bell" in such expressions as "get the bell," "lead the bell," "stop the bell," "call the bell."

Bell sharp: Applied to mules that become especially attached to the "bell" horse.

Blind: A hood of leather, made to cover the eyes of a pack mule when loading the animal or tightening the load.

Boot: Term applied to the end pieces of aparejo.

Boot bar: A section of wood representing the finished product, when the boot of the aparejo is properly filled with hay by the skilled packer, and provided with slots to receive ribs of wood. (In connection with the saddle bar, the boot bar holds the ribs in place, thus stiffening the aparejo.)

Brake: To brake a pack; to brake a load—signifying the act of working the packs close together and into their proper relative positions after they have been tied together by a sling rope.

Bunch: A puffing up of the skin.

Cargo: The loads carried by a pack train, when spoken of collectively. To "form cargo," i.e., to arrange in an orderly and convenient manner an aggregation of loads.

Cargador: An individual who, in the organization of a pack train, is next in importance after the pack master. He has to do with making up and forming the cargo, equalizing the packs, caring for mules, repairing aparejos, etc.

Carrier piece: A fold of leather sewed in between the back and belly pieces of aparejo at rear, to which, by means of lacing, the crupper is attached, and which thus serves to support the crupper and prevent it from hanging too low on the mule's buttocks.

Center stitch line: The stitch line which divides the aparejo into two equal parts.

Cinch (cincha): A broad canvas band, by means of which the aparejo is secured on the mule's back.

Collar: That portion of the aparejo which lies over the mule's withers. It is so shaped as to relieve the mule of all pressure on the withers.

Corona: A saddle pad, which is placed on the mule's back before the blanket and aparejo are put on. A numeral is placed on one of its sides to distinguish it.

Cover, aparejo (or sobre-jalma): A canvas covering attached to the aparejo to protect the leather from wear and tear. Called by packers a "sovereian hammer, soldier hammer."

Cover, pack: A section of heavy canvas employed to wrap therein, by means of rope, certain packages that may deteriorate by exposure to rain or dampness.

Cover, rigging: Covers used to protect the aparejos in camp or bivouac.

Cover, cargo: Canvas used to protect aggregation of loads, termed the "cargo," in camp or bivouac.

Cover, feed: Canvas laid on the ground at the picket line, on which grain is placed for feeding the animals.

Crupper: A leather band attached to the front facing and carrier pieces of the aparejo, and fitting under the mule's tail, its purpose being to steady the aparejo, and to prevent it from slipping to the front.

Deadman: A holdfast, sunk in the ground, to which the picket line is attached.

Diamond hitch: Name applied to the lashing, by means of which the load is secured to the aparejo, the two ropes forming a diamond or lozenge on top of the load.

Dock piece: That portion of the crupper that fits under the animal's tail; also applied to that portion of the animal's tail under which the dock of the crupper rests.

Drag tails: Term applied to mules that are farthest away from the "bell" when traveling; also applied to a lazy packer.

Facings: Additional pieces or strips of leather, applied to certain parts of the aparejo to strengthen them.

"Go:" Term used by the "near" to the "off" packer, when hitch is formed and ready to be tightened (Near side—left side; off side—right side.)

Hand-hole: Hole made in the belly piece of the aparejo in the center of each side, to enable the packer to insert the hay or grass that forms the padding.

"Hold:" Signal by the "near" to the "off" packer to hold his pack in position, while the "near" packer brakes the load.

Lair: Term applied to the rope used in securing pack covers around pack. Hence, to "lair;" "to lair up;" meaning to secure the pack cover to the pack by means of the lair rope.

Line up: Meaning to cause the pack mules to take position at rear of the rigging on the proper flank of the "bell" horse.

Load: A pack or packs forming the burden for one pack mule. Hence, "to load up," meaning to place the loads, as formed in cargo, on the pack mules.

Pack: In the ordinary case, that portion of the load carried on one side of the mule's back. A load, however, may consist of a single pack or of several packs, depending on the nature of the articles to be packed, or the exigencies of the service.

Pack up: Meaning to load up; to place the loads, as formed in cargo, on the pack mules.

Packer, first-class: One skilled in the art of preparing cargo; loading a pack mule; adjusting a load so that it will balance evenly on the mule's back, etc.; one familiar with the "diamond" and other hitches used in securing loads, and versed in the usages and customes of the pack service.

Packer, second-class: A novice in the art of packing.

Pack master: A master in the art of packing; one who has charge of a pack train.

Ribbing up: Placing in an aparejo the sticks, or whatever may be used to give stiffness to the sides of the aparejo.

Rigging: Term applied to the aparejos in a pack train; particularly when it is desired to refer to them in a collective sense.

Saddle bar: A section of wood representing the finished product when the saddle of the aparejo is properly filled with hay or similar material, by the skilled packer, and provided with slots to receive ribs of wood. In connection with the boot bar, the saddle bar holds the ribs in place, by means of which the aparejo is stiffened.

Set up: To set up an aparejo, meaning to prepare it for use by inserting the ribs, and then padding it with hay, so as to adjust it properly to the shape of the mule's back.

Settle: To adjust packs to their places on the aparejo, as in the case of simple box loads. Here it is not necessary to brake the load, i.e., to work the near pack up and down, until it is in place, as the two packs may readily be settled on the aparejo so as to ride evenly.

Shoe: Term applied to the protecting sticks of the aparejo cover.

Sling: Term applied to the rope used in tying the packs together on the mule's back prior to being lashed. Hence, "to sling" the load; "to cross sling;" "to double sling;" and "to double cross sling."

Snap up: To tie animals together by their halter shanks, while standing at the rigging.

Stem or snap: Names sometimes applied to halter shanks.

Sticks, protecting: Used on the aparejo cover to stiffen the ends. Sometimes called shoes.

Sticks, tamping: Used in tamping hay, etc., in the corners of the aparejo.

Tie: Signal from the "off" to the "near" packer that all slack has been rendered on the running rope. Also signal from the "near" to the "off" packer for the latter to secure the end of the rope, on completion of the hitch.

"Tied:" Signal from the "near" to the "off" packer, in slinging the load, that the "square" knot has been tied.

Trail: A path, usually narrow; hence incumbent upon animals of a train to move in single file. "To trail" means to follow in single file after the "bell" horse.

Train, pack: A pack train is an organization comprising fifty pack animals, a proper complement of men, and a complete equipment.

16

COMMUNICATIONS IN THE CAMPAIGN OF 1886

Though smoke signals, signal fires, and flashes with a piece of metal were crude methods of communication, these Apache "telegrams" were confounding the Federal troops during the campaign of 1886. To make matters worse for General George Crook, who was in charge of the campaign at the time, the Apaches had found a clever method of knocking out the Army's telegraph system. They would cut the wire and "splice" it with wet rawhide, which, when dried, formed an almost invisible patch that could hardly be detected by the repair crews who rode the lines. Crook's failure to force the surrender of Geronimo was beginning to irritate his superior, General Philip Sheridan. Sheridan was now sitting in Washington, flushed over his victory in the South, and was little inclined to accept Crook's excuses.

Sheridan was a hero in Washington. He had broken the back of the Confederacy, and thought he could probably do the same with the Apache. Crook's suggestion that they imprison the Indians in eastern prison camps for two years, and then return them to the reservation, met with Sheridan's disdain. It was Sheridan, after all, who was said to have muttered, "The only good Indian is a dead Indian." He ordered Crook to fight until there was unconditional surrender, undercutting an agreement that Crook was finalizing with the Apache. After an exchange of explosive missives between Crook and Sheridan, Crook rescinded his offer of a two-year exile, and Geronimo and Naiche (another renegade) rode off to their mountain hideout, tired of lies, full of mescal, and feeling meaner than a tromped-on polecat.

Then on March 31, 1886, Sheridan fired off a telegram berating Crook: "It seems strange that Geronimo and party could have escaped without knowledge of the scouts." Crook was clearly in trouble. He relied on his trusty scouts and believed that the Apache campaign could never be successful without them. Now, with Geronimo and Naiche camped in the mountains, any control Crook might have had over the Apache was gone. Crook had nearly reached an agreement with the Indians, but Sheridan refused to back him up. Crook was almost as angry as Geronimo, and resigned on April Fools Day.

The very next day, General Nelson A. Miles, stationed at Fort Leavenworth, Kansas, was sent to replace Crook at the Department of Arizona, and to take up the battle with the Apache. With Miles came a change in strategy: no more Apache scouts, and no more Indian volunteers. More Regular Army troops were rushed into the fray and then sent to the border areas to contain the Apache, who frequently left and reentered the United States.

Miles attacked the communication problem. He had seen the Indians' clever job of splicing the telegraph wires with rawhide, and he knew that without a reliable means of communication, it would be very hard to contain the Apache. The telegraph lines were extremely vulnerable. Miles listened to the soldiers' tales of gloom and doom with a measure of patience, replying that the Federals were, after all, superior in intelligence and technology, and that they ought to be able to equal the cunning of the Indian.

In 1886, General Nelson Miles made considerable use of the heliograph during his Indian campaigns in the Southwest, where many stations were established and utilized until 1890. This web of stations was anchored high in the hills and mountains southwest of Fort Huachuca, extended up through the heart of Arizona to Fort Whipple, and embraced the western half of the Territory of New Mexico. Flashes from these mirrors could be seen from 30 to 100 miles away. (Photo courtesy of the Signal Corps, National Archives.)

Miles had heard of the heliograph, an instrument employing a sighting rod and mirrors, that transmitted messages by Morse code, from station to station, by means of the sun's rays. In a way, this was similar to one of the methods of the Apaches—using sunlight and bright flashes. But the heliograph systematized the operation, and could send messages many miles farther. Miles's installation of the heliograph was the largest one to be attempted at that time. On April 20, 1886, he sent the following orders that clearly indicated his insistence on using the new technology. This quote is from his autobiography, *Personal Recollections of Nelson A. Miles*[1]:

> The chief object of the troops will be to capture or destroy any band of hostile Apache Indians found in this section of the country. . . . To better facilitate this duty, and afford as far as practicable protection to the scattered settlements, the territory is subdivided into districts of observation as shown upon maps furnished by the Department engineer officer, and will place under commanding officers to be hereafter designated. . . . The signal detachments will be placed upon the highest peaks and prominent lookouts, to discover any movements of Indians and to transmit messages between the different camps.

He also recollects the following in his autobiography:

> I had it in mind to utilize for our benefit and their discomfiture the very elements that had been the greatest obstacles in that whole country to their subjugation, namely the high mountain ranges, the glaring, burning sunlight, and an atmosphere void of moisture. I therefore requested the chief signal officers and men, and the best instruments and appliances that were attainable. I also directed my engineer officer to block out the country in such a way that we might establish a network of points of observation and communication over that entire country. Posts were established over the country most frequented by the Apaches, a district some two hundred miles wide by three hundred miles long, north and south. On the high mountain peaks of this region, I posted strong guards of infantry supplied with casks of water and provisions enough to last them for thirty days in case of siege. They were provided with the best field glasses and telescopes that could be obtained, and also with the best heliostats.
>
> The heliostat is a little invention of an English officer which had been used in India many years before. My attention was first directed to it nearly twenty years ago when in the office of the chief signal officer of the Army, General Myer, who then had six of these instruments. As they were not being used, I suggested that he send them to me at the cantonment on the Yellowstone, now Fort Keogh, Montana, and I there established the first line in this country, from Fort Keogh to Fort Custer. I afterward used them experimentally in the Department of the Columbia between Vancouver Barracks and Mount Hood a distance in an air line of fifty miles. I now determined to test them to their full extent and make practical use of them in the Department of Arizona.

Miles requested twelve additional operators plus equipment from the Signal Corps School near Washington, D.C., as only a very few of his soldiers knew Morse code well enough to send and receive messages. Washington sent eleven operators, and, during May and June of 1886, shipments of thirty-four heliographs, including Mance, Garner, and Grugan models. In addition to the heliographs, Washington also supplied ten telescopes and thirty marine binoculars. Miles continues in his autobiography:

> I was much gratified to receive the hearty support of General Hazen in sending me skilled men; and within a short time these stations were fixed on the high mountain peaks. It was remarkable what advantage they gave us in observing the movements of the Indians or of the troops in the valleys below, and in reporting it promptly to the central station or headquarters; also in communicating with the various commands, posts and stations in the field. At one time, when the system was in full operation, to test its efficiency a message of twenty-five words was sent from the extreme eastern to the extreme western station, over a zigzag course of four hundred miles, and the answer was received in four hours, the total distance traversed being about eight hundred miles. Between these two points for a part of the distance there was telegraphic communication, yet the message could not have been sent by telegraph and courier and answer received as quickly as it was by this method.
>
> The importance of the work done by the heliostat in the Apache campaign makes it worthy of a more extended notice than has yet been accorded it. The method of signaling by it is very simple. By alternately imposing and removing some object in front of the mirror which forms the principal part of the instrument, long or short flashes of light are made which indicate words and letters to the eye in the same way that the telegraph indicates them to the ear. The mirrors are usually mounted on a tripod, and the distance through which this

method of communication may be carried depends on the clearness of the atmosphere and the size of the mirrors.

As General Miles noted, the heliostat had been used, or at least tested, by Chief Signal Officer Albert J. Myers. In 1879, Myers commented that the use of direct light flashes or flashes from mirrors "has been known for a long time." He explained, "Many years ago messages were in this way transmitted . . . in the ordnance service of England—a distance said to have been over ninety miles, and sun-flashes from the heliotrope, or sun-flash turner, an instrument used in surveys, have very often . . . been used for conveying brief messages between parties accompanying surveyors and engineers, as in the survey of Lake Superior."[2]

Several of these early devices were tested during the Civil War, using flashing lights at night. It was suggested that an instrument could be used to send signals by reflecting sunlight, but the difficulty of transporting the fragile yet cumbersome instruments had prevented large-scale testing.

Myers's position was that the heliograph was useful, but only as an auxiliary to other methods.

But the heliograph had been used before. According to the *Encyclopedia Britannica*, the device was invented by Sir Henry Christopher Mance (1840–1926), while working in the Persian Gulf Telegraph Department of the Indian Government after the era of the American Civil War. While the instrument was never really accepted by the Indian Office because it was fragile, it was used in military campaigns in the frontiers of India and in South Africa, where the sunlight was strong and continuous. It was also used in Manchuria during the Russo-Japanese War (1904–05). Acetylene lamps were used at night, and both shutter and movable mirror versions of the heliograph were used in daylight. Despite the oft-noted fragility of the equipment, it was carried on pack animals without undue difficulty.

The use of the heliograph during the Apache campaigns fulfilled three main functions: Information was dispatched within the troop system, telegraph messages were also relayed from the point where they were received to areas where there were no telegraph wires, and the heliograph and telegraph were used together for extra assurance.

We know that messages were relayed that told of troop deployment before Geronimo's surrender. In April and May of 1886, some Apaches attempted to reenter the United States. This information was

During July of 1886, 432 messages were sent and received by various stations, keeping post commanders in touch with one another in a matter of hours instead of days. (Photo courtesy of the Signal Corps, National Archives.)

In addition to surveying both Indian and troop maneuvers, the heliograph was also used by the soldiers to dispatch personal messages from one station to another. (Photo courtesy of the Arizona Historical Society Library.)

relayed by heliograph, getting tactical orders to officers in the field, which thereby prevented the reentry. Clearly, Miles was more aware of the locations of various commands, especially those operating in Mexico, than he could have been had he depended on telegraphs with couriers to fill in the blind spots.

In his autobiography, Miles reports Geronimo as being flabbergasted at the accomplishments of the heliograph. However, the wily Indian may have been faking his surprise to see what else he could find out. The heliograph stations were well fortified to withstand possible Indian attack, but, for some reason, none of them were attacked. In an entry in his diary (also from his autobiography), Miles tells of a meeting with Geronimo in Skeleton Canyon. The dates of the meeting were noted as September 3 and 4.

> I told him [Geronimo] that we had the use of steam, and could move troops with great rapidity. . . . That we also had the telegraph and heliostat, both superior to any of their methods of communication. . . . I said to Geronimo, "We can watch your movements and send messages over the tops of mountains in a small part of one day, and over a distance which it would take a man mounted on a swift pony twenty days to travel." Geronimo's face assumed an air of curiosity and incredulity. . . . As I have previously had occasion to remark, when an Indian sees something that he cannot comprehend, he attributes it to some superior power beyond his knowledge and control. [Geronimo] told me he had observed these flashes upon the mountain heights, and believing them to be spirits, had avoided them by going around those points of the mountains never realizing that it was a subtle power used by his enemies. . . .

(In a demonstration of the heliograph, Miles had a message sent to Fort Bowie inquiring for Geronimo whether his brother was well, and a reply was returned shortly.)

> This struck the savage with awe, and evidently made a strong impression upon him. I noticed that he said something to one of the warriors close by him, at which the warrior quietly turned upon his heel, walked back a short distance to where his pony was lariated, jumped on his back and rode rapidly back in the direction of the mountains from whence Geronimo had come.

(Miles then asked what Geronimo had said to the warrior.)

> The interpreter replied, "He told him to go and tell Nachez that there was a power here which he could not understand; and to come in, and come quick." The heliostat had performed its last and

> best work, and in a few hours Nachez came riding down from the mountains with his band of warriors and their families and came into camp, though with much hesitation and reserve.

There are, however, some holes in Miles's dramatic story. Some authors have noted that Nachez didn't surrender that way at all, and there is the matter of Miles's sketch of the heliograph in his book. The sketch shows a heliograph that is not representative of the models available at that time, and, what's more, the map in the book purporting to describe the 1886 heliograph system is actually a description of the 1890 practice maneuver.

Nevertheless, the heliograph was described by others as successful, and several Army notables, including Lieutenants Dravo and Wood, were sent to plan an extended system. Practice lines were established at Fort Apache, as well as Forts Bowie, Huachuca, Union, and Mohave. At these forts, classes also were held to train officers in the use and repair of the systems and instruments.

Much of the interest in the heliograph was a result of Miles's capture of Geronimo, and the resulting end to the Apache hostile action. Miles wrote the following (reprinted in his autobiography) to his wife after the capture, on September 7, 1886:

> We have at last been most successful. I am making a clean sweep of the hostile Apache out of this country and it has given a feeling of relief and security to thousands of homes that they have never felt before. . . . It is a brilliant ending of a difficult problem.

After the Apache action was over, interest in the heliograph continued, and larger districts were defined, with junior officers getting a chance at command. By the spring of 1890, a large operation was being planned by Colonel William J. Volkmar, assistant adjutant general and chief signal officer for the Department of Arizona. Volkmar intended to establish stations from Whipple Barracks in Arizona to Fort Stanton, New Mexico. Heliographs were sent from the Signal Corp's headquarters, including the newer Maus models as well as older devices, and official forms were devised to standardize procedures. But time was not on the side of the heliograph, which disappeared from use around 1900, to be replaced by methods that were as far ahead of the heliograph as that instrument was ahead of Geronimo's smoke signals.

Notes

[1]Published by Werner, 1896.

[2]*A Manual of Signals for the Use of Signal Officers in the Field*, Government Printing Office, 1879.

A Brief History of the Morse Telegraph

Samuel F. B. Morse (1791–1872), the inventor of the telegraph, was an American portrait painter with a keen interest in the new science of electricity. In 1832, while returning from Europe aboard the packet *Sully*, he conceived the idea of using electricity and magnetism to convey messages over wires.

In 1844 Morse completed a practical, working telegraph line between Washington and Baltimore. The historic message "What Hath God Wrought!" was transmitted on May 24, 1844. The original Morse apparatus recorded dots and dashes on a moving paper tape. By 1850 operators had learned to read by sound and this became the normal method of operation. The transcontinental line was completed in 1861.

Morse's invention ranks as one of the greatest of all time. In addition, it stands as a monument to the skill of the men and women who, as operators, made the Morse system practical and kept it going for over 100 years.

Telegraph Codes

	AMERICAN MORSE CODE	CONTINENTAL CODE
A	•—	•—
B	—•••	—•••
C	•• •	—•—•
D	—••	—••
E	•	•
F	•—•	••—•
G	——•	——•
H	••••	••••
I	••	••
J	—•—•	•———
K	—•—	—•—
L	⸺	•—••
M	——	——
N	—•	—•
O	• •	———
P	•••••	•——•
Q	••—•	——•—
R	• ••	•—•
S	•••	•••
T	—	—
U	••—	••—
V	•••—	•••—
W	•——	•——
X	•—••	—••—
Y	•• ••	—•——
Z	••• •	——••
&	• •••	

Figures

	AMERICAN MORSE CODE	CONTINENTAL CODE
1	•——•	•————
2	••—••	••———
3	•••—•	•••——
4	••••—	••••—
5	———	•••••
6	••••••	—••••
7	——••	——•••
8	—••••	———••
9	—••—	————•
0	⸻	—————

Punctuation

American Morse Code:

(.)	••——••
(,)	•—•—
(?)	—••—•
(:)	—•— • •
(;)	••• ••
(-)	•••• •—••
(!)	———•
(')	••—• •—••
(/)	••— —
(	••••• —•
)	••••• •• ••
(")	••—• —•
(")	••—• —•—•

Continental Code:

(.)	•—•—•—
(,)	——••——
(?)	••——••
(:)	———•••
(;)	—•—•—•
(-)	—••••—
(!)	None at present
(')	•————•
(/)	—••—•
()	—•——•—
(")	•—••—•

17

THE HELIOGRAPH

The following description of the heliograph appeared in the *Signal Corps Manual*, published in 1908 by the Government Printing Office.

The heliograph is an instrument designed for the purpose of transmitting signals by means of the sun's rays.

Historical—Experiments with the heliograph with a view to its adoption as a part of the visual signaling equipment of the United States Army were commenced as early as 1878. The reported successful use of the instrument by the British in India about this time lead to the importation of two heliographs of the Mance pattern. A series of experiments with these machines

The heliograph was first tested in Arizona at Fort Whipple in 1877. Heliograph stations were anchored at Fort Huachuca and extended through the heart of Arizona and the western half of the territory of New Mexico. The heliograph was used extensively during the Apache campaigns of 1885–87. (Photo courtesy of the U.S. Signal Corps, National Archives.)

At the heliograph stations, the mirrors helped keep the men all freshly shaven. (Photo courtesy of the U.S. Signal Corps, National Archives.)

conducted for the purpose of eliminating certain objectionable features finally resulted in the evolution of the present type of service heliograph.

The early English heliograph was not provided with a shutter, the flash being directed on the distant station by means of a movable mirror controlled by a key. The great objection to this type of instrument was the impossibility of maintaining accurate adjustment during the transmission of signals due to the fact that the manipulation of the mirror tended to throw the flash constantly out of alignment. To overcome this, the American heliograph has been provided with a screen designed to operate as a shutter and control the flash reflected from an immobile mirror.

Description—the service heliograph equipment of the Signal Corps consists of:

A sole-leather pouch with shoulder strap containing:

1 sun mirror
1 station mirror — Enclosed in a wooden box.

1 screen, 1 sighting rod, 1 screw-driver.

A small pouch, sliding by 2 loops upon the strap of the larger pouch, containing 1 mirror bar.

A skeleton leather case containing 2 tripods.

The mirrors are each 4½-inch squares of plate glass supported by sheet brass and cardboard backings, and mounted in brass retaining frames. At the center of each mirror there is an unsilvered spot three thirty-seconds of an inch in diameter and holes corresponding to these spots are drilled in the backing. The sun mirror differs from the station mirror only in that it has a paper disk pasted upon its face covering the unsilvered spot. The mirror frames are carried by brass supports provided at the bases with conical projections accurately turned to fit the sockets of the mirror bar and grooved at the ends to receive the clamping spring. Each support is fitted with a tangent screw and worm wheel attachment functioned to control the motion of the mirror frame about its horizontal axis.

The mirror bar is a bronze casting provided at the center with a clamp threaded to fit the screw of the tripod. By releasing the clamp the bar may be moved independently of the screw and adjusted to any desired position. Conical sockets for the reception of the mirror supports are provided at the ends of the mirror bar. These sockets work freely in the bar and, being actuated by a tangent screw and worm wheel, serve to regulate the motion of the mirror frame about its vertical axis. Clamp springs, for engaging and securing the ends of the mirror frame supports, are attached at each end of the bar.

The screen is a brass frame 6½ inches square, in which six segments or leaves are mounted in such a way as to form a shutter. The leaves are designed to turn through arcs of 90° on horizontal axes, unanimity of movement being secured by connections made with a common crank bar. The crank bar is operated by a key and retractile spring which serve to reveal and cut off the flash. A set screw and check nut at the lower edge of the screen frame limits the motion of the crank bar and the opening of the leaves. A threaded base support furnishes the means of attaching the screen frame to the tripod.

The sighting rod is a brass rod 6½ inches long, carrying at the upper end a front sight and a movable disk. About the rod is fitted a moveable bronze collar, coned and grooved to take the socket and clamping spring of the mirror bar. A milled edged bronze washer serves to clamp the collar to the rod at any desired point.

The tripods are similar in all respects, the screw of either threading into the mirror bar or screen frame. Each tripod is provided with a hook at the base of the head, allowing the suspension of a weight when great stability is required.

Assembling—There are two ways of assembling the heliograph and the position of the sun is the guide in determining which of the two should, in any given case, be employed. When the sun is in front of the operator (that is, in front of a plane through his position at right angles to the line joining the stations) the sun mirror only is required; with the sun in rear of this plane both mirrors should be used. With one mirror the rays of the sun are reflected directly from the sun mirror to the distant station; with two mirrors, the rays are reflected from the sun mirror to the station mirror, and thence to the distant station.

With one mirror: Firmly set one of the tripods upon the ground; attach the mirror bar to the tripod; insert and clamp in the sockets the sun mirror and sighting rod, the latter having the disk turned down. At a distance of about 6 inches, sight through the center of the unsilvered spot in the mirror and turn the mirror bar, raising or lowering the sighting rod until the center of the mirror, the extreme point of the sighting rod, and the distant station are accurately in line. Firmly clamp the mirror bar to the tripod, taking care not to disturb the alignment, and turn up the disk of the sighting rod. The mirror is then moved by means of the tangent screws until the "shadow spot" falls upon the paper disk in the sighting rod, after which the flash will be visible at the distant station. The "shadow spot" is readily found by holding a sheet of paper or the hand about 6 inches in front of the mirror, and should be constantly kept in view until located upon the disk. The screen is attached to a tripod and established close to, and in front of, the sighting disk, in such a way as to intercept the flash.

With two mirrors: Firmly set one of the tripods on the ground; clamp the mirror bar diagonally across the line of vision to the distant station; clamp the sun mirror facing the sun to one end of the mirror bar and the station mirror facing the distant station. Stooping down, the head near and in rear of the station mirror, turn the sun mirror by means of its tangent screws until the whole of the station mirror is seen reflected in the

The type of telegraph the Army used from 1870 through 1889, consisting of a Bunnell Company relay, an Electrical Construction and Maintenance Company sounder, and a Knox and Shain Company camelback key. (Photo courtesy of the Gill Schlehman collection.)

sun mirror and the unsilvered spot and the reflection of the paper disk accurately cover each other. Still looking into the sun mirror, adjust the station mirror by means of the tangent screws until the reflection of the distant station is brought exactly in line with the top of the reflection of the disk and the top of the unsilvered spot of the sun mirror; after this the station mirror must not be touched. Now step behind the sun mirror and adjust it by means of the tangent screws so that the "shadow spot" falls upon the center of the paper disk on the station mirror. The flash will then be visible at the distant station. The screen and its tripod are established as described in the single mirror assembling.

Alternate method with two mirrors: Clamp the mirror bar diagonally across the line of vision to the distant station, with the sun mirror and the station mirror approximately facing the sun and distant station, respectively.

Look through the small hole in the sun mirror and turn the station mirror on its vertical and horizontal axes until the paper disk on the station mirror accurately covers the distant station.

Standing behind the sun mirror, turn it on its horizontal and vertical axes by means of the tangent screw attachments until the shadow spot falls upon the paper disk on the station mirror.

Adjustment—Perfect adjustment is maintained only by keeping the "shadow spot" uninterruptedly in the center of the paper disk, and as this "spot" continually changes its position with the apparent movement of the sun, one signalman should be in constant attendance on the tangent screws of the sun mirror. Movement imparted by these screws to the mirror does not disturb the alignment, as its center (the unsilvered spot) is at the intersection of the axes of revolution. Extra care bestowed upon preliminary adjustment is repaid by increased brilliancy of flash. With the alignment absolutely assured and the "shadow spot" at the center of the disk, the axis of the cone of reflected rays is coincident with the line of sight and the distant station receives the greatest intensity of light. Remember the distant observer is unquestionably the better judge as to the character of the flash received; and if therefore, adjustment is called for when the "shadow spot" is at the center of the disk, the alignment is probably at fault and should be looked after at once. In setting up the tripods always see that the legs have a sufficient spread to give a secure base and on yielding soil press firmly into the ground. Keep the head of the tripod as nearly level as possible and in high wind ballast by hanging a substantial weight to the hook. See that the screen completely obscures the flash; also that the flash passes entire when the screen is opened. This feature of the adjustment is partially regulated by the set screw attached to the screen frame. The retractile spring should sharply return all the leaves of the screen to their normal positions when the key is released. Failure to respond promptly is obviated by strengthening or replacing the spring.

Operation—It is of the utmost importance that uniformity in mechanical movement of the screen be cultivated, as lack of rhythm in the signals of the sender entails "breaks" and delay on the part of the receiver. Dark backgrounds should, when practicable, be selected for heliograph stations, as the signals can be most easily distinguished against them.

To find a distant station, its position being unknown, reverse the catch holding the station mirror and with the hand turn the mirror very slowly at the horizon over the full azimuth distance in which the distant station may possibly lie. This should be repeated not less than twice, after which, within a reasonable time, there being no response, the mirror will be directed upon a point nearer the home station and the same process repeated. With care and intelligence it is quite probable that, a station being within range and watching for signals from a distant station with which it may be desired to exchange messages, this method will rarely fail to find the sought-for station.

The exact direction of either station searching for the other being unknown, that station which first perceives that it is being called will adjust its flash upon the distant station to enable it when this light is observed to make proper adjustments. If the position of each station is known to the other, the station first ready for signaling will direct a steady flash upon the distant station to enable the latter to see not only that the first station is ready for work, but to enable the distant station to adjust its flash upon the first station.

Smoked or colored glasses are issued for the purpose of relieving the strain on the eyes produced by reading heliograph signals.

Care of apparatus—Minor parts of the instrument should be dismounted only to effect repairs, for which spare parts are furnished on requisition. Steel parts should be kept oiled and free from rust. Tangent screws and bearings should be frequently inspected for dust or grit. Mirrors should invariably be wiped clean before using. In case of accident to the sun mirror, the station mirror can be made available for substitution therefore by removing the paper disk. If the tripod legs become loose at the head joints, tighten the assembling screws with the screw-driver.

Powers and limitations of the heliograph—Portability, great range, comparative rapidity of operation, and the invisibility of the signals except to observers located approximately on a right line joining the stations between which communication is had, are some of the advantages derived from using the heliograph in visual signaling.

The principal disadvantage results from the entire dependence of the instrument upon the presence of sunlight. The normal working range of the heliograph is about 30 miles, though instances of its having attained ranges many times greater than this are of record. The heliograph can be depended upon to transmit from five to twelve words per minute.

APPENDIX
BIBLIOGRAPHIES
ACKNOWLEDGMENTS
INDEX

APPENDIX: THE 1885 UNIFORM CHANGEOVER—WITH PLATES

REPORT OF THE QUARTERMASTER-GENERAL TO THE SECRETARY OF WAR BEGINNING OF THE SECOND SESSION OF THE FORTY-EIGHTH CONGRESS VOLUME I

QUARTERMASTER-GENERAL'S OFFICE,
Washington, D.C., October 9, 1884

Sir: I have the honor to submit the annual report of the operations of the Quartermaster's Department during the fiscal year ending June 30, 1884:

The tables, statements, abstracts, etc., which accompany this report will be found to give the items of appropriations, expenditures, disbursements, etc., in all their details.

Duties of the Quartermaster's Department

Under sections 219 and 220, Revised Statutes, and the authority of the Secretary of War, the Quartermaster's Department transports troops, munitions of war, equipments, military property, and all articles of supply from the places of purchase to the several armies, garrisons, posts and recruiting places; provides for the safe keeping of such articles, the distribution, adequate and timely supply of the same to the regimental quartermasters and to such officers as may by virtue of the Secretary of War's regulations be intrusted with the same; and the officers of this department pay for store-rent and storage necessary for keeping such supplies.

By section 1133 it is further made—

The duty of the officers of the Quartermaster's Department, under the direction of the Secretary of War, to purchase and distribute to the Army all military stores and supplies requisite for its use which other corps are not directed by law to provide; to furnish means of transportation for the Army, its military stores and supplies, and to provide for and pay all incidental expenses of the military service which other corps are not directed to provide for and pay.

Section 1139 provides that—

The Quartermaster-General, under the direction of the Secretary of War, shall prescribe and enforce a system of accountability for all quartermaster's supplies (furnished to the Army or to officers, seamen, and marines).

By acts approved June 18, 1866, and July 28, 1866, the provisions of this act were extended to include the counties of Berkeley and Jefferson, West Virginia, and the loyal citizens of the State of Tennessee.

And further, it is provided by the acts of Congress and the regulations founded thereon, that the Quartermaster's Department shall secure grounds for national cemeteries, to preserve the graves of all soldiers who fell in battle, died of disease in the field or hospital, in the rebellion, from desecration; to secure suitable burial places for all honorably discharged soldiers, sailors, or marines who served during the late war, either in the regular or volunteer forces, dying subsequent to the passage of this act (approved March 3, 1873), in a national cemetery free of cost.

Provision is also made by law for the Quartermaster's Department to furnish suitable headstones to mark the graves of all soldiers, sailors, or marines, who have served during the late war, whose burial is provided for as above, or who may have been buried in private cemeteries.

Under these several acts, above recited, and other of like import, the Quartermaster's Department provides the means of transportation by land and water for troops and materials of war for the Army (but not for the transportation of the arms for the militia of the several States); it transports the property for other Executive Departments, on proper requisition, the outlay therefor being reimbursed to the appropriation for the department; it provides wagons, ambulances, carts, saddles, and horse equipments (except for the cavalry), and harness (except that used by the artillery).

This department provides vessels for water transportation; wharves; constructs and repairs roads or military purposes; pays tolls; and builds all necessary military bridges. It provides and distributes clothing, tents, and equipage; fuel, forage, stationery, lumber, straw for bedding for men and animals, and all material for camps and for shelter of troops and stores; furniture for barracks, such as bunks, benches, chairs, tables, and lockers; heating and cooking stoves for use in public barracks and quarters; tools for mechanics and laborers in the Quartermaster's Department, and lights for all military posts and buildings. It builds barracks, quarters, storehouses, and hospitals; provides, by hire or purchase, grounds for military encampments and buildings; supplies periodicals and newspapers, or school books in lieu of periodicals, if desired, to the post libraries for the use of enlisted men. It also provides grounds for cemeteries, and for the burial of officers and soldiers therein; lodges for superintendents of cemeteries, and, generally, for fencing, marking by suitable stones, and care of graves of soldiers who die in service on duty throughout the country.

Under the provisions of section 219, Revised Statutes, "other officers" than "regimental quartermasters," to the average number of 106, have been detailed in the Quartermaster's Department in doing its duties in various ways in the care and "distribution of the stores of the Quartermaster's Department, under the Secretary of War and his regulations."

These officers are justly entitled to extra pay for this extra service, and continued efforts have been made for some years to get their extra pay allowed from the Pay Department of the Army. The attempt, however, to compensate them from that source has not met with success, and the unjust discrimination still exists between officers doing extra duty in the Commissary Department and those doing duty in the Quartermaster's Department. It is recommended that authority to pay $10 per month to all line officers properly detailed (by any commander of a department or division) who actually renders consecutive service not less than thirty days at any one time, by the Quartermaster-General, from the appropriation for regular supplies; provided, that the total sum of such payments hereafter for any one year shall not exceed $25,000. This recommendation is made for the reason that this service relates mainly to the care and distribution of these supplies to the Army as provided by law.

Stations of Officers of the Quartermaster's Department Serving with Troops in the Southwest

Department of the Missouri

Brig. Gen. C. C. Augur, U.S.A., commanding; headquarters, Fort Leavenworth, Kansas.

Maj. James Gilliss, quartermaster, U.S.A., chief quartermaster.

Maj. J. H. Belcher, quartermaster, U.S.A., Denver, Colorado.

Capt. J. V. Furey, assistant quartermaster, U.S.A., Santa Fe, New Mexico.

Capt. L. E. Campbell, assistant quartermaster, U.S.A., Fort Leavenworth, Kansas.

Capt. J. W. Pullman, assistant quartermaster, U.S.A., Fort Wingate, New Mexico.

Department of Texas

Brig. Gen. D. S. Stanley, U.S.A., commanding; headquarters, San Antonio, Texas.

Maj. J. G. C. Lee, quartermaster, U.S.A., chief quartermaster.

Capt. John Simpson, assistant quartermaster, U.S.A., San Antonio, Texas.

Division of the Pacific and Department of California

Maj. Gen. John Pope, U.S.A., commanding; headquarters, Presidio of San Francisco, California.

Col. J. D. Bingham, assistant quartermaster-general, U.S.A., chief quartermaster.

Maj. George H. Weeks, quartermaster, U.S.A., in charge of depot, San Francisco, California.

Capt. C. F. Humphrey, assistant quartermaster, U.S.A., Presidio of San Francisco, California.

Department of Arizona

Brig. Gen. George Crook, U.S.A., commanding; headquarters, Whipple Barracks, Arizona.

Maj. A. J. McGonnigle, quartermaster, U.S.A., chief quartermaster.

Capt. C. W. Williams, assistant quartermaster, U.S.A., Whipple Depot, Arizona.

Capt. D. H. Floyd, assistant quartermaster, U.S.A., Fort Huachuca, Arizona.

Clothing and Equipage Supplies

This branch is in charge of Capt. John F. Rodgers, M.S.K., U.S. Army. It supplies the Army with clothing and equipage, which is purchased and manufactured at the general clothing depots at Philadelphia, PA, Jeffersonville, IN, San Francisco, CA, and at the Military Prison at Fort Leavenworth, KS. The supplies have been ample and fully up to the required standards.

The amount appropriated by Congress was $1,400,000, and there were deposited to the credit of the appropriation $136,753.48 on account of clothing overdrawn by enlisted men, or from sales to officers. One million four hundred and ninety thousand, seventy-one dollars and fifty cents have been expended on account of purchases and manufactures. The balance in the Treasury on the 30th of June, 1884, was $46,681.98, which, together with future credits, will be needed to pay outstanding indebtedness on account of clothing contracts entered into during the fiscal year. The principal articles of clothing and equipage issued during the last fiscal year were: 7,040 helmets, 11,760 cork helmets, 28,960 forage caps, 12,248 campaign hats, 8,000 overcoats, 2,000 uniform dress coats, 36,523 blouses, 7,369 canvas sack coats, 7,716 stable frocks, 13,189 pairs overalls, 68,987 pairs of trousers, 6,381 pairs canvas trousers, 33,047 pairs suspenders, 45,004 dark-blue shirts, 58,294 undershirts, 80,923 pairs of drawers, 119,885 pairs of woolen, and 127,061 pairs of cotton stockings, 209,547 pairs of Berlin gloves, 3,979 pairs woolen mittens, 10,160 pairs fur gauntlets, 18,445 pairs of boots, 23,382 pairs shoes, 4,400 pairs Arctic overshoes, and 31,135 woolen blankets. Much time and attention has been given during the last fiscal year to the improvement of the various articles of clothing and equipage issued to the Army. The following are the principal changes:

The sizes of trousers and blouses have been increased from five to twelve for the former and from five to six for the latter. It is hoped that the enlisted men can be easily fitted with these new sizes. So far as they have been tried they have met with favor. Canvas overcoats lined with blankets have been adopted, and will hereafter be issued to the Army at extreme northern posts, in place of the buffalo overcoats, which have become very costly, owing to the scarcity of the buffalo pelt.

Overcoats, uniform dress coats, and blouses, as well as trousers, will hereafter be issued unmade whenever desired. This will enable the troops to properly fit their persons and save the first cost of making, but the introduction of the new sizes will, it is thought, in time do away with the unmade clothing.

The Secretary of War having approved the recommendation of the Quartermaster-General, $5 additional per annum in the first year of every enlistment will be allowed to each enlisted man for the purpose of having his new clothing altered to properly fit his person.

Materials of finer texture have been procured for issue to non-commissioned officers of the Army from which to make their uniforms. This, together with chevrons made of gold lace, will add materially to the attractiveness and appearance of the non-commissioned officers' full dress.

Action looking toward improvement in the fit and cut of the uniform dress coat, has also been taken and will be concluded, so soon as a proposed change in the facings of infantry dress coats shall have been decided upon.

A long felt want has been met by the adoption of fatigue coats and trousers, which are to be issued to all enlisted men on fatigue and extra duty without cost. These garments are made from the surplus shelter-tents in store which have been dyed to a dark brown color. The introduction of this kind of clothing has met with general favor throughout the Army. It protects the uniform clothing while the men are not employed on strictly military duty. The same material is utilized in the manufacture of warm lined canvas caps and gauntlets, which are issued to troops serving in northern latitudes. The caps have a lining of blanket, and are intended as a substitute for the fur cap heretofore supplied. The canvas gauntlets are to be issued to men employed at outdoor work, such as cutting wood, ice, etc.

Leather gauntlets will hereafter be issued to mounted troops. A supply is now being procured for issue.

Sewed post and field shoes will be issued to the Army as soon as the stock of brass-screwed shoes shall be exhausted. A supply is now being made at the Military Prison at Fort Leavenworth, Kansas.

Sewed boots of a different pattern have also been adopted and will likewise be issued to mounted men exclusively. The patterns of overcoats have also been revised and improved. They will, in the future, be provided with detachable capes.

The fur campaign hat of a drab color has finally been adopted, and will hereafter be purchased and issued to the enlisted men in lieu of the black wool hat which has been so much objected to.

Suspenders have been added to the clothing supply table.

Tents of improved pattern have also been introduced for the use of the Army. The common or "A" tents have been provided with walls two feet high, and the corners of these walls have been made so that they can be laced. This will give the enlisted men more room and allow the walls to be opened or closed at will, thus giving better ventilation. The new tents have been patented in the interest of the Government. All tents will hereafter be provided with ventilators. Modifications have also been made in the conical wall tents, adding to their usefulness and comfort.

The pattern of barrack chairs has been modified and improved thereby.

Mattresses, pillows, sheets, and pillow-slips have also been introduced for trial. Purchases are made gradually and issues will be continued from time to time, until the whole Army shall have been provided with them.

Barrack bags, made from dyed shelter tents, have been provided. They are to be issued to the enlisted men to pack their clothing in, and to preserve it from injury.

New company, regimental, and post books have been devised. A supply has been procured, and they are now ready for issue.

A complete set of uniforms for officers and enlisted men has been procured and sent to the International Health Exhibition at London, England.

Under special authority of the honorable the Secretary of War, all the surplus equipage in store at the general depots of the Quartermaster's Department has been disposed of by sale. This action was found necessary, owing to the fact that the stores had, from long storage, deteriorated. The amount realized from these sales was $73,969.10. The expenses of these sales were $930.73.

Four hundred and eighteen hospital tents were issued to the sufferers from the overflow of the Ohio River.

Under instructions from the War Department to the commanding general, Division of the Pacific, a limited quantity of condemned clothing has been issued to certain destitute Chiricahuas Indians, from the San Francisco depot.

Forty-two thousand three hundred and eighteen overcoats, 4 uniform coats, 346 blouses, 1,223 pairs overalls, 320 pairs trousers, 31 shirts, 36 pairs drawers, and 5 pairs woolen stockings, all condemned and old patterns, and the property of the National Home for Disabled Volunteer Soldiers, under the act of Congress of March 31, 1881, have been transferred to the Home during the last fiscal year.

Two hundred hospital tents, valued at $12 each, have been issued under directions of the Secretary of War to the authorities of the State of Nebraska, forming a charge against the appropriation for arming and equipping the militia of the States and Territories.

A reserve stock of 1,500 suits complete of uniforms has been ordered set aside at each of the depots at Philadelphia, Jeffersonville, and San Francisco, to be in readiness for issue at any time in case of a sudden emergency.

The cutting of clothing, heretofore done by days' work, has been for some time and will hereafter be paid for by the piece; a trial of several months at the principal depots having demonstrated that this new system has given satisfaction to both the employees and the Government.

New standards for the following articles of clothing and equipage were adopted; dark blue overshirts, trousers, blouses, cavalry standards, woolen blankets, barrack bags, canvas caps, sewed boots and shoes, overcoats, books, kersey, cotton duck, leather gauntlets, mosquito bars, canvas fatigue clothing, gold lace chevrons, suspenders, fur campaign hats, forage caps, Berlin gloves, axes, scrubbing brushes, dark blue blouse flannel, Italian cloth, black padding, canvas padding, black silesia, corset jeans, cotton rope, gilling line, tent slips, galvanized-iron rings, brass grommets, manila rope, thread, cotton twine, silk thread, and twist and sewing cotton.

The following specifications have been amended, adopted, and distributed to officers of the Quartermaster's Department, viz: suspenders, canvas overcoats, chairs, overshirts, fur hats, trousers, blouses, woolen blankets, cavalry standards, conical, wall, and improved common tents; the latter of two kinds, closed and laced corners, hospital tents, wall tents, canvas caps, boots, field and post shoes, leather gauntlets, canvas coats and trousers, and mosquito bars. A set of plates illustrating the various articles of clothing and equipage now supplied by the Quartermaster's Department to the Army of the United States, giving measurements and dimensions of each article, will be found with the report of Captain Rodgers. For further and more detailed information upon the subject of the supply of clothing and equipage, attention is invited to the report and accompanying tabular statements of that officer.

WAR DEPARTMENT,
QUARTERMASTER-GENERAL'S OFFICE,
Washington, D.C., September 6, 1884

GENERAL: I have the honor to submit the annual report of the Clothing Supply Branch of this office for the fiscal year ending June 30, 1884.

The supplies of clothing and equipage procured at the principal purchasing and manufacturing depots at Philadelphia, PA, Jeffersonville, IN, San Francisco, CA, and at the Military Prison at Fort Leavenworth, KS, have been ample, and the Army has been fully supplied with everything necessary to its comfort and utility.

The articles procured have passed a rigid inspection, and it is believed that they were fully up to the required standards and specifications.

No complaints as to inferior quality of any of them have reached this office.

The following are the principal articles issued to the Army during the last fiscal year:

Helmets		7,040
Cork helmets		11,760
Forage caps		28,960
Campaign hats		12,248
Overcoats		8,000
Uniform coats		2,000
Blouses		36,523
Canvas sack coats		7,369
Stable frocks		7,716
Overalls	pairs	13,189
Trousers	do	68,987
Canvas trousers		6,381
Suspenders	pairs	33,047
Dark-blue flannel overshirts		45,004
Knit undershirts		58,294
Drawers	pairs	80,923
Woolen stockings	do	119,885
Cotton stockings	do	127,061
Berlin gloves	do	209,547
Woolen mittens	do	3,979
Fur gauntlets	do	10,160
Brass-screwed boots	do	18,445
Brass-screwed shoes	do	23,382
Arctic overshoes		4,400
Woolen blankets		31,135

The accompanying Statement A gives a general resume of the condition of the stock of clothing, equipage, and materials on hand at the general depots of the Quartermaster's Department on the 30th June, 1883, the quantities received from all sources during the last fiscal year, the quantities transferred, sold, expended, and issued to the Army, also the quantities available for issue on the 30th June, 1884.

Statement B herewith shows in minute detail the articles of clothing, equipage, and materials purchased by the Quartermaster's Department and paid for from appropriation for clothing and equipage during the last fiscal year. It shows how the various articles were procured, whether by contract or otherwise, of whom they were purchased, and the price paid for each article.

The appropriation for the purchase of clothing and equipage for the last fiscal year was $1,400,000, and deposits to the credit of the appropriation from sales to officers and on account of clothing overdrawn by enlisted men amounted to $136,753.48. Of these amounts, there were remitted to officers for purchases and manufactures $1,490,071.50, leaving a balance of $46,681.98 in the Treasury of the United States, all of which, together with such credits as may yet be made to last year's appropriation, will be needed in the liquidation of contracts not finally closed. Attention in this connection is respectfully invited to the accompanying marked Statements C and D respectively.

The Quartermaster-General has given much time and study to the needs of the enlisted men of the Army, and devoted his personal attention and constant supervision to the improvements which he deemed advantageous and necessary for its comfort and efficiency. It is thought that they have never been so serviceable and acceptable in the history of the Army.

The aim of the Quartermaster-General to ameliorate the condition of the enlisted men, to make them content, and awaken that soldierly pride so necessary to a proper discipline, has been satisfactorily inaugurated, and will undoubtedly in time bring forth the desired results.

The following are the principal improvements which have been instituted and partly carried into effect, viz:

Trousers and Blouses

These two articles of clothing have heretofor been supplied to the Army in five sizes. As a consequence, it became a matter of great difficulty, if not an utter impossibility, to properly fit the men with the patterns of clothing as furnished. An ordinary man can go into any ready-made clothing store and be fairly fitted. Why should this not be done with the enlisted men of the Army, who, as a rule, are between the ages of twenty and forty-five years, and consequently well proportioned? The officers in charge of the depots at Philadelphia, PA, and San Francisco, CA, were directed to study this question, and the result has been the adoption of new patterns, making twelve sizes for the trousers and six for the blouses.

These new sizes will be issued as soon as the stock of these articles conforming to the old measurements shall have become exhausted by issue. The few articles made according to the new sizes, and which have been distributed for trial, have met with great favor.

Overcoats Lined with Blanket

Owing to the scarcity of the buffalo pelt, the cost of the buffalo overcoats heretofore issued to the Army on the extreme northern frontier had advanced to such an extent that it became necessary to look about for an acceptable substitute. This, it is believed, has been found. An overcoat of water-proof duck, lined with a heavy blanket cloth specially manufactured for the purpose, having a high collar and being somewhat lighter than the buffalo coat, has been adopted, and will in the future, whenever the stock of buffalo coats is exhausted, be issued exclusively. The new coat is considered equally as warm as fur, and less costly.

Unmade Clothing

Authority has been obtained from the War Department to issue to the enlisted men unmade clothing, if so desired. This will enable the troops to properly fit the clothing to their persons, and, as they are charged only with the value of the materials, they are credited in their annual money allowance with the cost of the made garments. It is thought that after the Army has become fully acquainted with the merits of the made clothing of the new sizes about to be introduced, that the demand for unmade clothing will decrease to a greater extent, if not cease altogether.

In order that the enlisted men, who have always been more or less subjected to considerable expense in having the clothing issued to them by the Quartermaster's Department altered and fitted to their persons, the Quartermaster-General recommended to the honorable Secretary of War that an extra money allowance of $5 be given to each enlisted man for the first year of enlistment, in addition to the money allowance to which he is now entitled by law and regulations. This new regulation has been approved and announced to the Army in general orders.

Authority has also been obtained from the War Department to purchase materials of finer texture, such as cloth, flannel, and kersey, for issue to the non-commissioned officers of the Army, out of which to make their uniforms. A supply of finer goods has been procured, and is now held subject to requisition. This, it is hoped, will also be appreciated by officers of the Army, who, under existing regulations, may purchase of these materials for their own personal use.

To make the uniforms of the non-commissioned officers as attractive as possible, the Quartermaster-General obtained permission from the honorable the Secretary of War to issue gold lace chevrons, to be worn upon the uniform dress coats. Samples of gold lace were obtained, and one similar to that in use in the British army has been selected as the standard. Contract for a supply of this quality of lace has been awarded, and deliveries are now being made at the Philadelphia depot, and the manufacture of the chevrons commenced.

Great care is taken in the inspection of the lace, and the purchasing officer was instructed to have it assayed. This has been done from time to time, and the lace is reported to be equal to the requirements and standards. The manufacture of the gold chevrons requires greater skill than those made of cloth, and it will therefore take some time before the supply for the whole Army will be completed.

The Army once supplied, no difficulty will, it is thought, be experienced in filling future requisitions with promptness and dispatch.

Uniform Dress Coats

Action looking towards the improvements in the patterns of the uniform coats has also been taken, but certain proposed changes in the color of facings and mode of trimming, which suggested themselves, have thus far delayed final results. Frequent complaints have reached this office that the sky-blue facings of the infantry, upon being exposed to the air and sun, faded so rapidly that a new facing soon became necessary. The Quartermaster-General therefore recommended to the War Department that white be adopted for sky-blue. No decision has been arrived at.

Actual service having demonstrated the fact that the side loops on the uniform dress coats were a useless appendage, instructions have been given the officers in charge of manufacturing depots to omit them hereafter and to remove them from the coats already manufactured.

Canvas Fatigue Clothing

Most, if not all the enlisted men, as is well known to every one connected with the Army, are employed on fatigue, extra and daily duty. Such duty is very trying on the uniform clothing of the men, exposing it to hard usage and incidental wear and tear. At some posts the clothing issued under existing allowances is ample; at others, owing to the nature of this extra work, it is not.

The Quartermaster-General, fully aware of this fact, made it one of the first acts of his administration to devise a suit of canvas clothing, suitable for the military service, and similar to the working clothes worn by miners in the Western States and Territories.

The officer in command of the Philadelphia depot of the Quartermaster's Department, with the sanction of the honorable Secretary of War, was directed to have some of the shelter tents—of which there is a large number in store, few of which are used for the purpose for which they were originally intended—dyed to a brown color. Out of these dyed tents coats and trousers are made and issued to the Army free of expense to the enlisted men at the rate of one suit per annum. This clothing remains the property of the United States, the same as fur overcoats, which are used for the protection of life and limb.

Two kinds of coats, one a plaited blouse, the other a sack coat, were manufactured and sent out for trial.

The result has demonstrated the fact that only the sack coat ought to be provided, and hence only the latter is supplied. These fatigue garments are made of six sizes, and there will be no difficulty in properly fitting the men. From reports already received it appears that this clothing is universally liked. It will prove of great benefit, not alone that the men will save their clothing for strictly military duty, but that their appearance will also be neater and cleaner.

Canvas Caps and Gauntlets

The same dyed material, only waterproofed, has also been utilized in manufacturing caps, with heavy blanket lining, which will be substituted for the muskrat caps heretofore purchased and supplied. These caps, besides being warmer, are less costly. They will be issued gratuitously to the enlisted men serving in extreme northern latitudes, together with canvas mittens to be used on fatigue duty, handling ice, etc. These mittens are not lined, and the enlisted men who require warm gauntlets are permitted under existing regulations to purchase muskrat gloves at cost price.

Leather Gauntlets

A desideratum, long felt, has been supplied by obtaining the authority from the honorable Secretary of War to supply leather gauntlets to all mounted men of the Army. It has been possible to do this by rearranging the allowance of Berlin gloves. By giving the mounted men annually one pair of the latter, sufficient for parade purposes if deemed necessary, and three pairs of leather gauntlets during an enlistment of five years, this attractive and useful article has been added to the equipment of the mounted men without additional cost to the Government.

Shoes

Under authority of the War Department the patterns of sewed shoes referred to in my last annual report have been adopted for all arms of the service. They are to be known to the service as the "post" and "field" shoes. They are made of two widths, "A" and "B." The "post" shoes have uppers of calf, and are quite pliable. The "field" shoes have "wax" uppers, come well up over the ankle, and have a metallic patent buckle. A supply of both kinds of shoes is now being manufactured at the Military Prison at Fort Leavenworth, KS, but the issue cannot and ought not to be commenced until the supply of brass-screwed shoes on hand at the general depots and posts shall have been exhausted. A general order to that effect has been issued to the Army. The five hundred sewed shoes, representing both the "post" and "field" shoes, manufactured during the previous fiscal year, have been distributed for trial, and from reports received it appears that they have given satisfaction.

Bvt. Col. A. P. Blunt, the commandant of the military Prison at Fort Leavenworth, having suggested a service shoe of a different pattern than the "field" shoe, five hundred pairs, to be known as the "campaign" shoe, have been ordered made, and they will be sent out for trial after a six months' seasoning.

Shoes with Flexible Soles

The invention of Mr. F. Kearney, having been brought to the attention of the Quartermaster-General, permission was obtained from the War Department to manufacture 200 pairs "field" shoes with flexible soles. They were made at the Military Prison and distributed for trial. From reports received it is ascertained that they are not adapted to the military service.

Boots

Under former custom and usage boots have been supplied to troops of all arms of the service. The pattern of the "field" shoe to be supplied being considered sufficiently high to cover and protect the ankle, the issue of boots, after the present supply of brass screwed is exhausted, will be confined exclusively to the mounted service. It has thus been practical to change the pattern by making the leg come up higher and better adapted for riding purposes. The uppers will be of "wax upper," the legs of pebble grained leather.

It is hoped that the difficult question of providing comfortable and serviceable foot-gear, suitable for Army purposes, has been solved.

Overcoats

The patterns of overcoats have also been revised. They are made so as to better fit the person. The cuffs have been removed, the sleeves made wider, and the cape is made detachable by means of hooks and eyes.

The kersey-lined canvas overcoats, otherwise known as the "Miles" overcoats, which the enlisted men declined to draw, have been distributed, under authority of the honorable the Secretary of War, to posts in the Department of Dakota for gratuitous issue to the men, the same as in the case of fur overcoats.

Campaign Hats

The black woolen campaign hat has been a source of much complaint. The objections made to the quality, and especially to the color, were of such nature that it has been determined to substitute a drab-colored fur hat. A few of the latter have in former years been procured and distributed for trial. Reports show that they are very much preferred. The drab hats will therefore be purchased exclusively hereafter.

Forage Caps

A limited number of forage caps, having leather crowns, have been purchased and sent out for trial in active service, it having been represented that they were superior to the regulation caps with paste-board crowns. Reports upon their merits have not yet been received at this office.

Cap Ornaments

It is a well-known fact that the cap ornaments now furnished are of necessity quite frail in their construction, especially on the back, where the loops are soldered to the body. They are easily broken, and the enlisted men are resorting to various methods to fasten the letters and numbers to the devices, so as to avoid breakage in cleaning and fastening to the cap. The Department has been studying this subject, and experiments are now making to improve the ornaments without being compelled to provide a special die for each company of the service—quite a heavy expenditure.

Suspenders

To supply a long-felt want, the Secretary of War approved the recommendation of the Quartermaster-General that the enlisted men be supplied with suspenders at the rate of one pair per year. They have been made part of the soldiers' clothing allowance, and the Army has been fully supplied with them. They are strong and durable, and appear to give general satisfaction.

Coat Buttons

New and more clearly defined buttons have also been adopted. These will, until the stock of buttons of the old kind is exhausted, be exclusively used on the uniform dress coats. A number of . . .

Shank Buttons

have also been procured. They have been fastened to some of the trousers manufactured at the Philadelphia and San Francisco depots and sent out for trial. Reports as to their comparative value have been called for.

Berlin Gloves

Active service having demonstrated the fact that the system of issuing the Berlin gloves singly instead of by pairs has led to accumulation at almost every post, throughout the country, steps have been taken to properly size up and complete those on hand. Issues will hereafter be made only by pairs.

Numbers on Coat Collars

It having been represented to the Quartermaster-General that the metallic number and insignia worn on the collars of the uniform dress coats were not desirable, owing to the fact that they were soiling and tearing the facings, and that they were unnecessary because the numbers and insignia were also worn on the caps and helmets, the Quartermaster-General recommended that they be omitted from the coats. This recommendation has, however, not been approved by higher authority.

Experimental Clothing

Articles of clothing are frequently sent out for trial by troops in active service. This is done to ascertain the value of whatever improvements it is desirable to test. These trials being for the benefit of the department, it is thought that the value of the clothing should not form a charge against the money clothing allowance of the enlisted men. The honorable Secretary of War has therefore approved the recommendation of this office that the clothing issued for purely experimental purposes be not charged against the soldiers.

Marking Clothing

The stencil-plates heretofore issued to the Army for the purpose of marking the clothing of the enlisted men have been reported upon as not entirely satisfactory, and steps have been taken to procure numbers and stamps having the company and number of regiment upon it, one for each company in the service, which are considered far superior and better adapted to the purpose for which they are intended. Steel dies with which to mark the leather equipments are supplied by the Ordnance Department.

Tents

The common or "A" tents heretofore in use have been improved by adding a wall of 2 feet in height, thus giving greater space and corresponding comfort to the occupants. The walls of the corners of these improved tents are manufactured either closed entirely or open with loops attached, so as to admit of closing the corners at will. The tents with laced corners are intended for issue to troops stationed south of Saint Louis, while the tents with closed corners are intended for issue to troops stationed north of Saint Louis. The merits of the tents with laced corners consist in that the walls, while the tent is pitched, can be elevated, thus allowing the air to freely enter the tent. Both kinds of these improved common tents have been provided with ventilators.

The Quartermaster-General has patented these tents in the interest of the department.

The conical-wall tents, for use of officers, have been changed so as to reduce the diameter of the roof from 17 feet 6 inches to 16 feet 5 inches, and to decrease the height of the tent from 12 to 10 feet.

Barrack Chairs

Complaint having been made that the legs of the barrack chairs were not thick enough at those parts through which the iron rods are to pass, the standards and specifications have been changed and the thickness of the legs increased.

Mattresses and Pillows

Heretofore the enlisted men were supplied with bed-sacks and pillow-sacks to be filled with straw or hay for their bedding. The Quartermaster-General, desirous of improving the condition of the enlisted men whenever practicable with a due regard to economy and efficiency, obtained the sanction of the War Department to supply mattresses, pillows, bed-sheets, and pillow-cases.

Samples of various kinds were procured, and a mattress and pillow stuffed with cotton linters adopted. Limited purchases of these articles have been made and will be continued from time to time as the condition of the appropriation will permit. Issues have thus far been made to recruiting depots, and requisitions called for from posts in the Division of the Atlantic. As soon as these posts shall have been supplied, issues will be extended west, until the whole Army shall have been equipped. Such commands as may still prefer the bed and pillow sacks can continue to draw them.

Barrack Bags

A number of bags made of the surplus shelter tents, dyed brown, and having lacing strings, have been distributed to some of the posts. They are to be used by the enlisted men to pack away their woolen clothing and to protect it from the ravages of moths.

Books

The company, regimental, and post books purchased during the war had, from long storage, become deteriorated to such an extent that it became necessary to lay in a new supply. In doing so, an understanding was arrived at with the Adjutant-General of the Army as to the particular books each of the Departments was to supply. A general order upon this matter has been promulgated, and the Quartermaster's Department is ready to furnish the books immediately upon the receipt of proper requisitions.

Corn Brooms and Scrubbing-Brushes

No provision having been made by regulations for the issue of brooms to offices and storehouses, the regulations, upon the recommendation of the Quartermaster-General, have been so amended as to permit the issue of six brooms per annum to the offices of the post commanders and post quartermasters, also to quartermasters' warehouses. Each officer of the Army is also permitted to purchase six brooms and three scrubbing-brushes for use in his quarters.

General Operations of Last Fiscal Year

A complete set of articles of clothing and equipage for officers and men of the United States Army has been shipped to London, England, for exhibit by this department at the International Health Exhibition, and, at the request of the German minister accredited to this Government, a complete set of infantry uniforms and equipments has been sent to the German Government at Berlin.

Clothing for Destitute Indians

Under instructions communicated by the War Department to the Commanding General, Division of the Pacific, on the 19th of January last, the issue of a limited quantity of the condemned, obsolete, and unserviceable clothing on hand at the San Francisco depot, not to exceed one garment, was authorized each of the destitute Chiricahuas.

Clothing for National Homes

The following articles of old pattern clothing, which, under the act of March 3, 1881, are the property of the National Home for Disabled Volunteers, have been transferred to the President of the Home during the last fiscal year, having been kept at the Philadelphia depot, subject to his orders, viz: 42,318 overcoats, 4 uniform coats, 346 blouses, 1,223 pairs overalls, 320 pairs trousers, 31 shirts, 36 pairs drawers, and 5 pairs woolen stockings.

Tents for State of Nebraska

Under the order of the honorable the Secretary of War, 200 hospital tents, with poles and pins, but without flies, were turned over to the Governor of the State of Nebraska. The value of the tents ($12 each) were to be charged against the appropriation for arming and equipping the militia of the States and Territories.

Tents to Sufferers from the Overflow of the Ohio River

The accompanying Statement F shows the number of hospital tents issued during the last fiscal year, under joint resolution of Congress of February 11, 1884, to the sufferers from the overflow of the Ohio River. Of the 418 tents issued, 14 have been returned as not required.

The issue of these tents, as well as those turned over to the State of Nebraska, has absorbed the stock of hospital tents left on hand at the close of the war, and the few still remaining in depot will be required for the actual necessities of the service.

"Doecker" Felt Tents

As reported in my last annual report, three of these tents had arrived from abroad. They were submitted to a board of officers, and are found not to be adapted to the military service of the United States.

Sale of Surplus Equipage

It having been ascertained that the large surplus stock of equipage in depot since 1865 had, from long storage, deteriorated to such an extent as to render it, if kept much longer, almost valueless, authority was obtained from the honorable the Secretary of War to sell the same, after reserving a five years' supply, to the highest bidders. These sales have been made, and the accompanying statement E shows in detail the quantities of each article sold, where sold, prices realized, and expenses of sale. The latter were $930.73, and the total amount realized $73,969.10, which has been covered into the Treasury and credited to miscellaneous receipts. The expenses of the sale have been paid from the appropriation for clothing and equipage.

Reserve Stock of Clothing

In order that the department may be fully prepared to meet at any time any sudden demand that may be made upon it, instructions have been given to set aside at each of the general depots of the Quartermaster's Department at Philadelphia, PA, Jeffersonville, IN, and San Francisco, CA, 1,500 suits of clothing. This reserve stock is to be kept separate from all other supplies, and although issues in limited quantities will be made therefrom to prevent it from becoming shelf and shop worn and obsolete, care will be taken to constantly replenish it and keep it up to the required number of suits.

Cutting Clothing by Piece-Work

The attention of the Quartermaster-General having been called to the fact that it was thought to be more advantageous to the Government to pay for cutting the garments manufactured by the Quartermaster's Department by piece, instead of day's work, the officers in charge of depots were instructed to make the change proposed. After a trial of several months, and having met with no opposition on the part of the employees, showing conclusively that the new mode of remuneration may be considered as satisfactory, it has been adopted.

Standards

New standards for the following articles of clothing, equipage, and materials have been established, sealed, and distributed to the purchasing and manufacturing department during the last fiscal year:

Dark-blue overshirts, trousers, blouses, cavalry standards, woolen blankets, barrack bags, canvas caps, sewed boots, shoes, overcoats; books for companies, regiments, and posts; kersey, cotton duck, leather gauntlets, mosquito bars, canvas clothing, gold lace, suspenders, fur campaign hats, forage caps, Berlin gloves, axes, scrubbing-brushes, dark-blue blouse flannel, Italian cloth, black padding, canvas padding, black silesia, colored jeans, cotton rope, gilling line, tent slips, galvanized iron rings, brass grommets, manila rope, thread, cotton twine, chevron silk, machine silk, silk twist, sewing silk, machine thread, lap thread, and Willimantic cotton.

Specifications . . .

for the following articles have been either amended or adopted during the fiscal year. Copies of all of them are submitted herewith, marked N, viz:

Suspenders, canvas overcoats (blanket lined), barrack chairs, overshirts, fur campaign hats, trousers, blouses, woolen blankets, cavalry standards, conical wall tents, improved common tents with laced corners, improved common tents with closed corners, hospital tents, wall tents, canvas caps, boots, "post" shoes, "field" shoes, leather gauntlets, canvas sack-coats, canvas trousers, and mosquito bars.

L—Statement showing average prices at which the various articles of clothing and equipage are charged to the Army of the United States.

ARTICLES	PRICE	ARTICLES	PRICE
Helmet without trimmings	$1.25	Crescent	.03
Helmet hair plumes	46	Wreath and caduceus	05
Helmet cord and band	49	Fur cap	1 15
Helmet top piece or base	03	Letters, brass	01
Helmet socket for plume	17	Numbers, brass	01
Helmet spike	07	Overcoat:	
Helmet eagle	05	Made	9 70
Helmet scroll and rings . . . pairs	02	Unmade	7 70
Helmet side buttons . . . do	01	Uniform dress coats:	
Helmet device for shield of		Non-commissioned staff,	
eagle . . . do	02	made	8 89
Helmet number	01	Non-commissioned staff,	
Cork helmet	1 42	unmade	5 89
Fatigue or campaign hat:		Engineers, musicians, made	9 49
Black, wool	65	Engineers, privates, made	8 89
Drab, fur	1 79	Engineers, musicians, unmade	5 99
Cord and tassel	07	Engineers, privates, unmade	5 89
Forage cap	55	Musicians, mounted, made	9 30
Crossed sabers for caps	02	Musicians, mounted, unmade	5 80
Crossed cannons for caps	02	Privates, mounted, made	8 70
Crossed rifles for caps	02	Privates, mounted, unmade	5 70
Shell and flame	02	Musicians, foot, made	9 44
Bugle	02	Musicians, foot, unmade	5 94
Castle	02	Privates, foot, made	8 84

ARTICLES	PRICE
Privates, foot, unmade	$5.84
Crescent for coats	02
Castle for coats	03
Shell and flame for coats	03
Caduceus for coats	02
Blouse:	
Made	2 93
Unmade	2 18
Stable frock	0 61
Overalls:	
Engineers	1 31
Mounted	52
Trousers, heavy:	
Mounted, made per pair	3 46
Mounted, unmade do	2 46
Foot, made do	2 71
Foot, unmade do	1 96
Trousers, light	
Mounted, made do	3 28
Mounted, unmade do	2 28
Foot, made do	2 58
Foot, unmade do	1 83
Suspenders do	17
Dark blue overshirts	2 29
Knit undershirts	56
Drawers per pair	55
Stockings:	
Woolen do	24
Cotton do	10
Berlin gloves do	12
Leather gauntlets do	1 21
Fur gauntlets do	1 98
Woolen mittens do	32
Boots:	
Brass-screwed do	2 73
Sewed do	4 32
Shoes:	
Brass-screwed do	1 76
Sewed, "post" do	3 25
Sewed, "field" do	2 88
Arctic overshoes do	2 33
Blankets:	
Woolen	3 98
Rubber	1 13
Ponchos, rubber	1 55
Chevrons:	
Cloth, hospital stewards per pair	87
Cloth, non-commissioned staff and color & first sergeants per pair	73
Cloth, sergeants do	39
Cloth, corporals do	.31
Cloth, service, peace do	23
Cloth, service, war do	34
Cloth, pioneers & farriers do	72
Device for Signal Corps do	28
Chevrons, gold lace:	
Post quartermasters & ordnance sergeants per pair	3 00
Hospital stewards do	2 66
Commissary-sergeants do	3 68
Sergeant-majors do	4 55
Quartermaster-sergeants, engineers per pair	3 73
Quartermaster-sergeants all other arms per pair	4 44
Chief trumpeters per pair	4 43
Principal musicians do	3 68
Saddler-sergeants do	4 38
Color & first sergeants do	3 49
Sergeants do	2 67
Corporals do	1 79
Service, peace or war do	82
Stripes for trousers:	
Non-commissioned staff do	37
Sergeants, engineers do	66
Sergeants, all other arms do	29
Corporals, engineers do	50
Corporals, all other arms do	19
Musicians, engineers do	1 12
Musicians, all other arms do	38
Iron bunk, without slats	4 50
Bed sacks	76
Pillow sacks	16
Mattresses	2 24
Pillow	32
Bed sheets	33
Pillow cases	11
Barrack bag	46
Mosquito bar	81
Iron pot	1 50
Camp kettle	38
Mess pan	25
Ax	60
Ax-helve	15
Ax-sling	31
Hatchet	40
Hatchet-helve	03
Hatchet-sling	25
Spade	48
Shovel, short-handled	37
Shovel, long-handled	37
Pick-ax	63

ARTICLES	PRICE	ARTICLES	PRICE
Pick-ax helve	.07	Tent pins, wall	.89
Drum, complete	6 75	Tent, wall, complete	21 30
Drum, head-batter	52	Tent, common, closed corners	7 25
Drum, head-snare	38	Tent, common, laced corners	7 41
Drum-sling	49	Tent poles, common	1 00
Drum sticks, pairs	11	Tent pins, common	38
Drum stick carriages	23	Tent, common, closed corners, complete	8 63
Drum-snares . . . per set	11	Tent, common, laced corners, complete	8 79
Drum case	29	Tent, shelter, half	1 00
Fife	17	Tent poles, shelter	40
Trumpet, with extra mouth piece	1 88	Tent pins, shelter	12
Trumpet cord and tassel	45	Tent, shelter, complete	3 32
Trumpet crook	44	Tent pin, hospital, large or small	04
Trumpet, extra mouth piece	25	Tent pin, wall, large	04
Books:		Tent pin, wall, small or common	02½
Company letters sent	2 25	Tent pin, shelter	02
Index company letters sent	1 40	Flag:	
Company order	1 50	Garrison	37 00
Company letters received	2 40	Post	12 00
Index company letters received	1 40	Storm and recruiting	3 45
Regimental order	5 50	Flag-hallards:	
Regimental letters received	6 65	Garrison and post	1 32
Index regimental letters received	1 40	Recruiting	26
Regimental letters sent	6 65	Colors:	
Index regimental letters sent	1 40	National	79 00
Post general order	5 50	Regimental	135 00
Post special order	5 50	Standard	125 00
Post letters received	5 78	Guidon	5 95
Index post letters received	1 40	Color belt and sling	1 57
Post letters sent	5 55	Camp color	79
Index post letters sent	1 40	Stencil plates . . . per set	1 05
Tent, conical wall, complete	28 00	Scrubbing brush	15
Tent, Sibley	19 98	Corn broom	25
Tent pole, conical wall or Sibley	1 00	Barrack chair, raw-hide seat	1 34
Tent, tripod	2 25	Barrack chair, poplar seat	1 01
Tent pins, conical wall or Sibley	1 18	Shoe file	25
Tent, Sibley, complete	24 41	Card holder for bunks	01
Tent, hospital	29 35	Buffalo overcoat	12 95
Tent-fly, hospital	9 12	Canvas overcoat, blanket-lined	11 40
Tent poles, hospital	3 90	Canvas fatigue coat	85
Tent pins, hospital . . . per set	1 68	Canvas fatigue trousers . . per pair	87
Tent, hospital, complete	44 05	Canvas cap or hood	1 05
Tent, wall	14 10	Canvas mittens . . . per pair	13
Tent, wall, fly	4 32		
Tent poles, wall . . . per set	2 00		

Respectfully submitted.

JOHN F. RODGERS,
Captain and Military Storekeeper, United States Army.

M.—Drawings of each article of clothing and equipage supplied by the Quartermaster's Department to the Army, giving measurements and dimensions of each article and details of each section of each garment manufactured by the Quartermaster's Department.

77 plates folioed in black ink, 1 to 75.

N.—Specifications for clothing, equipage, and materials for the manufacture of clothing and equipage, adopted or amended and distributed to the officers of the Quartermaster's Department during the fiscal year ending June 30, 1884.

Specifications for Suspenders

Front straps—The front straps are to be made of nonelastic webbing ¾ inch broad, to have thirteen cords, and to be of weight and quality of the standard sample. They are to be attached directly to the buckle in the manner known as "cantab," and before they are sewed together; to be 9½ inches long, and overlap each other to an extent that will give sufficient "play" or change of length of the two straps that are fastened together. The button-hole is to be woven into the strap and must be at least half an inch from the extremity of the strap.

Shoulder straps—The shoulder-straps are to be made of one continuous piece of nonelastic webbing folded and bent upon itself in the middle, as per sample. They are to be 1⅜ inches broad, of same weight, and be equal in quality in every respect to the standard sample; to be regular in width and weaving, and to have a figure woven on them equal to sample. The extremities to be neatly bound.

Back straps—The back straps are to be made of elastic rubber web, to have twenty-two cards, and to be 1¼ inches broad. The rubber thread is to be that made by the East Hampton Rubber Co., or other equally as good, of the size known to the trade as No. 28, and to be freshly manufactured. The button-holes are to be woven into the strap and to be at least ⅞ of an inch from the extremity of the strap or end. The straps are to be neatly woven, with a smooth even face, and edges to be neatly bound at the ends, the binding to extend up one-half the length of button hole on each side.

Buckle—The buckle is to be made in one piece and be stamped from sheet brass of weight equal to that on sample, and to have three prongs. It must have an opening sufficient to accommodate the shoulder straps, and two smaller openings or slots of a size that will allow the cantab straps to freely play or move through it. Each slot must have an anti-friction roller to prevent the wear of the strap upon the buckle, as on sample. Both the friction rollers and the prongs must be made from brass, well nickel-plated.

Re-enforce straps—The back straps to be united to the shoulder straps by two rows of stitching, as shown on sample. The shoulder straps are also to be fastened together in the back by a re-enforce or strengthening piece made from web similar to the shoulder straps, of the size and shape of sample, with its cut edges bound, the strengthening piece securely sewed to the shoulder straps, as in sample. The front straps will be sewed by four lines of stitching, nearly forming a square, as per sample.

Button hole strengthening—All the button holes are to be strengthened by being whipped or oversewed at their wearing extremities, to the extent of the sample.

Lengths—The suspenders are to be of three lengths, and to measure from button hole to button hole 36 inches, 38 inches, and 40 inches, respectively, in the following proportions per 100 pairs: 60 pairs 26-inch, 20 pairs 38-inch, and 20 pairs 40-inch, measuring from the extremes of the front and back button holes.

Thread—All the thread used in sewing the suspenders must be made from the sea island cotton and be of the best quality.

Color—All the parts of the suspenders must be of the same color and must be "fast" color, and as per sample.

Packing—The suspenders must be neatly packed in paper boxes, one dozen of same size in a box.

Each pair of suspenders is to have the length of same stamped or stenciled in black or blue color on the reverse side of the strengthening strap (without, however, defacing the outer side), in letters and figures ⅜ of an inch long, as follows: 40-in., 38-in., 36-in.

Adopted September 4, 1883.

S. B. HOLABIRD,
Quartermaster-General, U.S.A.

1760, Q.M.G.O., 1883,
C. & Eq. Suppl.

Specifications for Canvas Overcoats, Blanket-Lined

Material—The overcoats to be made of 10-ounce brown cotton duck, lined throughout (body, sleeves, and collar) with heavy blanket cloth.

Shape—To be double-breasted, frock skirt, slashed at the back to within about 8 inches of the waist-belt; pockets on both sides covered with flaps 4 inches by 8 inches, lined with blanket cloth, to be worn either inside or out. Large collar, fastened by a strap (of brown duck) about 5½ inches by 1¾ inches, with button hole at each end.

Buttons—The coats to have ten rubber buttons 1⅛ inches in diameter, five on each breast, placed equidistant, starting 1 inch below the collar seam. The collar to have three rubber buttons ¾ inch in diameter, one on each side, to fasten the collar when turned up, and one to take up the strap of collar when it is turned down.

Loops—The loops by which the coat is buttoned across the breast to be about 6 inches long, made of ¼-inch black mohair cord, and secured to the coat under the buttons.

Waist belt—To be made of the same material as the body of the coat, 3 inches wide, to fasten with a Japanned iron buckle or slide, and to be supported on each side of the coat by supporters, made of the same material, placed over the side seams.

Sizes

	No. 1	No. 2	No. 3	No. 4
	Inches	Inches	Inches	Inches
Length of coats	50	52	54	56
Breadth of back	9¼	9½	10	10½
Length of sleeve	33	34	35	36
Width of collar	5½	5¾	6	6½
Width of breast	40	42	44	46
Width of waist	36	38	40	42

Adopted October 24, 1883, and conforming to standard sample approved October 13, 1883.

2135, Q.M.G.O., 1883,
C. & Eq. Suppl.

S. B. HOLABIRD,
Quartermaster-General, U.S.A.

Specifications for Overshirts

Materials—Dark blue wool flannel, Army standard, and hard-rubber buttons, 23 ligne.

Patterns—To be according to sample, loose, with falling collar (without band), single plait 2 inches wide on front, and with cuffs. Two outside "patch" breast pockets about 7 inches deep by 6 inches wide, rounded at bottoms. The side seams open about 9 inches from bottom, and secured at top of opening with a stay of white cotton binding well stitched on the inside. Buttons and button holes to be at each of the following places, viz: One at the throat, two on the front plait equidistant between the throat and bottom of opening, one at the center of the mouth of each pocket, and one on each cuff, making seven in all. Corners of cuffs and bottom of shirt to be rounded off.

Dimensions—Depth of collar for average size about 3 inches in front and 2¼ inches behind; of cuff about 2½ inches; of front plait about 14 inches.

Sizes—To be of five sizes, measuring as follows:

	No. 1	No. 2	No. 3	No. 4	No. 5
	Inches	Inches	Inches	Inches	Inches
Length of shirt	33	33	34	35	36
Length of sleeve	32½	33	34	35	36
Collar	15	15½	16¼	17	17½
Cuff	7½	8	8½	9	9½

Adopted November 26, 1883, in lieu of specifications adopted April 12, 1883, which are hereby canceled.

2349, Q.M.G.O., 1883,
C. & Eq. Suppl.

S. B. HOLABIRD,
Quartermaster-General, U.S.A.

Specifications for Fur Campaign Hats

Mixture—To be composed of two-thirds best coney and one-third fine blown nutria.

Weight—Hat bodies to be weighed—4¾ ounces heavy.

Shape—Block to be 5¾ inches deep to center of tip.

Brim—To be 2¾ inches wide in front and rear, and 3 inches wide at sides; to be of double thickness, and to have two rows of stitching, as shown on sample.

Color—To be a drab or other suitable color, as per sample.

Trimmings—To be trimmed with 8-ligne union band—same quality as on hat—to be sewed on by hand. Sweat to be an imported lined leather, 2¼ inches wide, sewed to the reed by zigzag stitch. A wire-gauze ventilator to be on each side of the hat, 3½ inches from brim—to be of size as on sample hat.

The hats to be doe (sic) finished, as per sample.

To be packed three hats in each bandbox.

Adopted December 14, 1883.

Specifications for Trousers

Material—Sky-blue kersey, Army standard.

For foot troops—To be cut and made in accordance with the standard patterns and samples approved January 16, 1884. To have side pockets, and a hip pocket on the right side. The bottoms to be lined with canvas.

For mounted troops—To be similar to those for footmen, with the addition of a re-enforce or saddle-piece of the same material on seat and legs. Four buttons at bottom of each leg, two on each side, for straps.

Size	Waist	Seat	Crotch	Outside seam	Inside seam	Knee	Bottom
	Inches	Inches	Inches	Inches	Inches	Inches	Inches
1	31	36	23	41	31	17½	19
2	32	36	23	40	30	17½	19
3	32	37	23	43	33	17¾	19¾
4	32	38	24	42	32	18	19¾
5	33	38	24	41¼	31	18¼	19¾
6	33	39	24	44½	34	18¼	19¾
7	34	39	25	42½	32	18½	20¼
8	34	40	25½	45½	35	18½	20¼
9	36	41	26	42¾	32	19	20½
10	36	41	26	44	33	19	20½
11	38	43	26	45	34	19½	21
12	40	44	26½	44¼	33	19½	21

Adopted January 16, 1884, in lieu of specifications of October 9, 1882, which are hereby canceled.

(41 F.—1884.)
5547 W—43

S. B. HOLABIRD,
Quartermaster-General, U.S.A.

Specifications for Blouses

Material—Dark blue wool flannel, Army standard; gray, twilled, mixed flannel lining for body, and unbleached muslin lining for sleeves.

Pattern—To be a single-breasted sack coat, with falling collar, and having five regulation buttons in front from neck to waist. To have two inside breast pockets.

To be cut and made in accordance with the standard patterns and samples approved January 16, 1884.

Size	Breast	Length	Waist	Collar	Length of sleeve
	Inches	Inches	Inches	Inches	Inches
1	34	28	32	16	31
2	35	28¼	33	16½	31½
3	36	29	34	17	32½
4	38	30	36	18	33
5	40	31¾	38	19	34
6	42	32¾	40	19½	34½

Adopted January 16, 1884, in lieu of specifications of May 19, 1883, which are hereby canceled.

S. B. HOLABIRD,
Quartermaster-General, U.S.A.

(41 F.—1884.)

Specifications for Woolen Blankets

Each blanket to be 7 feet long and 5 feet 6 inches wide, and to weigh not less than 5 pounds. To be gray in color, and made of pure long-staple wool, free from shoddy, reworked wool or cotton, or any impure materials. The warp to be of not lower grade than three-eighths blood-bred wool; the filling or woof to be of not lower grade than one-half blood-bred wool; to have the letters "U.S." in dark blue, 4 inches long, in the center; to bear a strain of not less than 25 pounds per inch for the warp, and 30 pounds per inch for the woof, without tearing, and to have not less than 22 threads of warp and 25 threads of filling or woof to the inch. The threads to be well driven up. The stripes at ends of blanket to be dark blue, of pure indigo dye.

Note—It is immaterial whether the letters "U.S." be stamped on the blanket or woven into the fabric; their color must be pure indigo dye.

Adopted February 5, 1884, in lieu of specifications adopted August 23, 1876, which are hereby canceled.

S. B. HOLABIRD,
Quartermaster-General, U.S.A.

(279 F.—1884.)

Specifications for Cavalry Standards

Material—To be made of a single thickness of seamless blue banner silk.

Dimensions—To be 2 feet 5 inches long (exclusive of casing for the lance of the same material) by 2 feet 3 inches long on the lance.

Design—To bear the coat of arms of the United States as on the design sketch for cavalry standard approved by the Quartermaster-General, and which may be described as follows:

An eagle with outstretched wings, on its breast a U.S. shield; in the right talon an olive branch with red berries, and in his left ten arrows bunched. A red scroll held in eagle's beak, with the letters "E Pluribus Unum" in yellow; over the scroll a group of thirteen stars surmounted by an arc of diverging sun rays. Below the eagle a red scroll with the figures and letters "U.S. Cavalry" in yellow.

Embroidery—The design, letters, and figures to be embroidered in silk, the same on both sides of the standard.

The standard to be trimmed on three sides with United States silk knitted fringe 2½ inches deep.

The lance to be 9 feet long, including metal spear and ferule.

Adopted February 4, 1884.

S. B. HOLABIRD,
Quartermaster-General, U.S.A.

(280 F.—1884.)

Specifications for Conical Wall Tents

Material—Body of tent to be made of standard 12-ounce cotton duck, and the sod cloth of standard 8-ounce cotton duck, 28½ inches wide. Eave lines of 6-thread manila line (large), and foot lines of 9-thread manila line.

Work—To be made in a workmanlike manner, with not less than 2½ stitches of equal length to the inch, made with a double thread of 5-fold cotton twine well waxed. The seams to be not less than 1 inch in width, and no slack taken in them.

Form and dimensions—The roof to be in the form of a frustum of a cone, 16 feet 5 inches in diameter at the base, 18 inches in diameter at the top. Wall to be 2 feet high. Height, when pitched, to top of roof 10 feet. Eaves to be 2 inches wide, and tabling at bottom 2½ inches wide. The angle from the top to the eave 10 feet 6½ inches.

Top—The top opening at the top to be formed with a galvanized-iron ring 18 inches in diameter, over which the duck shall be firmly stitched and reenforced down the roof to a depth of 8½ inches. Six ¾-inch grommet holes around the top, equal distances just below the ring, to be reenforced with leather in which to hook the chains which support the tent on the pole.

Plate and chains—The plate to be 4 inches in diameter and ¼ inch in thickness, with six ⅜-inch holes around the edge at equal distances and countersunk, and a ⅝-inch hole in the center. Chains, six in number, to be 14 inches long, including hook, made of machine chain No. 1. All to be of galvanized iron.

Door—Doorway to be 7 feet high measured along the seam, 13¼ inches wide at top, 25¼ inches at bottom. The door of two equal pieces in area to the doorway, and joined at opposite sides of the same so as to lap and form double thickness when closed. Tabling on edge to be 2 inches when finished.

Door fastenings—To consist of five No. 5 conical pointed brass grommets on each side, placed at equal distances of 16 inches from the top of door to the eave, and 18 inches from the eave down on the wall holes to be worked on the seams, the same distance, with ⅝-inch galvanized iron rings; door lines of ¼-inch cotton rope 3 feet long and whipped on both ends, to be seized in the middle with a knot on each side of the hold, that the door may be tied either inside or outside. Two ⅝-inch holes, worked 8 inches above the lap of the door, with two ¼-inch cotton lines, 1 foot long in the clear, with a "Mathew Walker" knot on one end and properly whipped on the other end; one hold ½-inch worked on each side at the bottom, with one 6-thread manila line 3 feet long for door line.

Sod cloth—The sod cloth to be 8¾ inches wide in the clear and to extend around the inside of the tent from door to door.

Grommet holes—Twenty-four in number, worked on the seams of the foot of the tent over ¾-inch galvanized malleable-iron rings, and twenty-four ½-inch holes to be worked on the seams of the eaves over galvanized iron rings, the holes to be worked with 4-thread five-fold cotton twine well waxed.

Hood—Conical hood open at side, and having hole in apex, worked over ⅞-inch galvanized iron ring, to admit spindle of pole; to extend down the roof at least 6 inches below the top, with five ½-inch holes worked over galvanized iron rings; at the bottom four lines, which are to be made of 6-thread manila line, 16 feet long and spliced in the holes and properly whipped on the end.

Eave lines—Twenty-four in number, to be 6-thread manila line and to be 6 feet 6 inches long, with eave 4 inches spliced on one end and properly whipped on the other. To be furnished with a metallic slip No. 2.

Foot lines—Twenty-four in number, to be 4 inches long, and to be in the form of a loop passing through a single grommet hole, stopped by a "Mathew Walker" knot.

Adopted February 8, 1884, in lieu of specifications of November 5, 1880, which are hereby canceled.

S. B. HOLABIRD,
(87 F.—1884.) Quartermaster-General, U.S.A.

Specifications for Improved Common Tents with Wall (Laced Corners)

Dimensions when finished:	Ft.	Ins.
Height when pitched	6	10
Length of ridge	6	10
Width	8	4
Height of wall	2	0
Width of eave	0	2
Height of door	5	6
Width of door at top	0	3
Width of door at bottom	1	0

Material and workmanship—To be made of standard cotton duck 28½ inches in width, clear of all imperfections, and weighing 10 ounces to the linear yard, and in a workmanlike manner, with not less than 2½ stitches of equal length to the inch, made with a double thread of five-fold cotton twine well waxed. The seams to be not less than 1 inch in width, and no slack taken in them.

Door and stay pieces—To be of the same material as to body of the tent. Stay pieces on the ridge to be 6½ inches square; those on the corners of the eaves to be 16 inches long and 6 inches wide, to be divided 8 inches up and 8 inches down on the wall; three pieces 2 inches square to be placed on the side of the end to strengthen door-line holes. Stay pieces triangular in shape stitched across each end next to the ridge, extending 5 inches below the ridge.

Grommets—Made with galvanized malleable iron rings, to be worked in all the holes, and be well made with four-thread five-fold cotton twine well waxed. Eight grommets on the eaves, four on each side of the tent, worked on the seams, size ½-inch; fifteen ¾-inch, worked on the foot of the tent; one ¾-inch, worked on each end of ridge 1⅜ inches from the end to the center of hole; three ⅝-inch, worked on the seam of the door at an equal distance of 16 inches from the foot of the tent; three ⅝-inch on the opposite side at the same distance, and one ½-inch, worked at the bottom corner of the door.

Brass grommets—Six in number, to be placed on both sides of the door at an equal distance of 16 inches from the bottom. To be of sheet brass No. 3.

Sod cloth—To be 8¾ inches wide clear from the tabling, and to extend around the tent from door to door. To be made of standard 8-ounce cotton duck.

Foot stops—Fifteen in number, to be made in form of a loop 4 inches long in the clear, of 9-thread manila line, both ends passing through a single hole worked in the tabling at the seams and held by the "Mathew Walker" knot. Tabling on the foot to be 2 inches wide when finished; on the side of the door, 1½ inches wide.

Door lines—To be 3 feet long, made of 6-thread manila line, small.

Door fastenings—To consist of three double strings of ¼-inch cotton rope 1 foot long in the clear, passing through the grommets worked on the seam, and three on the side of the end for the purpose of tying the door inside; to be secured by a "Mathew Walker" knot.

Eave lines—Eight in number, made of 6-thread manila line (large), to be 5 feet long in the clear, with an eye spliced on one end 4 inches long, the other properly whipped and furnished with a metallic slip No. 3.

Wall lines—For typing up the wall, to be made of No. 3 gilling line, nineteen in number, to be 24 inches long, properly whipped on both ends; four to be placed on each side of the tent in the seams of the wall under the eave, passing through with a knot on the inside and stay stitched on the outside; four to be placed on the front end, three on the back end, and one at each corner, as shown in the standard sample.

Laced corners—The tabling on the end and side at each corner to be 1½ inches wide; five ⅜-inch holes to be worked on each corner, over galvanized iron rings, 5 inches apart, the lower one taking distance from the center of the grommet hole on the foot of the tent; the opposite side to have five sheet brass grommets No. 3 placed at the same distance apart, so that the corners may be laced up by means of loops made of No. 3 gilling line, 5¼ inches long, with the "Mathew Walker" knot on one end; one ¾-inch grommet hole worked on each corner for foot-stops.

Ventilator—An aperture 3 inches wide and six inches long, one in the front and one in the back end of the tent, placed 6 inches from the top and 2 inches from the center, on the right side of each end. The aperture to be reenforced with the same material as the body of the tent, and to be overstitched with twine. A flap or curtain on the inside, 6 inches wide and 10 inches long, to be made of two-ply 8-ounce cotton duck, stitched around the edge, with one No. 1 sheet brass grommet placed at the top for the purpose of tying it up; to close the opening, strings made of No. 2 gilling line to be used for tying the curtain in place.

Adopted February 8, 1884.

S. B. HOLABIRD,
(87 F.—1884.) Quartermaster-General, U.S.A.

Specifications for Improved Common Tents with Wall (Closed Corners)

Dimensions when finished:	Ft.	Ins.
Height when pitched	6	10
Length of ridge	6	10
Width	8	4
Height of wall	2	0
Width of eave	0	2
Height of door	5	6
Width of door at top	0	3
Width of door at bottom	1	0

Material and workmanship—To be made of standard cotton duck 28½ inches in width, clear of all imperfections, and weighing 10 ounces to the linear yard, and in a workmanlike manner, with not less than 2½ stitches of equal length to the inch, made with a double thread of five-fold cotton twine well waxed. The seams to be not less than 1 inch in width, and no slack taken in them.

Door and stay pieces—To be of the same material as to body of the tent. Stay pieces on the ridge to be 6½ inches square; those on the corners of the eaves to be 16 inches long and 6 inches wide, to be divided 8 inches up and 8 inches down on the wall; three pieces 2 inches square to be placed on the side of the end to strengthen door-line holes. Stay pieces triangular in shape stitched across each end next to the ridge, extending 5 inches below the ridge.

Grommets—Made with galvanized malleable iron rings, to be worked in all the holes, and be well made with four-thread five-fold cotton twine well waxed. Eight grommets on the eaves, four on each side of the tent, worked on the seams, size ½-inch; fifteen ¾-inch, worked on the foot of the tent; one ¾-inch, worked on each end of ridge 1⅜ inches from the end to the center of hole; three ⅝-inch, worked on the seam of the door at an equal distance of 16 inches from the foot of the tent; three ⅝-inch on the opposite side at the same distance, and one ½-inch, worked at the bottom corner of the door.

Brass grommets—Six in number, to be placed on both sides of the door at an equal distance of 16 inches from the bottom. To be of sheet brass No. 3.

Sod cloth—To be 8¾ inches wide clear from the tabling, and to extend around the tent from door to door. To be made of standard 8-ounce cotton duck.

Foot stops—Fifteen in number, to be made in form of a loop 4 inches long in the clear, of 9-thread manila line, both ends passing through a single hole worked in the tabling at the seams and held by the "Mathew Walker" knot. Tabling on the foot to be 2 inches wide when finished; on the side of the door, 1½ inches wide.

Door lines—To be 3 feet long, made of 6-thread manila line, small.

Door fastenings—To consist of three double strings of ¼-inch cotton rope 1 foot long in the clear, passing through the grommets worked on the seam, and three on the side of the end for the purpose of tying the door inside; to be secured by a "Mathew Walker" knot.

Eave lines—Eight in number, made of 6-thread manila line (large), to be 5 feet long in the clear, with an eye spliced on one end 4 inches long, the other properly whipped and furnished with a metallic slip No. 3.

Wall lines—For tying up the wall, to be made of No. 3 gilling line, fifteen in number, to be 24 inches long, properly whipped on both ends; four to be placed on each side of the tent in the seams of the wall under the eave, passing through with a knot on the inside and stay stitched on the outside; four to be placed on the front end, three on the back end, and one at each corner, as shown in the standard sample.

Ventilator—An aperture 3 inches wide and 6 inches long, one in the front and one in the back end of the tent, placed 6 inches from the top and 2 inches from the center, on the right side of each end. The aperture to be reenforced with the same material as the body of the tent, and to be overstitched with twine. A flap or curtain on the inside, 6 inches wide and 10 inches long, to be made of two-ply 8-ounce cotton duck, stitched around the edge, with one No. 1 sheet brass grommet placed at the top for the purpose of tying it up; to close the opening, strings made of No. 2 gilling line to be used for tying the curtain in place.

Adopted February 8, 1884.

S. B. HOLABIRD,
(87 F.—1884.) Quartermaster-General, U.S.A.

Specifications for Hospital Tents

Dimensions—When finished; Height when pitched, 11 feet; length of ridge, 14 feet; width when pitched, 14 feet 6 inches; height of wall when pitched, 4 feet 6 inches; wall eaves, 3 inches in width; height of door when pitched, 9 feet; width of door when pitched, 18 inches at bottom and 10 inches at top; from top of ridge to wall, 9 feet 10 inches.

Material—To be made of cotton duck, 28½ inches wide, clear of all imperfection, and weighing 12 ounces to the linear yard.

Work—To be made in a workmanlike manner, with not less than two and one-half stitches of equal length to the inch, made with double thread of fivefold cotton twine well waxed. The seams not less than 1 inch in width, and no slack taken in them.

Grommets—Grommets made with malleable iron rings, galvanized, must be worked in all the holes, and be well made, with 4-thread fivefold cotton twine well waxed. Sizes of grommets; For eaves, ½-inch rings; for foot-stops, ⅝-inch rings; and for ridge, ⅞-inch rings; the latter to be worked so that the center will measure 2¼ inches from edge of roof, so as to be in correct position to receive spindle of upright poles.

Door and stay pieces—Door and stay pieces to be of the same material as the tent. The stay pieces on end and ridge of tent to be 1 foot square, those at the corners of tent, at angle of roof and wall, to be 8 inches wide, let into the tabling at the eaves, and extending 8 inches up the roof and 8 inches down the wall.

Extension cloth—The extension cloth, 13 inches wide in the clear, to be of the same material as the tent, and stitched to it with 2 rows of flat stitching. Grommets of the required sizes to be worked in proper places for upright spindle and for eave lines.

Sod cloth—The sod cloth to be 8-ounce cotton duck, 12 inches in width in the clear from the tabling and underlying it 2¼ inches, and to extend from door to door around all sides of the tent.

Tabling—The tabling on foot of tent, when finished, to be 2½ inches in width.

Ventilator—An aperture 5 inches wide and 10 inches long, one in the front and one in the back end of the tent, placed 6 inches from the top and 2 inches from the center on the right side of each end. The aperture to be reenforced with 10 ounce cotton duck, and to have the edges turned in and stitched all around. A flap or curtain on the inside 8 inches wide and 14 inches long, finished; to be made of two-ply 8-ounce cotton duck, stitched around the edges; to have one "No. 1" sheet brass grommet placed at the top for the purpose of tying it up to close the opening; strings made of "No. 2" gilling line, to be used for tying the curtain in place.

Guy lines—Two guy lines, of 12-thread manila line, soft and pliable, each 30 feet long in the clear.

Eave lines—Eave lines, fourteen in number, to be 9-thread manila line (large), and to be 10 feet 6 inches long in the clear. To be "spliced" in the eaves, and each line to be furnished with a metallic slip of Army standard.

Door lines—Door lines, of 6-thread manila line 3 feet long in the clear.

Door fastenings—Door fastenings, as shown in sample tent, to consist of four double door strings of ¼-inch cotton rope, 1 foot long on each side, passing through the door seam and secured by a stop knot and a stay stitch. Brass grommets to be in corresponding positions on edge of door piece, in which to tie the door cords. A 2-inch tabling to be made on edge of door.

Foot stops—Foot stops, twenty-six in number, to be loops 4½ inches long in the clear, of 6-thread ratlin, both ends passing through a single grommet worked in the tabling at seams, and to be held by what is known as the "Mathew Walker" knot. Ends to be whipped with cotton twine well waxed.

The tabling at bottom, the sod cloth, and the foot stops to be so arranged that the sod cloth falls inside and the foot stops outside the tent.

All lines to be well whipped 1 inch from their ends with waxed twine and properly knotted.

Adopted February 18, 1884, in lieu of specifications adopted March 12, 1879, which are hereby canceled.

S. B. HOLABIRD,

(317 F.—1884.) Quartermaster-General, U.S.A.

Specifications for Wall Tents

Dimensions—Height, 8 feet 6 inches; length of ridge, 9 feet; width, 9 feet; height of wall, 3 feet 9 inches; wall eaves, 2 inches wide; height of door, 7 feet; width of door, 12 inches at bottom, 4 inches at top; from top of ridge to wall, 6 feet 6 inches.

Material—To be made of cotton duck, 28½ inches wide, clear of all imperfections, and weighing 12 ounces to the linear yard.

Work—To be made in a workmanlike manner, with not less than 2½ stitches of equal length to the inch, made with double thread of fivefold cotton twine well waxed, the seams to be not less than 1 inch in width, and no slack taken in them.

Grommets—Grommets made with malleable iron rings, galvanized; must be worked in all the holes, and be well made, with 4-thread fivefold cotton twine well waxed. Sizes of grommets: For eaves, ½-inch rings; for foot stops, ⅝-inch rings; and for ridge, ¾-inch rings; the latter to be worked so that the center will measure 1¼ inches from edge of roof, so as to be in correct position to receive spindle of upright poles.

Door and stay pieces—Door and stay pieces to be of the same material as the tent. Stay pieces on ends and ridge of tent to be 6½ inches square; those at corners of tent, at angle of roof and wall, to be 8 inches wide, let into the tabling at the eaves, and extending 8 inches up the roof and 8 inches down the wall.

Back stay—A band or strip 4 inches wide, of the same material as the tent, to be stitched across the back of the tent on the inside, entering into and being stitched with the corner seams at the juncture of the roof and wall.

Sod cloth—The sod cloth to be of 8-ounce cotton duck, 9 inches wide in the clear from the tabling, and to extend from door to door around both sides and ends of the tent.

Tabling—The tabling on the foot of the tent, when finished, to be 2½ inches in width.

Ventilator—An aperture 4 inches wide and 8 inches long, one in the front and one in the back end of the tent, placed 6 inches from the top and 2 inches from the center, on the right side of each end. The aperture to be reenforced with 10-ounce cotton duck and to have the edges turned in and stitched all around. A flap or curtain on the inside 8 inches wide and 14 inches long, finished; to be made of two-ply 8-ounce cotton duck, stitched around the edges; to have one "No. 1" sheet brass grommet placed at the top for the purpose of tying it up to close the opening; strings made of "No. 2" gilling line to be used for tying the curtain in place.

Door lines—The door lines to be of 6-thread manila line (large), 3 feet long in the clear.

Door fastening—Door fastening, as shown in sample tent, to consist of four double door strings of ¼-inch cotton rope 1 foot long on each side, passing through the door seam and secured by a stop knot and a stay stitch. Brass grommets to be in corresponding position on edge of door piece in which to tie the door cords. A 2-inch tabling to be made on the edge of the door.

Foot stops—Foot stops, seventeen in number, to be loops 4½ inches long in the clear, of 6-thread ratlin, both ends passing through a single grommet worked in the tabling at seam, and to be held by what is known as the "Mathew Walker" knot. Ends to be whipped with cotton twine well waxed.

Eave lines—Eave lines, ten in number, to be of 6-thread manila line (large), and be 8 feet long in the clear. To be "spliced" in the eaves, and each line to be furnished with a metallic slip of Army standard.

The tabling at bottom, the sod cloth, and the foot stops to be so arranged that the sod cloth falls inside and the foot stops outside the tent.

All lines to be well whipped 1 inch from the end with waxed twine and properly knotted.

Adopted February 18, 1884, in lieu of specifications adopted February 15, 1879, which are hereby canceled.

S. B. HOLABIRD,
(317 F.—1884.) Quartermaster-General, U.S.A.

Specifications for Overcoats

Material—Sky-blue kersey, 22 ounce, Army standard. Lining for body, dark blue flannel to weigh 11½ ounces to the 6/4 linear yard. Flannel for cape lining, Army standard, to weigh 10 ounces to the 6/4 linear yard, and to be of the following colors, viz: For hospital stewards, emerald green; for commissary sergeants, gray; for ordnance, crimson; for engineers and artillery, scarlet; for signal service, orange; for infantry, dark blue; for cavalry, yellow. Sleeve lining, colored jeans.

Pattern—To be double-breasted, with cape, and having five regulation brass buttons, large, on each breast. The cape to be adjustable by means of seven hooks beneath the collar of the coat, and seven eyes upon the cape; to have seven regulation brass buttons, small.

Workmanship—To be cut and made in conformity with the standard patterns and samples.

Size	Coat Length	Cape Length	Breast Measure	Waist Measure	Sleeve Length	Collar Length
	Inches	Inches	Inches	Inches	Inches	Inches
1	44½	24½	36	34	32½	17
2	45	25½	38	36	33	17½
3	46	26½	41	39	33½	18½
4	47	27½	44	42	34	19½
5	48	28½	45	44	34½	20
6	49	29	46	46	35	20½

Adopted March 8, 1884, in lieu of specifications adopted February 6, 1880, which are hereby canceled.

(559 F.—1884.) S. B. HOLABIRD,
Quartermaster-General, U.S.A.

Specifications for Canvas Caps

Material—To be made of 6-ounce cotton duck, dyed brown, lined with light blanket cloth next to the duck, and with light-colored cotton jean in the inside; to have two buttons on the cape to button at the throat, on one, vest size, brown "lasting" button on the top for finish. The visor and edges bound with ¾ brown cotton tape.

Style—Skull cap with extension, forming a cape reaching to the shoulders and meeting in front, covering the throat, and buttoning together with two buttons. A visor of the same material bound with ¾ brown cotton tape sewed on the forehead (to be worn up or down as desired), and having hook and eye to fasten it when turned up.

Workmanship—To be cut and made in conformity with the sealed standard sample adopted this date.

Adopted April 17, 1884.

Specifications for Boots

To be worked square with the last on which they are made; the edges to be finished with pressers, without heel-ball, and must measure at least half a size (outside) more than they are marked.

The upper leather to be of the best oak-tanned from slaughter-hides. The leg to be finished on the grain, and the foot to be wax upper. The soles to be best oak-tanned from "straight" Texas hides, or from South American (commonly called "Spanish") dry hides. No split leather to be used.

The width of the soles across the ball of the foot to be graduated as follows, and to be in proportion throughout: No. 5, 3 4/8 inches; No. 6, 3⅝ inches; No. 7, 3 6/8 inches; No. 8, 3⅞ inches; No. 9, 4 inches; No. 10, 4⅛ inches; No. 11, 4 2/8 inches; No. 12, 4⅜ inches.

The insteps and toes to measure as follows: No. 5, 9⅛, 8⅞ inches; No. 6, 9⅝, 9 inches; No. 7, 9⅝, 9⅜ inches; No. 8, 9⅞, 9 6/8 inches; No. 9, 10, 9⅞ inches; No.

10, 10 4/8, 10 inches; No. 11, 10 6/8, 10 3/8 inches; No. 12, 10 7/8, 10 5/8 inches.

The measurement for a No. 8 boot, standard, letter "A," is as follows, viz: heel, 13 1/8 inches; instep, 9 6/8 inches; ball or toe, 9 5/8 inches; length of legs, 20 inches in front, 14 1/2 inches back; width of leg at top, 16 inches; width of strap, 1 1/4 inches; length of strap, 7 inches; height of counter, 3 inches at back; length of heel, 3 inches; width of heel, 2 7/8 inches; width of sole or ball, 3 7/8 inches.

Straps to be made of calfskin leather and sewed on to the inside of the leg. They are to have not less than six stitches to the inch in the back seam, and to be stitched with three rows of silk on the front and counter.

To have the soles sewed with seven stitches to the inch on the welt, and four stitches to the inch on the inner sole; with not less than 12-cord flax thread on the inner sole, nor less than 10-cord flax thread on the welt.

Measurement for a No. 8 boot, standard, made on "B" last is, with the following exceptions, the same as that made on the "A" last: Heel, 13 1/4 inches: instep, 9 7/8 inches; ball or toe, 9 6/8 inches.

Adopted April 24, 1884, in lieu of those of February 25, 1878, which are hereby canceled.

S. B. HOLABIRD,
Quartermaster-General, U.S.A.

(783 F.—1884.)

Specifications for "Post" Shoes

To be worked square with the last on which they are made; the edges to be finished with pressers, without heel-ball, and to measure at least half a size (outside) more than they are marked.

The upper leather to be of the best oak-tanned American calfskin, and to weigh 4 pounds to the skin. Soles of the best quality, oak-tanned, from straight Texas hides, or from South American (commonly called "Spanish") dry hides. No split leather to be used.

The width of the soles across the ball of the foot to be graduated as follows, and to be in proportion throughout: No. 5, 3 3/8 inches; No. 6, 3 4/8 inches; No. 7, 3 5/8 inches; No. 8, 3 6/8 inches; No. 9, 3 7/8 inches; No. 10, 4 inches; No. 11, 4 1/8 inches; No. 12, 4 3/8 inches.

The instep and toe to measure as follows: For letter "A," No. 5, 8 5/8, 8 1/8 inches; No. 6, 8 7/8, 8 1/8 inches; No. 7, 9 1/8, 8 5/8 inches; No. 8, 9 3/8, 8 7/8 inches; No. 9, 9 5/8, 9 1/8 inches; No. 10, 9 7/8, 9 3/8 inches; No. 11, 10 1/8, 9 5/8 inches; No. 12, 10 3/8, 9 7/8 inches. For letter "B" 1/8 inch more.

The height of leg for a No. 8 shoe to be 6 1/4 inches. The upper to be cut without side seam; to have counter, side piece, strap, and crimped tongue stitched on with silk. To be laced in front, and to have metallic eyelets and hooks; to have the soles sewed with seven stitches to the inch on the welt, and four stitches to the inch on the inner sole, with not less than 12-cord flax thread on the inner sole nor less than 10-cord flax thread on the welt.

Adopted April 24, 1884, in lieu of those of March 8, 1876, which are hereby canceled.

S. B. HOLABIRD,
Quartermaster-General, U.S.A.

(559 F.—1884.)

Specifications for "Field" Shoes

To be worked square with the last on which they are made; the edges to be finished with pressers, without heel-ball, and to measure at least half a size (outside) more than they are marked.

The upper leather to be of the best oak-tanned from slaughter-hides. The soles to be of the best oak-tanned from straight Texas hides, or from South American (commonly called "Spanish") dry hides. No split leather to be used.

The width of the soles across the ball of the foot to be graduated as follows, and to be in proportion throughout: No. 5, 3 4/8 inches; No. 6, 3 5/8 inches; No. 7, 3 6/8 inches; No. 8, 3 7/8 inches; No. 9, 4 inches; No. 10, 4 1/8 inches; No. 11, 4 2/8 inches; No. 12, 4 3/8 inches.

The insteps and toes to measure as follows: For letter "A," No. 5, 9, 8 6/8 inches; No. 6, 9 4/8, 8 7/8 inches; No. 7, 9 4/8, 9 2/8 inches; No. 8, 9 6/8, 9 5/8 inches; No. 9, 9 7/8, 9 6/8 inches; No. 10, 10 3/8, 9 7/8 inches; No. 11, 10 5/8, 10 2/8 inches; No. 12, 10 6/8, 10 4/8 inches. For letter "B" 1/8 inch more.

The height of leg for a No. 8 shoe to be 8 inches, width of leg at top 6 1/2 inches, to have crimped front, with calfskin strap 2 1/2 inches long and 1/2 inch wide at back and front; to have close seam on the inside, and light calfskin gusset 5 inches long; to be closed with automatic buckle on the outside; the counter to be 2 1/2 inches high and to extend across side seams; to have not less than nine stitches to the inch on counter and straps. To have the soles sewed with seven stitches to the inch on the welt, and four stitches to the inch on the inner sole, with not less than 12-cord flax thread on the inner sole nor less than 10-cord flax thread on the welt.

Adopted April 24, 1884, in lieu of those of March 8, 1876, which are hereby canceled.

S. B. HOLABIRD,
Quartermaster-General, U.S.A.

(783 F.—1884.)

Specifications for Leather Gauntlets

To be made of Angora goat skin.

The gauntlet or cuff to be at least 4½ inches deep, and of sufficient fullness to admit cuff of coat.

The cuff to be lined with russet leather.

The gloves to be "table cut," and well stitched throughout with silk, and in quality of material and workmanship they must conform to the standard sample.

To be of five sizes, and put up in the following proportion to the 100 pairs: 10, 8; 30, 8½; 30, 9; 20, 9½; 10, 10.

Adopted May 21, 1884.

S. B. HOLABIRD,
Quartermaster-General, U.S.A.

(1087 F.—1884.)

Specifications for Conical Wall Tents

Material—Body of tent to be made of standard 12-ounce cotton duck, and the sod cloth of standard 8-ounce cotton duck, 28½ inches wide. Eave lines of 6-thread manila line (large), and foot lines of 9-thread manila line.

Work—To be made in a workmanlike manner, with not less than 2½ stitches of equal length to the inch, made with a double thread, of five-fold cotton twine well waxed. The seams to be not less than 1 inch in width, and no slack taken in them.

Form and dimensions—The roof to be in the form of a frustum of a cone, 16 feet 5 inches in diameter at the base, 18 inches in diameter at the top. Wall to be 3 feet high. Height, when pitched, to top of roof, 10 feet. Eaves to be 2 inches wide, and tabling at bottom 2½ inches wide. The angle from the top to the eave 10 feet 6½ inches.

Top—The top opening at the top to be formed with a galvanized iron ring 18 inches in diameter, over which the duck shall be firmly stitched and reinforced down the roof to a depth of 8½ inches. Six ¾-inch grommet holes around the top, equal distances just below the ring, to be reinforced with leather in which to hook the chains which support the tent on the pole.

Plate and chains—The plate to be 4 inches in diameter and ¼ inch in thickness, with six ⅜-inch holes around the edge at equal distances and countersunk, and a ⅝-inch hole in the center. Chains, six in number, to be 14 inches long, including hook, made of machine chain No. 1. All to be of galvanized iron.

Door—Doorway to be 7 feet high, measured along the seam, 13¼ inches wide at top, 25¼ inches at bottom. The door of two equal pieces in area to the doorway, and joined at opposite sides of the same so as to lap and form double thickness when closed. Tabling on edge to be two inches when finished.

Door fastenings—To consist of five No. 5 conical pointed brass grommets on each side, placed at equal distances of 16 inches from the top of the door to the eave, and 18 inches from the eave down on the wall holes, to be worked on the seams the same distance, with ⅝-inch galvanized iron rings; door lines of ¼-inch white cotton rope 3 feet long and whipped on both ends, to be seized in the middle with a knot on each side of the hole, that the door may be tied either inside or outside. Two ⅝-inch holes worked 8 inches above the lap of the door, with two ¼-inch cotton lines 1 foot long in the clear, with a "Mathew Walker" knot on one end and properly whipped on the other end; one hole ½ inch worked on each side at the bottom, with one 6-thread manila line 3 feet long for door line. Four lines 24 inches long, made of No. 3 manila line 3 feet long for door line. Four lines 24 inches long, made of No. 3 gilling line, placed on the eave on the inside of the tent on both sides of the door, for tying the doors back when open.

Sod cloth—The sod cloth to be 8¾ inches wide in the clear, and to extend around the inside of the tent from door to door.

Grommet holes—Twenty-four in number, worked on the seams at the foot of the tent over ¾-inch galvanized malleable iron rings, and twenty-four ½-inch holes to be worked on the seams of the eaves over galvanized iron rings, the holes to be worked with 4-thread five-fold cotton twine, well waxed.

Hood—Conical hood open at side, and having hole in apex, worked over ⅞-inch galvanized iron ring, to admit spindle of pole; to extend down the roof at least 6 inches below the top, with five ½-inch holes worked over galvanized iron rings at the bottom for lines, which are to be made of 6-thread manila line 16 feet long and spliced in the holes and properly whipped on the end.

Eave lines—Twenty-four in number, to be 6-thread manila line and to be 6 feet 6 inches long, with eye 4 inches spliced on one end and properly whipped on the other. To be furnished with a metallic slip No. 2.

Foot lines—Twenty-four in number, to be 4 inches long, and to be in the form of a loop passing through a single grommet hole, stopped by a "Mathew Walker" knot.

Wall lines—Twenty-four in number, to be 2 feet long, to be made of No. 3 gilling line whipped at both ends, and placed under the eaves on the seams for tying the wall up.

Adopted May 23, 1884, in lieu of specifications of February 8, 1884, which are hereby canceled.

S. B. HOLABIRD,
Quartermaster-General, U.S.A.

(1129 F.—1884.)

Specifications for Canvas Sack Coats

Material—Six-ounce cotton duck, dyed brown.

Pattern—To be a single-breasted sack coat, with falling collar, and having six india-rubber buttons in front from waist to neck; to have an outside pocket sewed on each breast.

Workmanship—To be cut and made in accordance with the standard patterns and samples.

Sizes	Breast measure	Waist measure	Length of coat	Length of sleeve	Length of collar
	Inches	Inches	Inches	Inches	Inches
1 ..	36	34	28	31½	17
2 ..	37	35	28½	32½	17½
3 ..	39	37	29	33	18
4 ..	41	39	29½	34	19
5 ..	42	40	30½	34¾	20
6 ..	44	43	31½	35	20¼

Adopted May 31, 1884.

S. B. HOLABIRD,
Quartermaster-General, U.S.A.

Specifications for Canvas Trousers

Material—Six-ounce cotton duck, dyed brown.

Pattern—To have slanting top pockets, a watch pocket, and a hip pocket on the right side, straps and buckles; waist-bands and flies faced with the same material the trousers are made of.

Workmanship—To be cut and made in accordance with the standard samples.

Sizes	Waist	Seat	Inside seam	Outside seam	Bottom
	Inches	Inches	Inches	Inches	Inches
1 ..	31	36	30½	40½	19½
2 ..	32	38	31	41½	20
3 ..	33	40	32	43½	20½
4 ..	34	42	33	44½	20½
5 ..	36	44	34	45½	21
6 ..	40	45	35	46½	21

Adopted May 31, 1884.

S. B. HOLABIRD,
Quartermaster-General, U.S.A.

Specifications for Mosquito Bars

Material—To be made of the best quality barred mosquito netting and white cotton tape, equal in quality to the same materials in the standard sample.

Dimensions—Seven feet long, 2 feet 8 inches wide, and 5 feet 8 inches high.

To be bound around top and down the four corners with white tape, and to have two strings of white tape 9 inches long, strongly sewed on each of the four upper corners, and to conform in all respects to the standard sample adopted May 23, 1884.

Adopted June 7, 1884.

S. B. HOLABIRD,
Quartermaster-General, U.S.A.

(1250 F.—1884.)

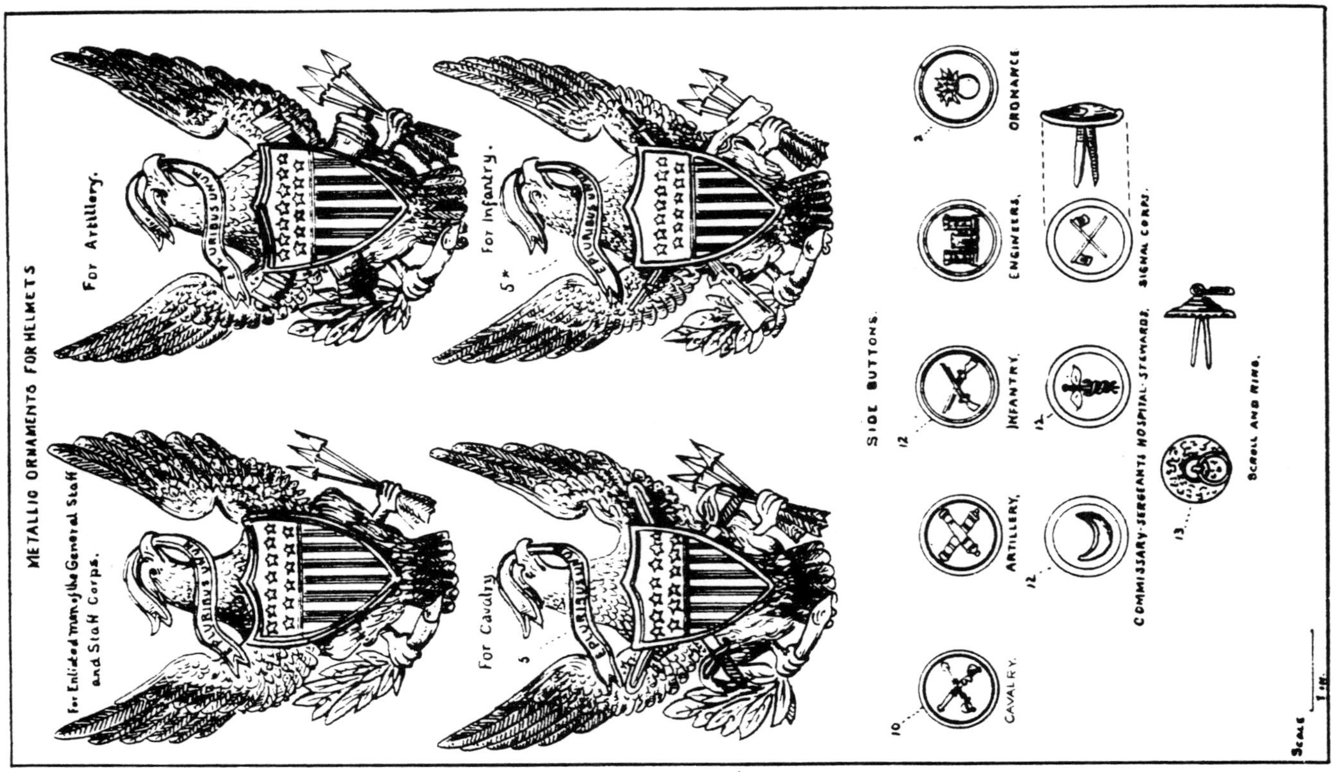
METALLIC ORNAMENTS FOR HELMETS
For Enlisted men of the General Staff and Staff Corps.
For Artillery.
For Cavalry
For Infantry.
SIDE BUTTONS.
CAVALRY.
ARTILLERY.
INFANTRY.
ENGINEERS.
ORDNANCE
COMMISSARY-SERGEANTS HOSPITAL-STEWARDS.
SIGNAL CORPS.
SCROLL AND RING.
SCALE 1 IN.

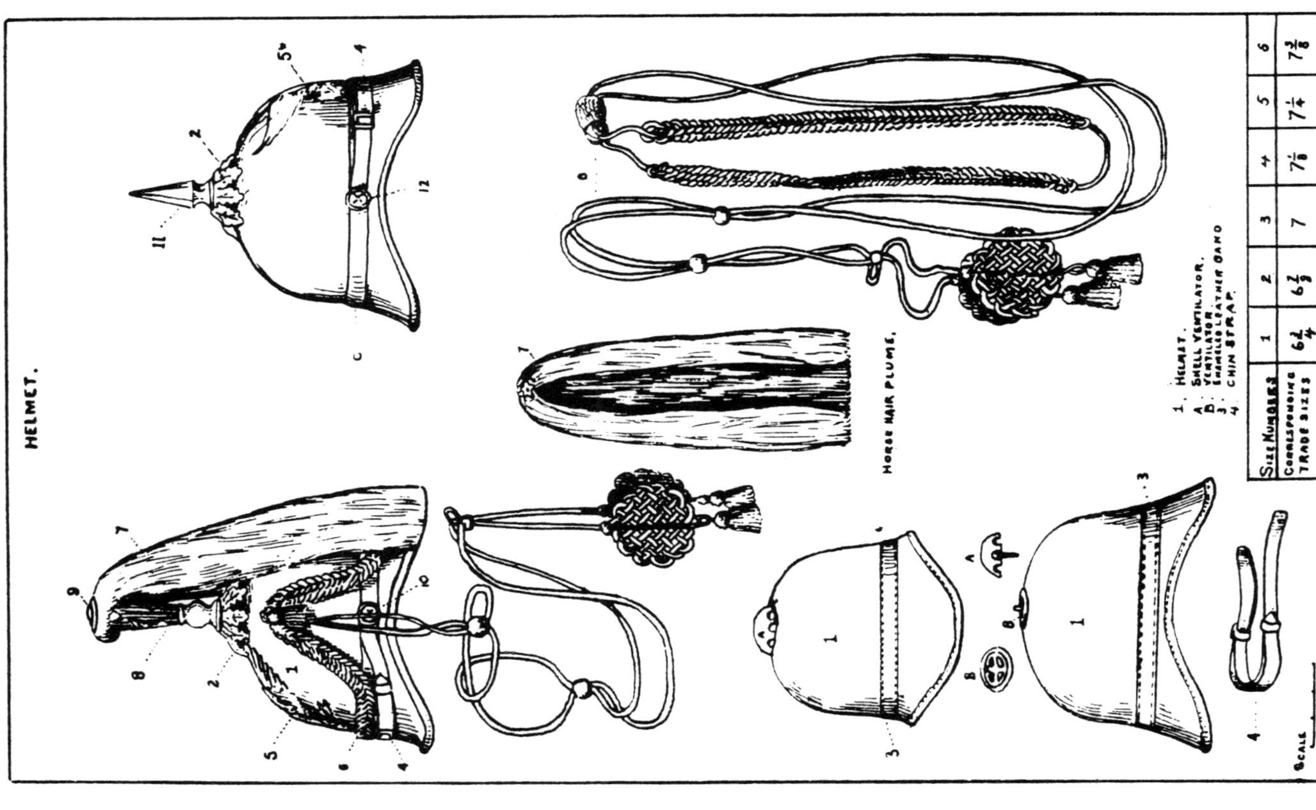
HELMET.
HORSE HAIR PLUME.
1. HELMET.
A. SHELL VENTILATOR.
B. VENTILATOR.
3. ENAMELLED LEATHER BAND
4. CHIN STRAP.
SIZE NUMBERS 1 2 3 4 5 6
CORRESPONDING TRADE SIZES 6 3/4 6 7/8 7 7 1/8 7 1/4 7 3/8
SCALE 2 INCHES

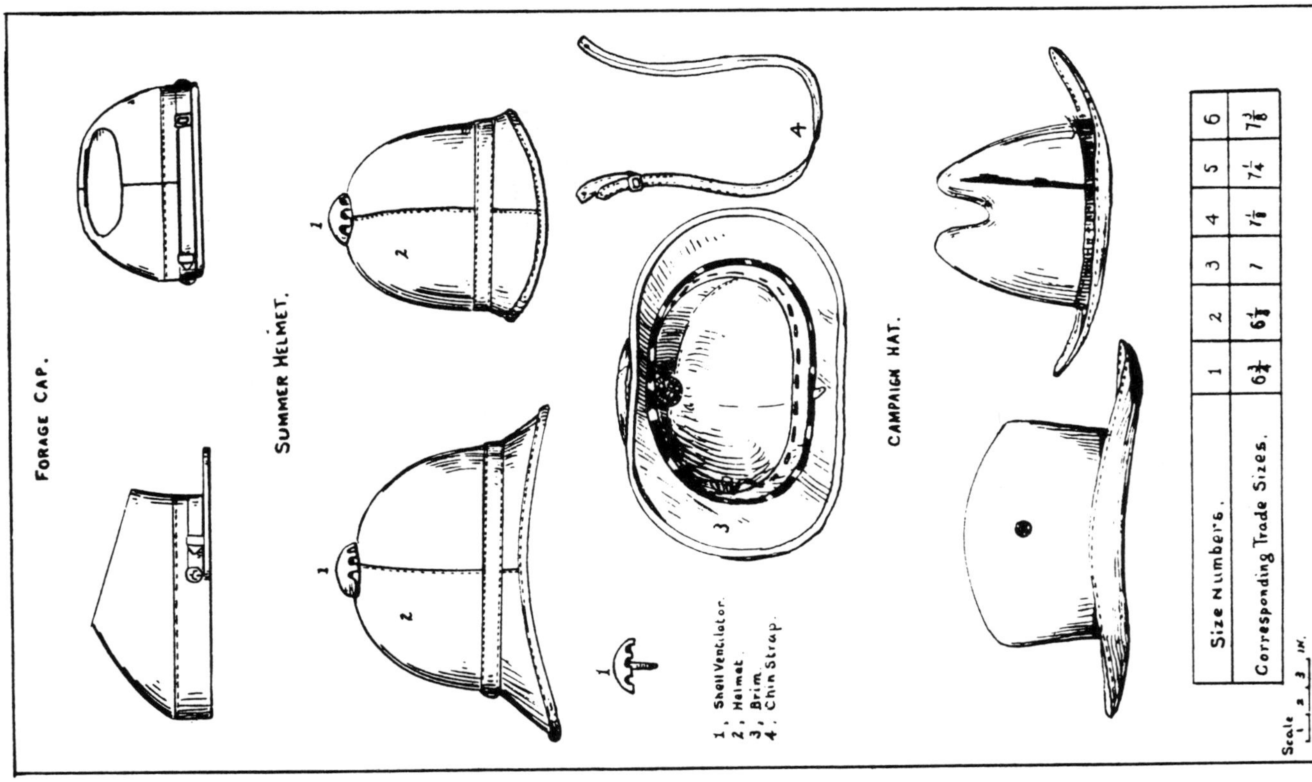
Forage Cap.
Summer Helmet.
1
2
1
2
4
3
Campaign Hat.
1. Shell Ventilator.
2. Helmet.
3. Brim.
4. Chin Strap.
Size Numbers. 1 2 3 4 5 6
Corresponding Trade Sizes. 6¾ 6⅞ 7 7⅛ 7¼ 7⅜
Scale 1 2 3 in.

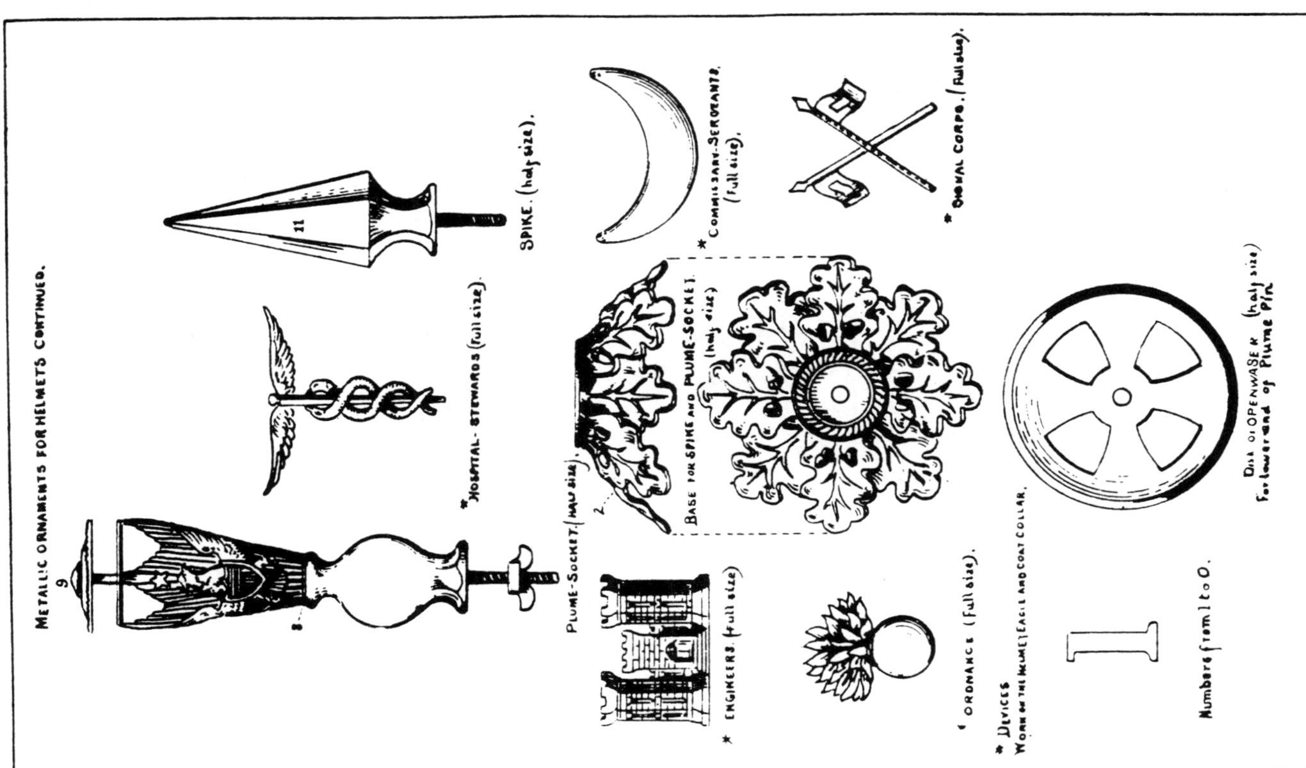
Metallic Ornaments for Helmets Continued.
9
8
11
Spike. (half size).
*Hospital-Stewards (full size).
Plume-Socket. (half size).
2
Base for Spike and Plume-Socket. (half size)
*Commissary-Sergeants. (full size).
*Signal Corps. (full size).
* Engineers. (full size)
* Ordnance (full size).
Disk of Openwork for lower end of Plume Pin. (half size)
Numbers from 1 to 0.
* Devices
Worn on the Helmet, Eagle and Coat Collar.

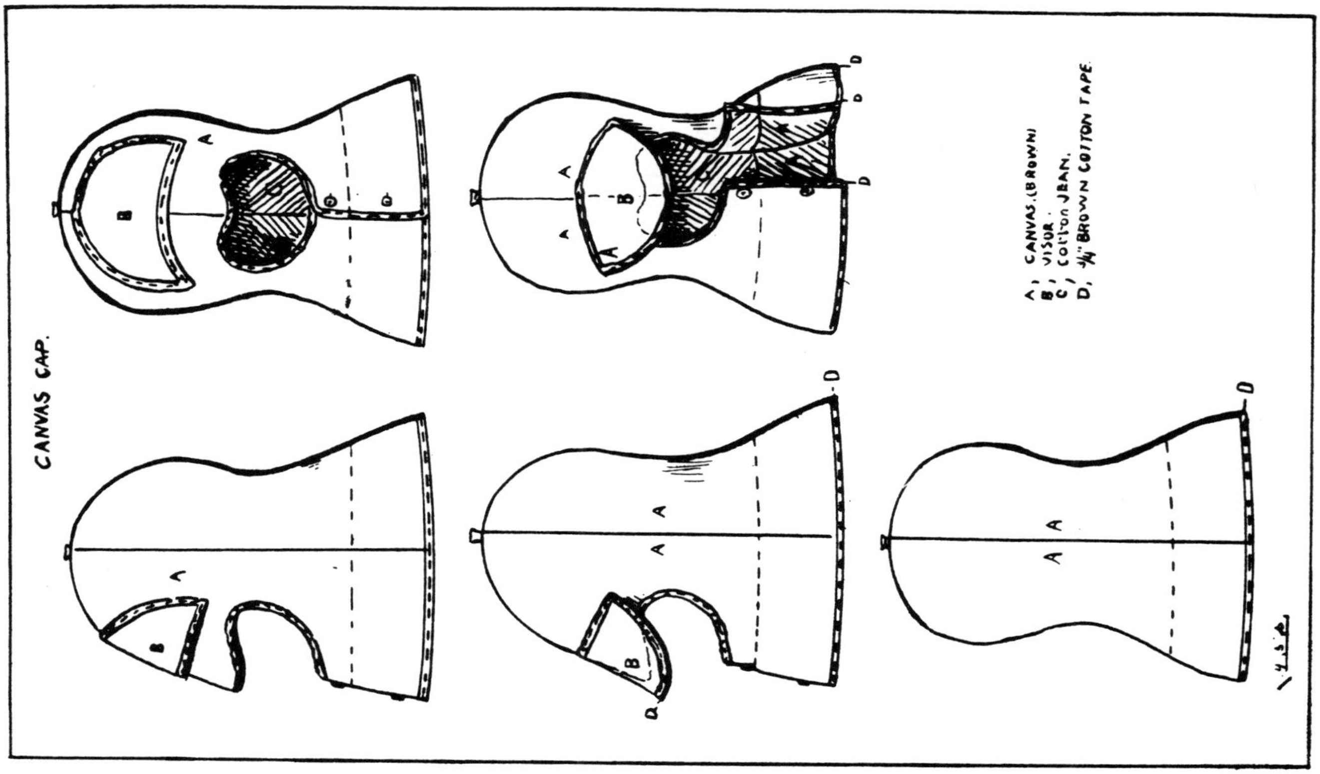
CANVAS CAP.
A, CANVAS.(BROWN)
B, VISOR.
C, COTTON JEAN.
D, 3/4" BROWN COTTON TAPE.

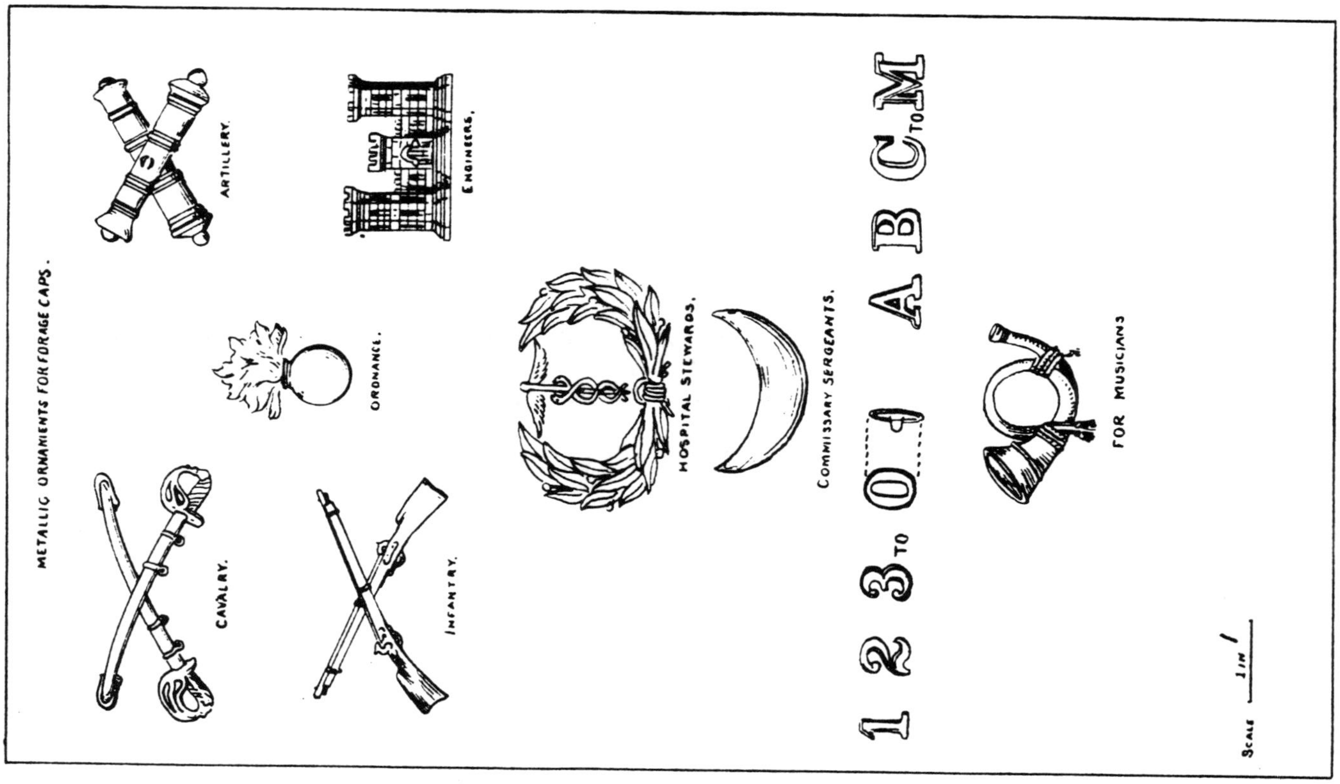
METALLIC ORNAMENTS FOR FORAGE CAPS.
CAVALRY.
INFANTRY.
ORDNANCE.
ARTILLERY.
ENGINEERS.
HOSPITAL STEWARDS.
COMMISSARY SERGEANTS.
1 2 3 TO 0
A B C TO M
FOR MUSICIANS
SCALE 1 IN

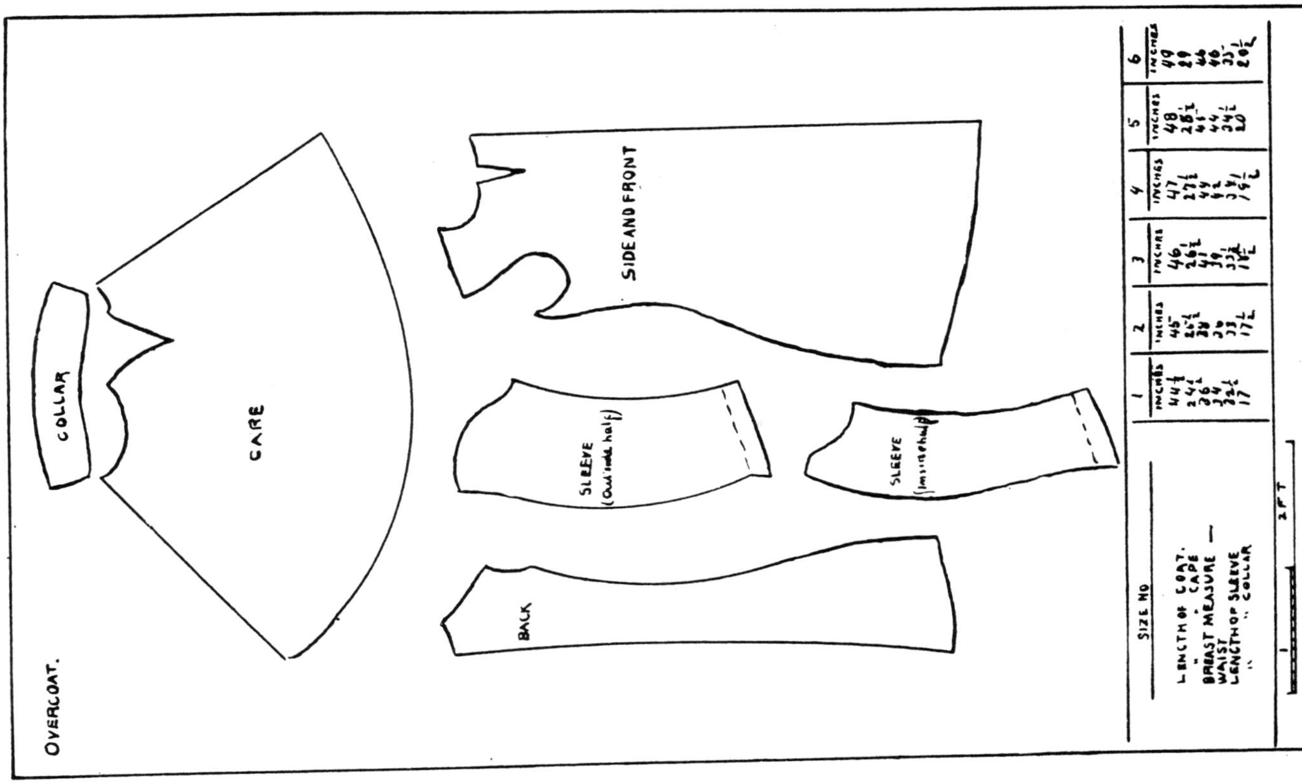

SIZE NO	1	2	3	4	5	6
	INCHES	INCHES	INCHES	INCHES	INCHES	INCHES
LENGTH OF COAT.	44½	45	46	47	48	49
" " CAPE	24½	25½	26½	27½	28½	29
BREAST MEASURE	36½	38	41	44	41	46
WAIST	34	36	39	42	44	46
LENGTH OF SLEEVE	32½	33	33½	34	34½	35
" " COLLAR	17	17½	18½	19½	20	20½

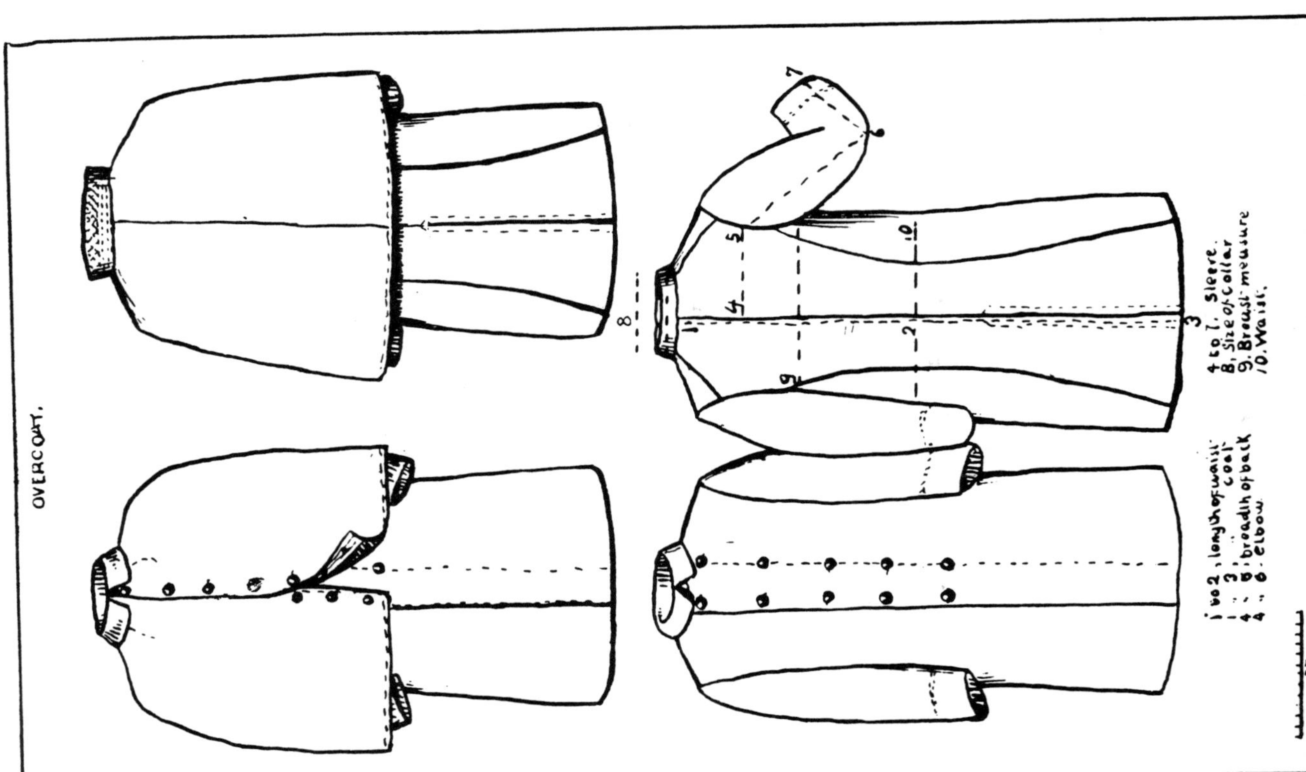

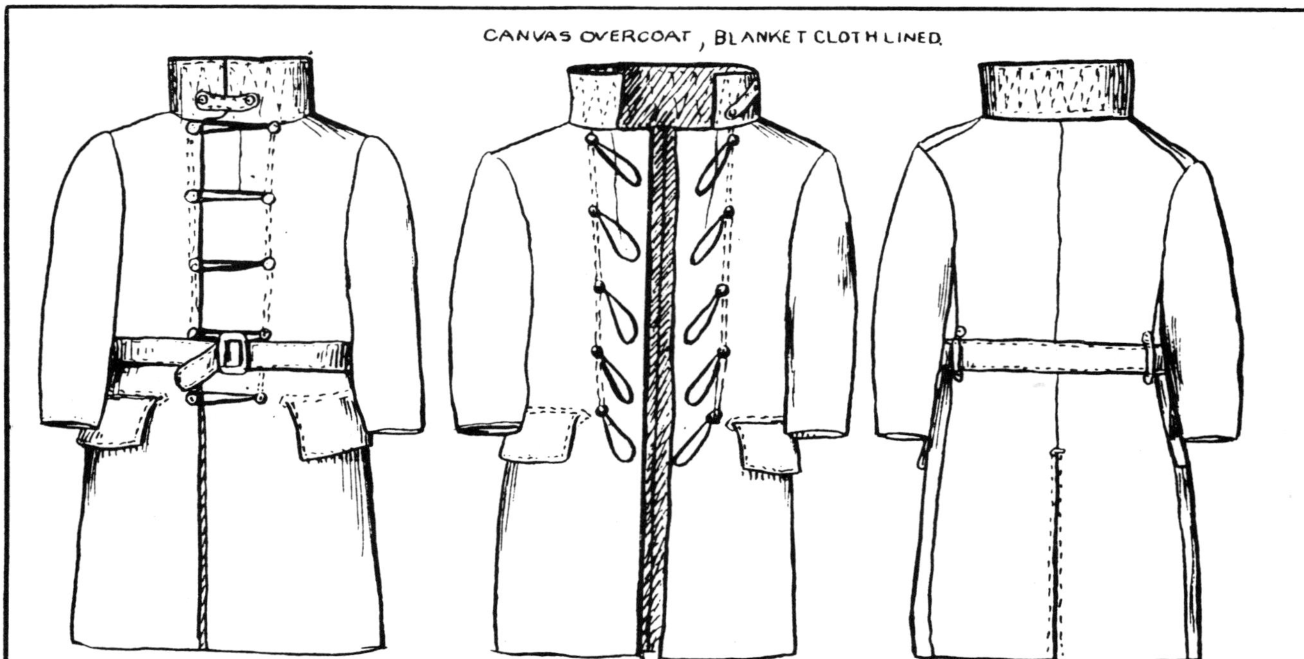

SIZES

	No 1	No 2	No 3	No 4
	Inches	Inches	Inches	Inches
Length of coat	50	52	54	56
Breadth of back	9¼	9½	10	10½
Length of sleeve	33	34	35	36

	No 1	No 2	No 3	No 4
	Inches	Inches	Inches	Inches
Width of Collar	5½	5¾	6	6¼
" " breast	40	42	44	46
" " Waist	36	38	40	42

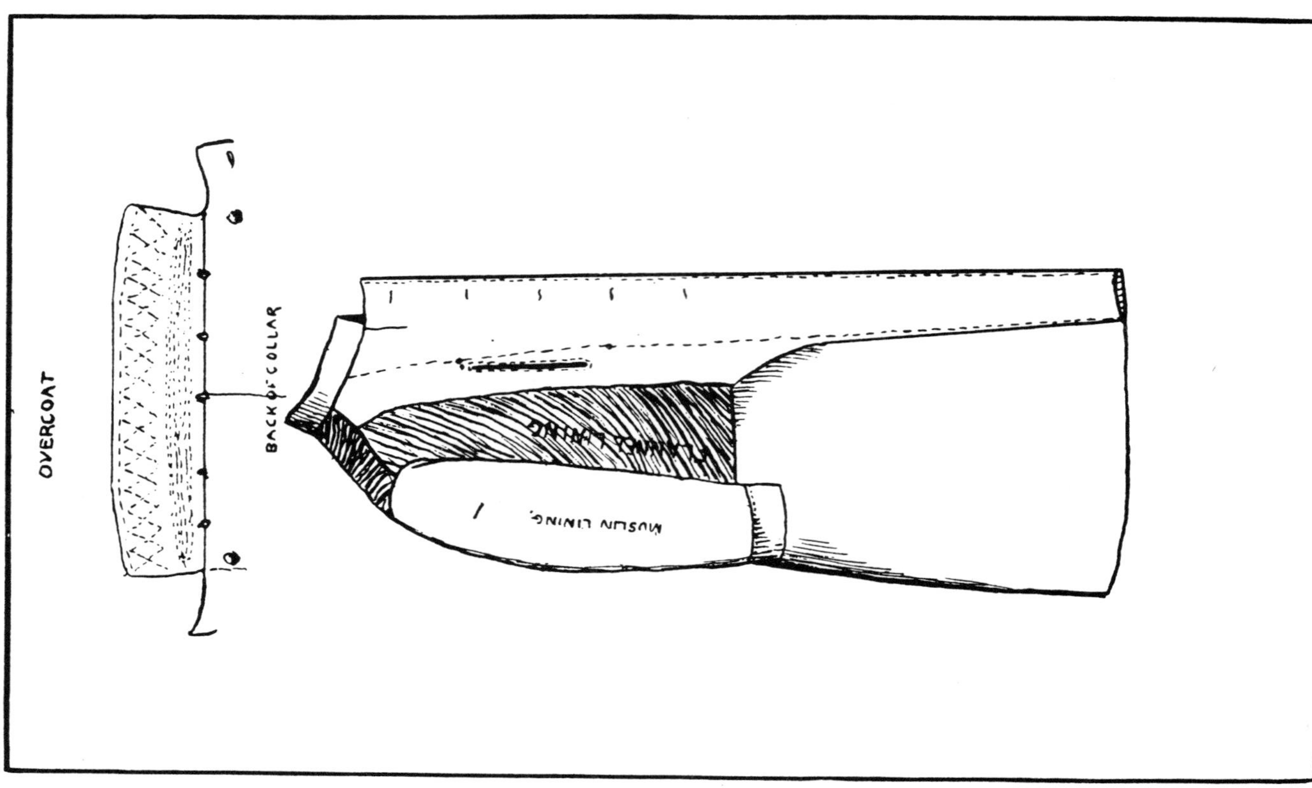

UNIFORM COAT
FOR FOOT TROOPS.

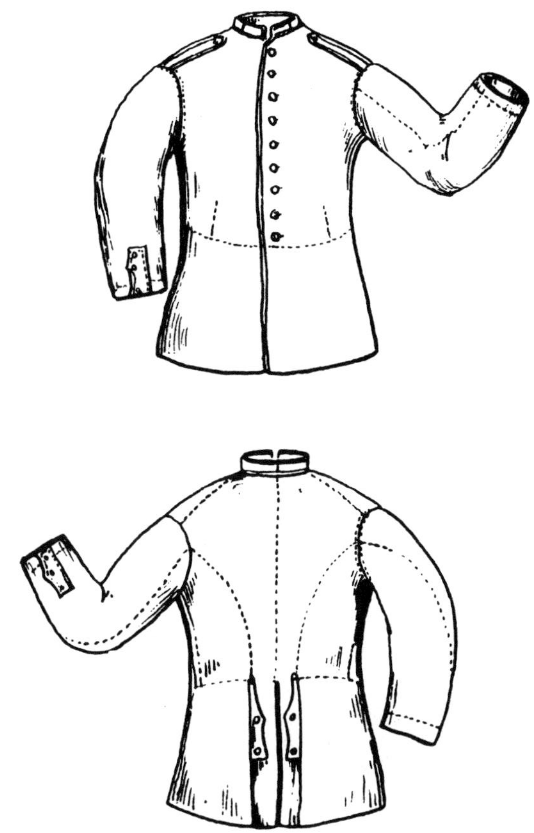

... Size ...	1	2	3	4	5
Lengh of Waiste	18 in	18¼ in	19 in	20 in	21 in
" " Coat.	29½"	30 "	31 .	32 .	33 "
" " Sleeve	32 .	32½.	34	34½	35 "
Collar	15	15¼.	16	16½.	17 "
Breast	33	36½.	39½.	42.	44 "
Waiste	31½.	33	35 .	37 "	41.
Sleeve hand	5½.	6 "	6 "	6½	6½ "

UNIFORM COAT
FOR CAVALRY MOUNTED

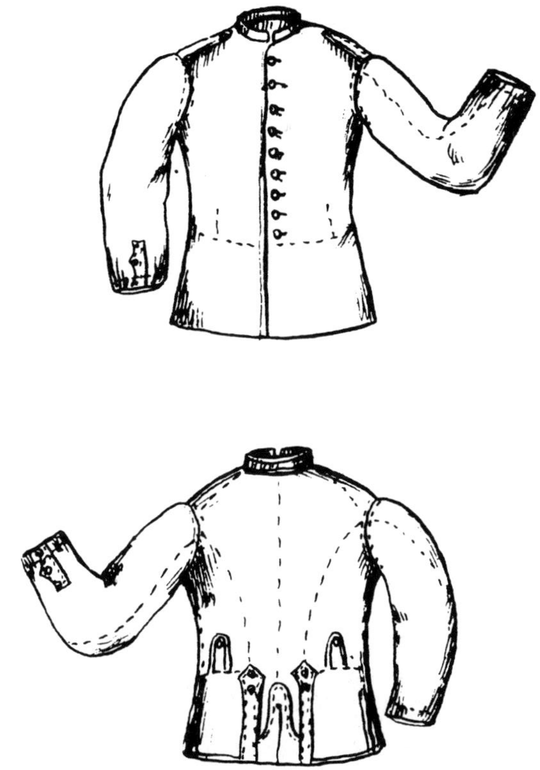

SIZE	1	2	3	4	5
Lenghof Waiste	18 in.	18½ in.	19 in.	20 in.	21 in
" "Coat	26 "	27 "	28 "	29 "	30 "
" "Sleeve	32 "	32 "	34	34 "	35 "
Collar	15 "	15¼"	16 "	16¼"	37"
Breast	35 "	36½"	39½	42"	44"
Waiste	31½"	33"	35"	37"	41"
Sleeve, hand	5½"	6"	6"	6½"	6½ "

BLOUSES.

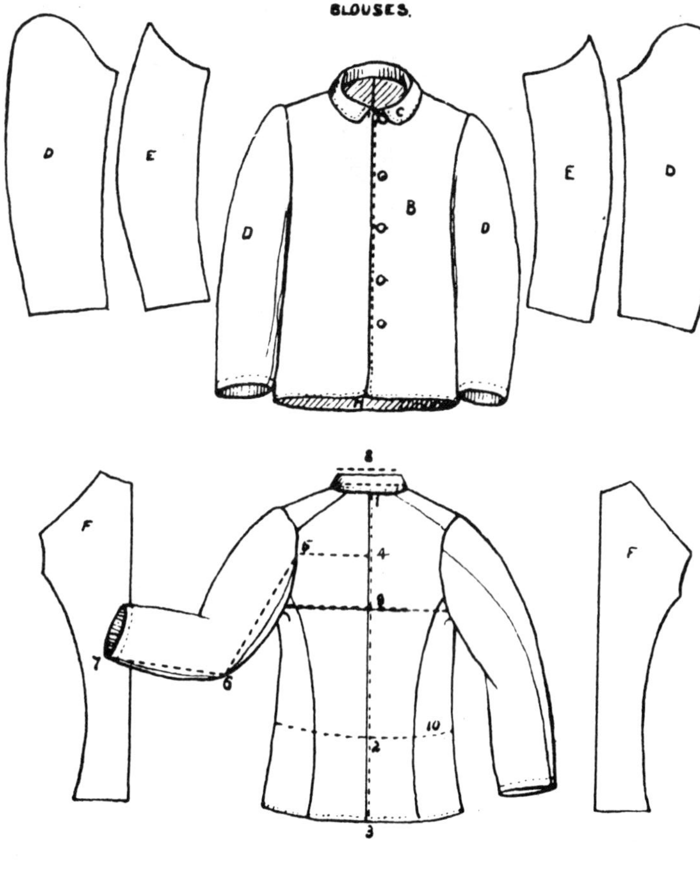

	1 to 3, Length.	4 to 7, Length of Sleeve.	8, Collar measure	9, Breast measure.	10, Waist measure.
	inches.	inches	inches.	inches.	inches
Size 1	28	31	16	34	32
" 2	28½	31½	16½	35	33
" 3	29	32½	17	36	34
" 4	30	33	18	38	36
" 5	31½	34	19	40	38
" 6	32½	34½	19½	42	40

BLOUSES continued.

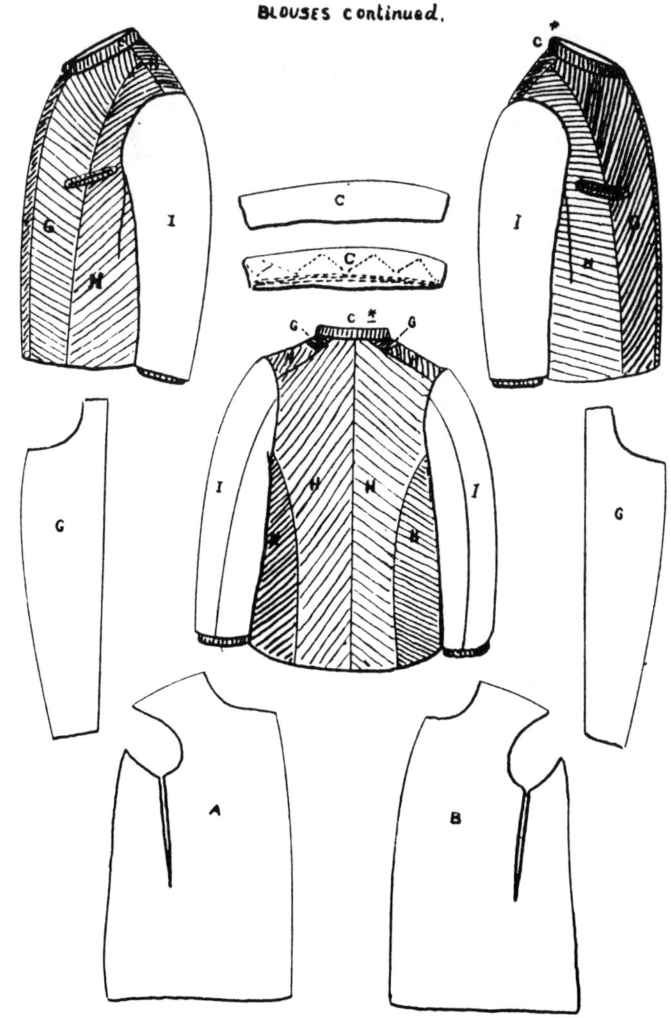

* Blouse inside out.

H. and I, Lining.
H, Gray twilled mixed flannel.
I, " Unbleached muslin.
G, Dark blue flannel.

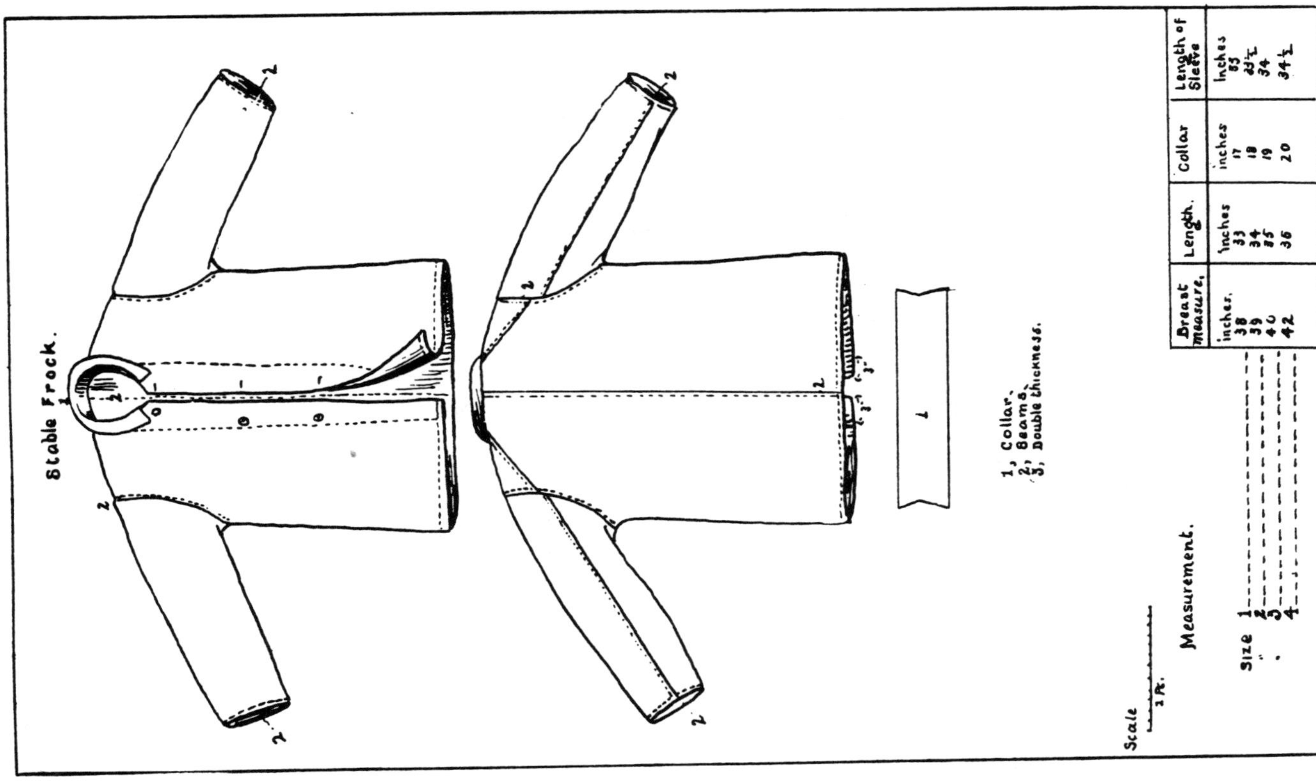
Stable Frock.
1, Collar,
2, Seams,
3, Double thickness.
Measurement.
Scale
1 ft.
Size 1
2
3
4
Breast Measure, inches. 38 39 40 42
Length. inches 33 34 35 36
Collar inches 17 18 19 20
Length of Sleeve inches 33 33½ 34 34½

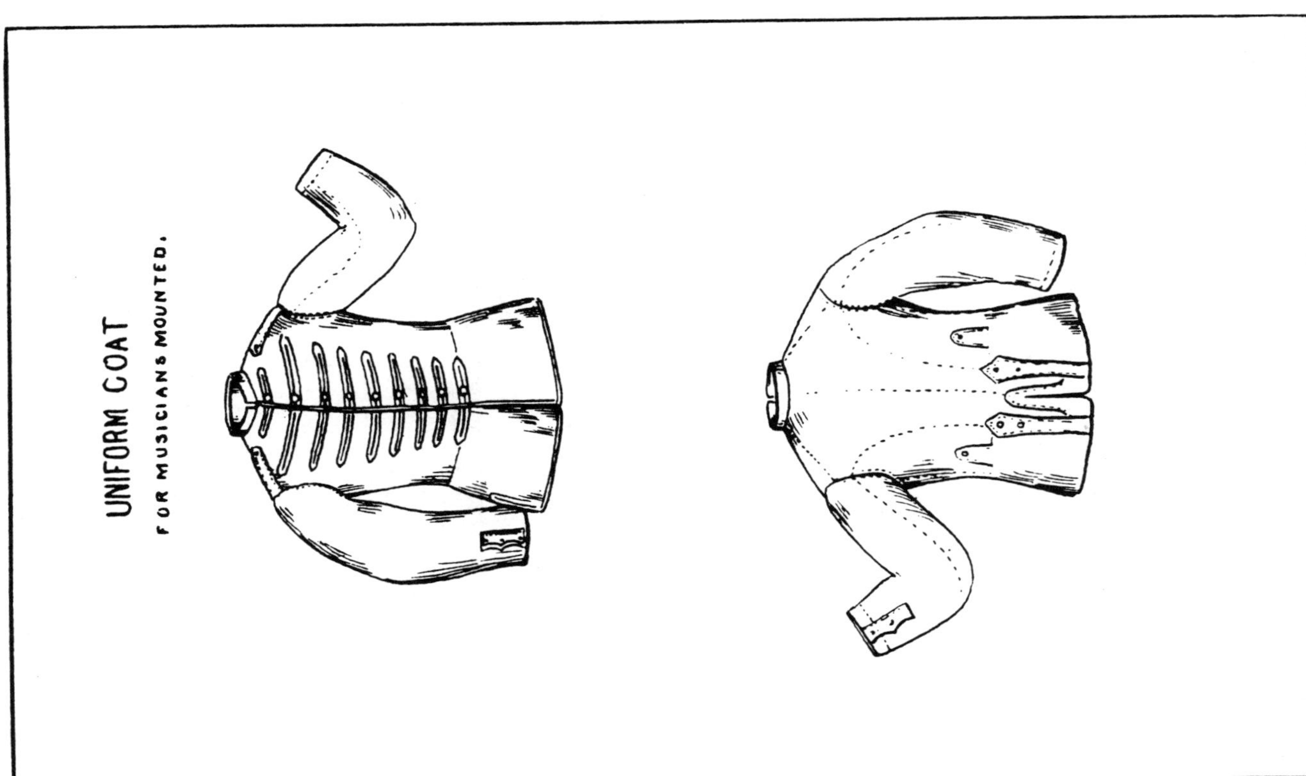
UNIFORM COAT
FOR MUSICIANS MOUNTED.

SIZE No 3
CANVASS-COAT

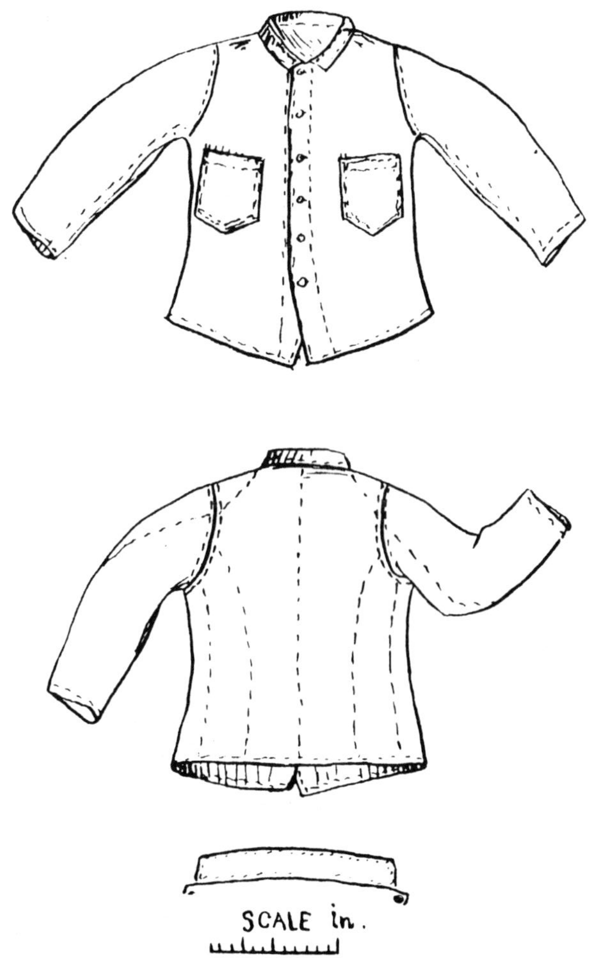

SIZE Numbers.	1	2	3.	4	5	6.
Breast	36 in	37 in	39 in	41 in	42 in	44 in
Collar	17 in	17½ in	18 in	19 in	20 in	20¼ in
Sleeve	31½ in	32½ in	33 in	34 in	34¾ in	35 in
coat Length	29 in	28½ in	29 in	29½ in	30½ in	31½ in

OVERALLS.
For Engineers.

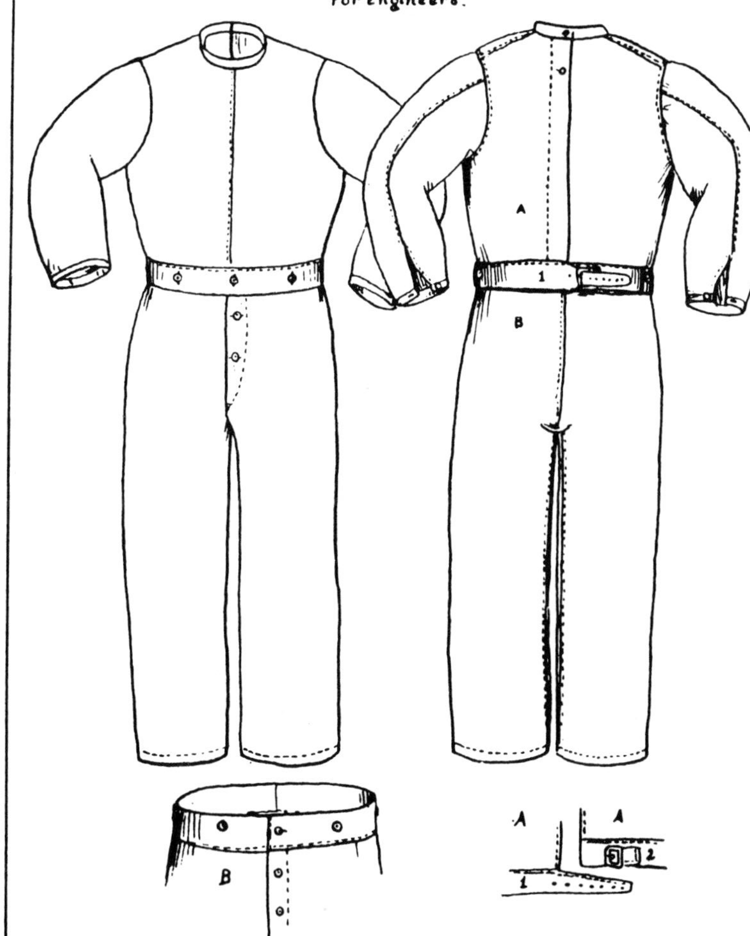

		No 1.	No 2	No. 3.	No. 4.	No. 5.
		Inches	Inches.	Inches.	Inches.	Inches.
Body	Breast Measure	38	39	41	43	45
	Waist	34	35	37	39	42
	Collar	17	18	18½	19	20
	Length of Sleeve	32½	33	33½	34	35
	Length of Body	18	18½	19	19½	21
Leg	Length of side seam	42	43	44	45	46
	Length of leg	31	32	33	34	35
	Waist	32	34	36	38	40
	Bottoms	20	20	20½	20½	21

Scale 1 ft.

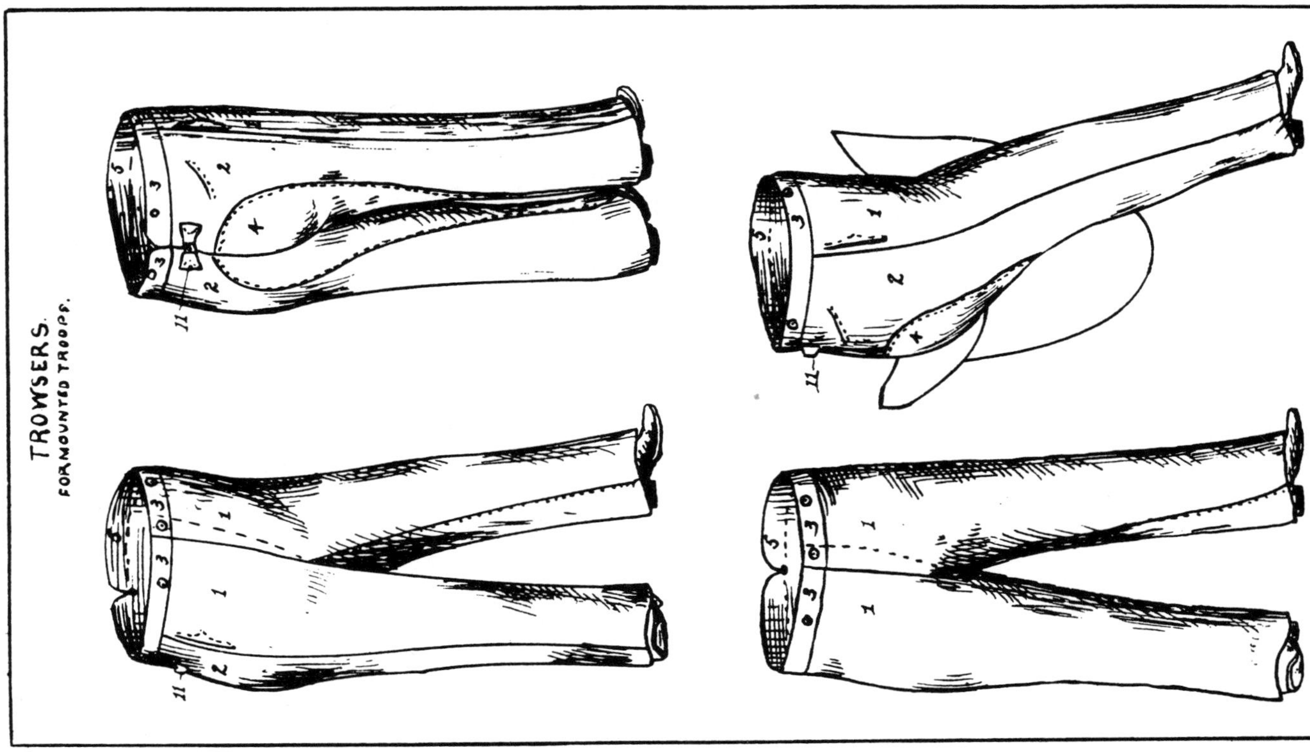
TROWSERS.
FOR MOUNTED TROOPS.

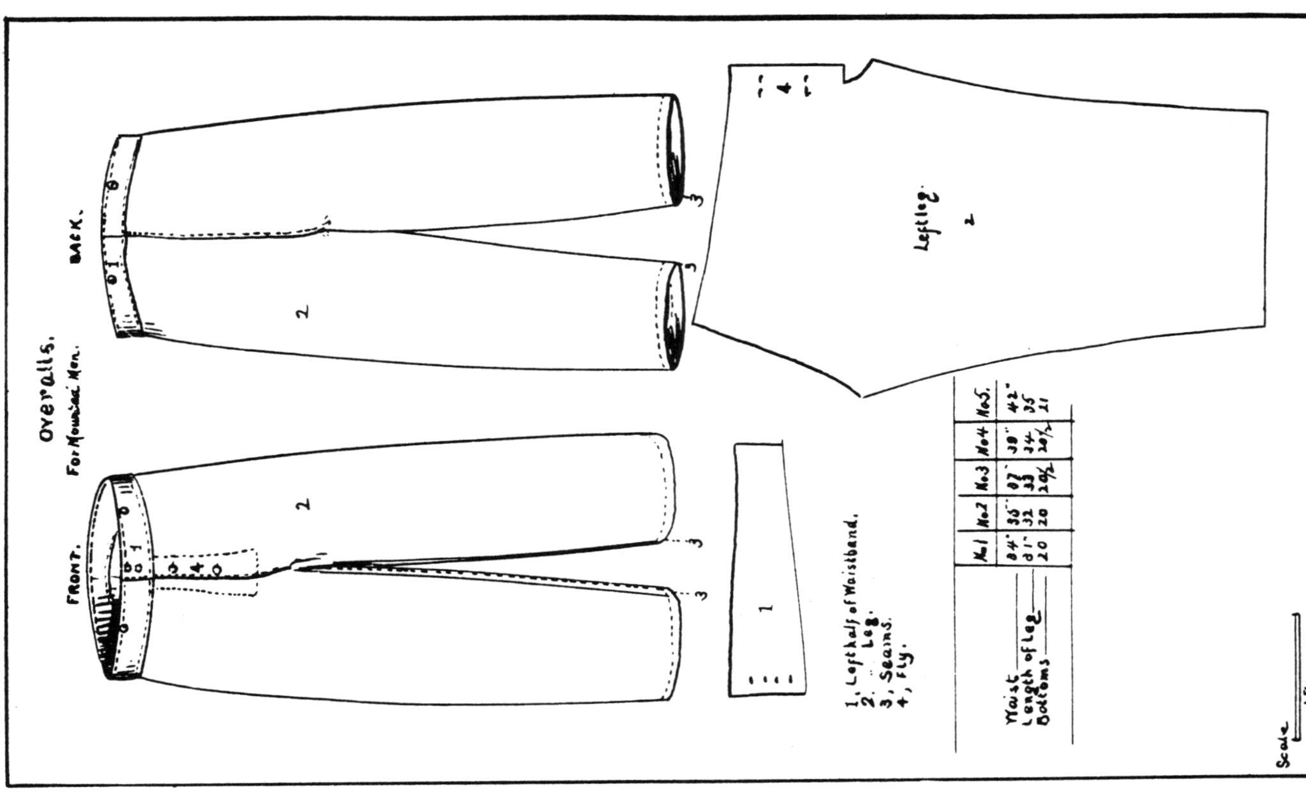
Overalls.
For Mounted Men.
FRONT.
BACK.
Left leg.
1, Left half of Waistband.
2, Leg.
3, Seams.
4, Fly.
Waist
Length of Leg
Bottoms
Scale
1 ft.

TROWSERS. FOR POOT TROOPS.

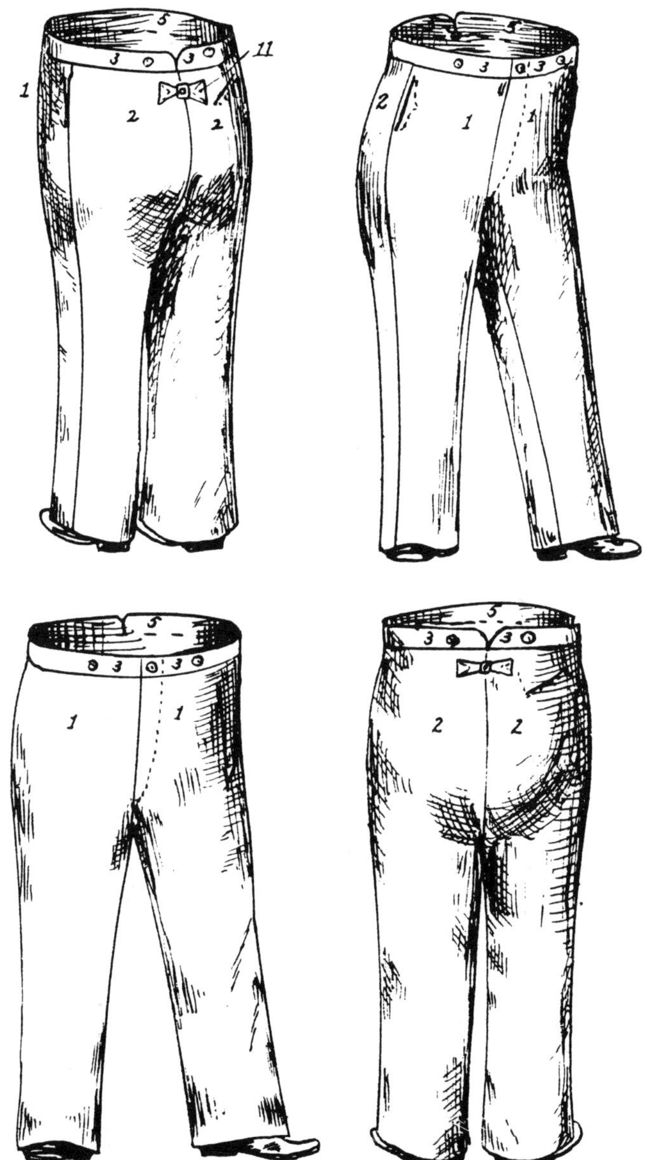

TROWSERS continued.

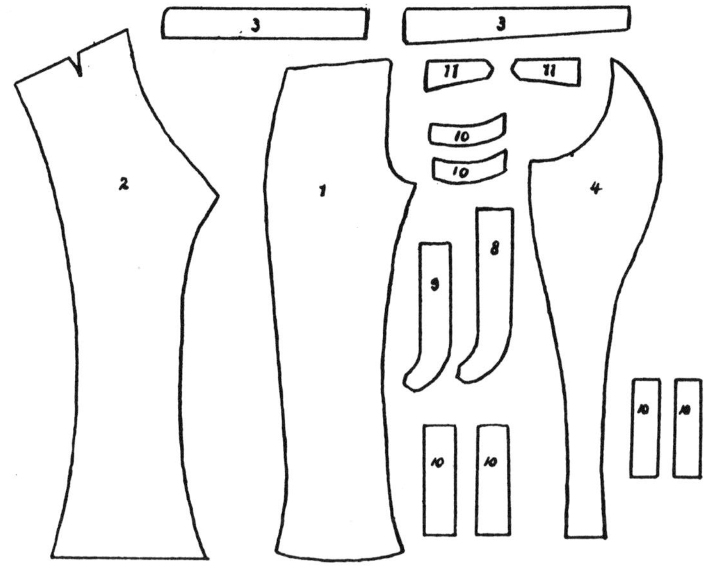

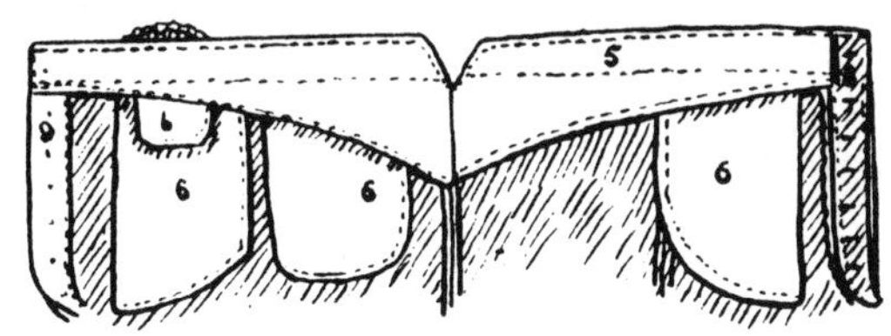

1. Front.
2. Back.
3. Waist.
4. Re-inforce or saddle piece.
5. Lining to Waist.
6. Pockets.
7. Canvas.
8 and 9 Fly pieces.
10. Re-inforce to Pockets.

Size.	Waist, inches	Seat. inches	Crotch. inches	Outside Seam. inches	Inside Seam. inches	Knee, inches	Bottom inches.
1	31	36	23	41	31	17½	19
2	32	36	23	40	30	17½	19
3	32	37	23	43	33	17¾	19¼
4	32	38	24	42	32	18	19½
5	33	38	24	41½	31	18¼	19¾
6	33	39	24	44½	34	18½	19¾
7	34	39	25	42½	32	18½	20¼
8	34	40	25½	45½	35	18¾	20¼
9	36	41	26	42½	32	19	20½
10	36	41	26	44	33	19	20½
11	38	43	26	46	34	19¼	21
12	40	44	26½	44½	36	19¼	21

Scale 1 ft.

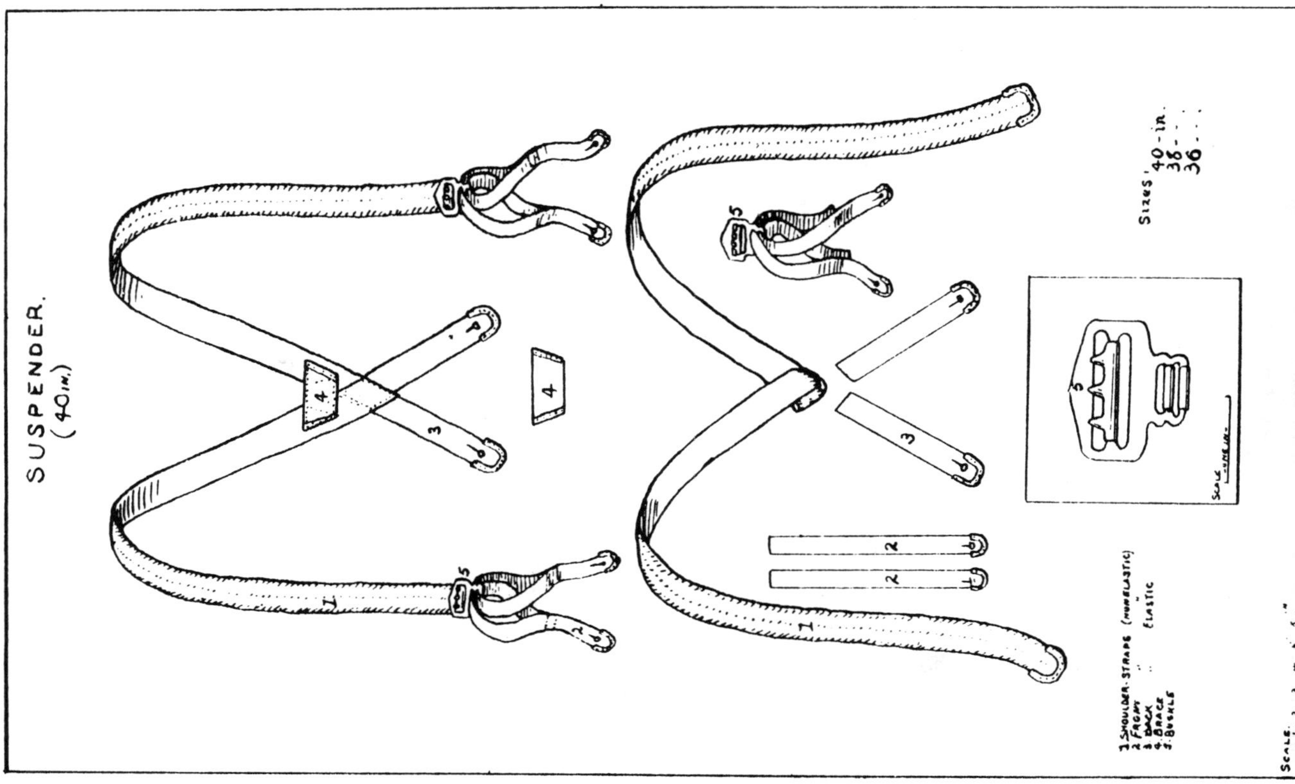
SUSPENDER.
(40 in.)
1 SHOULDER-STRAPS (NON ELASTIC)
2 FRONT " ELASTIC
3 BACK
4 BRACE
5 BUCKLE
SIZES 40 in.
38
36
SCALE

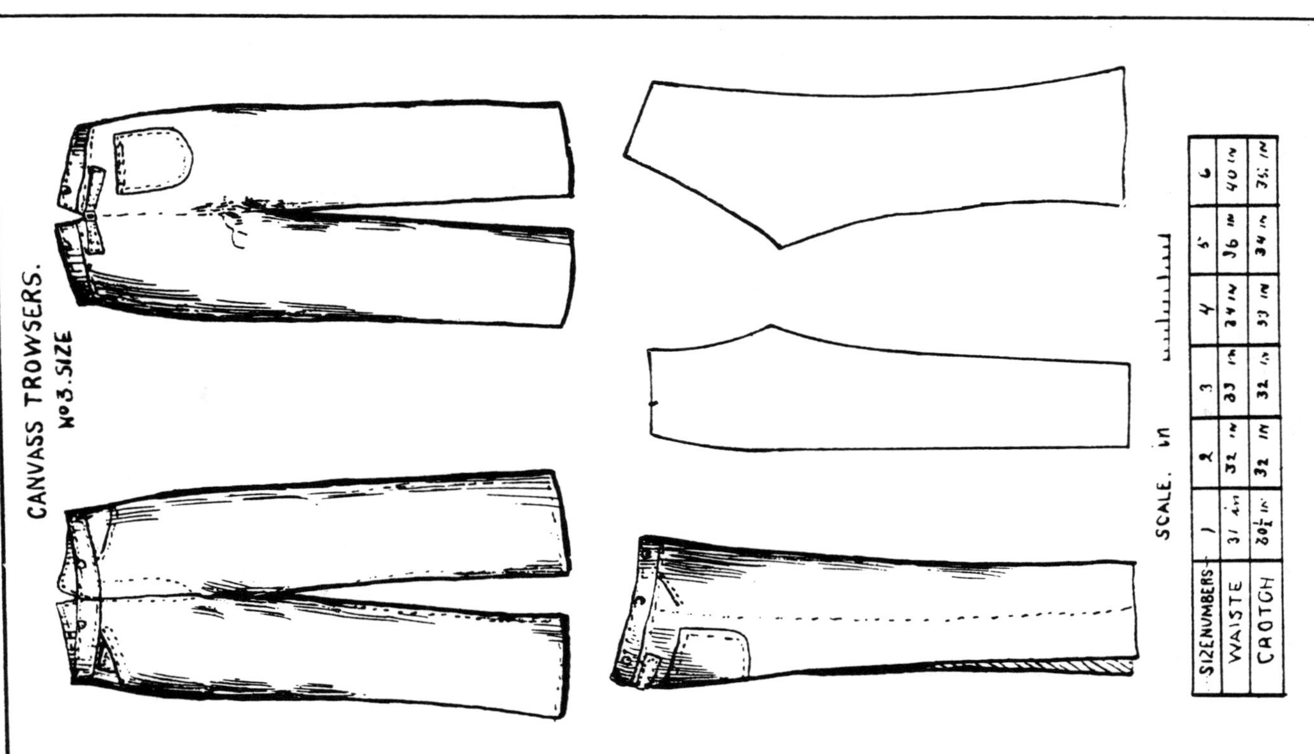
CANVASS TROWSERS.
No 3. SIZE
SCALE. in
SIZENUMBERS 1 2 3 4 5 6
WAISTE 31 in 32 in 33 in 34 in 36 in 40 in
CROTCH 30½ in 32 in 32 in 33 in 34 in 35½ in

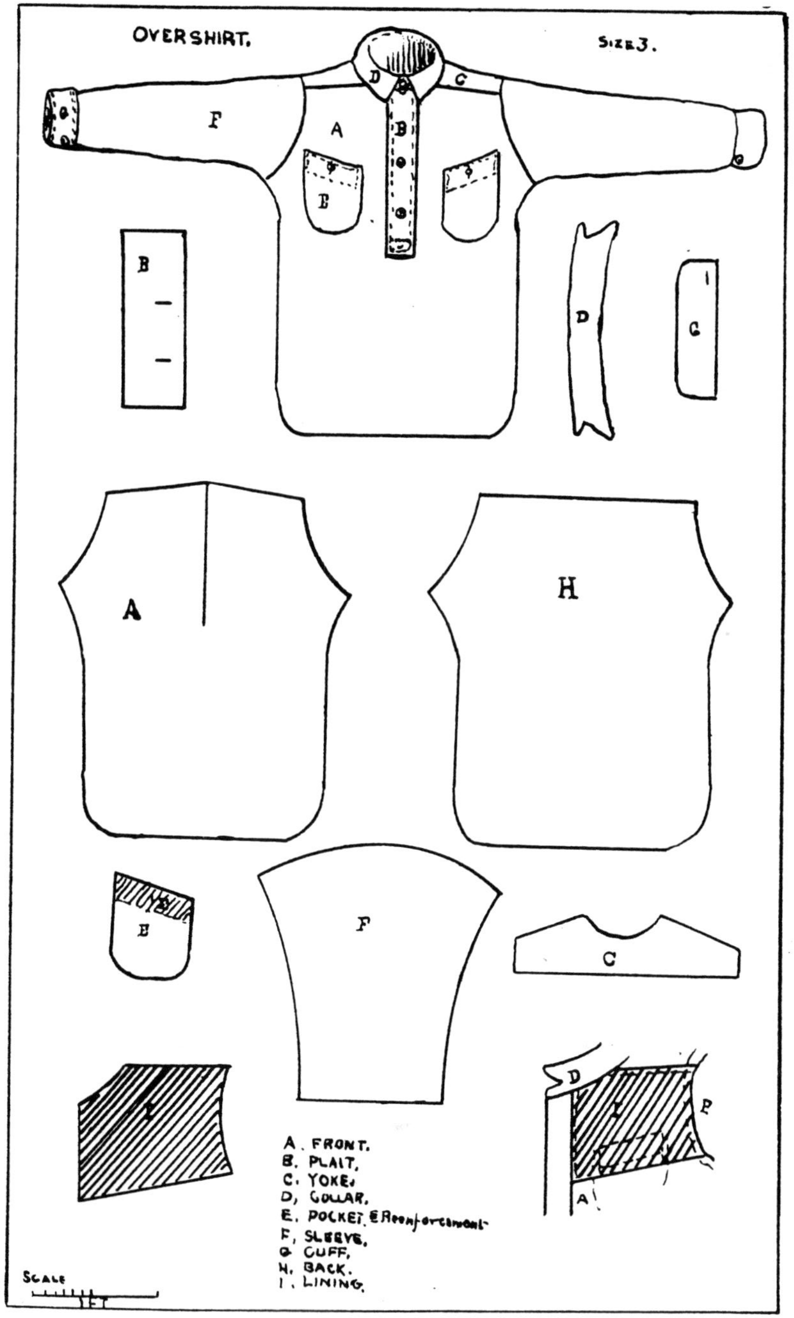

OVERSHIRT CONTINUED.

MEASUREMENT.

1 to 2, LENGTH OF BACK.
3 to 4, BREADTH OF BACK.
3 to 5, ELBOW.
3 to 6, SLEEVE.
7, SIZE OF COLLAR.
8, BREAST MEASURE.

Sizes.

	No. 1.	No. 2.	No. 3.	No. 4.	No. 5.
Length of Shirt	33 inches.	33 inches.	34 inches.	35 inches.	36 inches
" " Sleeve	32½ "	32 "	34 "	35 "	36 "
Collar	15 "	15½ "	16½ "	17 "	17½ "
Cuff	7½ "	8 "	8½ "	9 "	9½ "

UNDER SHIRT.

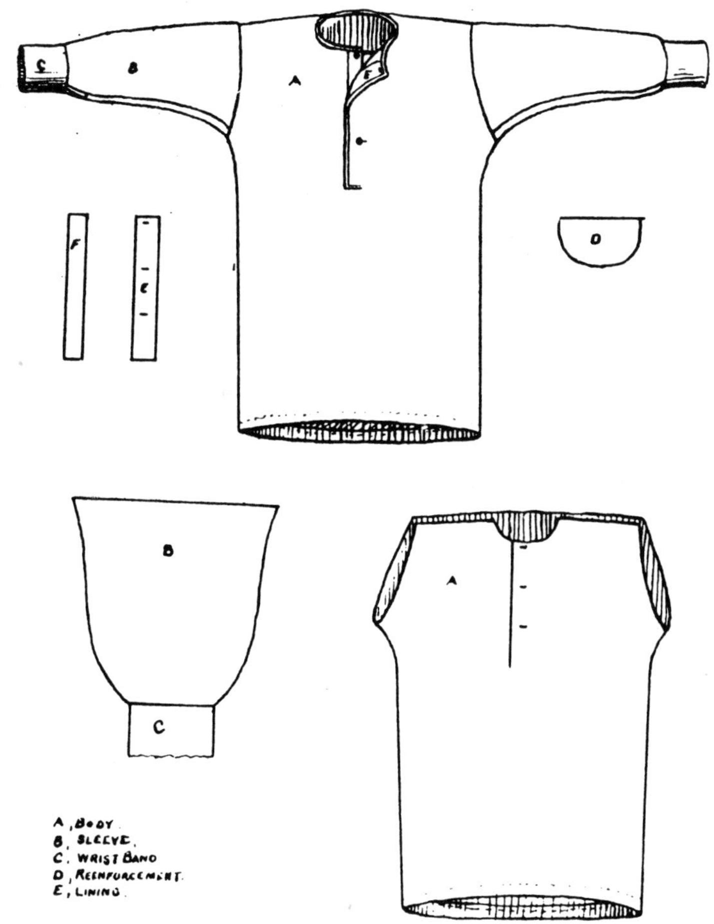

A, BODY.
B, SLEEVE.
C, WRIST BAND.
D, REENFORCEMENT.
E, LINING.

SCALE 1, 2, 3 INS

Size Numbers	1	2	3	4	5	6
Breast Measure	36 ins	38 ins.	40 ins.	42 ins	44 ins.	46 ins
Length of Shirt	31 ins	32 ins.	33 ins.	34 ins.	34 ins.	35 ins.
Weight	14 ozs.	15½ ozs.	16½ ozs	18 ozs.	19 ozs.	20 ozs.

DRAWERS.

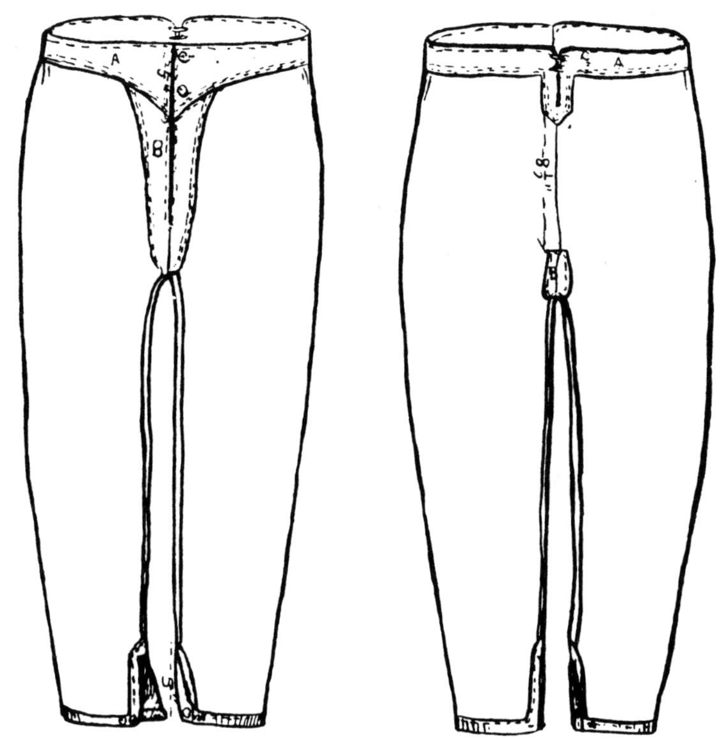

A, WAISTBAND.
B, FACINGS ARE ENFORCING PIECES.

	No1	No2	No3	No4	No5
	Inches	Inches	Inches	Inches	Inches
Length of side seam	39	40½	41½	43	45
Length of leg seam	29	30	31	32	33
Waist	31	32	34	36	38

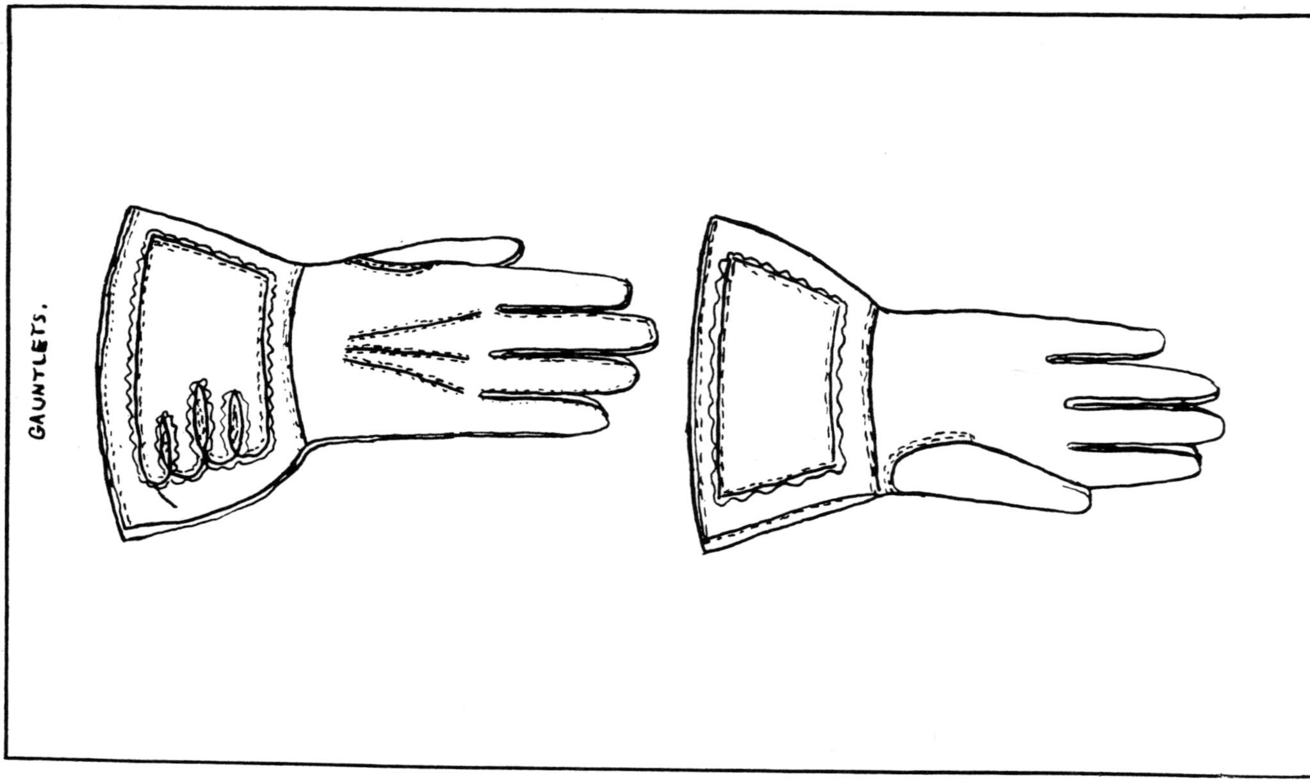
GAUNTLETS.

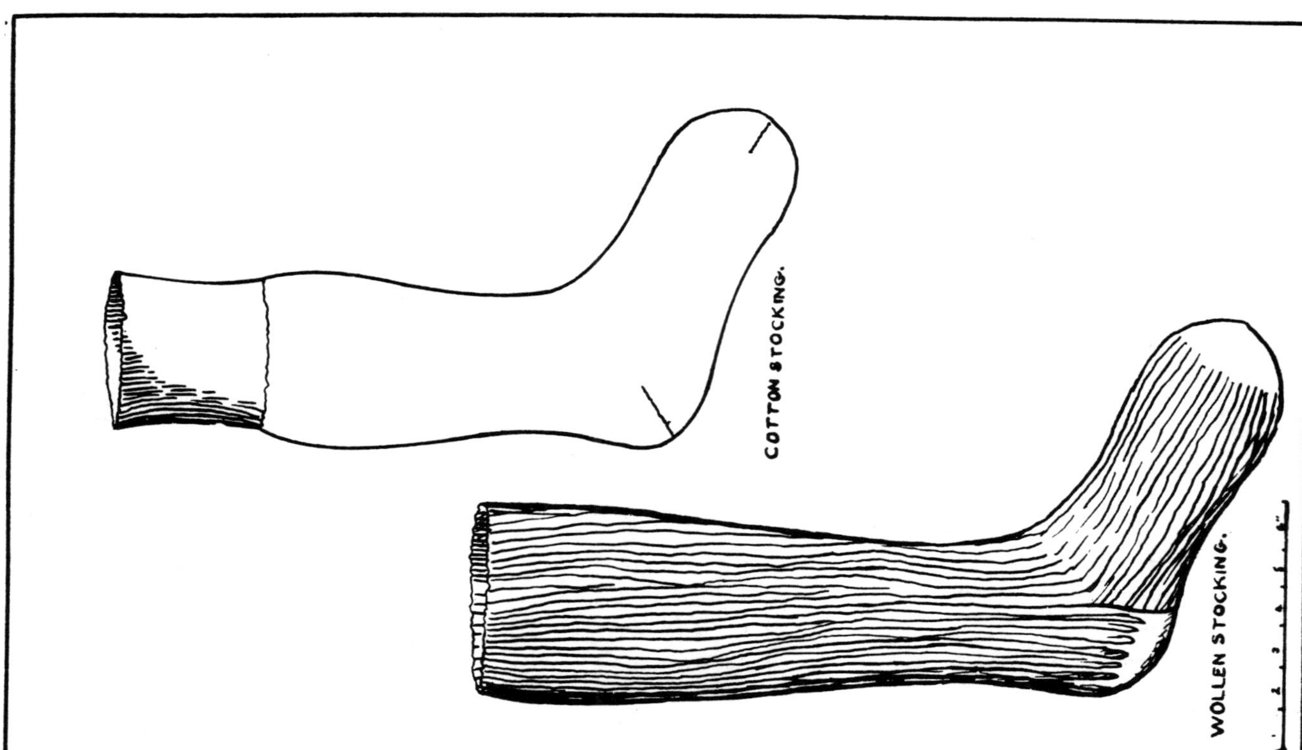
COTTON STOCKING.
WOLLEN STOCKING.

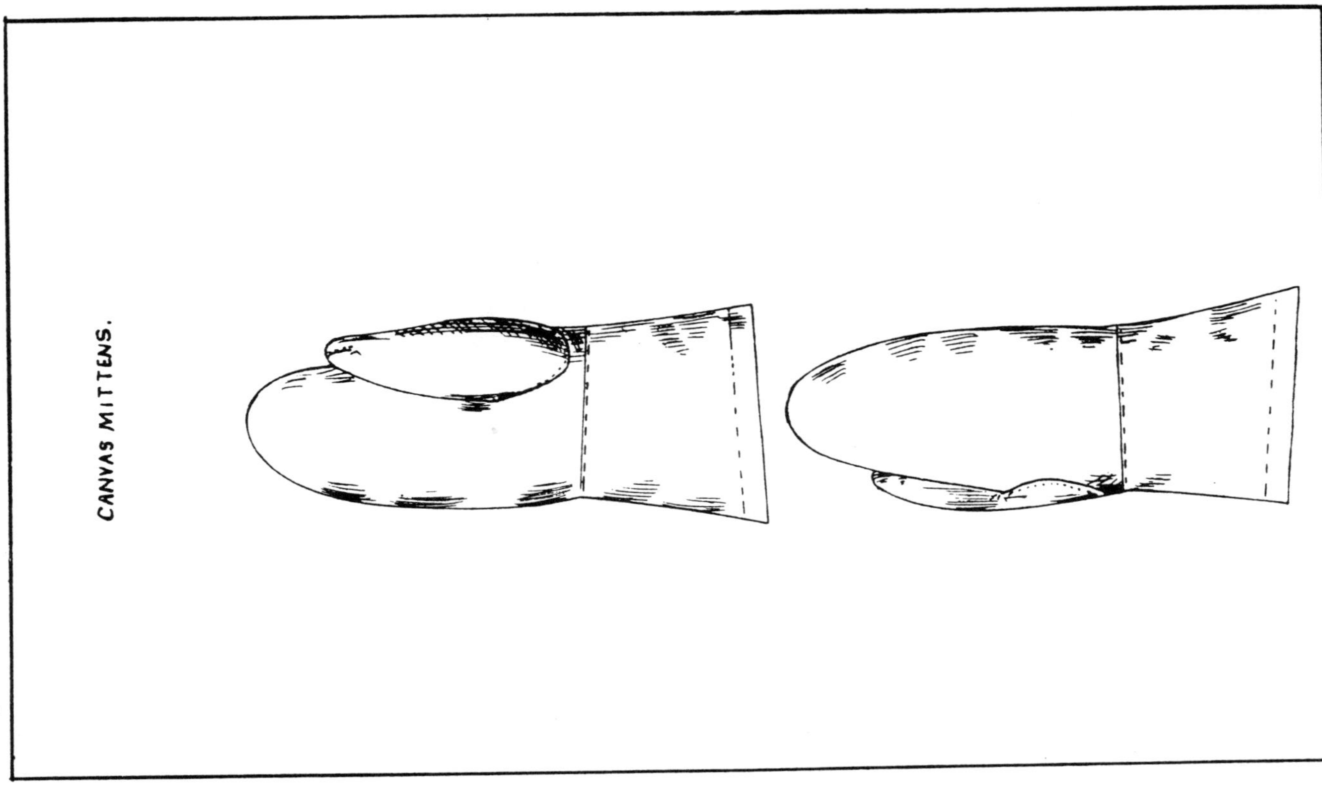
CANVAS MITTENS.

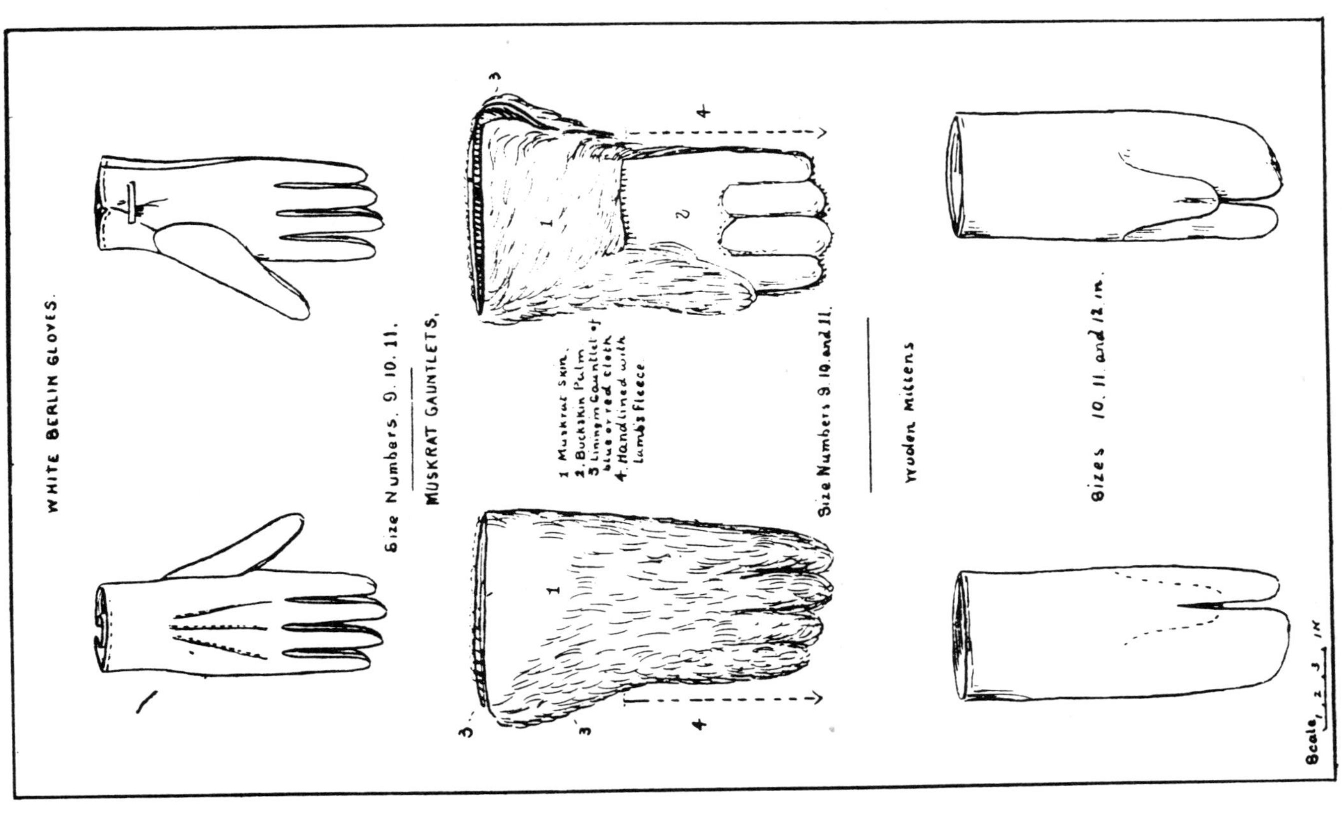
WHITE BERLIN GLOVES.
Size Numbers. 9. 10. 11.
MUSKRAT GAUNTLETS.
1 Muskrat Skin.
2. Buckskin Palm.
3 Lining in Gauntlet of blue or red cloth
4. Hand lined with Lambs fleece
Size Numbers 9. 10 and 11.
Woolen Mittens
Sizes 10. 11 and 12 in.
Scale 1 2 3 IN

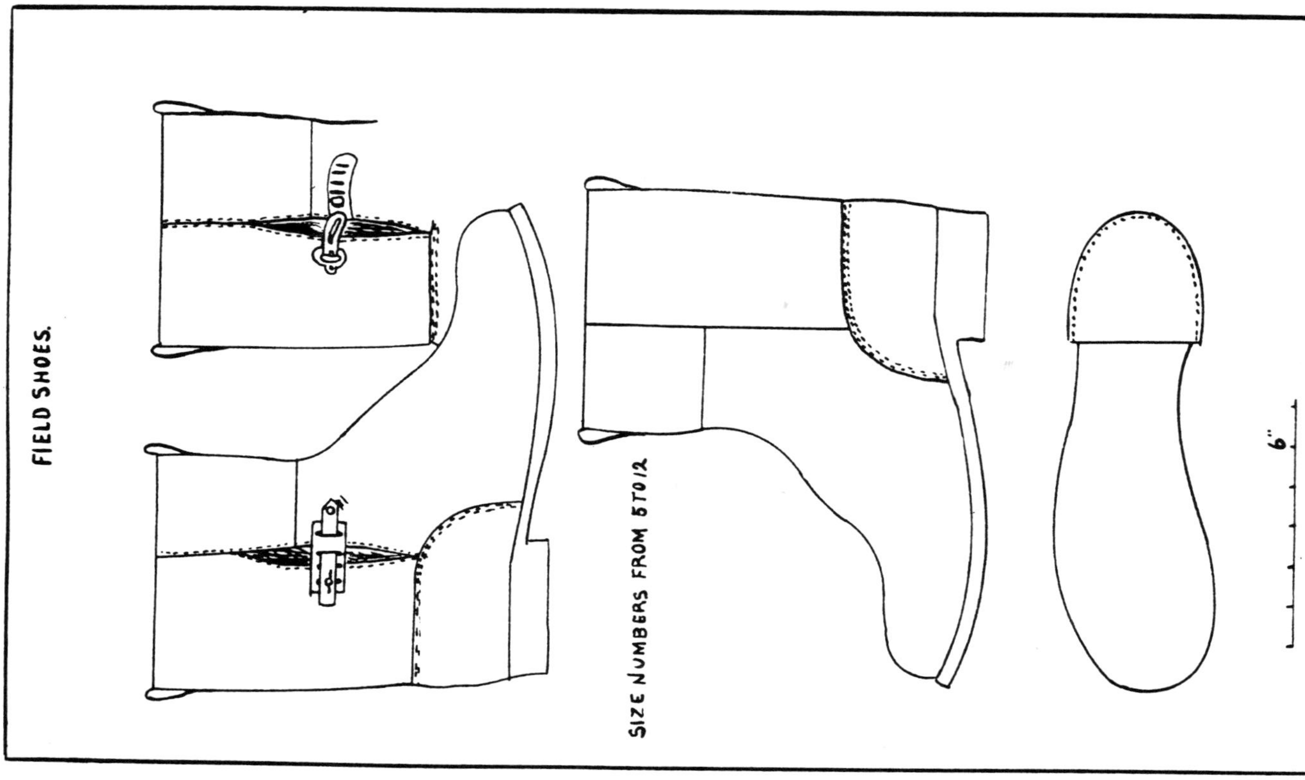
FIELD SHOES.
SIZE NUMBERS FROM 5 TO 12
6"

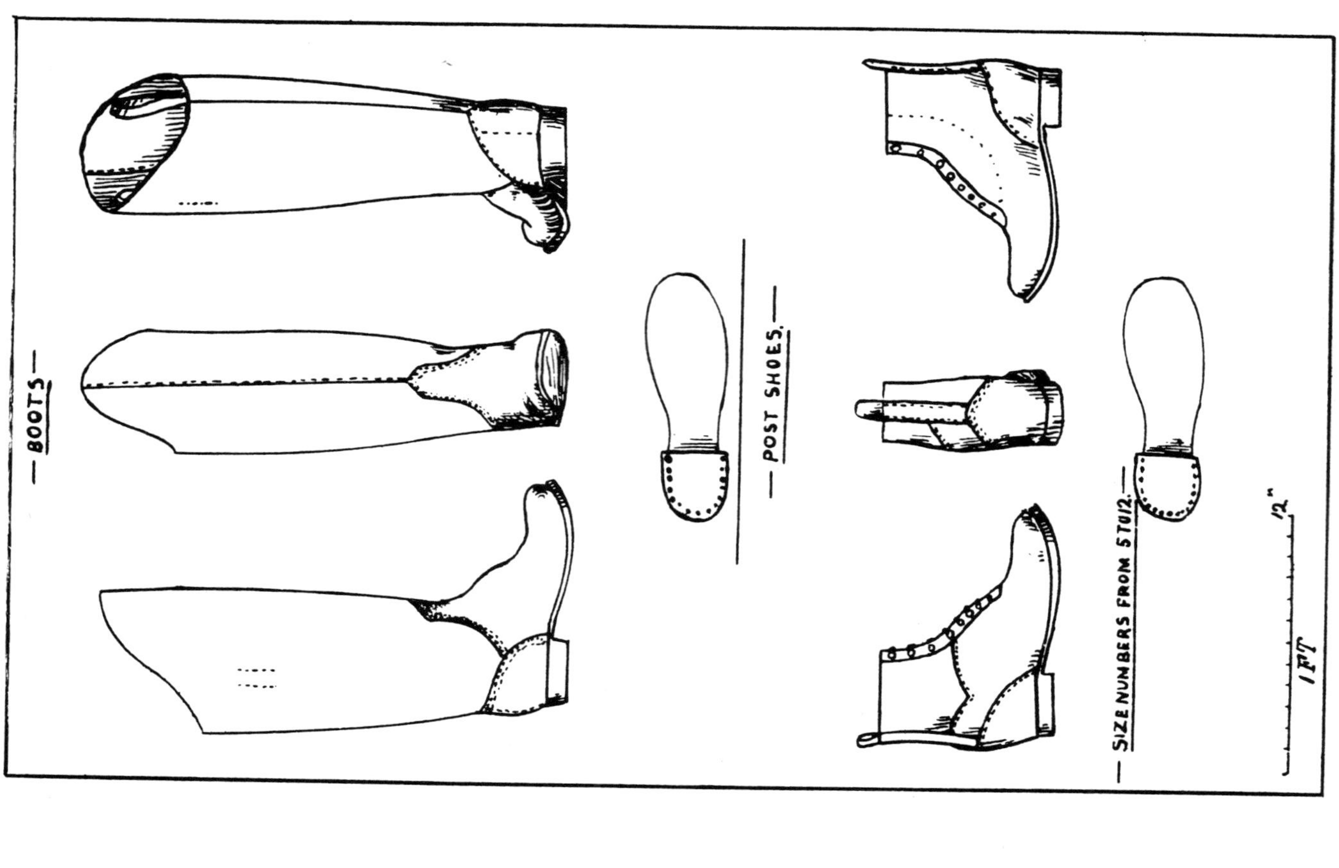
BOOTS
POST SHOES.
SIZE NUMBERS FROM 5 TO 12.
12"
1 FT

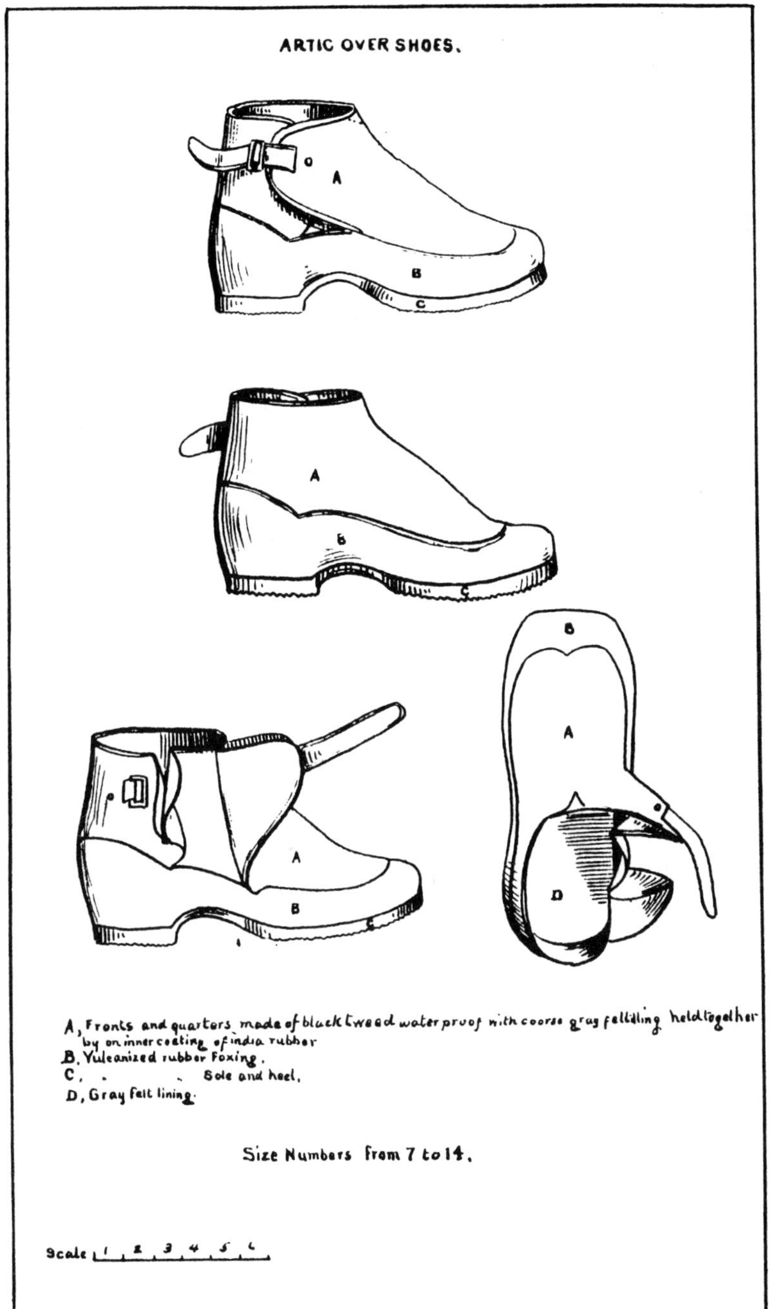
ARTIC OVER SHOES.
A
B
C
D
A, Fronts and quarters made of black tweed water proof with coorse gray feltding held together by an inner coating of india rubber
B, Vulcanized rubber Foxing.
C, " " Sole and heel.
D, Gray felt lining.
Size Numbers from 7 to 14.
Scale 1 2 3 4 5 6

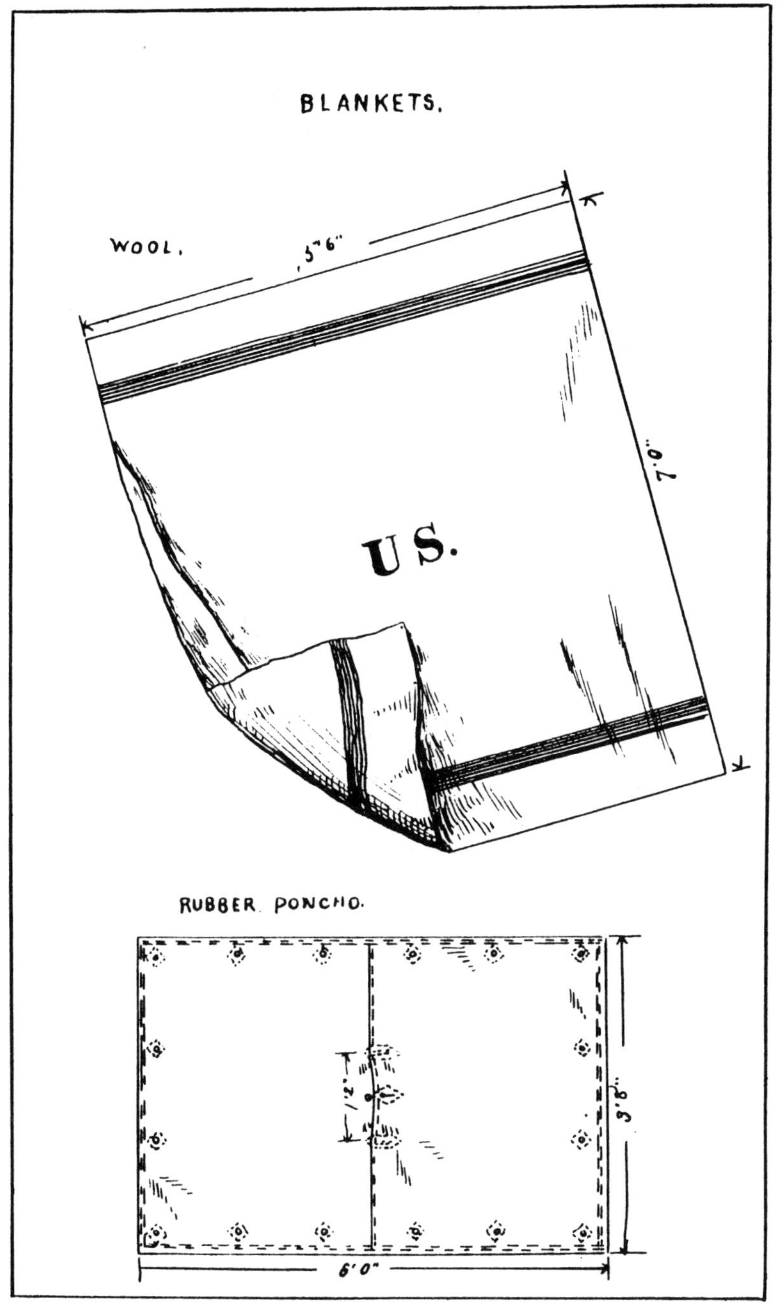
BLANKETS.
WOOL.
5'6"
7'0"
US.
RUBBER PONCHO.
1'2"
3'8"
6'0"

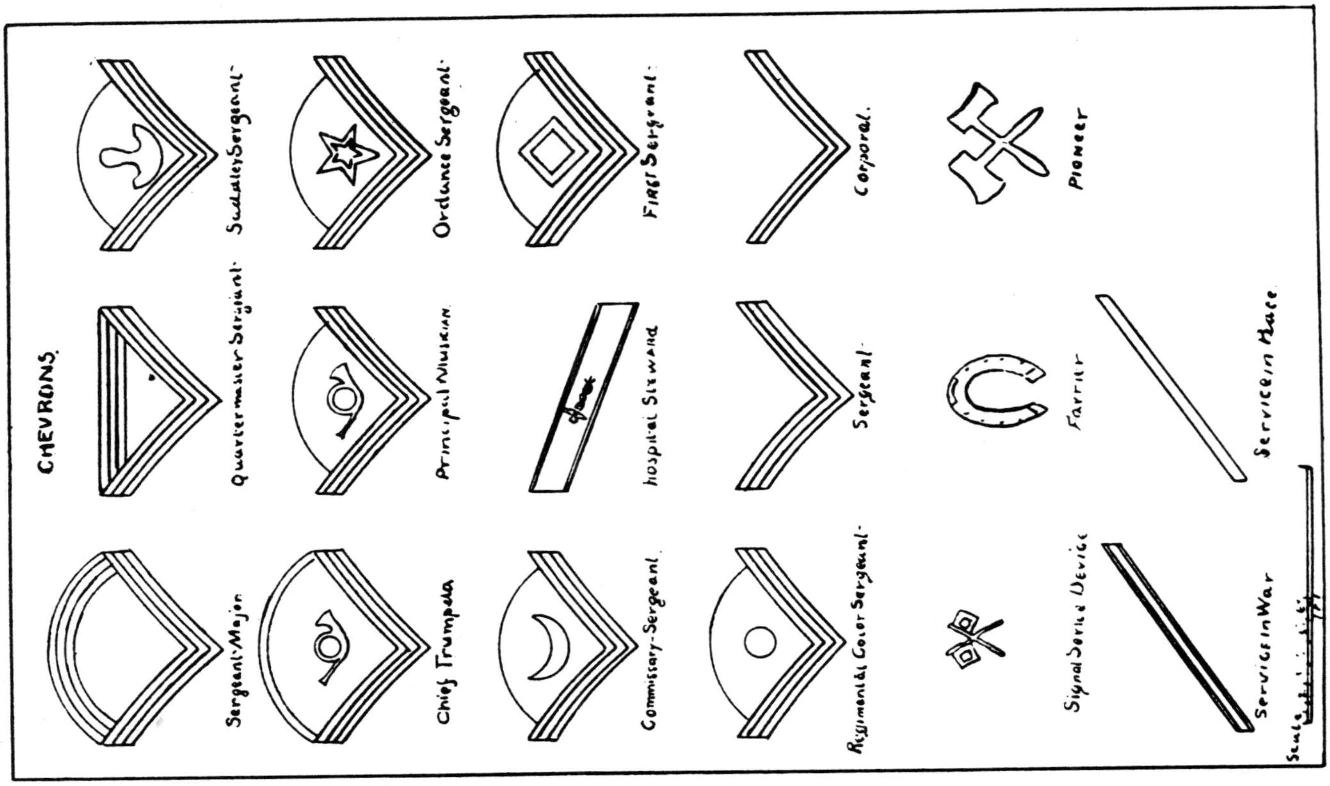
CHEVRONS
Sergeant-Major
Quartermaster-Sergeant
Saddler Sergeant
Chief Trumpeter
Principal Musician
Ordnance Sergeant
Commissary-Sergeant
hospital Steward
First Sergeant
Regimental Color Sergeant
Sergeant
Corporal
Signal Service Device
Farrier
Pioneer
Service in War
Service in Peace
Scale

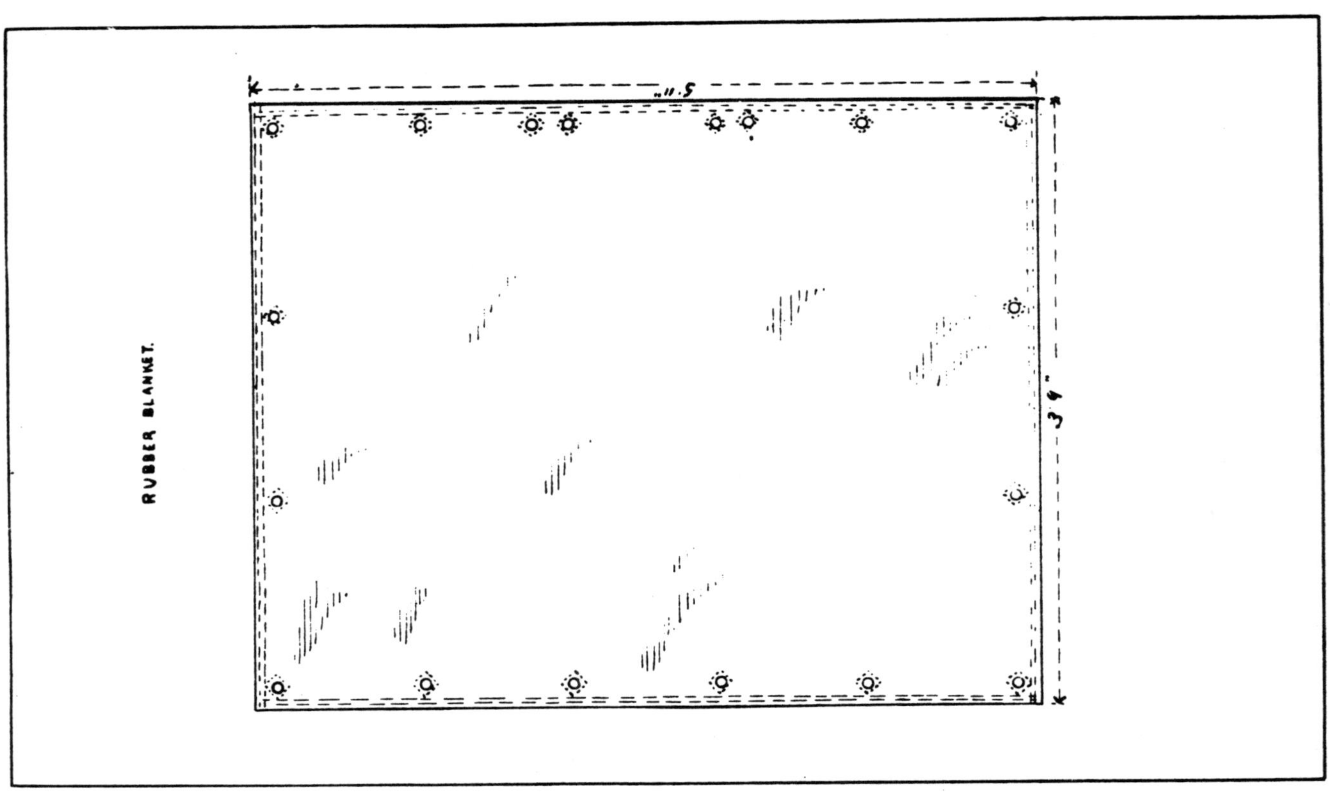
RUBBER BLANKET.

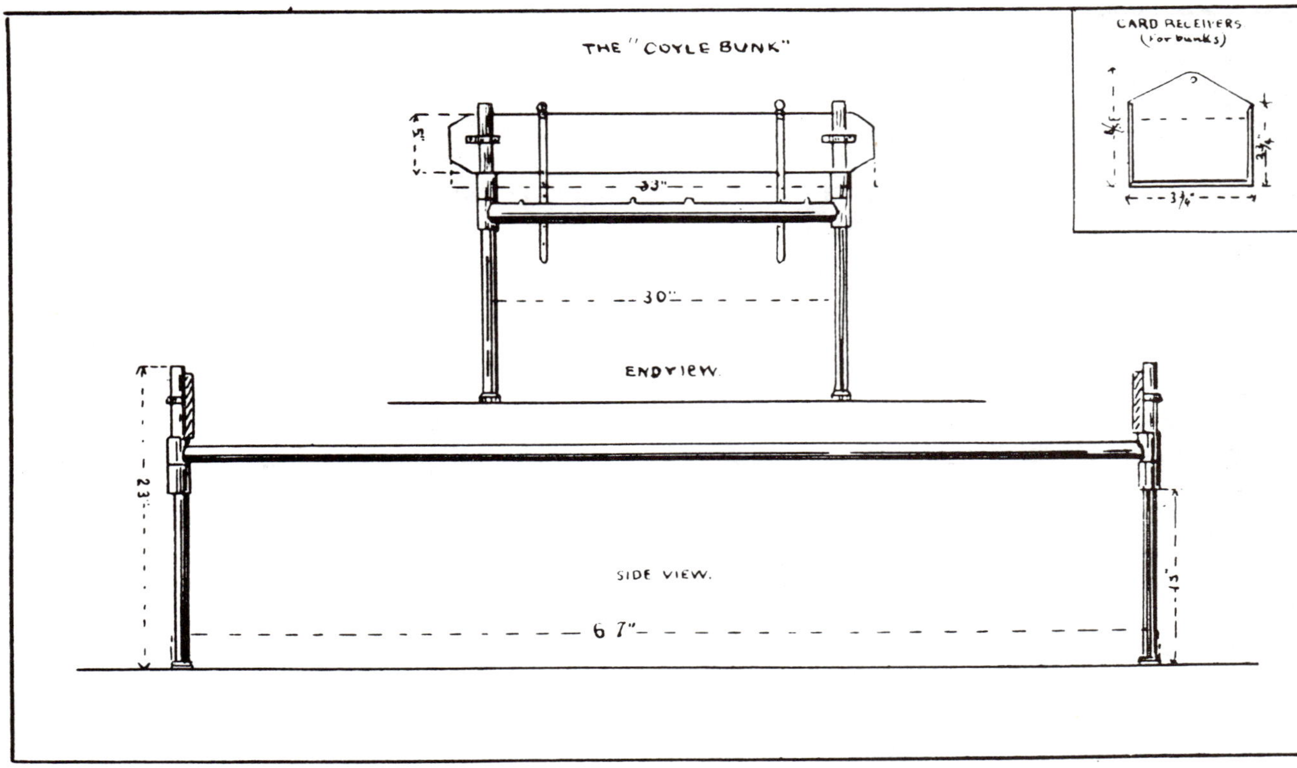
THE "COYLE BUNK"
END VIEW
SIDE VIEW
6 7"
30"
33"
23"
CARD RECEIVERS (for bunks)

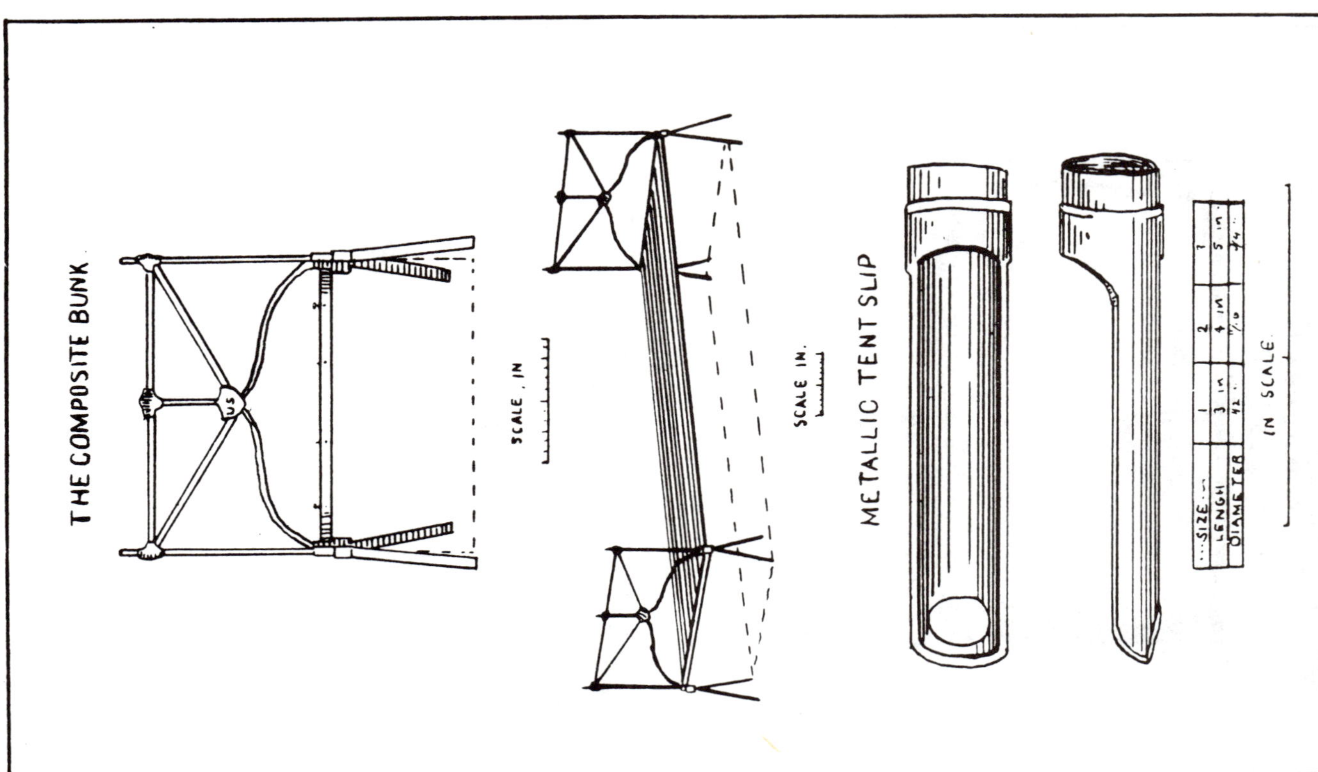
THE COMPOSITE BUNK
SCALE, IN
SCALE IN.
METALLIC TENT SLIP
IN SCALE

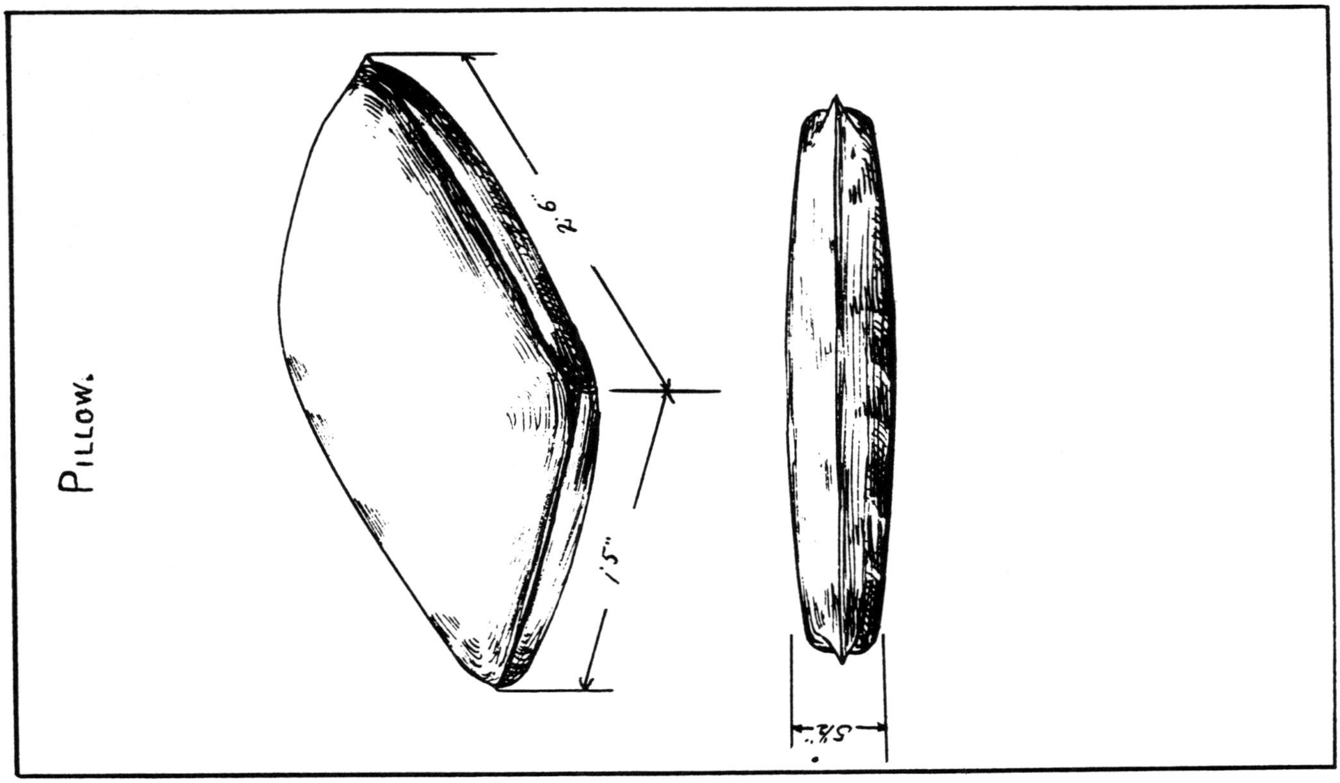
PILLOW.
2' 6"
1' 5"
5½"

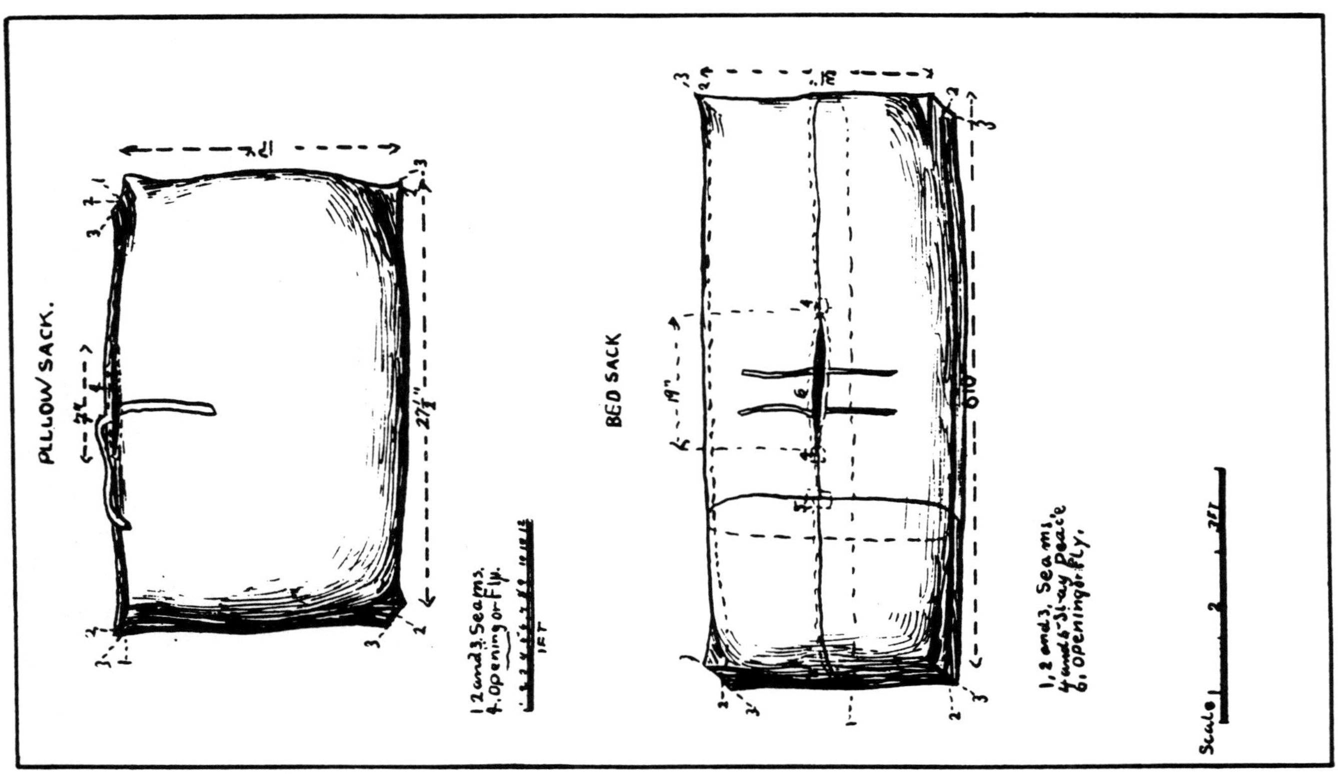
PILLOW SACK.
27½"
1, 2 and 3. Seams.
4. Opening or Fly.
1 FT
BED SACK
19"
1, 2 and 3. Seams,
4 and 5. Stay Peace
6. Opening or Fly.
Scale
2 FT

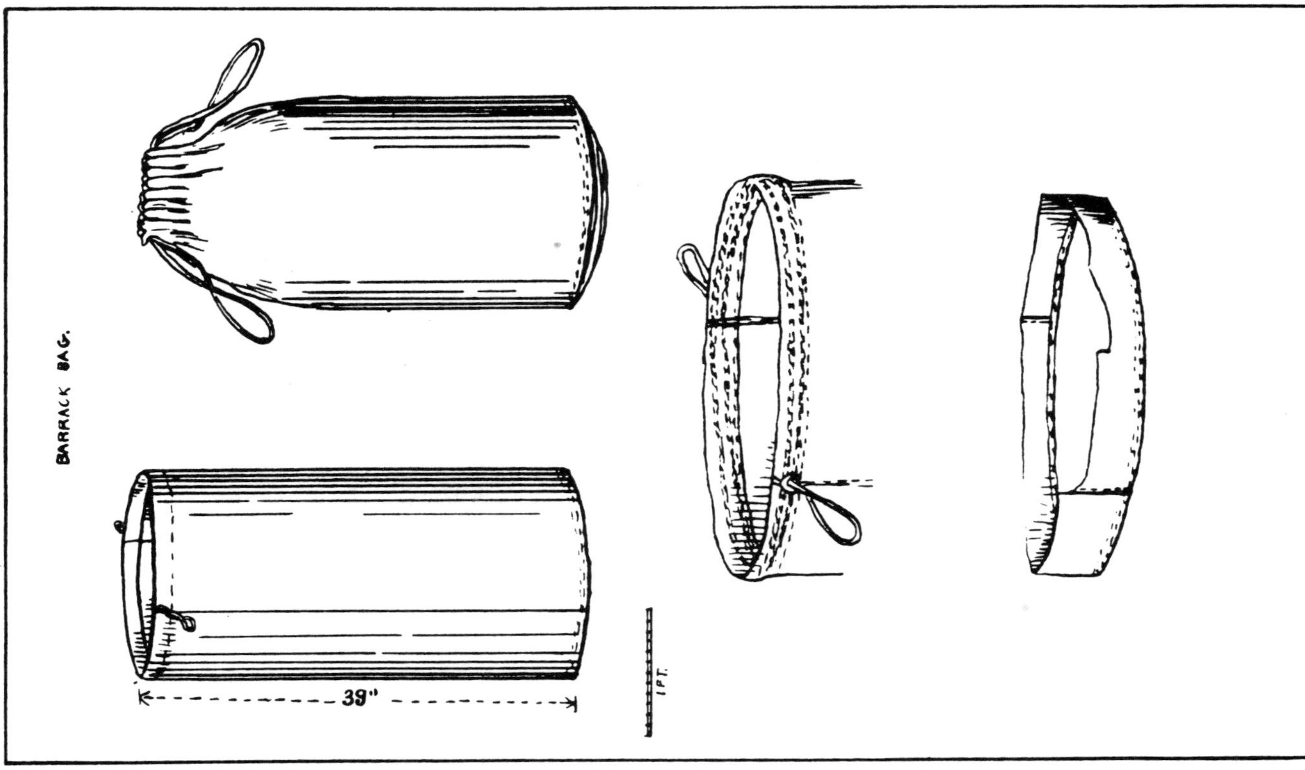
BARRACK BAG.
39"

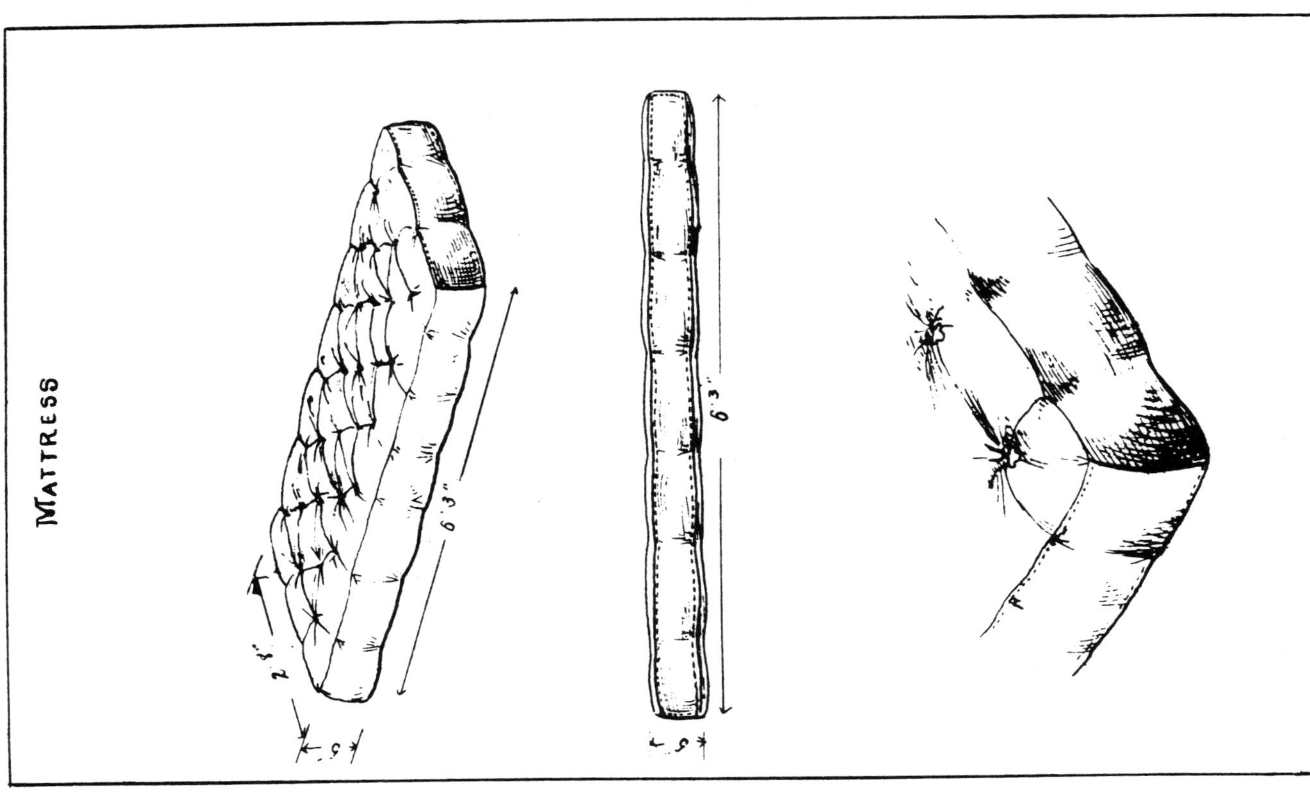
MATTRESS
6' 3"

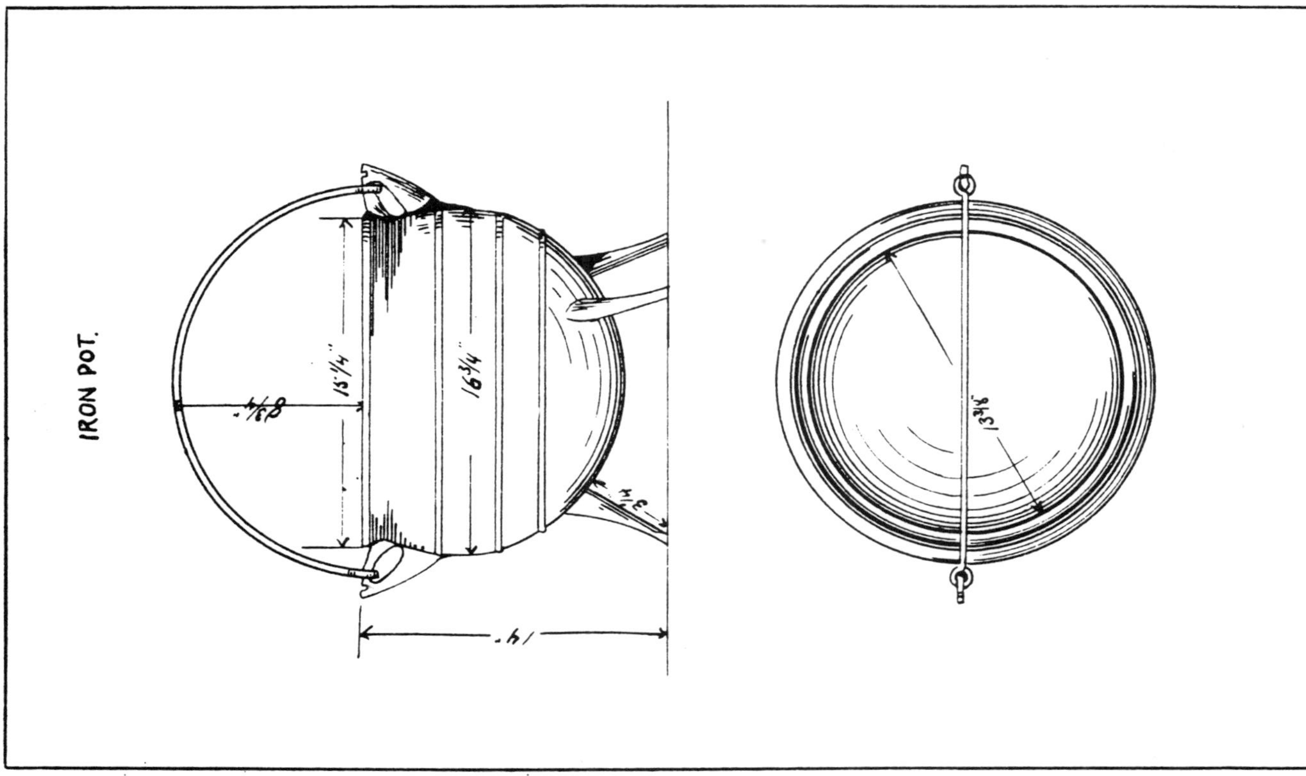
IRON POT.

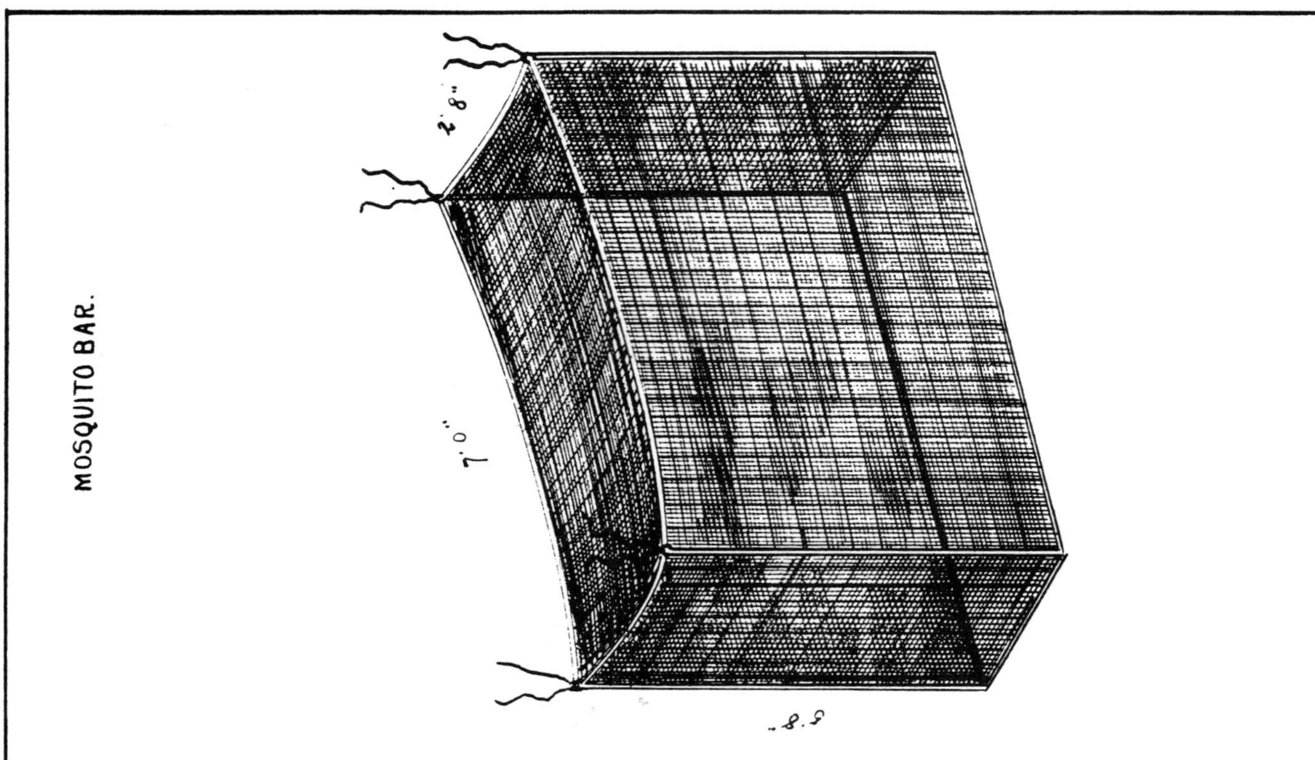
MOSQUITO BAR.

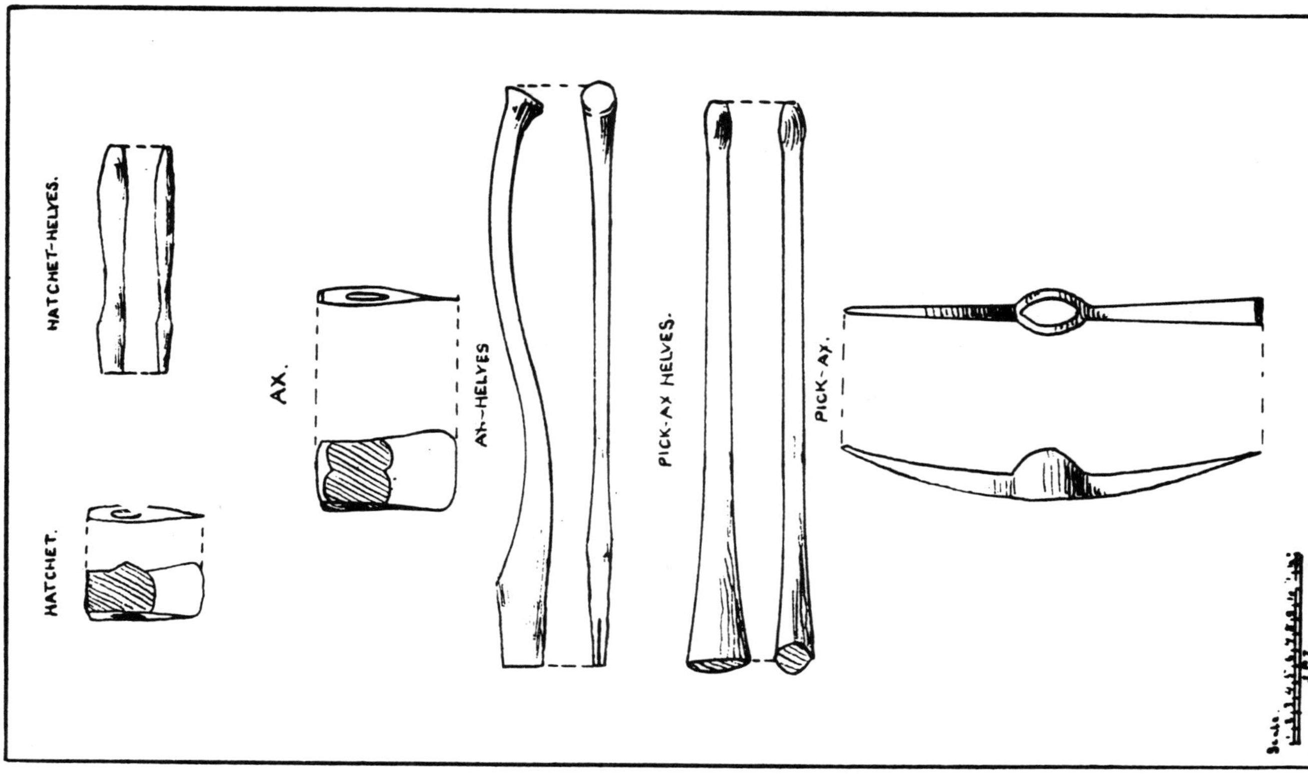
HATCHET-HELVES.
HATCHET.
AX.
AX-HELVES
PICK-AX HELVES.
PICK-AX.

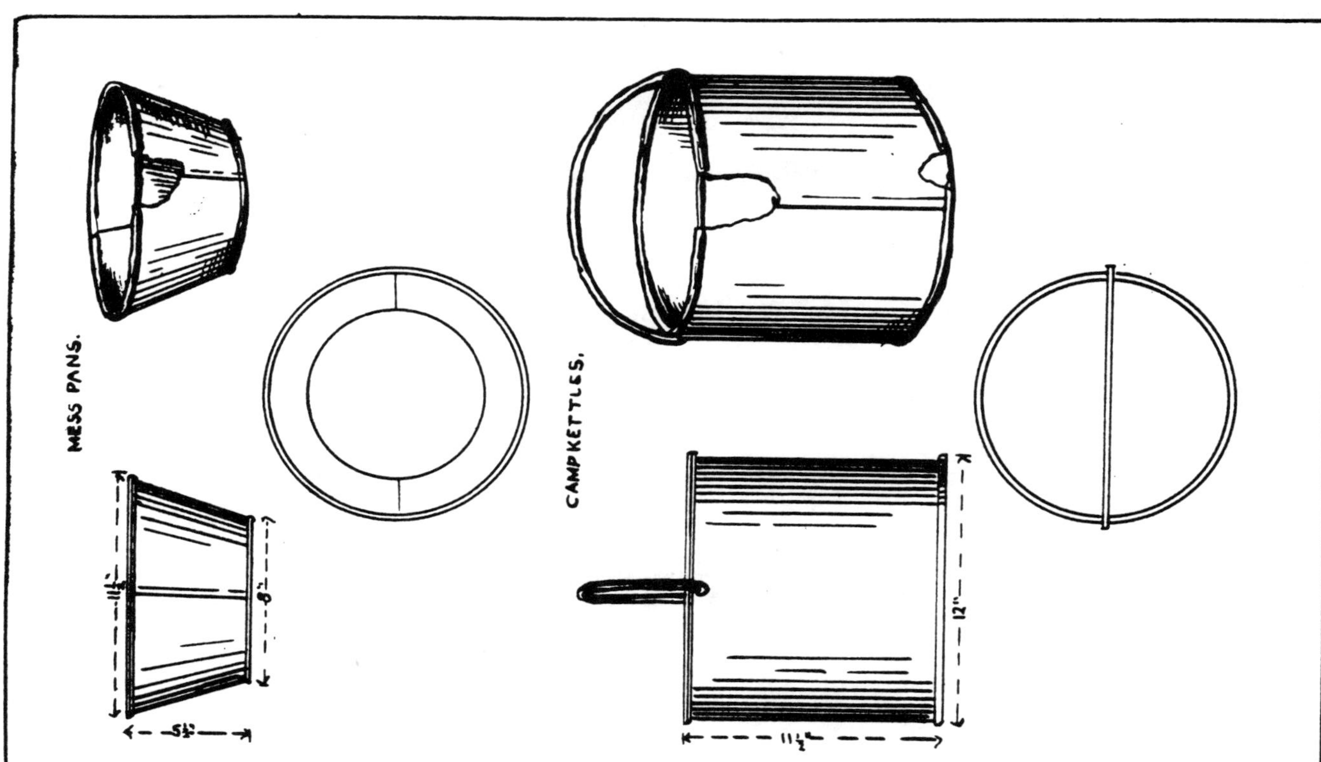
MESS PANS.
CAMPKETTLES.
12"
11½"

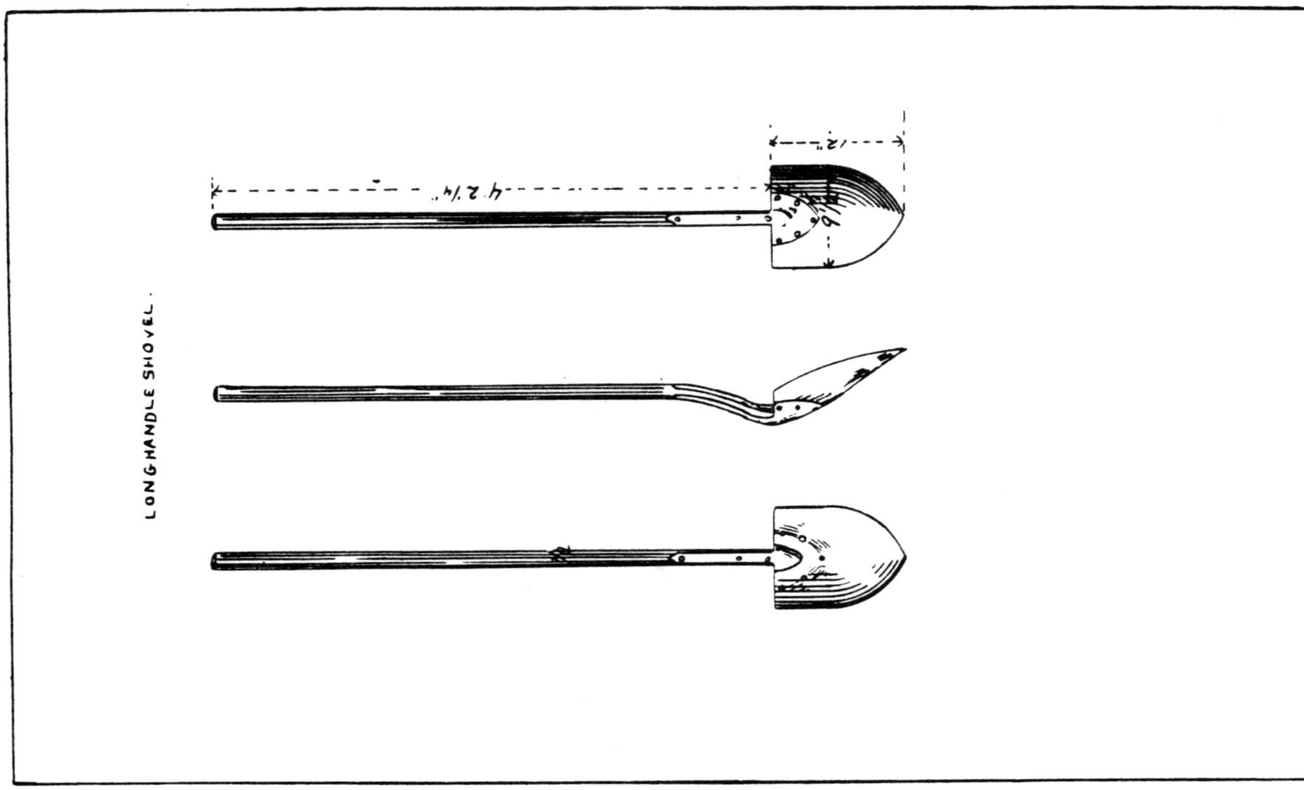
LONGHANDLE SHOVEL.

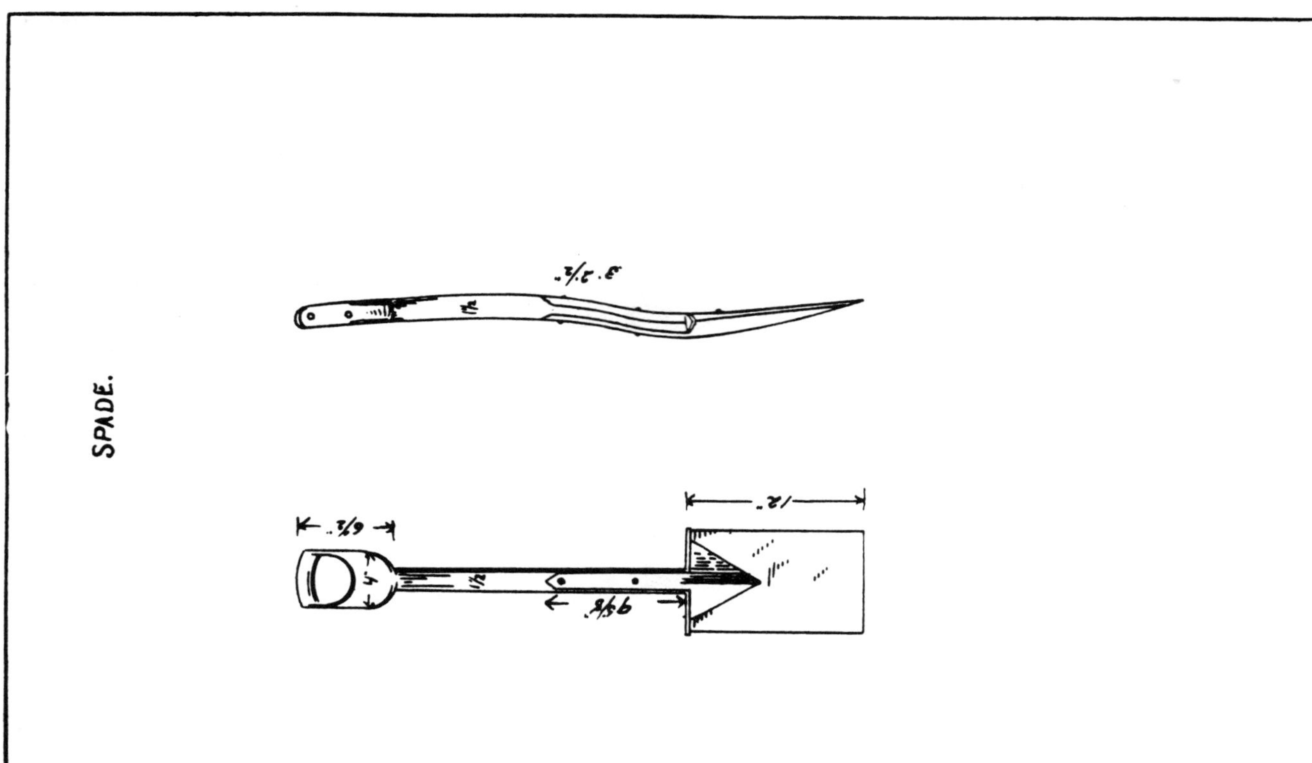
SPADE.

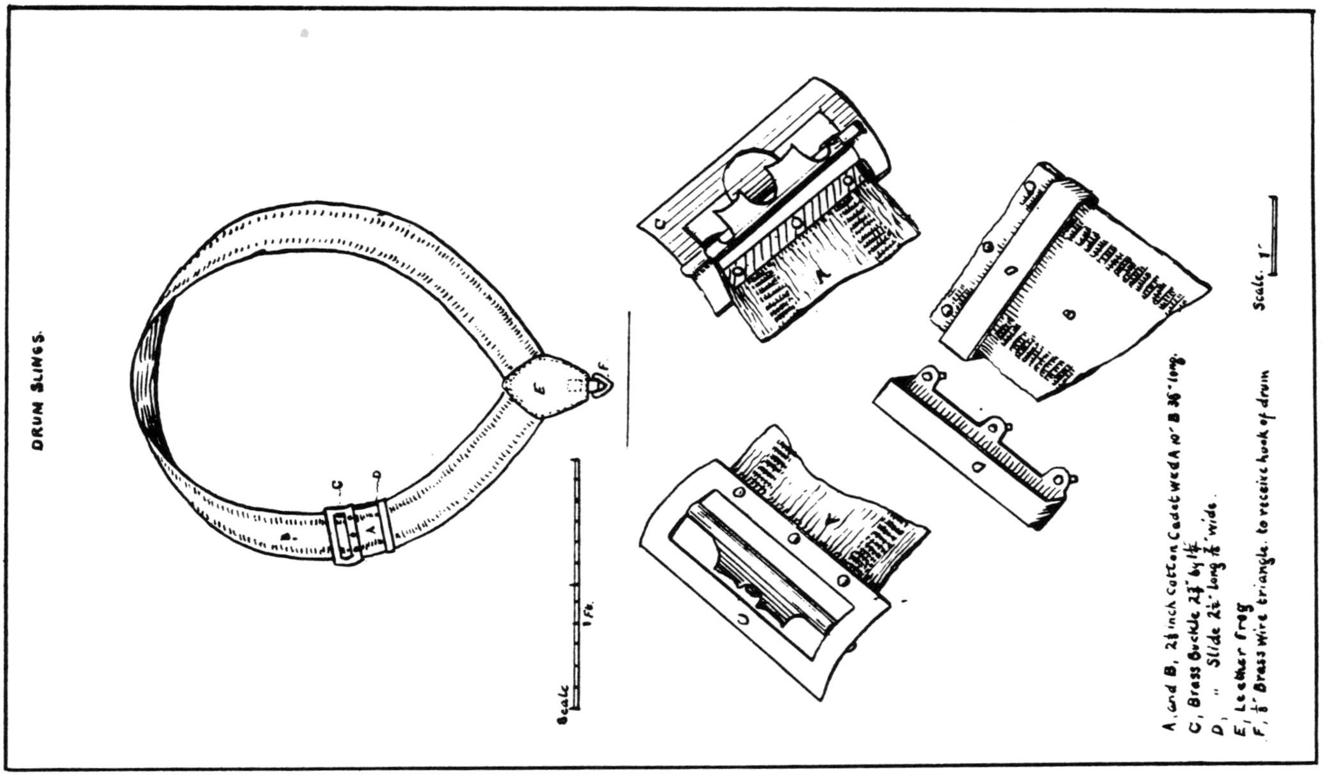
DRUM SLINGS.
Leather Frog
Scale 1 Ft.

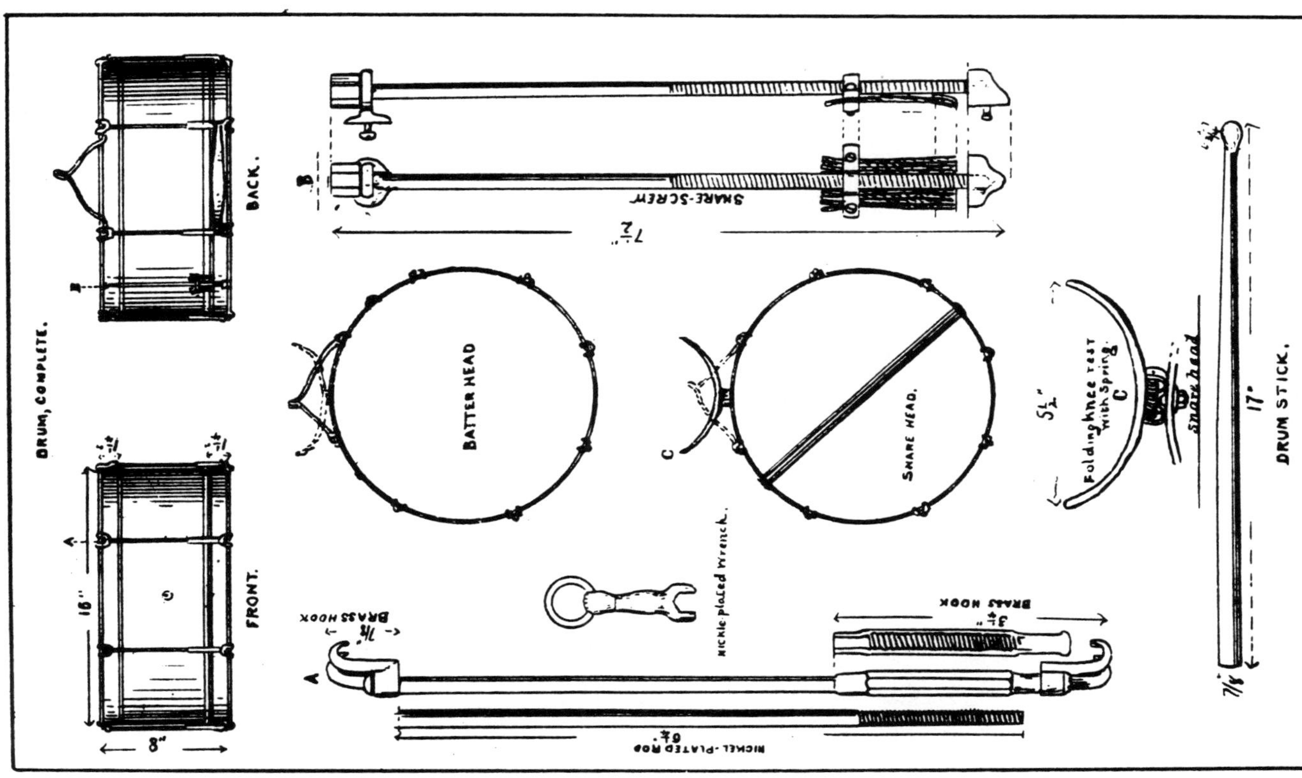
DRUM, COMPLETE.
FRONT.
BACK.
16"
8"
BATTER HEAD
SNARE HEAD.
SNARE-SCREW
7½"
BRASS HOOK
BRASS HOOK
NICKEL-PLATED ROD
Nickle plated Wrench
Folding knee rest with Spring
DRUM STICK.
17"

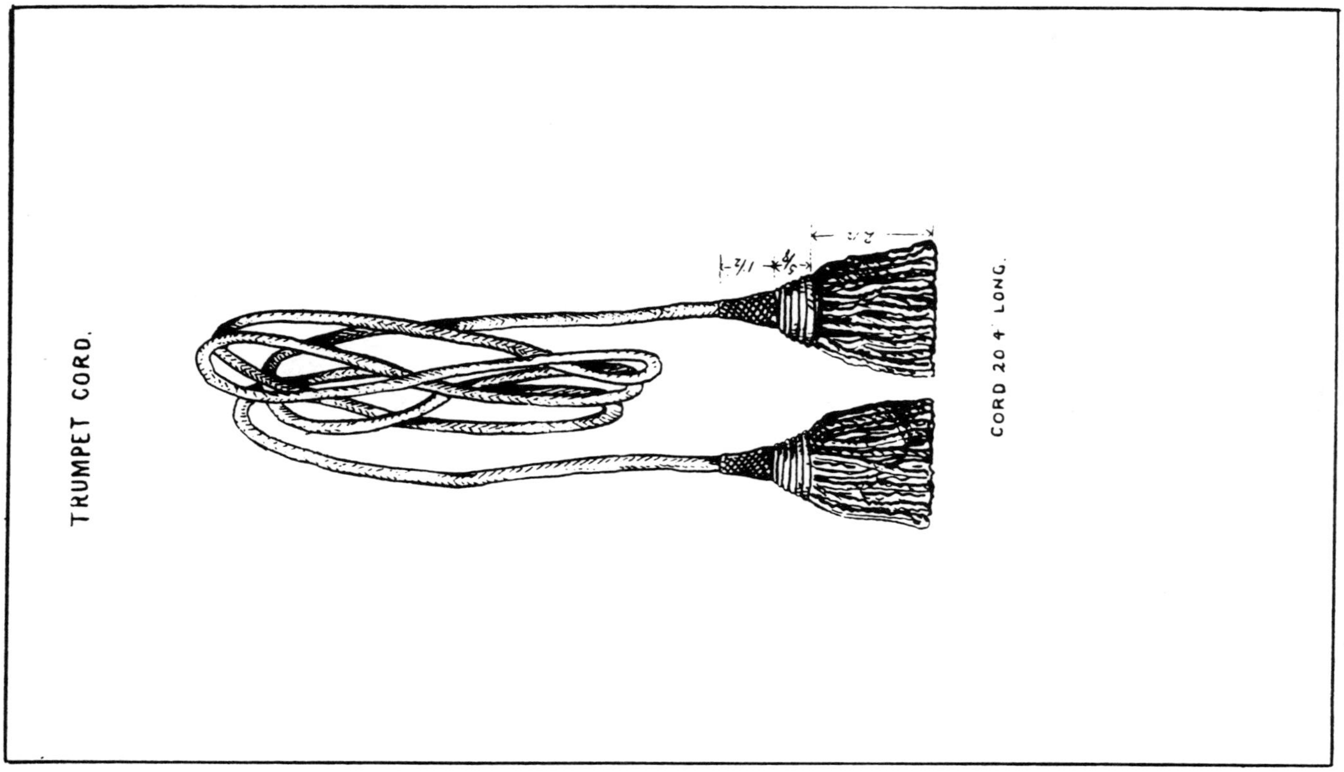
TRUMPET CORD.
CORD 20 4' LONG.

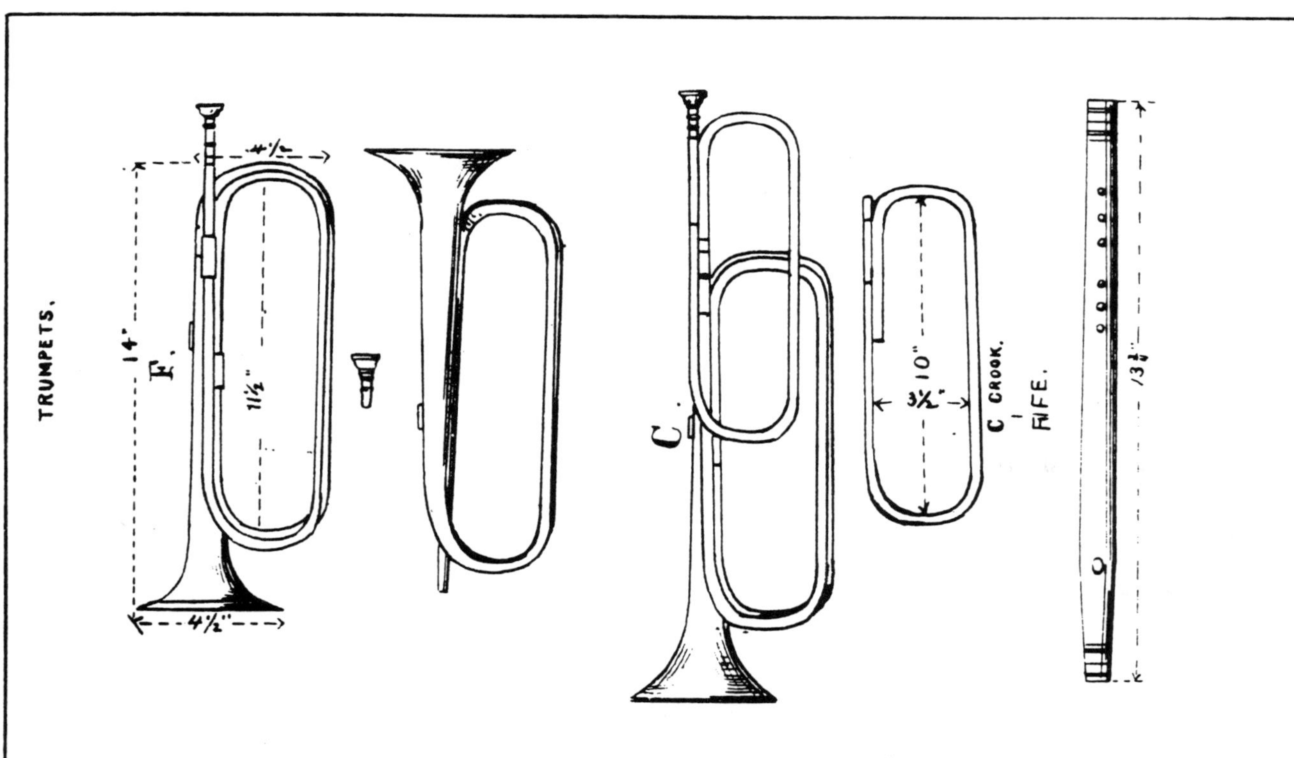
TRUMPETS.
14"
F.
11½"
4½"
C.
10"
3½"
C CROOK.
FIFE.
13¼"

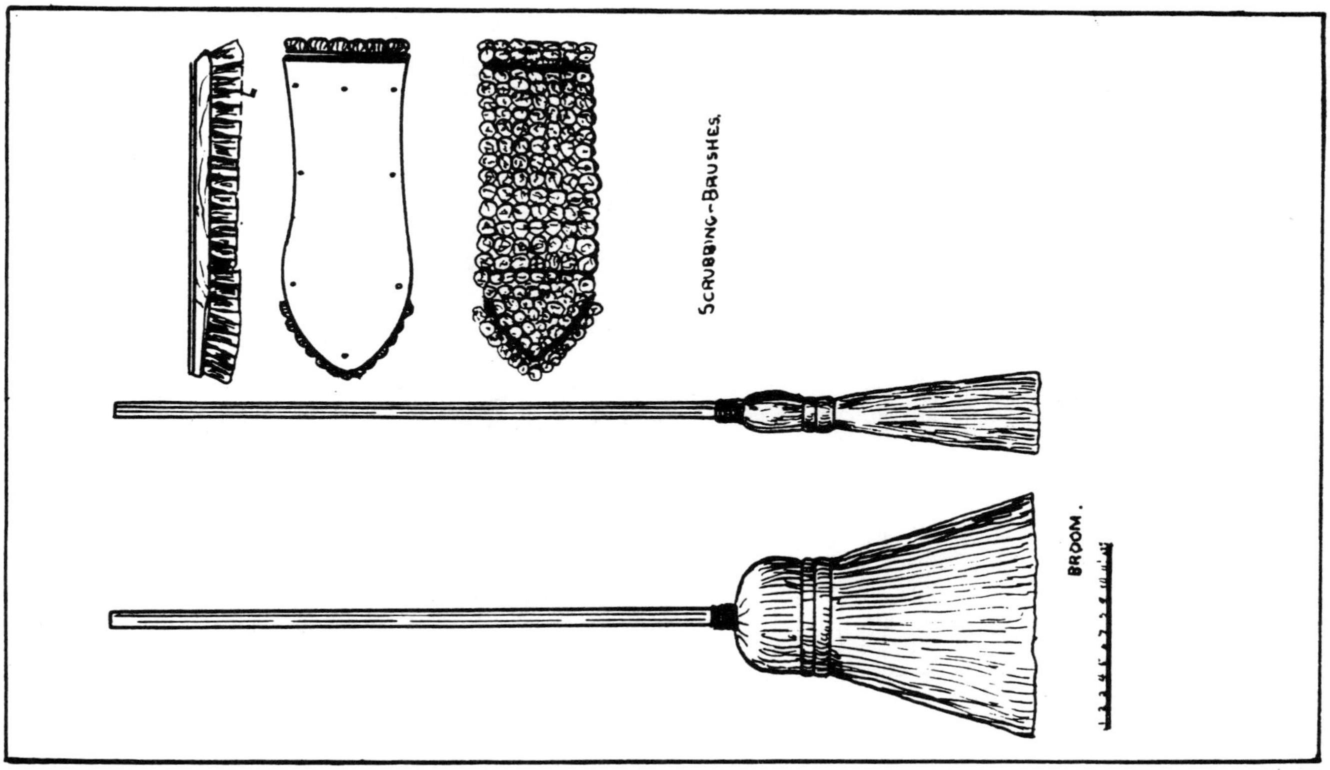
SCRUBBING-BRUSHES.
BROOM.

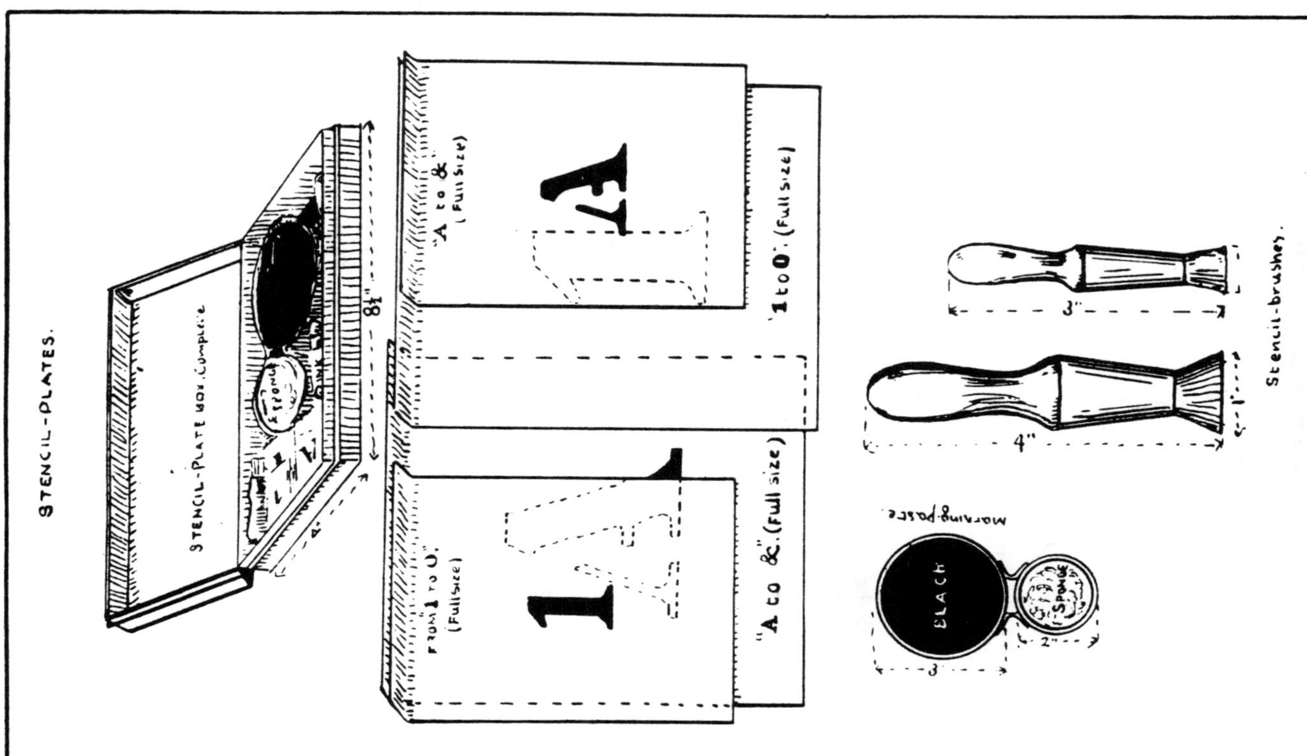
STENCIL-PLATES.
STENCIL-PLATE BOX, Complete
8½"
4"
"A to &" (Full size)
"1 to 0" (Full size)
FROM 1 TO 0. (Full size)
"A to &" (Full size)
Stencil-brushes.
3"
4"
1"
Marking-paste.
BLACK
SPONGE
3"
2"

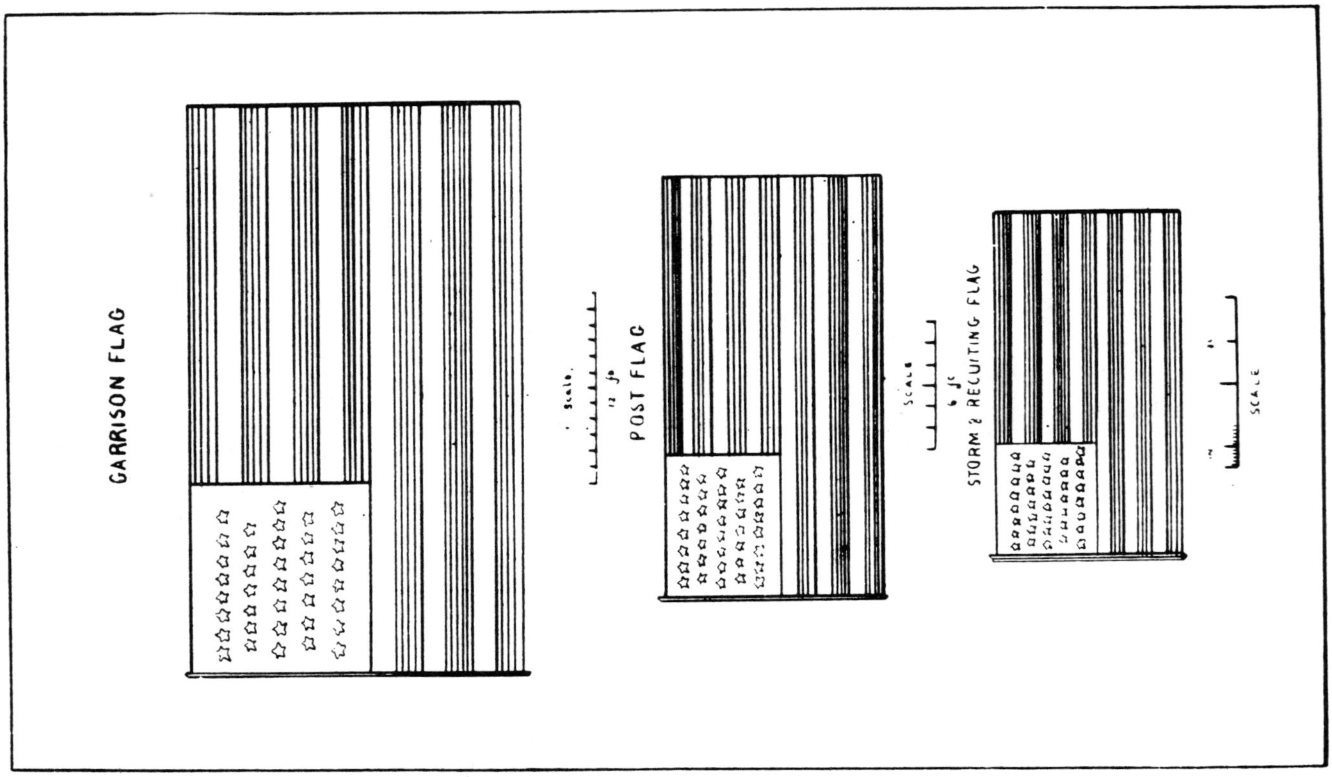
GARRISON FLAG
POST FLAG
STORM & RECUITING FLAG
SCALE

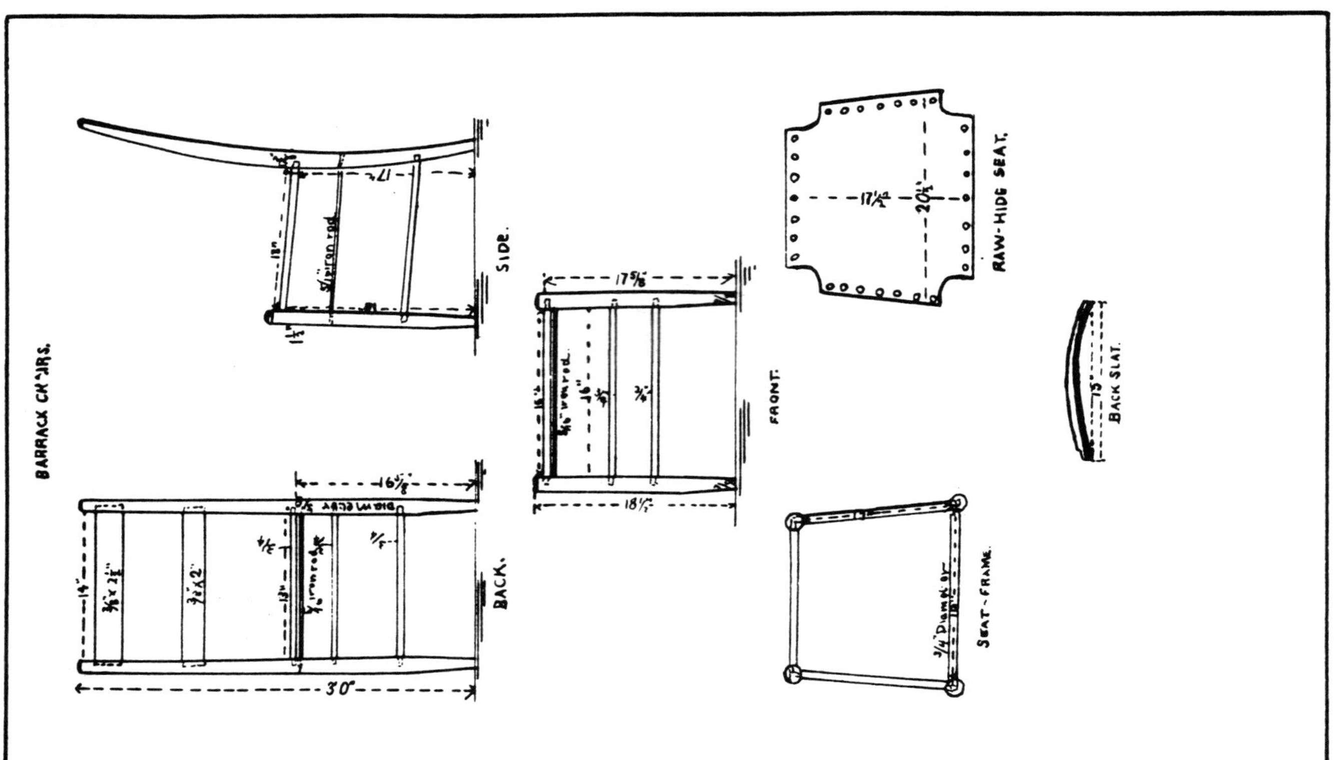
BARRACK CH'IRS.
SIDE.
BACK.
FRONT.
RAW-HIDE SEAT.
SEAT-FRAME.
BACK SLAT.
3'0"
16⅝"
17⅝"
18½"
17½"
20½"

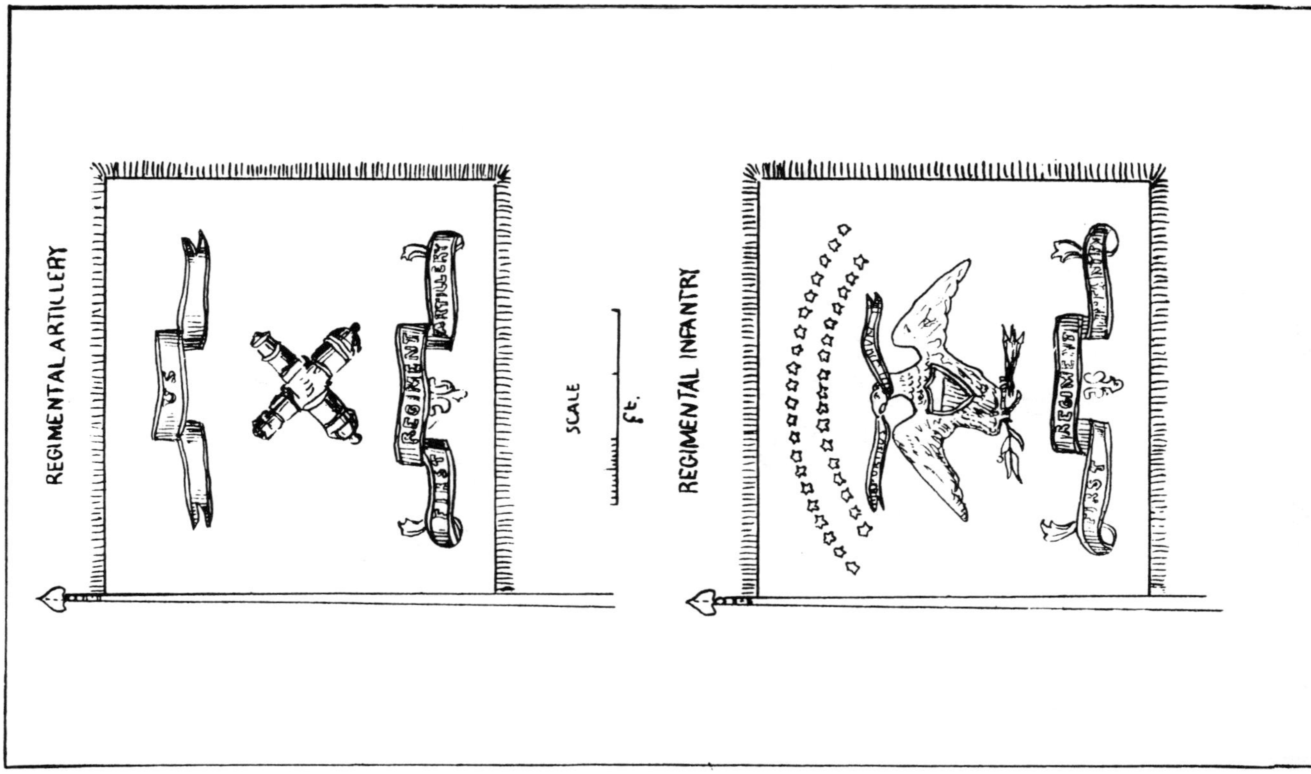
REGIMENTAL ARTILLERY
U.S
FIRST REGIMENT ARTILLERY
SCALE
ft.
REGIMENTAL INFANTRY
FIRST REGIMENT

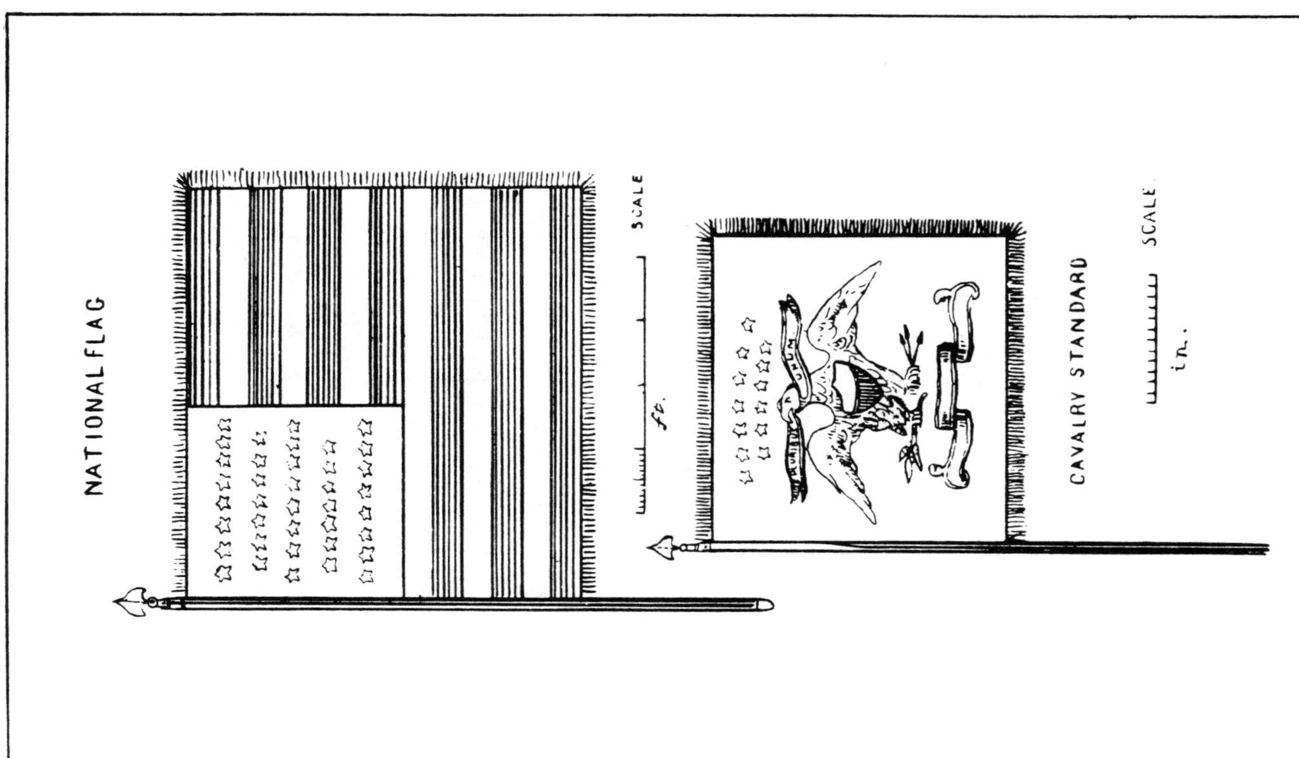
NATIONAL FLAG
SCALE
ft.
CAVALRY STANDARD
SCALE
in.

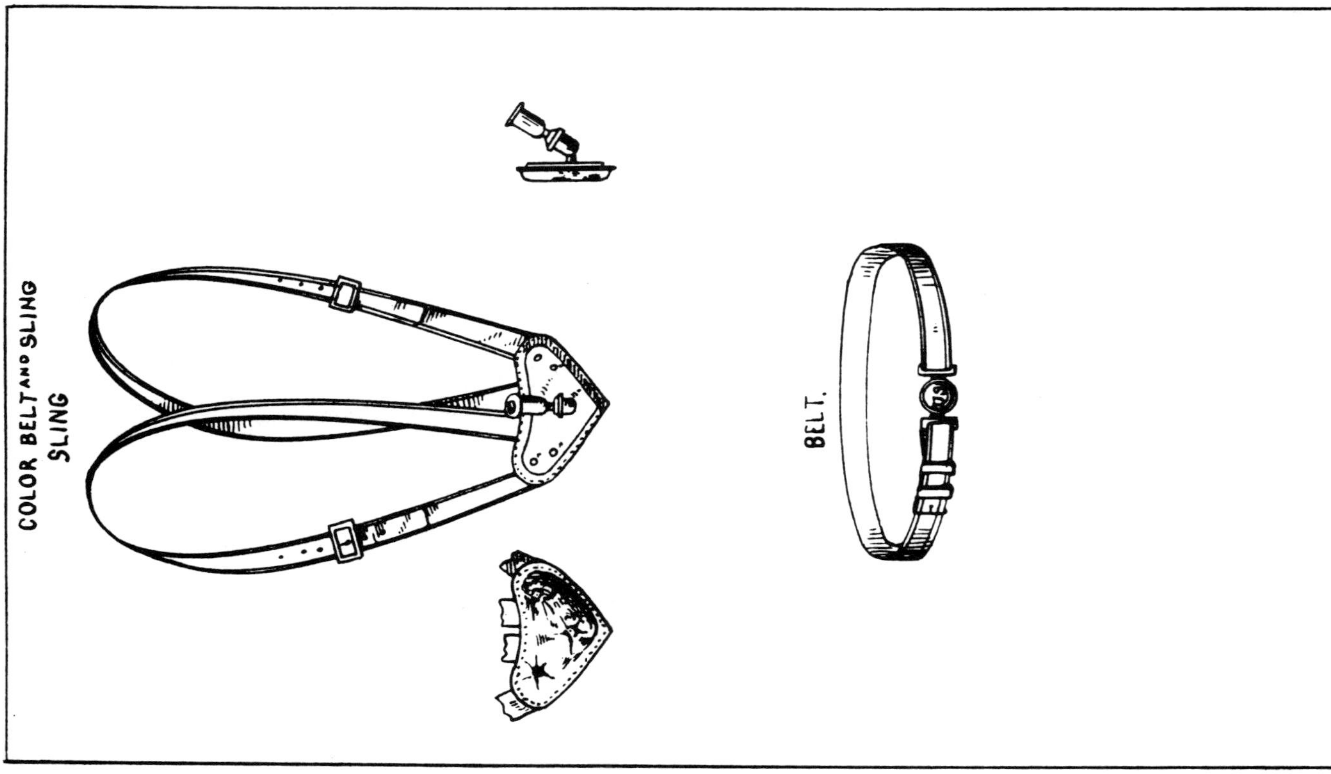
COLOR BELT AND SLING
SLING
BELT.

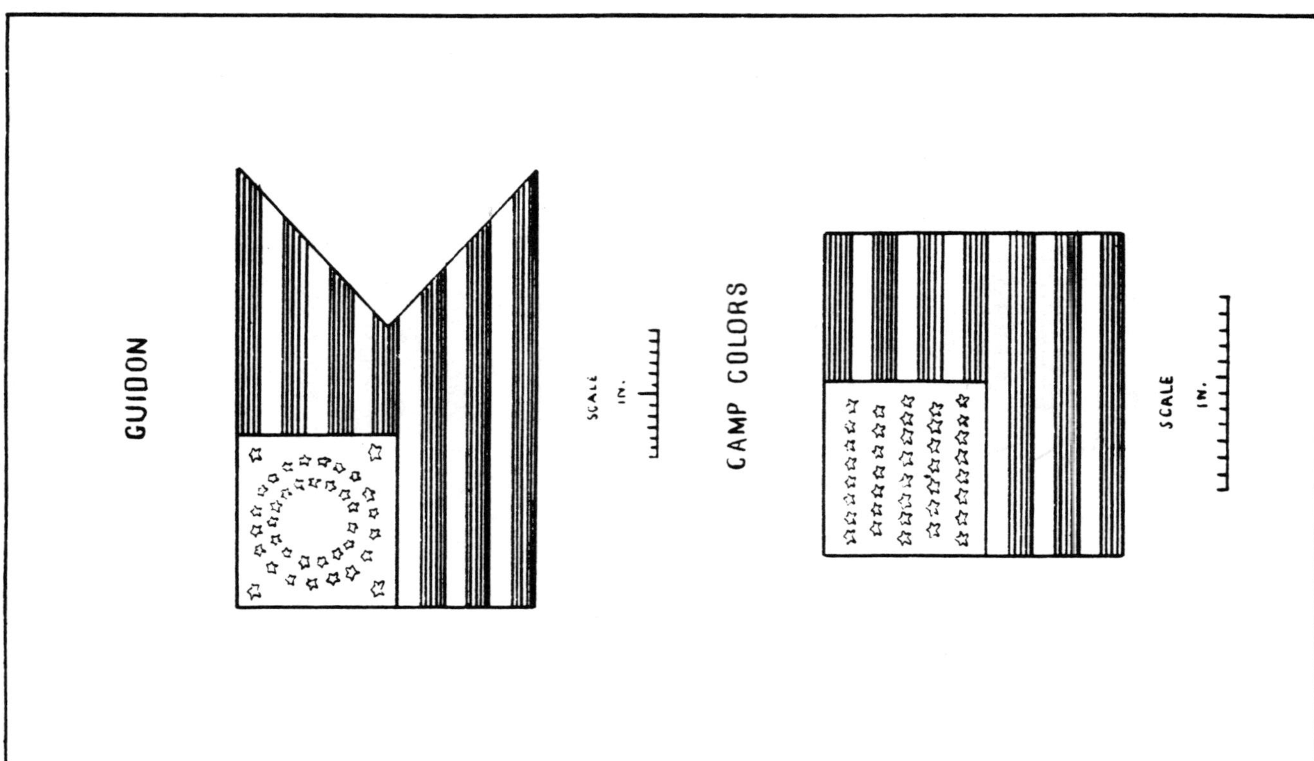
GUIDON
SCALE
IN.
CAMP COLORS
SCALE
IN.

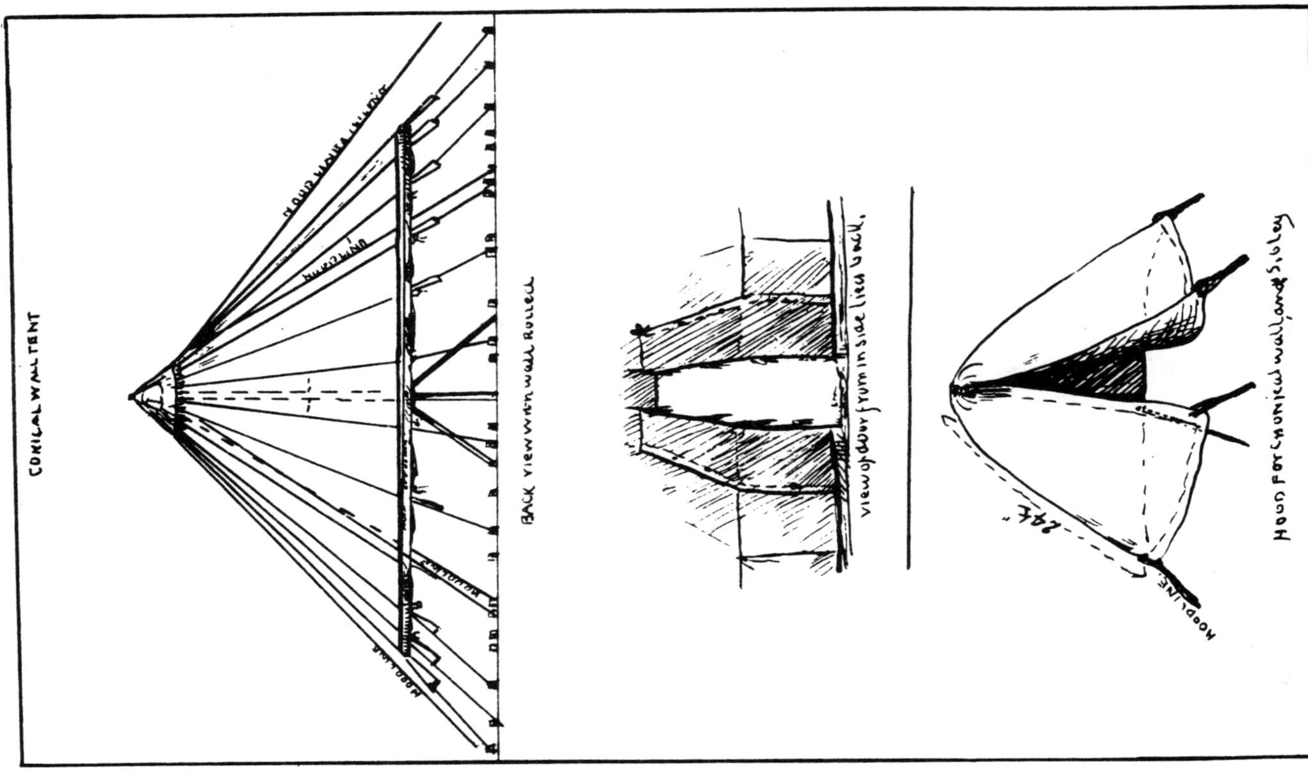
CONICAL WALL TENT
BACK VIEW WITH WALL ROLLED
View of door from inside tied back.
HOOD FOR CONICAL WALL and SIBLEY
HOODLINE
24"

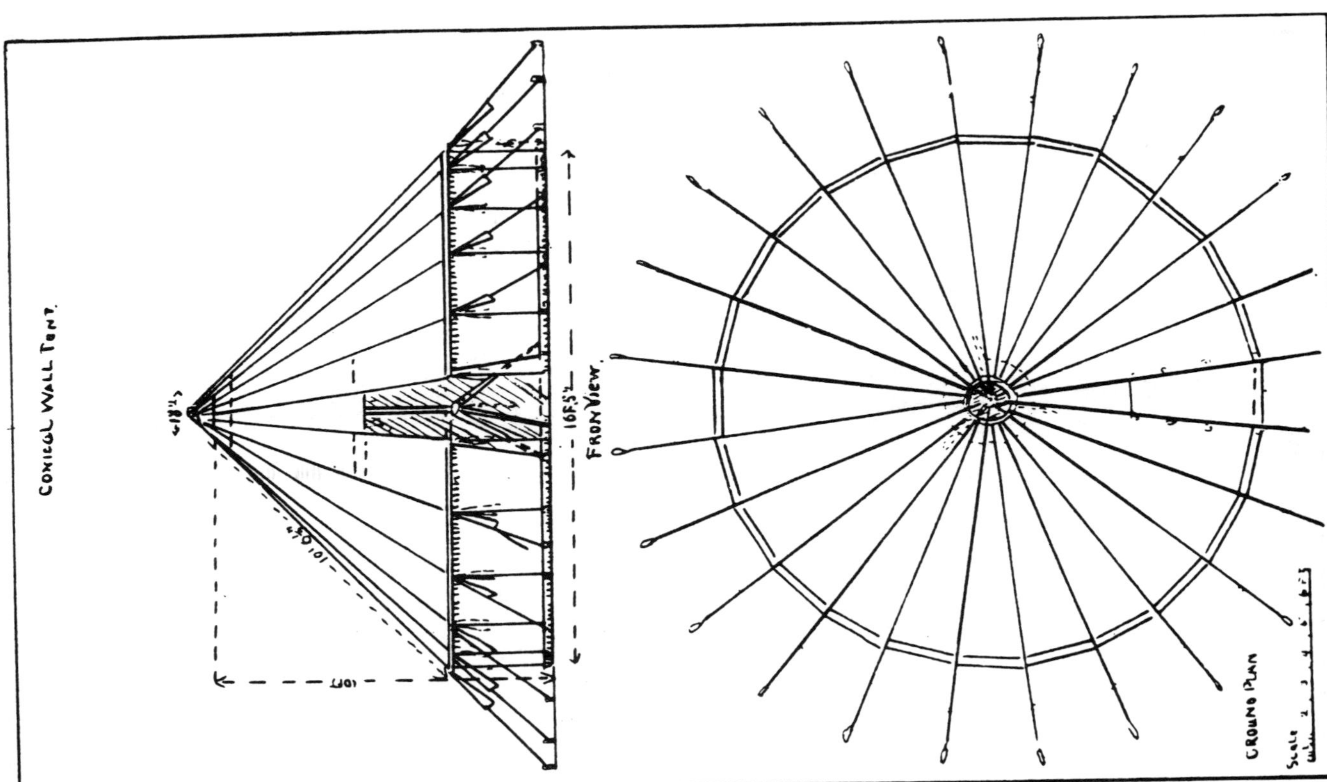
CONICAL WALL TENT.
FRONT VIEW.
16Ft 5½"
10Ft
GROUND PLAN
Scale

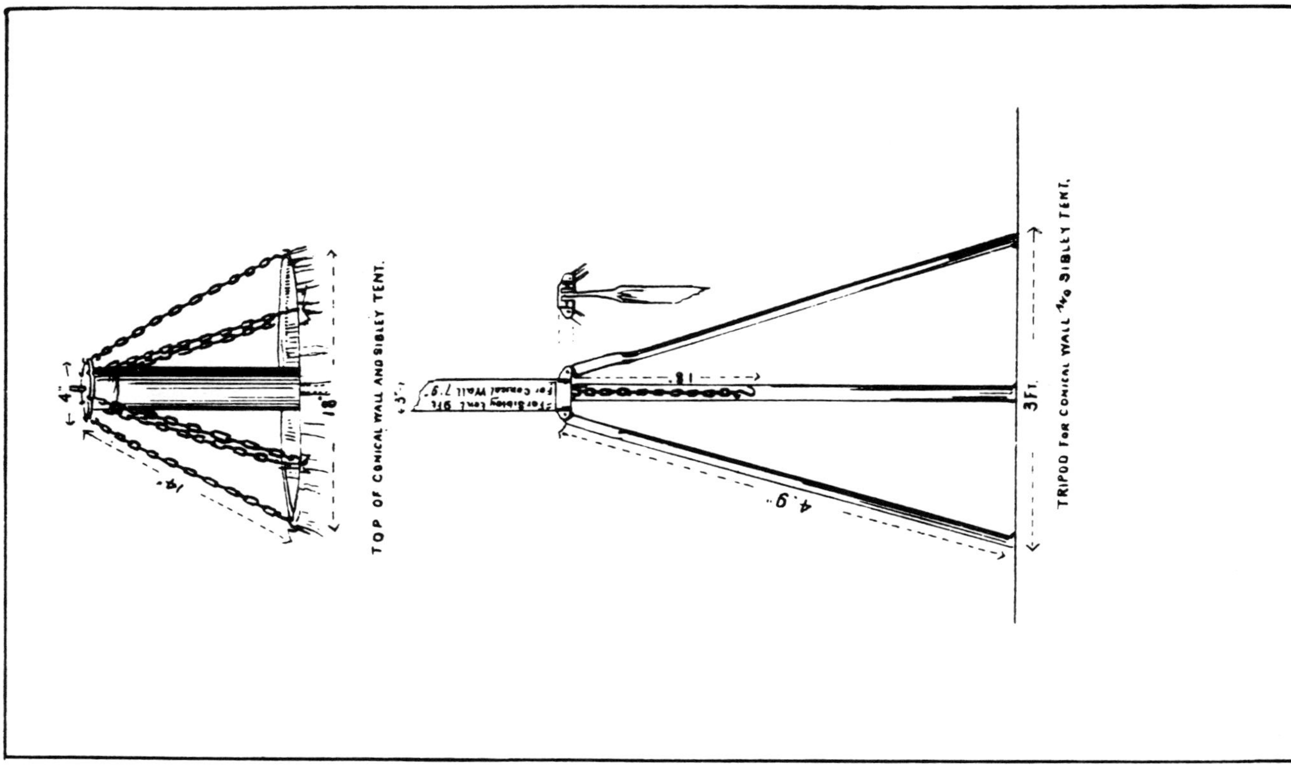
TOP OF CONICAL WALL AND SIBLEY TENT.
TRIPOD FOR CONICAL WALL AND SIBLEY TENT.

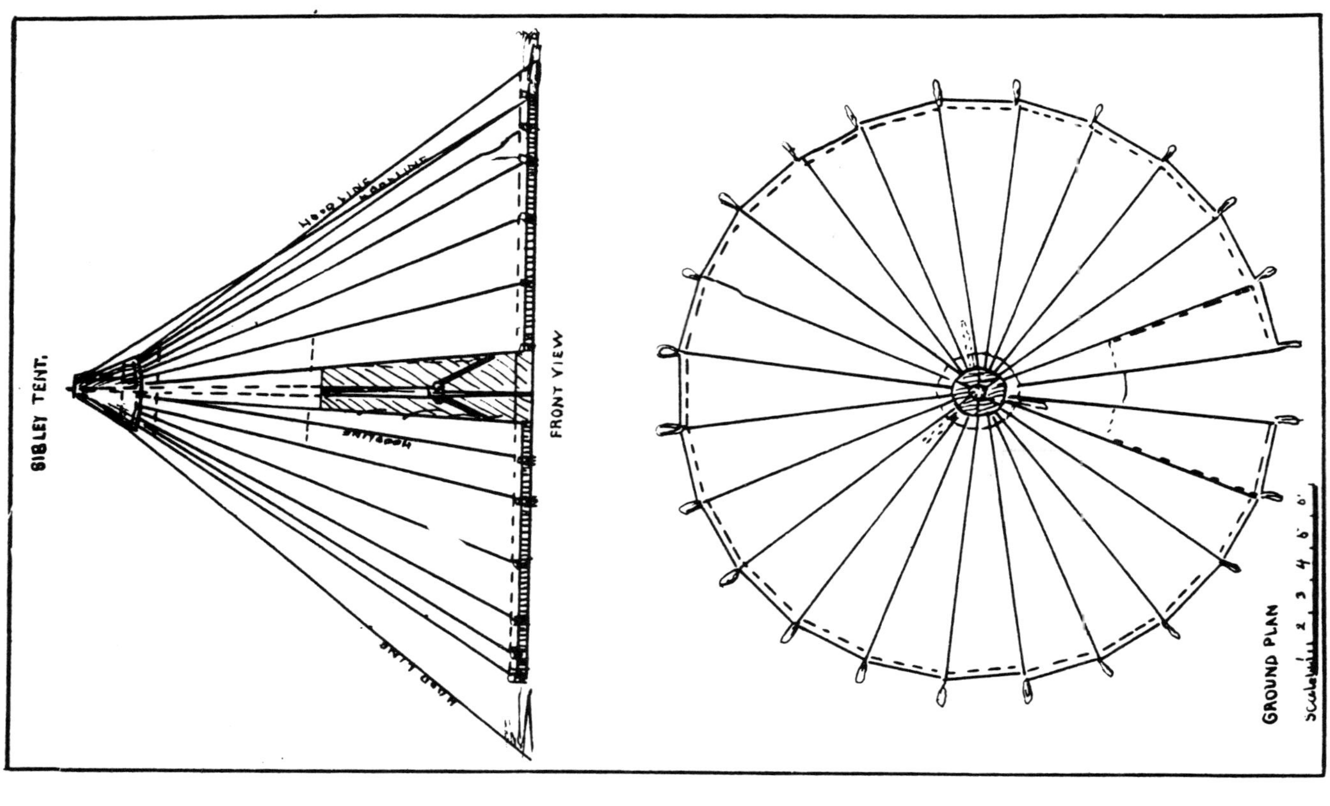
SIBLEY TENT.
FRONT VIEW
GROUND PLAN

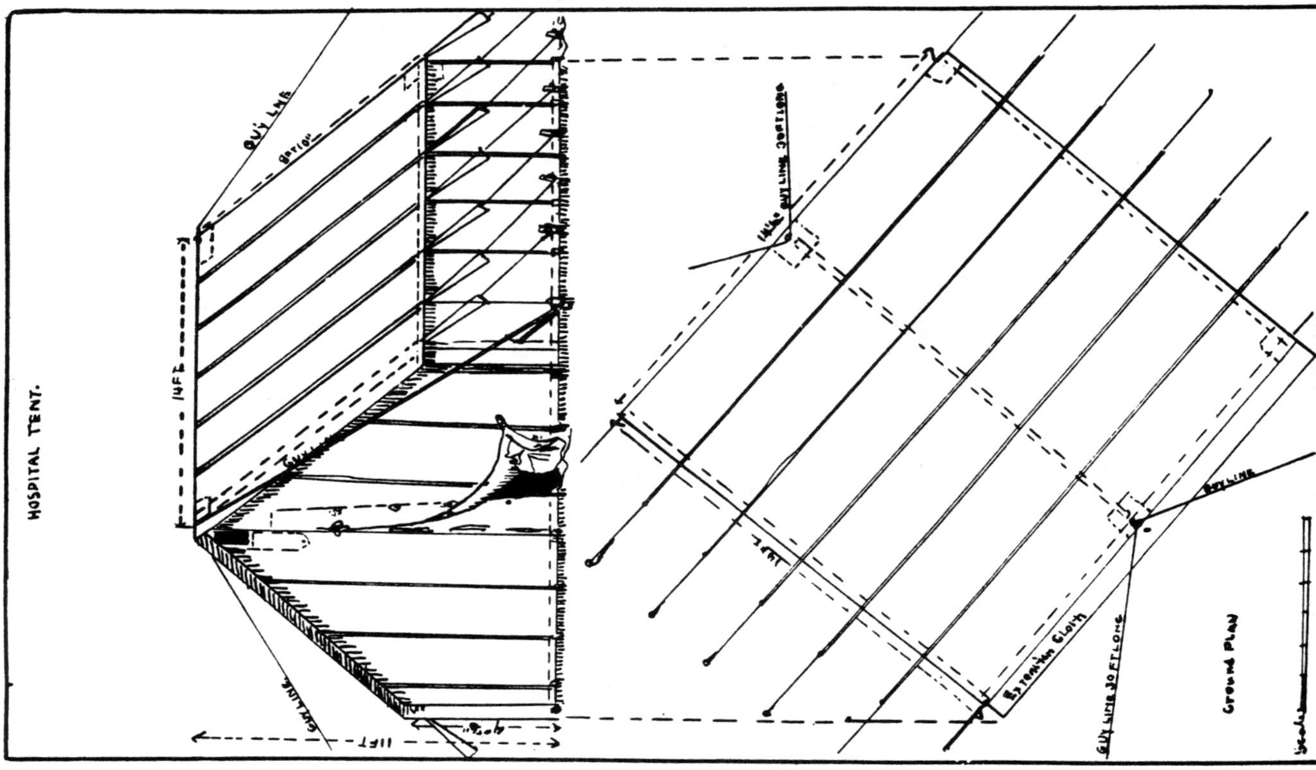
HOSPITAL TENT.
GUY LINE
14 Ft
GROUND PLAN
Extension Cloth
GUY LINE 30 FT LONG

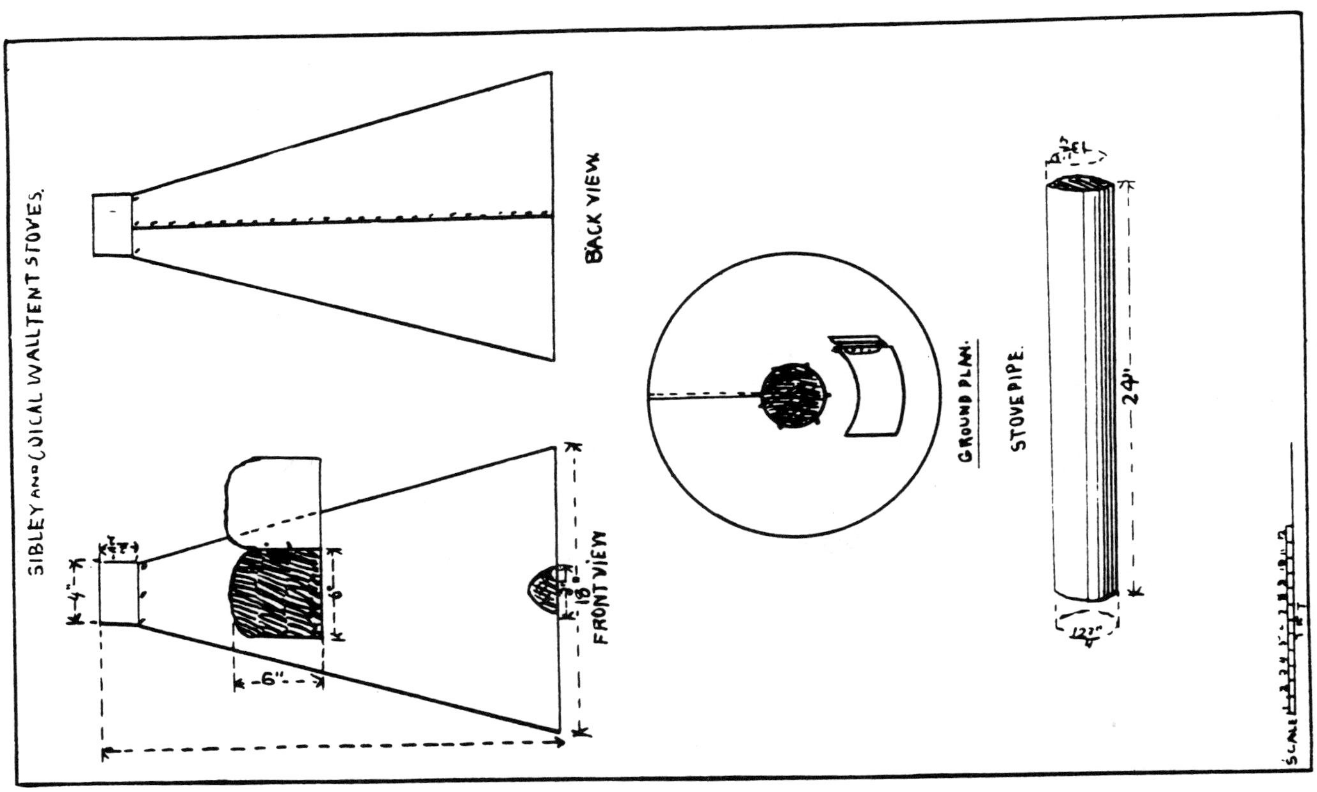
SIBLEY AND CONICAL WALLTENT STOVES.
BACK VIEW
FRONT VIEW
GROUND PLAN.
STOVEPIPE.
24"
6"

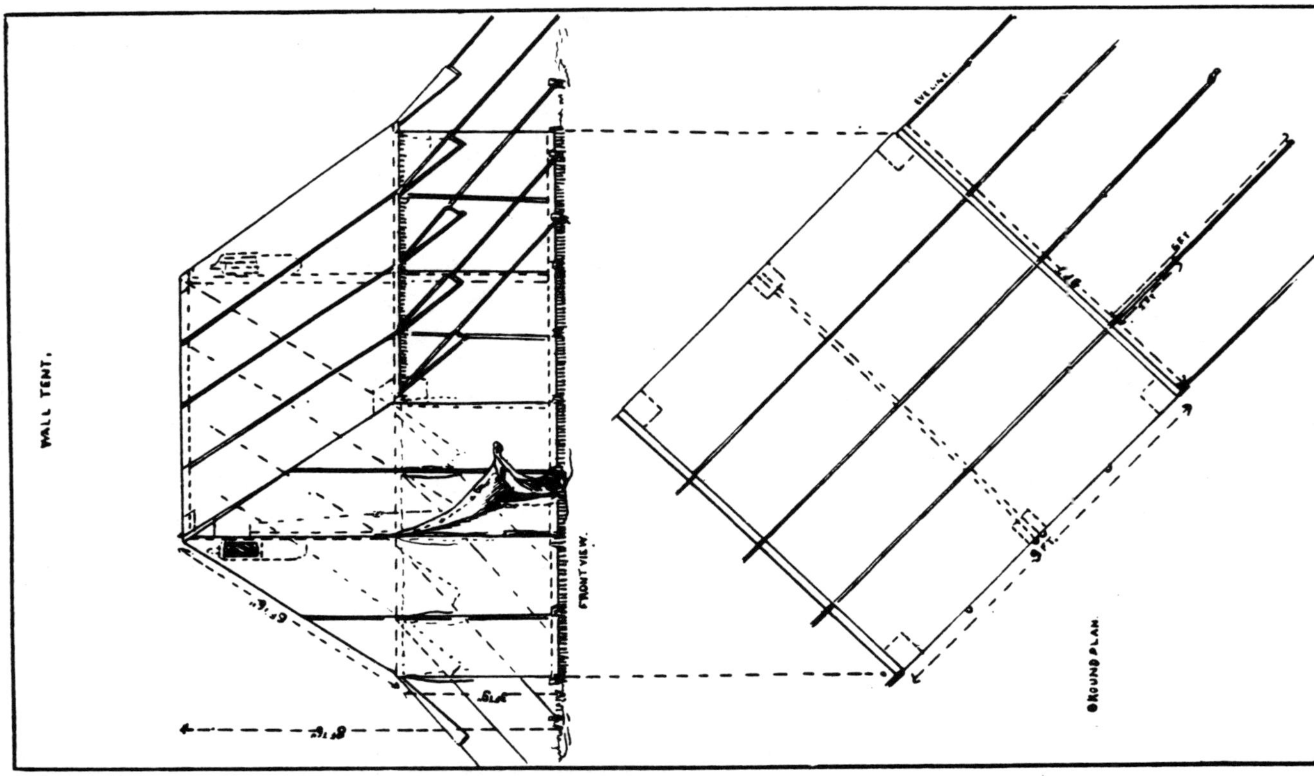
WALL TENT.
FRONT VIEW.
GROUND PLAN.

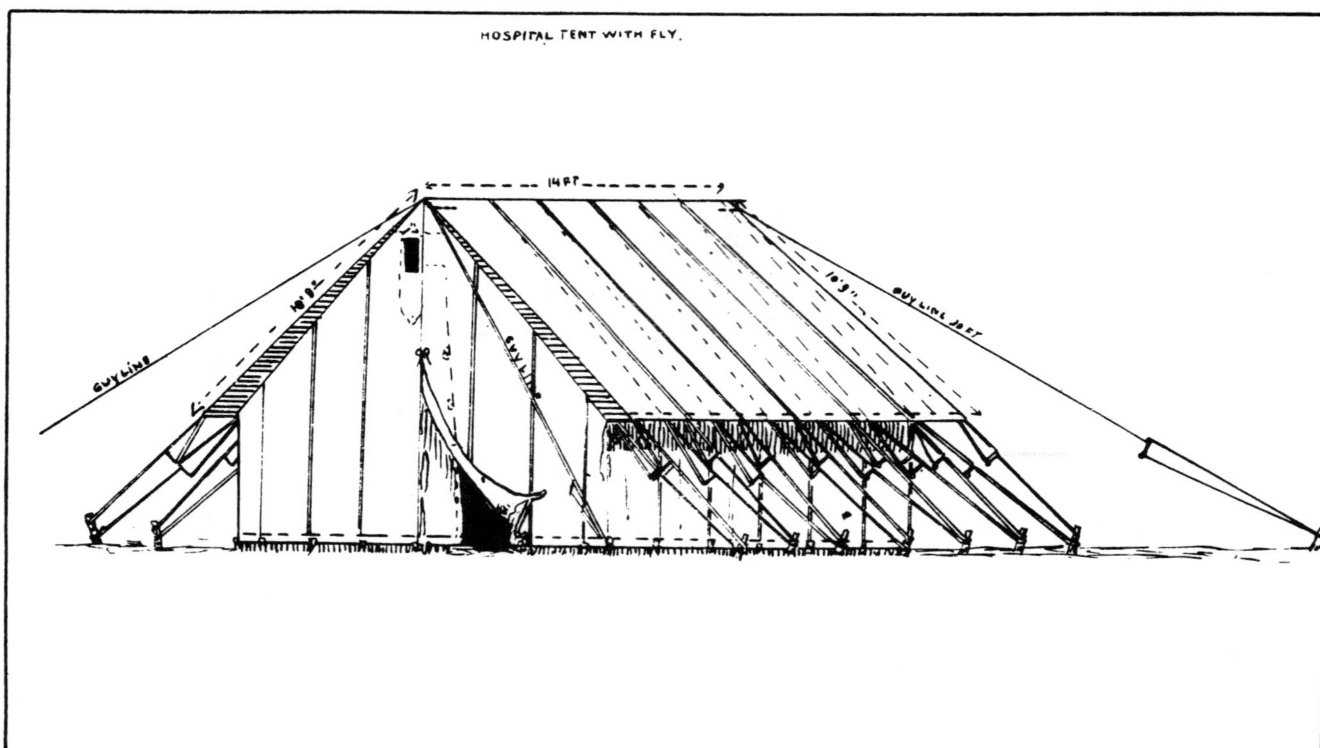
HOSPITAL TENT WITH FLY.
14 FT
GUY LINE
GUY LINE 30 FT

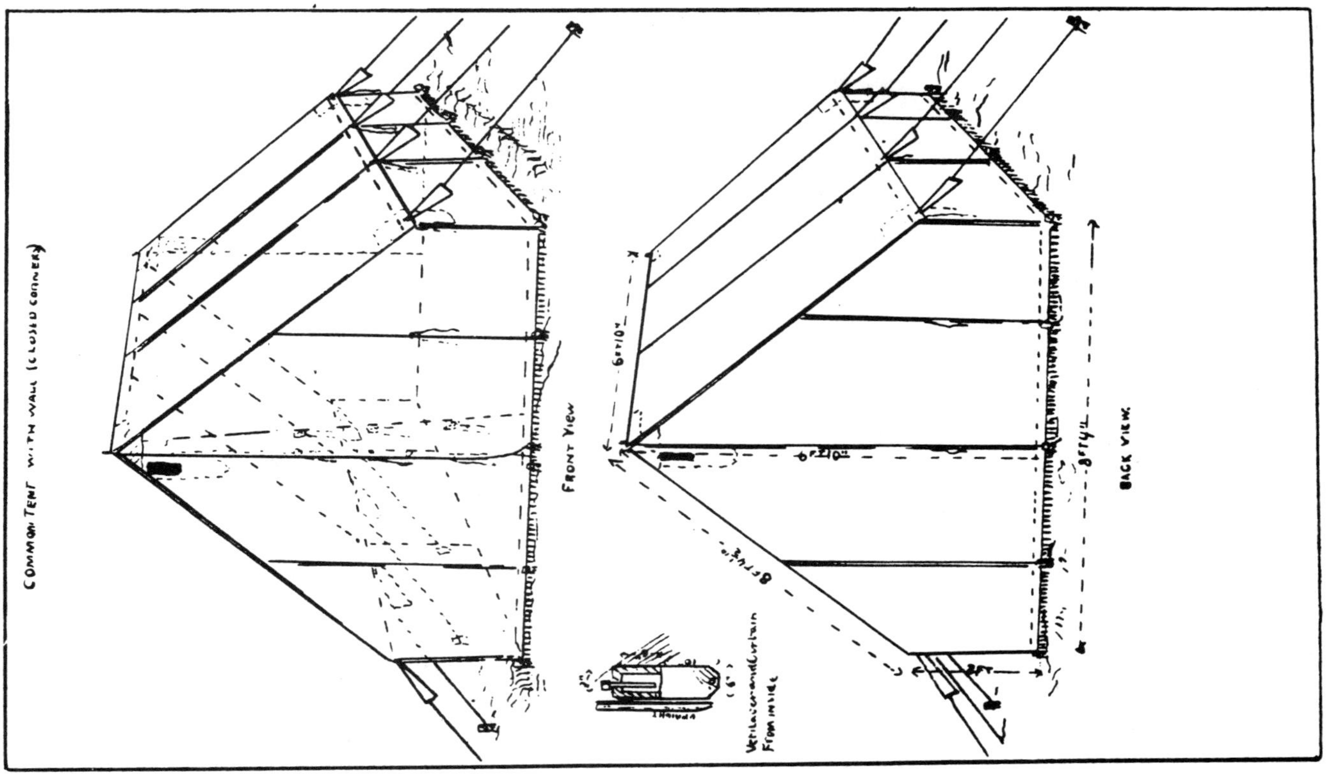
COMMON TENT WITH WALL (CLOSED CORNERS)
FRONT VIEW
BACK VIEW.
Ventilator and Curtain From inside

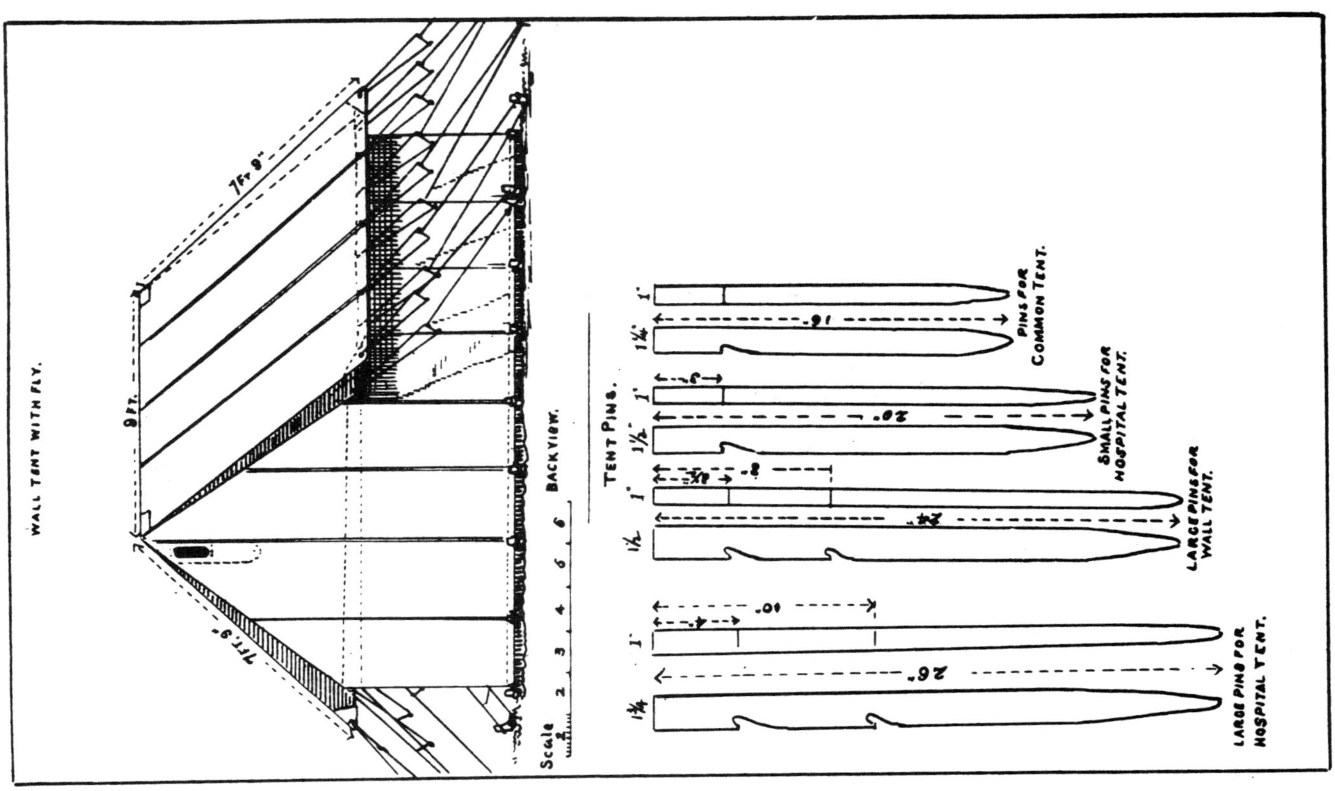
WALL TENT WITH FLY.
BACK VIEW.
Scale
TENT PINS.
PINS FOR COMMON TENT.
SMALL PINS FOR HOSPITAL TENT.
LARGE PINS FOR WALL TENT.
LARGE PINS FOR HOSPITAL TENT.

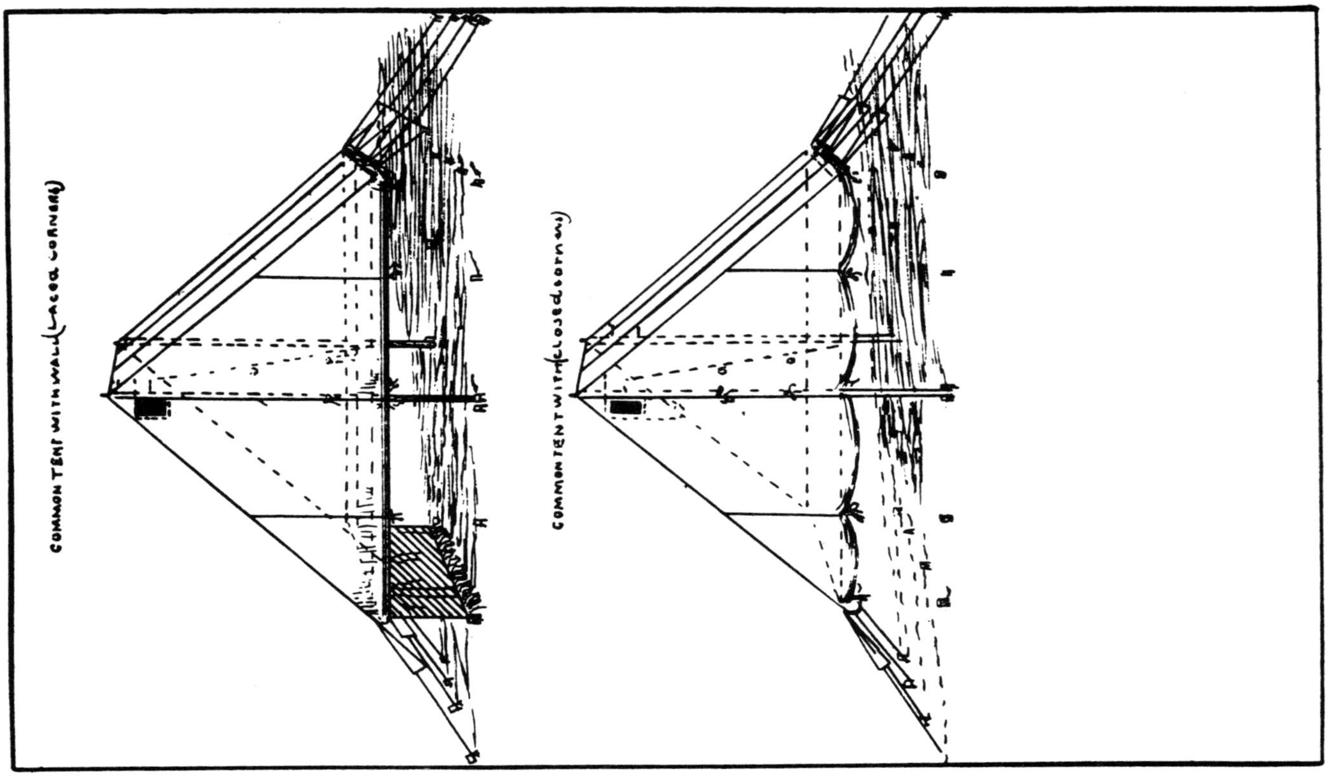
COMMON TENT WITH WALL (LACED CORNERS)
COMMON TENT WITH (CLOSED CORNERS)

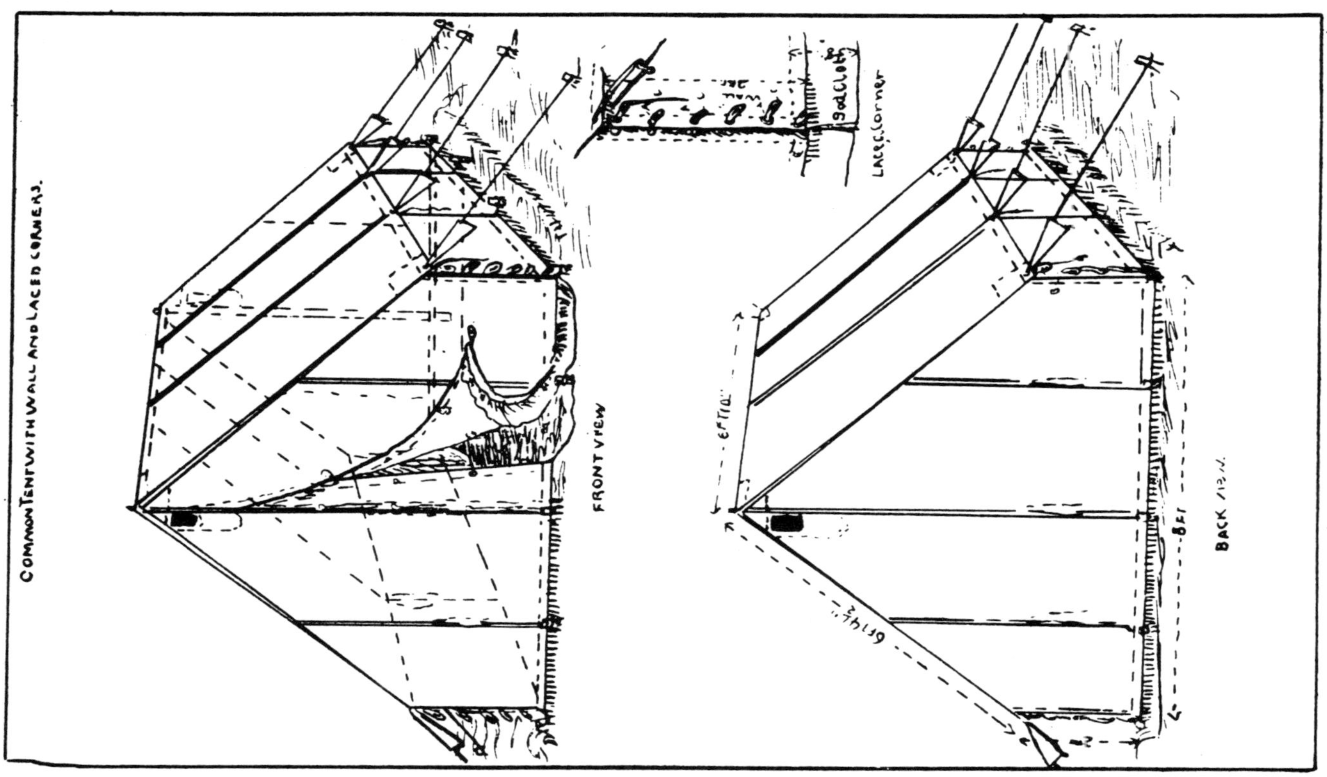
COMMON TENT WITH WALL AND LACED CORNERS.
FRONT VIEW
BACK VIEW
LACED CORNER
SOD CLOTH

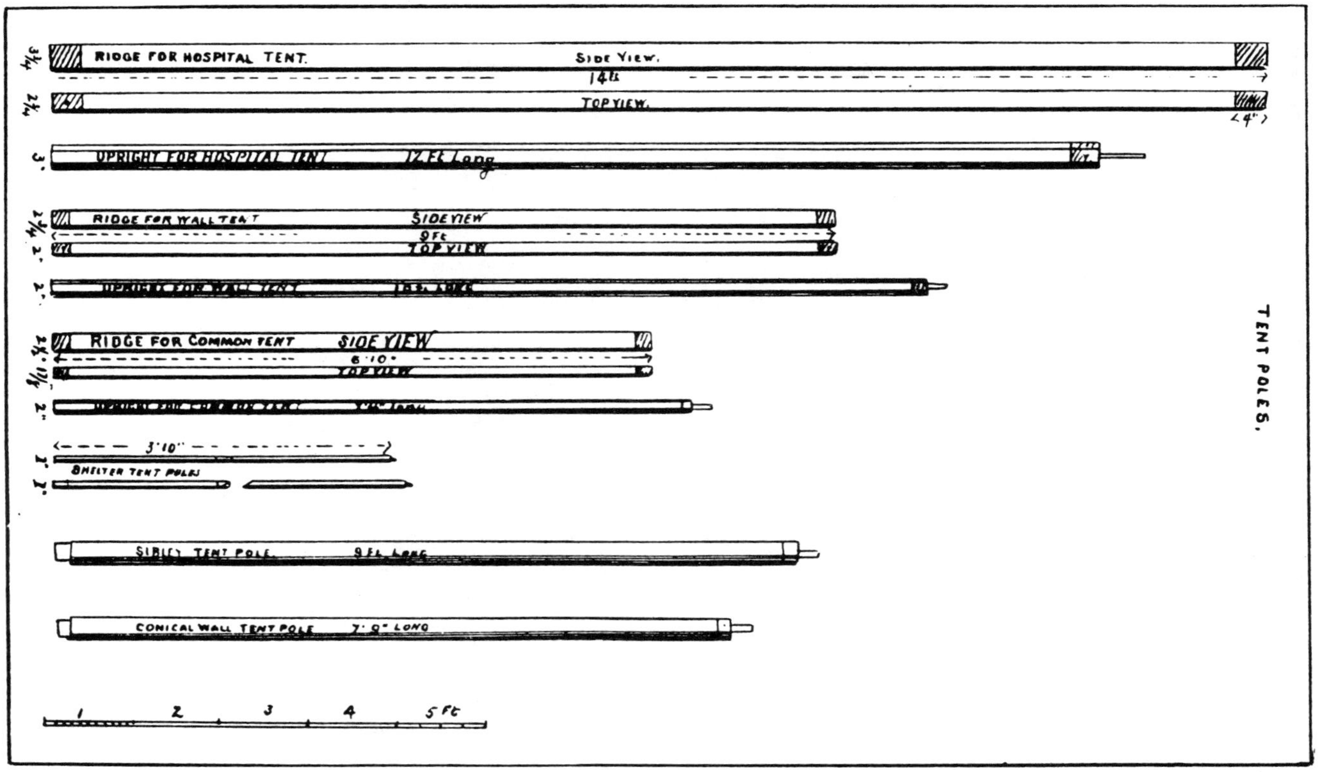
RIDGE FOR HOSPITAL TENT.
SIDE VIEW.
TOP VIEW.
UPRIGHT FOR HOSPITAL TENT
12 Ft Long
RIDGE FOR WALL TENT
SIDE VIEW
9 Ft
TOP VIEW
RIDGE FOR COMMON TENT
SIDE VIEW
6'10"
3'10"
SHELTER TENT POLES
TENT POLE.
9 Ft Long
CONICAL WALL TENT POLE
7'0" LONG
1
2
3
4
5 Ft
TENT POLES.

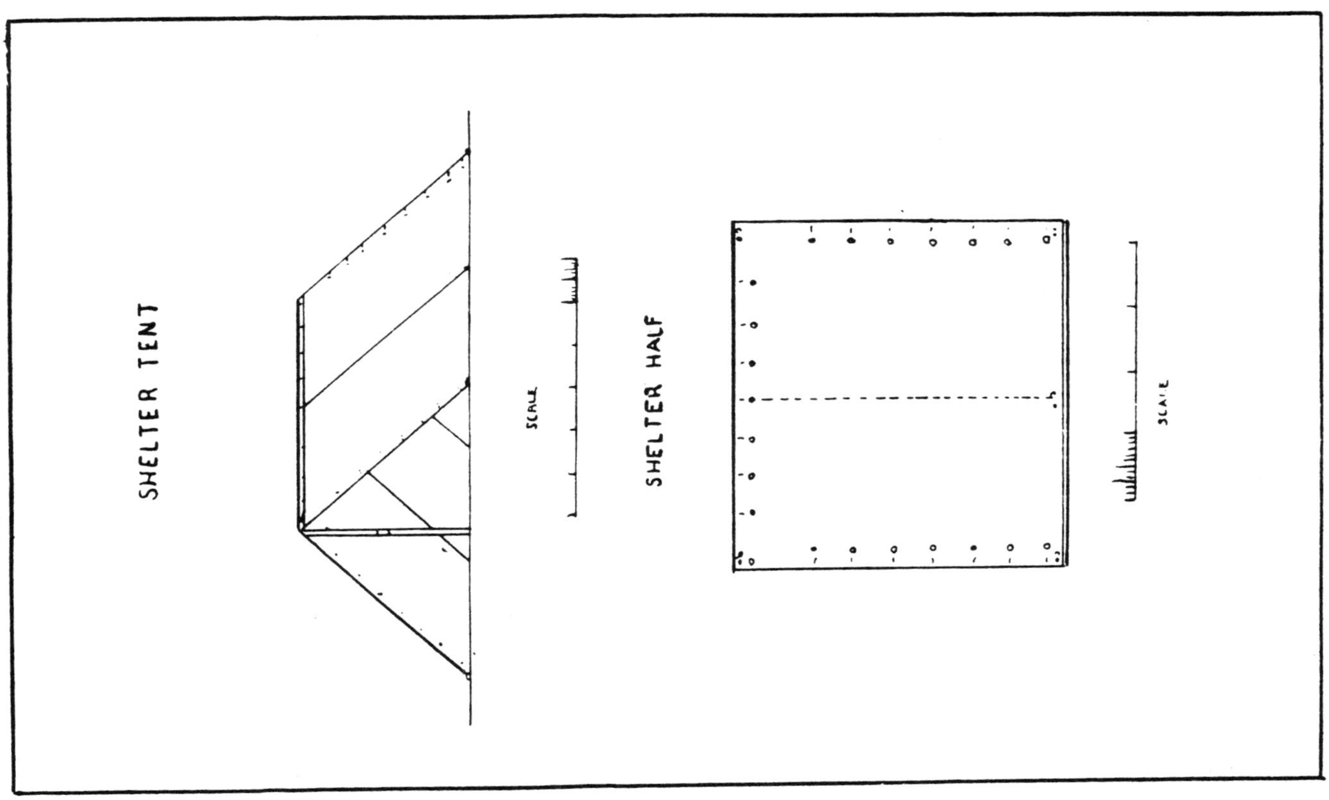
SHELTER TENT
SCALE
SHELTER HALF
SCALE

SPECIFICATIONS

FOR

BARRACK CHAIRS.

The legs, slats and rungs to be of clear white oak, ash or maple, well seasoned, $\frac{1}{4}$" or $\frac{5}{16}$" iron on each side, front and back; countersunk head on one end and a nut on the other.

The seat to be of raw-hide, secured with raw-hide thong lacing beneath.

The chairs to be delivered "knocked down," i.e. not put together, but packed in crates of convenient size for transportation by rail.

To be packed in boxes for shipment over the "Union Pacific Railway."

Adopted October 22, 1883, in lieu of Specifications adopted October 10, 1882, which are hereby canceled.

S. B. HOLABIRD,

Quartermaster General, U. S. A.

1945. Q. M. G. O. 1883. C. & Eq. Suppl.

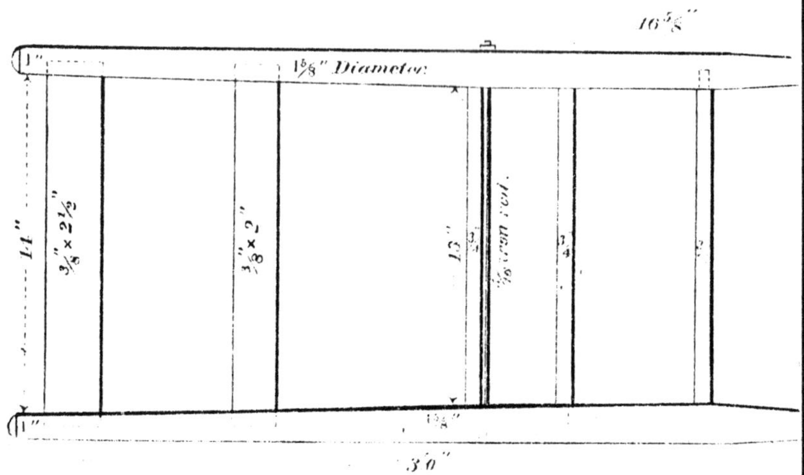

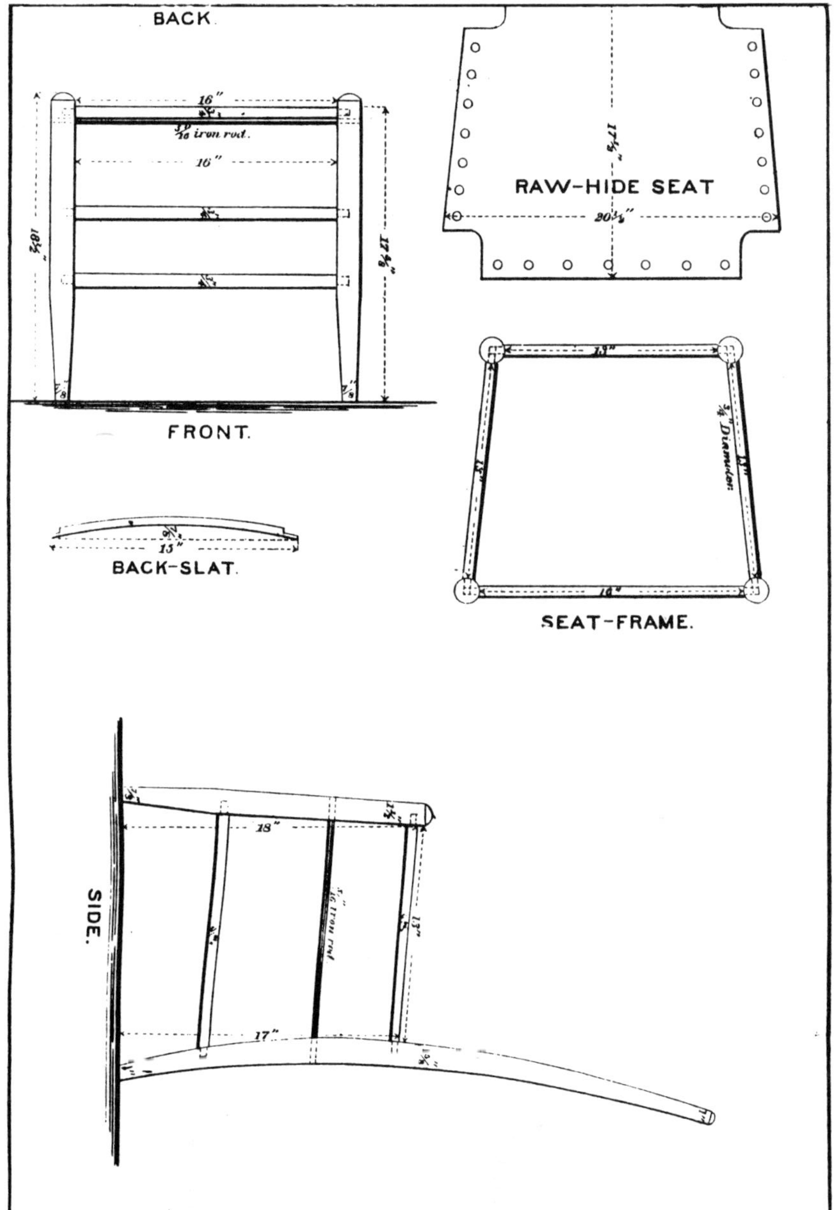

GENERAL BIBLIOGRAPHY

Agnew, S.C. *Garrisons of the Regular U.S. Army, New Mexico, 1846–1899*. Santa Fe: The Press of the Territorian, 1971.

Alliot, Hector. *Bibliography of Arizona*. Los Angeles: Southwest Museum, 1914.

Ashburn, P. M. *A History of the Medical Department of the United States Army*. Boston, 1929.

Ault, Phil. *Wires West*. New York: Dodd Meade, 1974.

Bailey, Lynn R. *The Long Walk: A History of the Navajo Wars, 1846–1868*. Los Angeles: Westernlore Press, 1964.

Bancroft, Hubert Howe. *History of Arizona and New Mexico, 1530–1888*. Vol. 17 of his *Works*. San Francisco, 1889.

Bannerman, Francis and sons. *Military Catalogue, 1943–1952*. New York, 1953.

Barnes, Will C. *Arizona Place Names*. Vol. 6, No. 1 of University of Arizona Bulletins. Tucson, 1935.

Barrett, S. M. *Geronimo's Story of His Life*. New York: Ballantine Books, 1970.

Bender, Averman B. *The March of the Empire: Frontier Defense in the Southwest, 1848–1860*. Lawrence, Kansas: University of Kansas Press, 1952.

Beyer, Walter F. and Keydel, Oscar F. *Deeds of Valor, 2 Vol*. Detroit: Perrien-Keydel Co., 1905.

Biddle, Ellen McGowan. *Reminiscences of a Soldier's Wife*. Philadelphia: Lippincott, 1907.

Bieber, Ralph H. (ed.). *Frontier Life in the Army, 1854–1861*, by Eugene Bandel. Glendale, Calif.: Arthur H. Clarke Co., 1932.

Billings, Dr. J. S. *Report on Barracks and Hospitals with Descriptions of Military Posts*. War Department: Surgeon General's Office, Circular No. 4. Washington, 1870.

Billings, John S. *A Report on the Hygiene of the United States Army with Descriptions of Military Posts*. Surgeon General's Office. Washington, 1875.

Bonsal, Stephen. *Edward Fitzgerald Beale: A Pioneer in the Path of Empire*. New York: Putnam, 1912.

Blount, Bertha. "The Apaches in U.S. History, 1846–1888." Master's thesis, University of California. Berkeley, 1918.

Bourke, John G. *An Apache Campaign in the Sierra Madre*. New York, 1886. Reissued by Scribners, 1958.

Bourke, John G. *On the Border with Crook*. New York: Charles Scribner's Sons, 1891. Reissued by Rio Grande Press, 1962.

Bourke, John G. "The Medicine Men of the Apache," *B. A. E. Ninth Annual Report, 1887–88*. Washington: Government Printing Office, 1892.

Boyd, Mrs. Orsemus B. *Cavalry Life in Tent and Field*. New York: J. S. Tait and Sons, 1894.

Brackett, Albert Gallatin. *History of the U.S. Cavalry*. 1865.

Brandes, Ray. "A Guide to the History of the U.S. Army Installations in Arizona, 1849–1886," *Arizona and the West*, Vol. 1. Spring 1959.

Brandes, Ray. *Frontier Military Posts of Arizona*. Globe, Ariz.: Dale Stuart King, 1960.

Brimlow, George F. *Cavalry Man Out of the West: Life of General William Carey Brown*. Caldwell, 1944.

Browne, J. Ross. *Adventures in the Apache Country*. New York: Harper, 1869.

Burnham, Frederick R. *Scouting on Two Continents*. New York, 1928.

Campion, J. S. Major. *On the Frontier: Reminiscences of Wild Sports, Personal Adventures and Strange Scenes*. London, 1878.

Carter, Lt. Col. W. H. *From Yorktown to Santiago with the 6th U.S. Cavalry*. Baltimore, 1900.

Carter, W. H. *The Life of Lieutenant-General Chaffee*. Chicago: University of Chicago Press, 1917.

Carter, W. H. *Old Army Sketches*. Baltimore, 1906.

Clum, Woodworth. *Apache Agent: The Story of John P. Clum*. New York: Houghton Mifflin, 1936.

Coe, Lewis. *Great Days of the Heliograph*. Crown Point, Ind., 1987.

Colyer, Vincent. *Peace with the Apaches of New Mexico and Arizona*. Washington, D.C., 1872.

Connell, Charles T. "The Apache Past and Present," (Tucson) *Citizen*. February 5 to July 31, 1921.

Connelley, William B. *Doniphan's Expedition*. Kansas City, Mo., 1907.

Cooke, Philip St. George. *Scenes and Adventures in the Army, or Romance of Military Life*. Philadelphia, 1857.

Cremony, John C. *Life Among the Apaches*. San Francisco, 1868. Reissued by Arizona Silhouettes, Tucson, 1951.

Crook, George. *Resume of Operations Against Apache Indians from 1882 to 1886*. Washington, D.C., 1886.

Cruse, Thomas. *Apache Days and After*. Caldwell, Idaho: Caxton, 1944.

Cullen, George W. *Biographical Register of the Officers and Graduates of the U.S. Military Academy*. Two vols. New York, 1868.

Daunt, Achilles. *With Pack and Rifle in the Far Southwest*. New York, 1886.

Davis, Britton. *The Truth about Geronimo*. New Haven: Yale University Press, 1929. Reprinted by Lakeside Press, 1951.

DeLong, Sidney. *The History of Arizona from the Earliest Times to 1903*. San Francisco, 1905.

Dorsey, R.S. *American Military Belts & Related Equipment*. Union City, Tenn.: Pioneer Press, 1984.

Downey, Fairfax. *Indian Fighting Army*. New York: Bantam Books, 1941.

Downey, Fairfax. *Indian Wars of the U.S. Army, 1776–1865*. New York: Doubleday, 1963.

Elliott, Wallace W. (comp.). *History of Arizona Territory*. San Francisco, 1884.

Emerson, William K. *Chevrons*. Washington: Smithsonian Institution Press, 1983.

Farish, Thomas E. *History of Arizona*. Eight vols. Phoenix, 1915–18.

Ferris, Robert G. *Soldier and Brave*. Washington: U.S. Dept. of Interior National Park Service, 1971.

Fish, Joseph. *History of Arizona*. Unpublished manuscript written in 1906 at Snowflake, Arizona, a copy kept at the Arizona Pioneers' Historical Society, Tucson.

Forsyth, George A. *The Story of the Soldier*. New York: Appleton, 1902.

Forsyth, George A. *Thrilling Days in Army Life*. New York: Harper, 1900.

Frazer, Robert W. (ed.) *Mansfield on the Condition of the Western Forts, 1853–1854*. Norman, Okla.: University of Oklahoma Press, 1963.

Fry, James B. *Army Sacrifices: Or Briefs from Official Pigeonholes*. New York: Van Nostrand, 1879.

Furber, George C. *The 12 Months Volunteer*. 1848.

Ganoe, William A. *The History of the United States Army*. New York, 1924.

Genung, Charles B. "About my experiences with the Colorado Indian Reservation and the Apaches, 1867," a manuscript on file at the Southwest Museum, Pasadena, Calif.

Genung, Charles B. "Apache Campaign under Lieutenant Morton," (1871), a manuscript on file at the Southwest Museum, Pasadena, Calif.

Gilmore, Harry. *Four Years in the Saddle*. 1866.

Glass, Edward L. N. *The History of the Tenth Cavalry, 1866–1921*. Tucson: Acme Printing Company, 1921.

Glisan, Rodney. *Journal of Army Life*. San Francisco, 1874.

Hackley, W. F.; Woodin, W. H.; Scranton, E. L. *History of Modern U.S. Military Small Arms Ammunition*. Vol. 1, 1880–1939. New York: Macmillan Co.

Hall, Sharlot M. *First Citizen of Prescott, Pauline Weaver: Trapper and Mountain Man*. (Introduction by Alpheu H. Favor—a booklet undated, without place of publication mentioned.)

Hamersly, Thomas H. S. (comp.). *Complete Regular Army Register of the United States for One Hundred Years, 1779–1879*. Washington, 1880.

Hamilton, Patrick. *The Resources of Arizona*. San Francisco, 1884.

Hamlin, Percy G. (ed.). *The Making of a Soldier: Letters of General R. S. Ewell*. Richmond, Va: Whittet & Shepperson, 1935.

Hammond, George P. (ed.). *Campaigns in the West, 1856–61, the Journals and Letters of John Van Dusen Dubois*. Tucson: Arizona Pioneers' Historical Society, 1949.

Hardin, A. M., Jr., *Light but Efficient*. Taylor Publishing, 1975.

Hayes, Jess C. *Apache Vengeance: The True Story of the Apache Kid*. Albuquerque: University of New Mexico Press, 1954.

Hein, Otto L. *Memories of Long Ago* (about General Crook). New York: Putnam, 1925.

Heitman, Francis B. (comp.). *Historical Register and Dictionary of the United States Army*. Two vols. Washington, 1903.

Herr, John K. and Wallace, Edward S. *The Story of the U.S. Cavalry, 1775–1942*. Boston, 1953.

Hinton, Richard J. *Handbook to Arizona: Its Resources, History, Towns, Mines, Ruins and Scenery*. San Francisco, 1878. Reissued by Arizona Silhouettes, Tucson, 1954.

Howard, James L. (ed.). *The Origins and Fortunes of Troop B*. Hartford, Conn., 1921.

Howard, O. O. "Account of General Howard's Missions to the Apaches and Navajos." Reprint from the *Washington Daily Morning Chronicle*, November 10, 1872.

Howard, O. O. *Famous Indian Chiefs I Have Known*. New York: Century Company, 1908.

Howard, O. O. *My Life and Experiences Among Our Hostile Indians*. Hartford, Conn., 1907.

Hunt, Aurora. *The Army of the Pacific: Its Operations in California, Texas, Arizona, New Mexico, Utah, Nevada, Oregon, Washington, Plains Region, Mexico, etc., 1860–1866*. Glendale, Calif.: Arthur H. Clarke Co., 1951.

Hunt, Aurora. *Major-General James Henry Carlton, Western Frontier Dragoon*. Glendale, Calif.: Arthur H. Clarke Co., 1958.

Kelly, George H. (comp.). *Legislative History (of) Arizona, 1861–1912*. Phoenix, 1926.

Kerby, Robert Lee. *The Confederate Invasion of New Mexico and Arizona, 1861–1962*. Los Angeles: Westmore Press, 1958.

King, Charles. *Campaigning with Crook*. Norman, Okla., 1964.

Lerwill, Leonard. *History of the U.S. Army Replacement System*. Washington: Government Printing Office, 1954.

Lockwood, Frank C. *The Apache Indians*. New York, 1938.

Lockwood, Frank C. *Pioneer Days in Arizona*. New York: MacMillan, 1932.

Lowe, Percival G. *Five Years a Dragoon*. 1906.

Mabee, F. Carleton. *Samuel F. B. Morse, the American Leonardo*. New York: Times Books, 1982.

Malloy, William M. (comp.) *Treaties, Conventions, International Acts, Protocols and Agreements Between the United States of America and Other Powers, 1776–1909*. Vols. 1 and 2 of 3 vol. Washington: Washington Public Office, 1910.

Manypenny, George W. *Our Indian Wards*. Cincinnati, 1880.

Marcy, Colonel R. B. *Thirty Years of Army Life on the Border*. New York: Harper and Brothers, 1866.

Marion, J. M. *Notes of Travel through the Territory of Arizona; being an account of the trip made by General George Stoneman and others in the autumn of 1870*. Prescott, Ariz.: Office of the Miner, 1870.

Mason, J. E. "The Use of Indian Scouts in the Apache Wars—1870–1886." Master's thesis, Indiana University, 1970.

Mazzanovich, Anton. *Trailing Geronimo*. Los Angeles, 1931.

McCall, George A. *Letters from the Frontier*. 1908.

McClintock, James H. *History of Arizona: Prehistoric, Aboriginal, Pioneer, Modern*. Vol. 1 of 3 vol. Chicago, 1961.

McClintock, James H. *Mormon Settlement in Arizona*. Phoenix, 1921.

McDowell, Major-General Irvin. *Outline Descriptions of Pacific Military Posts in the Military Division of the Pacific*. San Francisco, 1879.

"Mounted Riflemen: The Real Role of Cavalry in the Indian Wars," in *Probing the American West: Papers from the Santa Fe Conference*. Santa Fe: Museum of New Mexico Press, 1962.

Mowry, Sylvester. *Arizona and Sonora: The Geography, History, & Resources of the Silver Region of North America*. New York: Harper, 1864.

Orton, Richard H. (comp.). *Records of California Men in the War of the Rebellion, 1861–1867*. Sacramento, Calif., 1890.

Parker, Isabel Margaret. "Apache Troubles in the Southwest." Master's thesis, University of California, Berkeley, 1927.

Peplow, Edward H., Jr. *History of Arizona*. Vol. 1 of 3 vol. New York, 1958.

Pettis, George H. *Frontier Service during the Rebellions or a History of Company K, First Infantry, California Volunteers*. Providence, R.I.: The Society, 1885.

Price, George F. (comp.). *Across the Continent with the 5th Cavalry*. New York: Van Nostrand, 1883.

Pumpelly, Raphael. *Across America and Asia*. New York, 1870.

Reedstrom, E. Lisle. *Bugles, Banners, and Warbonnets*. Caxton, 1978. Second Printing. New York: Bonanza Press, 1986.

Reedstrom, E. Lisle. *Historical Dress of the Old West*. Poole, Dorset, England: Blandford Press, 1986.

Rickey, Don, Jr. *Forty Miles a Day on Beans and Hay*. Norman, Okla.: University of Oklahoma Press, 1963.

Robinson, Dorothy Fulwiler. "A Brief History of the Apaches from 1848–1864." Master's thesis, University of Southern California, Los Angeles, 1928.

Rodenbough, Theophilus Francis. *The Army of the United States*. New York: Maynard, Merrill and Co., 1896.

Rodenbough, Theophilus Francis. *Everglade to Canyon with the 2nd Dragoons*. New York: Van Nostrand, 1875.

Rodney, George Brydges. *As a Cavalryman Remembers*. Caldwell, Idaho: Caxton, 1944.

Royce, Charles C. "Indian Land Cessions in the United States," *Bureau of Ethnology: 18th Annual Report, 1896–1897*. Washington, 1898.

Russell, Don. *One Hundred and Three Fights and Scrimmages, the Story of Reuben F. Bernard*. Reprinted from *Cavalry Journal*, Washington, 1936, United States Cavalry Association.

Sacks, Benjamin. "New Evidence on the Bascom Affair." *Arizona and the West*. Vol. 4, 1962.

Safford, A. P. K. *The Territory of Arizona*. Tucson, 1874.

Sawyer, Charles W. *Our Rifles*. Boston, 1920.

Schmitt, Martin F. (ed.). *General George Crook: His Autobiography*. Norman, Okla.: University of Oklahoma Press, 1946.

Scheips, Paul J. "Will Croft Barnes, Soldier and Citizen of Arizona," *Arizona and the West*. Vol. 2, 1960.

Serven, James E. *Colt Firearms (1836–1954)*. Santa Ana, Calif., 1954.

Sharpe, Philip. *The Rifle in America*. New York, 1938.

Skinner, W. B. (Woody). "The Apache Rock Crumbles." Skinner Publishing, 1987.

Sloan, Richard E. *History of Arizona*. Vol 1 of 4 vol. Phoenix, 1930.

Smart, C. "Notes on the Tonto Apaches," *Smithsonian Report*, 1867.

Sparrow, John C. *History of Personal Demobilization*. Washington: Government Printing Office, 1951.

Spring, John A. "With the Regulars in Arizona in the Sixties." Washington: *National Tribune*, November 20, 1902.

Steele, James W. *Frontier Army Sketches*. 1883.

Summerhayes, Martha. *Vanished Arizona: Recollections of My Army Life*. Philadelphia: J. B. Lippincott Company, 1908.

Tevis, James H. *Arizona in the 50's*. Albuquerque: University of New Mexico Press, 1954.

Thompson, Robert L. *Wiring a Continent*. Princeton, N.J.: Princeton University Press, 1947.

Thrapp, Dan L. *Al Sieber, Chief of Scouts*. Norman, Okla.: University of Oklahoma Press, 1964.

Thrapp, Dan L. *General Crook and the Sierra Madre Adventure*. Oklahoma Press, 1972.

U.S. National Park Service. *Soldier and Brave*. New York: Harper and Row, 1963.

Webb, George C. *Chronological List of Engagements between the Regular Army of the United States and the Various Hostile Indians which occurred during the years 1790 to 1898 inclusive*. St. Joseph, Mo., 1939.

Wellman, Paul I. *Death in the Desert*. New York: Macmillan, 1935.

Wellman, Paul. *Indian Wars of the West*. New York: Doubleday, Inc., 1956.

Wells, Edmund. *Argonaut Tales*. New York: Grafton Press, 1927.

Woodward, Arthur (ed.). *On the Bloody Trail of Geronimo*. (An Account of Lt. John Bigelow, Jr.) Los Angeles: Westernlore Press, 1958.

Woodward, J. J., M.D. *The Hospital Steward's Manual*. Philadelphia: J.B. Lippincott & Co., 1863.

Woon, Basil D. (ed.). *Arizona's Yesterday: Being the Narrative of John H. Cady*. Patagonia, Arizona, 1915.

Worcester, Don E. *The Apaches, Eagles of the Southwest*. Oklahoma Press, 1979.

Wyllys, Rufus K. *Arizona: The History of the Frontier State*. Phoenix, 1950.

Zogbaum, Rufus F. *Horse, Foot and Dragoons*. New York: Harper, 1888.

Anonymous. "Military and Trading Posts, Missions, etc., within the Limits of . . . Arizona," *Bureau of American Ethnology: 17th Annual Report, 1895–1896*, part 1. Washington, 1897.

PERIODICAL BIBLIOGRAPHY

Ackerman, R. O. "The Spur Story," *Arizona Highways*, September, 1952.

Ackerman, R. O. "Weapons Westward!" *Arizona Highways*, January, 1952.

Baird, Major G. W. "General Miles' Indian Campaign," *Century Magazine*, Vol. 42, July, 1891, pp. 351–370.

Barnes, Will C. "The Apache's Last Stand in Arizona," *Arizona Historical Review*, Vol. 3, January 1931, pp. 36–57.

Barnes, Will C. "In the Apache Country," *Overland*, 2nd Series, February 1887, pp. 172–180.

Barney, James. "Merejildo Grijalva, noted Scout of the Apache Wars," *Sheriff's* magazine, Tucson, December 1951.

Barney, James M. "The Cochise Indian War in Arizona," *Sheriff's* magazine, Tucson, March 1954.

Barney, James M. "Colonel Edward E. Eyre, Cavalry Leader of the California Column," *Sheriff's* magazine, Tucson, March 1952.

Barney, James M. "Gi-ana-tah of the Mescalero Apaches," *Sheriff's* magazine, Tucson, March 1952.

Barney, James. M. "Tales of Apache Warfare," privately printed, Phoenix, 1933.

Barney, James M. "When General George Crook and General Nelson A. Miles left Arizona Territory," *Sheriff's* magazine, Tucson, June 1954.

Bateman, Cephas C. "A Group of Army Authors," *The Californian*, Vol. 4, October 1893. Historiography of Gen. O. O. Howard, John Bigelow, Jr., Capt. Charles King, and others.

Bender, Averam B. "Frontier Defense in the Territory of New Mexico, 1853–1861," *New Mexico Historical Review*, Vol. 9, October 1934, pp. 1–32.

Bender, Averam B. "Military Posts in the Southwest, 1848–1860," *New Mexico Historical Review*, Vol. 16, April 1941, pp. 125–147.

Bender, Averam B. "Military Transportation in the Southwest, 1848–1860," *New Mexico Historical Review*, Vol. 32, April 1957, pp. 123–150.

Bloom, Lansing B. (ed.). "Bourke on the Southwest," *New Mexico Historical Review*, Vols. 8–13, 1933–38.

Blount, Bertha. "The Apaches in the Southwest, 1846–1886," *Southwestern Historical Quarterly*, Vol. 23, July 1919, pp. 20–38.

Bourke, John G. "General Crook in the Indian Country," *Century Magazine*, Vol. 41, March 1891, pp. 643–660.

Brinckerhoff, Sidney B. "Military Headgear in the Southwest, 1846–1890," *Arizoniana*, Vol. 4, No. 4, 1963.

Brinckerhoff, Sidney B. "'Steadfast' Gregg in Arizona," *Arizoniana*, Vol. 5, No. 2, 1964.

"Camp Date Creek, A.T.: Army Outpost in the Yavapai Wars, 1867–1873," *The Westerners*, Tucson, 1964.

Carter, R. G. "Lawton's Capture of Geronimo . . .," *Collier's Weekly*, January 27, 1900, p. 8.

Caughey, John W. "Across the Continent with Kearney," *Westways* magazine, November 1946, p. 14.

Clendenen, Clarence C. "General James Henry Carleton," *New Mexico Historical Review*, Vol. 30, January 1955, pp. 23–43.

Clendenen, Clarence C. "An Unknown Chapter in Western History: Incidents in the History of the Column from California," *Westerners Brand Book: New York Possee*, Vol. 1, Summer 1954, pp. 11, 16–18.

Clum, John P. "The Apaches," *New Mexico Historical Review*, Vol. 4, April 1929, pp. 107–127.

Clum, John P. "Apache Misrule," *Arizona Historical*

Review, Vol. 4, April 1931, pp. 56–68; July 1931, pp. 52–64; October 1931, pp. 64–71.

Clum, John P. "Apache Years of the Man with the High Marble Dome," *Touring Topics*, Vol. 23, December 1931, pp. 14–17, 45–46.

Clum, John P. "Es-kim-in-zin," *New Mexico Historical Review*, Vol. 4, January 1929, pp. 1–26; Vol. 3, October 1928, pp. 399–420.

Clum, John P. "Fighting Geronimo, A Story of the Apache Indian Campaign of 1876," *Sunset* Magazine, Vol. 2, 1903, pp. 36–41.

Clum, John P. "Geronimo," *Arizona Historical Review*, Vol. 1, July 1928, pp. 14–49.

Clum, John P. "Victorio," *Arizona Historical Review*, Vol. 2, January 1930, pp. 74–90.

Cremony, John C. "The Apache Race," *Overland Monthly*, September 1868, pp. 201–209.

Cremony, John C. "Some Savages," *Overland Monthly*, Vol. 8, March 1872, pp. 201–210.

Crook, General George. "The Apache Problem," *Journal of the Military Service Institution of the United States*, Vol. 7, October 1886, pp. 257–269.

Daly, H. W. "The Geronimo Campaign," two parts, *Journal of the United States Cavalry Association*, July, October 1908.

Daly, H. W. "The Geronimo Campaign," *Arizona Historical Review*, Vol. 3, July 1930, pp. 26–44.

Dunlap, Horace E. "Tom Horn, Chief of Scouts," *Arizona Historical Review*, Vol. 2, July 1929, pp. 73–85.

Ellis, A. N. Dr., "Recollections of an Interview with Cochise, Chief of the Apaches," *Collections of the Kansas State Historical Society, 1913–1914*, Vol. 11, 1915, pp. 387–392.

Ellis, E. S. "Geronimo," *Frank Leslie's Popular Monthly*, November 1894, pp. 615–17.

Everett, Mary E. "The Disappointment of Cochise," *Southwest Magazine*, December 1894, p. 17.

Gatewood, Lieutenant Charles B. "The Account of Lieutenant Charles B. Gatewood's Part in the Final Surrender of Geronimo, Natches and the Hostile Chiricahua Apache Indians," (Bisbee) *Brewery Gulch Gazette*, May 19, 1933.

Gatewood, Lieutenant Charles B. "Campaigns against Victorio in 1879," *The Great Divide*, April 1894, p. 102.

Gatewood, Lieutenant Charles B. "Lieutenant Charles B. Gatewood and the Surrender of Geronimo," *Arizona Historical Review*, Vol. 4, April 1931, pp. 29–44.

Gatewood, Lieutenant Charles B. "Lieutenant Charles B. Gatewood 6th U.S. Cavalry and the Surrender of Geronimo," *Proceedings of the Annual Meeting and Dinner of the Order of Indian Wars of the U.S. held January 26, 1929*.

Gessler, E. A. and Schneider, H. "Origins of Military Uniforms," *CIBA Review*, August 1952.

Gregory, Leslie H. "John P. Clum," *Arizona Historical Review*, Vol. 5, August 1932, pp. 89–92 and Vol. 5, October 1932, pp. 188–197.

Hagemann, E. R. "Scout Out from Camp McDowell," *Arizoniana*, Vol. 5, No. 4, 1964.

Hanna, Robert. "With Crawford in Mexico," *Arizona Historical Review*, Vol. 6, April 1935, pp. 56–65.

Hunsaker, William J. "Lansford W. Hastings' Project for the Invasion and the Conquest of Arizona and New Mexico for the Southern Confederacy," *Arizona Historical Review*, Vol. 4, July 1931, pp. 5–12.

Hunter, Thomas Thompson. "Early Days in Arizona," *Arizona Historical Review*, Vol. 3, April 1930, pp. 105–120.

Huntington, Mary. "Last of the Scouts," *Westways*, Vol. 39, November 1947.

Irwin, Bernard J. D. "The Chiricahua Apache Indians: A Thrilling Incident in the Early History of Arizona Territory (the Bascom Affair)," *Infantry Journal*, April 1928.

Knox, M. B. "The Escape of the Apache Kid," *Arizona Historical Review*, Vol. 3, January 1931, pp. 77–87.

Leavell, Mary. "Life at an Army Post in Tucson," *Tempe Normal Student*, January 3, 1908.

Lockwood, Frank C. "Cochise, the Noble Warrior," *Arizona Highways*, February 1939.

Lockwood, Frank C. "Early Military Posts in Arizona," *Arizona Historical Review*, Vol. 2, January 1930, pp. 91–97.

Lockwood, Frank C. "John C. Cremony," *Westways*, March 1946.

Lummis, Charles F. "Apache Warrior," *The Kansas Magazine*, September 1886.

Mazzanovich, Anton, "Lieutenant Charles B. Gatewood," *Arizona Historical Review*, Vol. 2, July 1929, pp. 86–91.

McClintock, James H. "Fighting Apaches," *Sunset* magazine, Vol. 18, February 1907, p. 340.

McCracken, Harold, "Chronicler of the Old West: Frederick Remington," *Arizona Highways*, September 1950.

Merritt, Wesley. "Three Indian Campaigns," *Harper's* magazine, April 1890.

Miles, Nelson A. "On the Trail of Geronimo," *Cosmopolitan* magazine, July 1911, p. 249.

Mulligan, Raymond A. "Sixteen Days in Apache Pass," *The Kiva*, Vol. 24, No. 2, 1958.

Nickerson, T. S. "Geronimo's Last Raid," *Out West*, Vol. 9, March 1915, pp. 126–27.

Newhall, Beaumont. "Early Western Photographers," *Arizona Highways*, May 1946.

Ogle, Ralph H. "The Apache and the Government—1970's," *New Mexico Historical Review*, Vol. 33, April 1958, pp. 81–102.

Ogle, Ralph H. "Federal Control of the Western Apaches, 1848–1886," *New Mexico Historical Review*, Vol. 14, October 1939, pp. 309–365; Vol. 15, 1940, pp. 12–71, 188–248, 269–335.

Opler, Morris E. "A Chiricahua Apache's Account of the Geronimo Campaign of 1886," *New Mexico Historical Review*, Vol. 13, October 1938, pp. 360–86.

Otis, H. G. "The Apache Race," *Overland Monthly*, September 1868.

Peach, Edith, "The Early Indian Attacks in the Tonto Basin," *The Normal Student*, May 3, 1907.

Peterson, Thomas H., Jr. "Fort Lowell, A.T.: Army Post During the Apache Campaigns," *The Westerners*, Tucson, 1963.

Pettis, George H. "The California Column," *Papers of the New Mexico Historical Society*, No. 11, 1908.

Pettis, George H. "The California Column," *Arizona Historical Review*, Vol. 1, April 1928, pp. 80–96.

Pool, Frank M. "The Apache Kid," *Sheriff's* magazine, March 1947.

Raine, William McLeod, "The Apache Kid," *World Wide Magazine*, September 1904, p. 445.

Reedstrom, E. L. "Anson Mills' Cartridge Belts," *Guns Magazine Annual*, 1978.

Sandeman, John. "How I Met Victorio the Apache," *World Wide Magazine*, November 1901, p. 76.

Santee, Ross. "Among the Apaches," *Century*, February 1925, pp. 511–515.

Schwatka, T. "Among the Apaches," *Century*, May 1887, pp. 41–52.

Shipp, W. E. "Captain Crawford's Last Expedition," *Journal of the United States Cavalry Association*, December 1892, reprinted in the *Journal*, October 1908.

Smith, Cornelius C. "The Army and the Apache," *Arizona Historical Review*, Vol. 4, January 1932, pp. 62–70.

Smith, Cornelius C. "The Fight at Cibicu," *Arizona Highways*, May 1956.

Spring, J. A. "The Apache Indian," *The Great Divide*, December 1892.

Spring, John A. "A March to Arizona from California in 1866 (Reminiscence of . . .)," *Arizoniana*, Vol. 3, No. 3, 1962.

Stefen, Randy. "Indian Fighting Cavalryman," *Western Horseman*, March, April, May, and June 1963.

Tassin, A. G. "Among the Apaches," *Overland Monthly*, September, October 1889.

Tassin, A. G. "Reminiscences of Indian Scouting," *Overland Monthly*, August 1889, p. 151.

Toulouse, Joseph, "Military Forts in 1869," *Arizona Historical Review*, Vol. 6, July 1935, pp. 81–85.

Utley, Robert M. "The Surrender of Geronimo," *Arizoniana*, Vol. 4, No. 3, 1963.

Walker, Franklin. "Bohemian No. 1, Captain John Cremony," *Westways*, September 1937, pp. 22–23.

Wallace, Andrew. "General August V. Kautz in Arizona, 1874–1878," *Arizoniana*, Vol. 4, No. 4, 1963.

Walters, Lorenzo D. "Arizona," *Progressive Arizona Magazine*, January, pp. 5–6, 20; February, pp. 4, 18–19; March, pp. 16, 19; and April, p. 11; 1932.

Wharfield, H. B. "A Fight with the Yaquis at Bear Valley," *Arizoniana*, Vol. 4, No. 3, 1963.

Williamson, Dan R. "Al Sieber, Famous Scout of the Southwest," *Arizona Historical Review*, Vol. 3, January 1931, pp. 60–76.

Williamson, Dan R. "Story of Oskay De No Tah, the Flying Fighter," *Arizona Historical Review*, Vol. 3, October 1930, pp. 78–83.

Woodward, Arthur, "The Apache Scouts," *Masterkey*, July 1935.

Woodward, Arthur, "John Bourke on the Apaches," *Plateau*, Vol. 16, October 1943.

Wright, Harry Robinson. "In the Days of Geronimo—Some Incidents in the Apache Outbreak of 1885," *Pearson's*, February 1905, p. 196.

Wyllys, Rufus K. "Arizona and the Civil War," *Arizona Highways*, January 1951.

In addition, the following journals, manuals, and magazines are highly recommended:

Arizona and the West, a quarterly sponsored by the University of Arizona, Tucson, Arizona.

Arizona Highways Magazine, published monthly by the Arizona Highway Department. Address: Arizona Highways, Phoenix, Arizona.

Arizoniana, a quarterly published by the Arizona Pioneers' Historical Society, Tucson.

The Army Almanac, published by Stackpole Co., Harrisburg, Penn., 1959.

Army, Navy Journal, published by the Government Printing Office, Washington.

Cavalry Journal, published by the Government Printing Office, Washington.

Desert Magazine, published monthly at Palm Desert, California.

Journal of the U.S. Cavalry, published by the Government Printing Office, Washington.

The Kiva, a Journal of the Arizona Archaeological and Historical Society, published quarterly at Tucson, Arizona.

Manual of Pack Transportation, Quartermaster Corp., published by the Government Printing Office, Washington.

The Masterkey, published by the Southwest Museum, Highland Park, Los Angeles, California.

New Mexico Historical Review, published jointly by the Historical Society of New Mexico and the University of New Mexico, University Press, Albuquerque, New Mexico.

The Plateau, a quarterly, published by the Northern Arizona Society of Science and Art, Museum of Northern Arizona, Flagstaff, Arizona.

Upton's Cavalry Tactics, published by the Government Printing Office, Washington.

The Westerner's Brand Books of various corrals.

ACKNOWLEDGMENTS

For their indispensable assistance, I extend special thanks to the following people:

Bob Craig of Richmond, Indiana, a fellow bunkie, for sharing his library with me and for assisting me with research and posing before my cameras.

George A. Willhauck of North Hampton, New Hampshire, who has always taken the time to gather and save for me unusual news articles of the Old West period.

Ted Koelikamp of South Holland, Illinois, for the many newspaper articles from his collection covering the Geronimo Campaign.

My dear friends of many years, Mary and Bill Graf of Iowa City, Iowa, who share my interests in the Old West, and are always digging up special items in contemporary and out-of-print books.

Alan Feldstein of Park Forest, Illinois, for his research and contributions in the area of weapons.

Carl Breihan, a gifted writer, for taking time out of his busy schedule to furnish me with photos, historical data, and leads.

Carl G. Rumps of Hammond, Indiana, a Civil War reenactor and a historian on medical and surgical history during and after the Civil War, for generously sharing his research and photography.

Herb Peck, my good friend, for the many photographs with which he always keeps me supplied.

Dotty and Al Messina of Victor Studios, Merrillville, Indiana, my personal photographers.

Phil Spangenberger, associate editor of *Guns & Ammo* magazine, Los Angeles, California, for his courtesy in supplying me with many unpublished photos from his private collection as well as from his magazine.

Jerry Rakusan, editorial director of *Guns Magazine*, San Diego, California, and long-time friend, for his kind permission in releasing the many articles I have written for *Guns Magazine* in the past.

Richard House, former editor of *Roundup*, a publication of the Western Writers of America, for furnishing me with excellent photos of himself modelling as an Army scout and a bullwhacker.

Roger Reinke of Alexandria, Virginia, and Gil Schlehman of Downers Grove, Illinois, both collectors of early telegraphy material, who were very considerate in allowing me to use several photographs of theirs to accompany this text.

Lou Coe of Crown Point, Indiana, a personal friend, for the use of some of his work on heliographs.

My models again took the stage, posing for the many color plates in the book. A special thanks to historian Jim Nemeth of Harvey, Illinois, a cavalry buff and a western military artist in his own right; Phil Rodeghiero of Dalton, Illinois, who has become quite familiar with my studio, having also posed in uniform for various books of mine in the past.

Thanks also to the U.S. Army Military History Institute, Carlisle Barracks, Pennsylvania, and their special bibliographic series from 1860 to 1898.

For research and assistance and special attention in photocopying books, documents, and old photographs, I am indebted to the U.S. Army Medical Corps Museum, Walter Reed Hospital, Washington, DC; the U.S. Army Signal Corps, Fort Gordon, Georgia; the U.S. Army Field Artillery and Fort Sill Museum, Oklahoma; Arizona Archaeological and Historical Society, Arizona

State Museum, University of Arizona, Tucson; Arizona Historical Society, Tucson; Fort Huachuca Museum, Ft. Huachuca, Arizona; Smithsonian Institution, Washington, DC; National Archives, Washington, DC; Fort Davis National Historic Site, Fort Davis, Texas; and the Newbery Library, Chicago, Illinois.

I extend my gratitude to Barbara Burns, Head of Reference Services at the Crown Point Library, Crown Point, Indiana, and the Lake County Reference Library staff, Merrillville, Indiana. A wealth of source material would have been overlooked had it not been for the unsparing time, knowledge, and cooperative spirit of these people.

It is only fitting to mention the two dear young women who, over many long hours, helped to pull this manuscript together: my typist, Debbie Higgins, and my editor, Fran Katz, both of Crown Point, Indiana. I extend to them my appreciation for casting their critical editorial eye over the manuscript and for giving me useful suggestions for improvement.

Above all, I owe a debt of gratitude to my wife, Shirley Ellen Reedstrom, who took on the burden of outside chores during the planting and harvest seasons and maintained just about everything else around the farm so that I could continue working on this book.

To all those whom I have overlooked mentioning in a lapse of memory, my sincere thanks!

E. Lisle Reedstrom

INDEX